Mastering C++ Game Animation Programming

Enhance your skills with advanced game animation techniques in C++, OpenGL, and Vulkan

Michael Dunsky

Mastering C++ Game Animation Programming

Portfolio Director: Rohit Rajkumar

Relationship Lead: Neha Pande

Project Manager: Sandip Tadge

Content Engineer: Rashi Dubey

Technical Editor: Tejas Mhasvekar

Copy Editor: Safis Editing

Proofreader: Rashi Dubey

Indexer: Rekha Nair

Presentation Designer: Aparna Bhagat

Marketing Owner: Nivedita Pandey

Growth Lead: Namita Velgekar

First published: March 2025

Production reference: 2031225

Published by Packt Publishing Ltd.

Grosvenor House

11 St Paul's Square

Birmingham

B3 1RB, UK.

ISBN 978-1-83588-192-7

www.packt.com

No bits were harmed during development.

Contributors

About the author

Michael Dunsky is an electronics engineer, console porting programmer, and game developer with more than 20 years of programming experience. He started with BASIC at the young age of 14 and expanded his portfolio over the years to include assembly language, C, C++, Java, Py-thon, VHDL, OpenGL, GLSL, and Vulkan. During his career, he also gained extensive knowledge of Linux, virtual machines, server operation, and infrastructure automation. Michael holds a Master of Science degree in Computer Science from the FernUniversität in Hagen with a focus on computer graphics, parallel programming, and software systems.

Thanks to Marco and Morris for giving me the green light to create my second book, completed again in my spare time. And thanks to the team at Packt for the great support.

About the reviewers

Wanderson dos Santos Lopes is a seasoned software engineer with proven experience in both gameplay and server programming, specializing in C++ and Unreal Engine. With an extensive background in developing multiplayer mechanics and robust backend systems, he writes performance-first code and optimizes core software across platforms. His expertise in diagnosing and resolving bugs and implementing maintainable technologies has contributed to several high-profile gaming projects.

Bill Merrill acquired a BS in Computer Science from the University of California at Riverside and has been an engineer in the games industry for over 22 years, specializing in animation, AI, gameplay, and engine systems. In addition to several proprietary projects in robotics and simulation with Amazon, Bill has shipped numerous AAA games, from major franchises such as Silent Hill and Front Mission to original IPs such as Evolve and New World. He has also contributed to the industry through GDC talks and peer-reviewed contributions to the *Game AI Pro* book series. Bill now functions as a hands-on Technical Director working on a new, unannounced IP.

Table of Contents

Preface   **xxiii**

Free Benefits with Your Book xxx

Part I: Populating the World with the Game Character Models   1

Chapter 1: Working with Open Asset Import Library   3

Technical requirements 5

Getting the source code and the basic tools • 5

Getting the code using Git • 6

Getting the code as a ZIP file • 6

Installing the required tools and libraries for Windows • 6

Installing Visual Studio 2022 on Windows • 6

Enabling long path names on Windows • 7

Downloading Open Asset Import Library • 8

Configuring the build • 8

Installing the Vulkan SDK on Windows • 11

Compiling and starting the example code • 12

Installing the required tools and libraries for Linux • 13

Downloading Open Asset Import Library • 13

Installing a C++ compiler and the required libraries on Linux • 13

Compiling the examples via the command line on Linux • 14

Installing Eclipse on Linux • 15

Code organization in this book • 17

Animating game characters – a primer **18**

About nodes, bones, skeletal animation, and skinning • 18

Preparing the data for efficient usage • 20

Updating character data • 21

What is Open Asset Import Library? **22**

Loading a model file **25**

Loading embedded textures • 26

Parsing the node hierarchy • 27

Adding vertex buffers for the meshes • 29

Importing animations • 30

Checking the code for all the details • 30

Extending the UI with an Open File dialog **31**

Integrating the file dialog into CMakeLists.txt • 31

Using the ImGui file dialog • 32

Adding a filter to show only supported file types • 34

Adding a single filter • 34

Adding a group of filters • 34

Adding a regular expression-style filter • 34

Loading the model file • 35

Drawing the model to the screen • 36

Adding and removing model instances dynamically **36**

Reusing the bones for the sake of simplicity • 36

Storing instance-specific settings • 38

Dynamic model and instance management • 39

Drawing all instances • 42

Summary **44**

Practical sessions **44**

Additional resources **45**

Chapter 2: Moving Animation Calculations from CPU to GPU   47

Technical requirements 48

What are compute shaders and why should we love them? 48

The famous raster interrupt • 48

The rise of multi-core machines • 49

Hidden multi-core champions • 49

Welcome to the wonderful world of compute shaders • 50

Profiling animation performance 51

Locating the hotspots in the code • 53

Analyzing the current data representation • 54

Adjusting the data model • 56

Adding missing data for the compute shader • 58

Relocating data to another shader • 61

Doing the last preparations • 61

Moving the node computations to the GPU 62

Adding more shader storage buffers • 63

Calculating the node transforms in a shader • 63

Creating the final node matrices • 69

Finalizing the compute relocation • 72

Testing the implementation by scaling up 73

How to debug a compute shader 75

Summary 76

Practical sessions 76

Additional resources 77

Chapter 3: Adding a Visual Selection   79

Technical requirements 80

Implementing a "move to instance" function 80

Adding coordinate arrows • 80

Creating a button to center the selected instance • 85

Adding a highlight to the selected instance 87

Preparing the renderer to support highlights • 87

Adjusting logic to shaders and the UI • 89

Selecting a model instance with point and click 91

Pros and cons of shooting virtual rays • 91

Advantages of drawing the instance index into a texture • 92

Adjusting the framebuffer • 92

Creating a selection shader • 94

Reading a pixel from a texture • 95

Adding mouse button handling • 96

Assigning an index to each instance • 97

Selecting the instance at mouse positions • 98

Implementing a null object to allow deselection 100

What is a null object? • 100

Creating and using the AssimpModel null object • 101

Adjusting the user interface • 102

Summary 103

Practical sessions 104

Additional resources 104

Part II: Transforming the Model Viewer into an Animation Editor   107

Chapter 4: Enhancing Application Handling   109

Technical requirements 109

Switching between edit and view modes 110

Deciding what should be switched in view mode • 111

Adding the state variable plus code • 111

Toggling between the two modes and changing the title • 113

An outlook for future changes • 115

Reverting changes before applying 116

The basic idea • 116

Adding code and User Interface elements • 116

Drawbacks of the current solution • 118

Implementing undo and redo functionality 119

What do we need to create undo and redo? • 119

Creating a setting storage class • 120

Hooking up the storage class to the renderer • 121

Defining hotkeys for undo and redo • 122

Adding an ImGui menu to allow direct access • 122

Limits and enhancements of our undo/redo implementation • 123

Summary 124

Practical sessions 124

Additional resources 125

Chapter 5: Saving and Loading the Configuration   **127**

Technical requirements 128

Textual or binary file formats – pros and Cons 128

Saving and loading binary data • 128

Saving and loading textual data • 129

Choosing a text format to save our data 130

The INI file format • 131

The JSON file format • 131

The YAML file format • 132

Exploring the structure of a YAML file 133

The YAML node • 133

The YAML map • 133

The YAML sequence • 134

Combinations of maps and sequences • 134

Adding a YAML parser 135

Getting yaml-cpp • 135

Integrating yaml-cpp into the CMake build • 136

Adding the parser class • 137

   Using the node type of yaml-cpp • 137

   Accessing sequences and maps • 138

   Handling exceptions thrown by yaml-cpp • 139

Saving and loading the configuration file 139

Deciding what to store in the configuration file • 140

Overloading the output operator of the emitter • 141

Creating and writing the configuration file • 142

Adding a file dialog to the user interface • 144

Loading the configuration file back and parsing the nodes • 145

Cleaning up and recreating the scene from the saved values • 147

Strict or relaxed configuration file loading • 148

Common errors leading to corrupted files • 148

Loading a default configuration file at startup 149

Summary 150

Practical sessions 151

Additional resource 151

Chapter 6: Extending Camera Handling   153

Technical requirements 154

Adding multiple cameras 154

From a single camera to an array of cameras • 154

Extracting the camera settings • 155

Adjusting the renderer • 156

Defining a free camera as the default camera • 158

Adding and deleting cameras • 159

Adjusting camera configuration load and save • 162

Bumping the configuration file version • 164

Creating different camera types 164

Implementing first- and third-person cameras **166**

Retrieving the bone matrix for the first-person view • 167

Computing first-person camera parameters • 169

Moving the camera in a third-person view • 172

Disabling manual camera movement • 174

Limits of current first-/third-person cameras • 175

Adding stationary cameras **176**

Creating a stationary follow camera • 176

Switching between cameras and configurations **178**

Configuring keyboard shortcuts for camera selection • 178

Adding orthogonal projection • 179

User interface controls for the projection settings • 181

Summary **183**

Practical sessions **183**

Additional resources **185**

Part III: Tuning Character Animations

187

Chapter 7: Enhancing Animation Controls

189

Technical requirements **189**

Blending between animations with style **190**

The power of lookup tables • 190

Creating the lookup tables • 191

Uploading the data tables to the GPU • 194

Adjusting the renderer code and the compute shader • 196

Adding new states to the code **200**

Using bit fields and plain enums • 201

Extending model and instance settings • 202

Adding the idle/walk/run logic • 204

Using acceleration and deceleration • 206

Linking states and animations **209**

Mapping idle/walk/run animations • 209

Mapping actions to animation clips • 211

Defining allowed state changes • 213

Using a finite state machine to control the animation flow • 214

Saving and loading the states **217**

Storing the new data types • 218

Reading back the model settings in the renderer • 220

Summary **221**

Practical sessions **221**

Additional resources **223**

Chapter 8: An Introduction to Collision Detection   225

Technical requirements **226**

The complexities of collision detection **226**

Avoiding the naive way • 226

Using spatial partitioning to reduce complexity **227**

Grid • 227

Quadtree • 228

Octree • 228

Binary space partitioning • 229

K-d tree • 230

Bounding volume hierarchy • 231

Simplifying the instances for faster collision checks **232**

Axis-aligned bounding box • 232

Oriented bounding box • 233

Bounding circles and spheres • 234

Capsule • 234

Convex hull • 235

Bounding volume hierarchy • 236

Adding a quadtree to store nearby model instances 237

Adjusting the bounding box code • 237

Rewriting the quadtree code to fit our needs • 238

Calculating the instance bounding boxes • 240

Adding a three-dimensional bounding cube class • 240

Creating the AABB lookup tables • 242

Using the AABB in the model and renderer • 243

Creating a window to show the quadtree plus contents • 244

Retrieving the colliding instances and reacting to collisions • 245

Drawing the AABB debug lines • 246

Implementing bounding spheres 247

Creating the data for the bounding spheres • 248

Drawing bounding spheres • 251

Using the bounding spheres for collision detection • 253

Summary 255

Practical sessions 256

Additional resources 257

Chapter 9: Adding Behavior and Interaction 259

Technical requirements 260

Structures to control instance behavior 260

Adding a visual node editor 261

Integrating imnodes by using CMake • 262

Using imnodes to create UI elements • 263

Creating the imnodes context • 264

Setting default values for imnodes • 264

Creating the node editor • 264

Adding a simple node • 266

Creating imnodes attributes and ImGui elements in a node • 267

Maintaining links between nodes • 268

Creating graph node classes • 271

  Exploring the base class for graph nodes • 273

  Creating the wait node • 275

  Using callbacks to propagate changes • 278

  Creating a behavior struct and a storage class for the instances • 278

  Adding a node factory • 280

  Extending the node editor • 281

Saving and loading a node tree • 282

Extending the code to support behavior changes 285

Creating a node tree copy for every instance • 285

Connecting SingleInstanceBehavior and the renderer • 285

Adding events • 286

Limitations of the current implementation • 290

Adding interaction between instances 291

Creating interaction control properties • 291

Extending the handling code • 292

Drawing debug information • 294

Summary 295

Practical sessions 295

Additional resources 297

Chapter 10: Advanced Animation Blending   299

Technical requirements 299

How to animate facial expressions 300

Adding face animations to code and GPU shaders 302

Loading morph meshes • 302

Storing all morph meshes in a single buffer • 305

Adding face morph settings to the code • 307

Filling the per-instance buffer data in the renderer • 309

Extending the shader to draw face animations • 310

Finalizing the face animation code • 313

Adding UI elements to control face animations • 314

Saving and loading the new instance settings • 315

Using face animations in node trees 317

Adjusting the code for the new FaceAnim node • 318

Adding the FaceAnim node • 319

Enabling instance and renderer to react to face animation changes • 321

Limitations of morph target animations • 323

Implementing additive blending 324

How additive blending works • 325

Extending the code to support additive animations • 327

Creating mappings for the new head animations • 330

Adding a head animation node • 332

Saving and loading the head animation settings • 333

Summary 335

Practical sessions 336

Additional resources 337

Part IV: Enhancing Your Virtual World 339

Chapter 11: Loading a Game Map 341

Technical requirements 341

Differences between map and model data 342

Level data does not move around • 342

Using a separate collision detection for level data • 343

Level data may contain additional data • 343

Spatial division • 343

Lightmaps • 344

Navigation mesh • 344

Hierarchical level-of-detail • 344

Level data may be partial or incomplete • 344

Choosing a file format for a map 345

Using levels in file formats supported by Assimp • 345

Extending existing formats or creating a custom format • 346

Importing a game map 347

Adding a C++ class to hold the level data • 348

Adding callbacks and renderer code • 349

Extending the UI with level property controls • 350

Saving and loading the level configuration • 352

Converting the quadtree to an octree • 353

Creating an interactive octree view • 354

Adding interactivity • 354

Collecting the lines • 356

Calculating the view and drawing the lines • 357

Building an AABB for the level data • 359

Using non-animated models as assets • 361

Sending the level data to the GPU 363

Creating a new shader • 363

Drawing the level AABB • 365

Summary 368

Practical sessions 368

Additional resources 369

Chapter 12: Advanced Collision Detection   371

Technical requirements 372

Enhancing collision detection for level data 372

Adding a new octree type • 372

Filling the level data octree • 375

Detecting instance/level collisions • 378

Drawing debug lines • 380

Extending the node tree to support level geometry collisions • 382

Using gravity to keep the instances on the floor **383**

    Finding ground triangles in level data • 384

    Adding basic gravity • 386

    Keeping the instances on the ground triangles • 387

Adding inverse kinematics **391**

    The two types of kinematics • 392

    Understanding the FABRIK basics • 393

    Implementing the FABRIK inverse kinematics algorithm • 396

    Defining the node chain for the instance's feet • 399

    Adjusting the node positions • 400

        Keeping the node transformations separate • 401

        Adding the code for the animated instances • 402

        Creating the new world positions • 404

    Detecting feet-to-ground collisions • 405

    Running the FABRIK solver • 407

    Limitations of FABRIK • 409

Summary **409**

Practical sessions **410**

Additional resources **412**

Chapter 13: Adding Simple Navigation   **413**

Technical requirements **413**

An overview of different ways to navigate **414**

    Distance-based navigation • 414

    Graph-based navigation • 415

        DFS and BFS algorithms • 415

        Dijkstra's algorithm • 416

        A* algorithm • 416

    Mesh-based navigation • 417

        Navigation meshes • 417

        Area awareness system • 419

Using machine learning to generate navigation data • 420

The A* path-finding algorithm 421

Estimating the distance to the target • 421

Minimizing path costs • 422

Exploring the A*algorithm • 422

Implementing A*-based navigation • 424

Preparing the mesh triangles • 425

Adding the path-finding class • 426

Generating ground triangles • 428

Finding a path between two ground triangles • 431

Preparing the data • 431

Running the main loop • 432

Extracting the best node • 435

Backtracking the shortest path • 436

Adding navigation targets to the map 437

Adjusting model and instance • 437

Adding gravity for non-animated instances • 439

Saving and loading the new model and instance data • 440

Navigating instances to a target 441

Calculating the path to the target • 441

Rotating the instance to reach the target • 444

Adding debug lines for the path • 445

Summary 447

Practical sessions 448

Additional resources 449

Chapter 14: Creating Immersive Interactive Worlds   451

Technical requirements 452

Adding sound effects and background music 452

Using an audio library • 452

Simple DirectMedia Layer • 452

OpenAL • 453

PortAudio • 453

FMOD • 453

Playing sound effects • 453

The game character's footsteps • 453

Other character sounds • 454

Local sound sources • 454

Ambient sounds • 454

Weather effects • 454

Playing music • 454

Menu music • 454

Ambient music • 455

Adaptive music play • 455

Allowing custom music • 455

Hands-on: Implementing an audio manager • 455

Defining the high-level interface • 455

Using SDL for the low-level layer • 458

Controlling music replay • 462

Adding a callback for continuous music playback • 463

Playing sound effects • 464

Using the footstep sound effects in the renderer • 465

Extending the audio manager class • 467

Using the music player in the UI • 467

Alternative sound manager implementations • 468

Enhancing visuals **468**

Bringing colors to the world by using physically based rendering • 468

Adding transparency • 469

Looking up at a beautiful sky • 470

Playing with light and shadows • 471

Swimming in realistic water • 473

Adding stunning post-processing effects • 474

Upgrading to ray tracing • 475

Diving into virtual reality • 477

Hands-on: Adding a skybox to the virtual world • 478

   Exploring the technical details • 478

   Implementing the skybox • 480

   Drawing the skybox • 482

Extending immersion with daytime and weather **483**

Adding a day/night cycle • 484

Allowing forward time travel • 485

Playing in real time • 485

Worshipping the weather god • 485

Listening to the oracle of seasons • 486

Hands-on: Adding day and night • 486

   Implementing light control • 487

   Adding a UI control • 488

Summary **489**

Practical sessions **491**

Additional resources **492**

Other Books You May Enjoy   **497**

Index   **501**

Preface

Have you ever caught yourself watching your player character and the enemies in a first- or third-person game running and jumping around, firing and dodging, as you're pressing buttons and shooting at targets, and asked yourself:

Wait... how do all the characters stay on the ground? How do they know where the walls are? And how does the button know that it was pressed by me and not by my teammate?

To answer these questions, you would need to start up a modern 3D engine such as Unreal Engine, Unity, or Godot. You would play around with models and animations, levels, assets, menus, and other objects. By working your way through tutorials and videos, you would learn how to build a world similar to the game you love and be happy with what you have achieved.

But what if your hunger for the low-level details, for the implementation of several features, remains? Even after moving from visual programming to the underlying programming languages of the 3D engine, you are still not satisfied. The complexity of the code is way too heavy to learn just the basics from it. So, you are again on the road, searching for answers to those questions...

Does that sound familiar to you? Many game programmers start off with this kind of curiosity, a will to look "under the hood" of the things they see, and an urge to understand how models are animated and animations are blended. This might be how facial animations work or a simple "nodding" of the head is done, or how to make characters walk and run on the ground polygons of the level but not clip through walls.

This book aims to answer your questions about the implementation details of 3D game character animations. You will start off with nothing more than a basic OpenGL or Vulkan renderer to draw triangles to the screen – and then you will be guided all the way up the hill, from loading a single character model from a file to multiple instances of different models roaming around a game map, detecting and avoiding walls and other instances in the virtual world, following predefined paths, and being able to interact with another instance.

With the knowledge gained from this book, you will see the animations in games with a different pair of eyes, smiling a lot because you know how they're made.

Who this book is for

If you are already familiar with C++ and character animations but want to learn more about the implementation details and advanced character animation topics, similar to the animations found in 3D games, this book is for you.

What this book covers

Chapter 1, Working with Open Asset Import Library, gives an overview of the data structures of **Open Asset Import Library** (or **assimp**) and explains how to load a character model from a file. The fileloading process will be enhanced by adding an ImGui-based **Open File** dialog. In addition, code to add and remove model and instances at runtime will be covered.

Chapter 2, Moving Animation Calculations from CPU to GPU, introduces compute shaders to offload calculations to the graphics processor and store lookup data in GPU memory. By using the massively parallel architecture of the GPU, computing the node positions of all instances will be accelerated, and the CPU will be free again for other tasks.

Chapter 3, Adding a Visual Selection, explains how to support the user of the application in the task of character instance selection. As well as highlighting the currently selected instance on the screen, the ability to select any instance by using the mouse will be added.

Chapter 4, Enhancing Application Handling, introduces a separation of the application into a view mode and an edit mode with partially different configurations. Also, undo and redo operations will be implemented.

Chapter 5, Saving and Loading the Configuration, covers storing the current configuration of the application plus the loaded models and created instances in a YAML file, as well as loading the configuration from a file back into the application.

Chapter 6, Extending Camera Handling, shows how different camera types and configurations can be added. The new camera settings include orthogonal projection and first-person and third-person views.

Chapter 7, Enhancing Animation Controls, covers basic animation blending, action states, and linking the action states with the animation clips. By the end of the chapter, you will be able to control the instances using the keyboard and mouse, including additional actions such as jumping, rolling, or waving.

Chapter 8, An Introduction to Collision Detection, explains the path to instance/instance collision detection and the reaction to collisions, based on a quadtree, axis-aligned bounding boxes, and bounding spheres.

Chapter 9, Adding Behavior and Interaction, adds a node-based graphical editor to control instance behavior by creating and connecting simple nodes. The nodes will be extended to cover a configurable interaction between instances.

Chapter 10, Advanced Animation Blending, introduces face animations to express emotions and additive animation blending to move the head independently of the rest of the character model's body.

Chapter 11, Loading a Game Map, explains the differences between the dynamic character model instances and static level geometry, and how to load and process level data to achieve a good performance.

Chapter 12, Advanced Collision Detection, extends collision detection to the level geometry added in *Chapter 11*. Simple gravity will be added to keep the model instances on the level floor, and you will see how to avoid instance collisions with walls.

Chapter 13, Adding Simple Navigation, covers path-finding and navigation inside the loaded game map. A well-known path-finding algorithm will be used to let the instances roam around freely in the level.

Chapter 14, Creating Immersive Interactive Worlds, gives tips and resources on how to add more cool features to the character model editor, advancing the code step by step to a simple game engine.

To get the most out of this book

To get the most out of this book, you should have at least intermediate-level experience in C++ and knowledge about vector/matrix mathematics, as well as understanding the basics of skeletal animation. Any special or advanced features will be explained, and sources to learn more about these features are included in the chapters of their first usage. But you should be able to debug simple C++ problems by yourself (i.e., by using logging statements, or by attaching a debugger to the application).

The code is written for OpenGL 4.6 Core and Vulkan 1.1+. Both graphics APIs are widely supported in modern GPUs. The oldest graphics cards known to work with these API versions are the Intel HD 4000 series, made about 10 years ago.

Software covered in the book	OS requirements	
OpenGL 4.6 and Vulkan 1.1+	Windows or Linux	C++17 and above (upto C++26)

The example code presented in the book should compile on any desktop computer or laptop running a recent version of Windows and Linux. The code has been tested with the following combinations:

- Windows 10 with Visual Studio 2022
- Windows 10 with Eclipse 2024-09, using GCC from MSYS2
- Ubuntu 24.04 LTS with Eclipse 2024-09, using GCC or Clang
- Ubuntu 24.04 LTS, compiling on the command line, using GCC or Clang

If you are using the digital version of this book, we advise you to type the code yourself or access the code from the book's GitHub repository (a link is available in the next section). Doing so will help you avoid any potential errors related to the copying and pasting of code.

The full source code for the examples is available from the book's GitHub repository (a link is available in the next section). The chapters in the book contain only excerpts from the code, covering the important parts.

Download the example code files

You can download the example code files for this book from GitHub at https://github.com/PacktPublishing/Mastering-Cpp-Game-Animation-Programming. If there's an update to the code, it will be updated in the GitHub repository.

We also have other code bundles from our rich catalog of books and videos available at https://github.com/PacktPublishing. Check them out!

Download the color images

We also provide a PDF file that has color images of the screenshots/diagrams used in this book. You can download it here: https://packt.link/gbp/9781835881927.

Conventions used

There are a number of text conventions used throughout this book:

`CodeInText`: Indicates code words in text, database table names, folder names, filenames, file extensions, pathnames, dummy URLs, user input, and Twitter handles. For example: "Usually, you would use `nullptr` to signal the absence of an object instance."

Bold: Indicates a new term, an important word, or words that you see on the screen. For instance, words in menus or dialog boxes appear in the text like this. For example: "The **Import Model** button may seem a bit misplaced, but now we have the chance to change the functionality."

A block of code is set as follows:

```
std::shared_ptr<AssimpModel> nullModel = std::make_shared<AssimpModel>();
mModelInstData.miModelList.emplace_back(nullModel)
```

When we wish to draw your attention to a particular part of a code block, the relevant lines or items are set in bold:

```
mat4 worldPosSkinMat = worldPos[gl_InstanceID] * skinMat;
gl_Position = projection * view * worldPosSkinMat * vec4(aPos.x, aPos.y,
aPos.z, 1.0);
...
normal = transpose(inverse(worldPosSkinMat)) * vec4(aNormal.x, aNormal.y,
aNormal.z, 1.0);
```

Any command-line input or output is written as follows:

```
$ cd chapter01/01_assimp_opengl
$ mkdir build && cd build
$ cmake -G Ninja .. && ninja && ./Main
```

 Warnings or important notes appear like this.

 Tips and tricks appear like this.

Get in touch

Feedback from our readers is always welcome.

General feedback: Email feedback@packtpub.com and mention the book's title in the subject of your message. If you have questions about any aspect of this book, please email us at questions@packtpub.com.

Errata: Although we have taken every care to ensure the accuracy of our content, mistakes do happen. If you have found a mistake in this book, we would be grateful if you reported this to us. Please visit http://www.packtpub.com/submit-errata, click **Submit Errata**, and fill in the form.

Piracy: If you come across any illegal copies of our works in any form on the internet, we would be grateful if you would provide us with the location address or website name. Please contact us at copyright@packtpub.com with a link to the material.

If you are interested in becoming an author: If there is a topic that you have expertise in and you are interested in either writing or contributing to a book, please visit http://authors.packtpub.com.

Subscribe to Game Dev Assembly Newsletter!

We are excited to introduce Game Dev Assembly, our brand-new newsletter dedicated to everything game development. Whether you're a programmer, designer, artist, animator, or studio lead, you'll get exclusive insights, industry trends, and expert tips to help you build better games and grow your skills. Sign up today and become part of a growing community of creators, innovators, and game changers. https://packt.link/gamedev-newsletter

Scan the QR code to join instantly!

Join our community on Discord

Join our community's Discord space for discussions with the author and other readers:
`https://packt.link/cppgameanimation`

Share Your Thoughts

Once you've read *Mastering C++ Game Animation Programming*, we'd love to hear your thoughts! Scan the QR code below to go straight to the Amazon review page for this book and share your feedback.

`https://packt.link/r/1835881939`

Your review is important to us and the tech community and will help us make sure we're delivering excellent quality content.

Free Benefits with Your Book

This book comes with free benefits to support your learning. Activate them now for instant access (see the *"How to Unlock"* section for instructions).

Here's a quick overview of what you can instantly unlock with your purchase:

PDF and ePub Copies   Next-Gen Web-Based Reader

Access a DRM-free PDF copy of this book to read anywhere, on any device.

Use a DRM-free ePub version with your favorite e-reader.

Multi-device progress sync: Pick up where you left off, on any device.

Highlighting and notetaking: Capture ideas and turn reading into lasting knowledge.

Bookmarking: Save and revisit key sections whenever you need them.

Dark mode: Reduce eye strain by switching to dark or sepia themes.

How to Unlock

UNLOCK NOW

Scan the QR code (or go to packtpub.com/unlock). Search for this book by name, confirm the edition, and then follow the steps on the page.

Note: Keep your invoice handy. Purchases made directly from Packt don't require one.

Part 1

Populating the World with the Game Character Models

The first part of the book starts with an introduction to **Assimp**, the Open Asset Import Library. You will learn how to load a character model from a file, how to process the different elements of the character, such as meshes, textures, and nodes, and how to draw the model to the screen. You will also learn how to move the computational load to the GPU by using compute shaders, freeing the CPU for features introduced in the book. Finally, you will explore the idea and implementation of a visual selection, enabling you to select a model instance on the screen with a click of the mouse.

This part has the following chapters:

- *Chapter 1, Working with Open Asset Import Library*
- *Chapter 2, Moving Animation Calculations from CPU to GPU*
- *Chapter 3, Adding a Visual Selection*

1

Working with Open Asset Import Library

Welcome to *Mastering C++ Game Animations*! Are you the kind of person who looks at the animated models in a computer or console game, or a 3D animation tool, and asks yourself questions like:

> *How does this work? How do they do this? Could I do this myself, too?*

If so, this book will take you in the right direction to achieving this. In the next 14 chapters, you will learn how to create your own little game character model viewer.

The book starts with loading a file using Open Asset Import Library, converting the data structures from the importer library into more efficient data structures for rendering, and rendering the character model with a simple OpenGL or Vulkan renderer. You will also learn how to optimize data updates and rendering by relocating computational load to the GPU in the form of GPU-based lookup tables and compute shaders.

For the character animations, you will not only dive into normal animation blending but also be introduced to state-based animation control, additive animation blending to move the head independently of the rest of the body, and facial animations. You will also learn how to control the behavior of the instances by using a simplified version of behavior trees and implement interaction between the instances on the screen.

To give a proper home to the game characters, you will learn how to load a game map into the application. Moving around in the game map will be enhanced by adding collision detection, inverse kinematics for the character feet, and simple navigation to let the instances run around fully on their own in the virtual world.

In addition to the animations, features such as interactive selection by using the mouse, saving and loading the configuration to a file to allow working on larger virtual worlds, and handling different cameras in the virtual world are introduced. Also, a graphical, node-based configuration will be implemented, enabling you to change the behavior of the instances in a non-programming way.

With all these steps combined, your virtual characters in the virtual world will come closer to real game characters.

Every journey starts with the first step, so welcome to *Chapter 1*! This chapter will set the foundation for the animation application, as you will get an insight into how to load a model file from your computer into the program, position the instance in the vast emptiness of the virtual world, and play the animations that are included in the file. By the end of this chapter, your game character model will be able to jump, run, or walk on the screen, maybe surrounded by non-animated models or other static objects.

In this chapter, we will cover the following topics:

- Animating game characters – a primer
- What is Open Asset Import Library?
- Loading a model file
- Extending the UI with an Open File dialog
- Adding and removing model instances dynamically

As we will use open source software and platform-independent libraries in this book, you should be able to compile and run the code "out of the box" on Windows and Linux. You will find a detailed list of the required software and libraries, plus their installation, in the following *Technical requirements* section.

Free Benefits with Your Book

Your purchase includes a free PDF copy of this book along with other exclusive benefits. Check the *Free Benefits with Your Book* section in the Preface to unlock them instantly and maximize your learning experience.

Technical requirements

For this chapter, you will need the following:

- A PC with Windows or Linux, and the tools listed later in this section
- Git for source-code management
- A text editor (such as Notepad++ or Kate) or a full IDE (such as Visual Studio 2022 for Windows, or Eclipse/KDevelop for Linux)

Important note

A recent C++ compiler is required to compile the code. In the current CMake build system, C++17 is configured, but the code is known to work with newer C++ standards, up to and including C++26 (although the compiler must support those standards).

Now, let's get the source code for this book and start unpacking the code.

Getting the source code and the basic tools

The code for this book is hosted on GitHub, which you can find here:

https://github.com/PacktPublishing/Mastering-Cpp-Game-Animation-Programming

You need to install Git since the build system utilizes Git to download the third-party projects used in the examples.

On Linux systems, use your package manager. For Ubuntu, the following line installs Git:

```
sudo apt install git
```

On Windows, you can download Git here: https://git-scm.com/downloads.

To unpack the code, you can use any of the following two methods.

Getting the code using Git

To get the code in the book, you should use Git. Using Git offers you additional features, such as creating a local branch for your changes, keeping track of your progress, and comparing your updates to the example code. Also, you can easily revert changes if you have broken the code during the exploration of the source code, or while working on the practical sessions at the end of each chapter.

You can get a local checkout of the code in a specific location on your system either through the Git GUI, by cloning the repository in Visual Studio 2022, or by executing the following command in a CMD:

```
git clone https://github.com/PacktPublishing/Mastering-Cpp-Game-Animation-
Programming
```

Please make sure that you use a path without spaces or special characters such as umlauts as this might confuse some compilers and development environments.

Getting the code as a ZIP file

Although Git is recommended, you can also download the code as a ZIP file from GitHub. You will need to unpack the ZIP file to a location of your choice on your system. Also, make sure that the path the ZIP file is unpacked to contains no spaces or special characters.

Before we can use the code from the book, some tools and libraries must be installed. We will start with the Windows installation, followed by the Linux installation.

Installing the required tools and libraries for Windows

To compile the example code on a Windows machine, I recommend using Visual Studio 2022 as the IDE since it contains all you need for a quick start. Using other IDEs like Eclipse, Rider, or KDevelop is no problem as the build is managed by CMake, but you may need to install a C++ compiler like MSYS2 plus the compiler packages as an additional dependency.

Installing Visual Studio 2022 on Windows

If you want to use Visual Studio for the example files and don't have it installed yet, download the free Community Edition of Visual Studio at https://visualstudio.microsoft.com/de/downloads/.

Then, follow these steps:

1. Choose the **Desktop development with C++** option so that the C++ compiler and the other required tools are installed on your machine:

Figure 1.1: Installing the C++ desktop development in Visual Studio 2022

2. Then, under **Individual components**, also check the **C++ CMake tools for Windows** option:

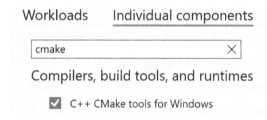

Figure 1.2: Check the box for CMake tools for Windows to be installed in Visual Studio 2022

3. Finish the installation of Visual Studio, start it, and skip the initial project selection screen.

Enabling long path names on Windows

When using a fresh installation of Windows 10 or 11, the maximum path length for files is 260 characters. Depending on the location of the folder containing the code for the book, Visual Studio 2022 might run into errors caused by paths for temporary build folders exceeding the 260 characters limit.

To enable long path names, the **Windows Registry** needs to be adjusted. A simple way is to create a text file with the .reg extension, for instance, long-paths.reg, and copy the following content to the file:

```
Windows Registry Editor Version 5.00
 [HKEY_LOCAL_MACHINE\SYSTEM\CurrentControlSet\Control\FileSystem]
 "LongPathsEnabled"=dword:00000001
```

A double-click on the file will automatically start the **Windows Registry Editor** to import the settings to the Windows Registry. After confirming both the **UAC** dialog and the following warning dialogs by clicking **Yes**, the Registry Editor will import the new settings.

Now, reboot the PC to activate the long path names and continue with the installations.

Downloading Open Asset Import Library

For Windows, Open Asset Import Library must be built and installed from the source files. Clone the repository from `https://github.com/assimp/assimp` in a new Visual Studio 2022 project, as shown in *Figure 1.3*:

Clone a repository

Enter a Git repository URL

Repository location

https://github.com/assimp/assimp

Path

C:\Users\Michael\Source\asset-importer

Figure 1.3: Cloning the asset importer GitHub repository within Visual Studio 2022

As an alternative, you can create a clone from a Git Bash, or via the Git GUI:

```
git clone https://github.com/assimp/assimp
```

Configuring the build

We need to make a few adjustments to create a static library instead of a dynamic library. Using a static library makes the build process easier for us, as we don't have to worry about an additional DLL file.

To change the CMake settings, choose the following option after right-clicking on the `CMakeLists.txt` file:

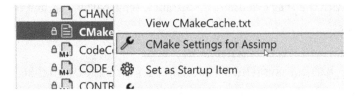

Figure 1.4: Changing the CMake settings for the asset importer

In the **Configuration** tab of Visual Studio 2022 that appears, change the configuration name to x64-RelWithDebInfo, and change the configuration type to RelWithDebInfo:

General

Configuration name:
A friendly name that identifies the configuration.

x64-RelWithDebInfo

Configuration type:
The build type to be used. "Debug" includes debug informa
debugging. This corresponds to CMAKE_BUILD_TYPE.

RelWithDebInfo

Figure 1.5: Modifying the current configuration of the asset importer

By using RelWithDebInfo, a release version with debug information will be created. The resulting executable will be optimized by the compiler, but the file still contains data to allow debugging the program in case of problems.

Next, change the following settings in the CMake settings. You can use the search field on the bottom left, named **Filter variables...**, to search for the specified setting:

- Disable building a shared library:

CMake variables and cache

Contains a name and value pair of CMake variables. Modified variables will be saved in CMakeSettings.json.
Save and generate CMake cache to load variables

☐ Show advanced variables | shared |

Name	Value	Save to JSON
BUILD_SHARED_LIBS	☐	☑

Figure 1.6: Switching the setting to create a static library

- Change the linking of the C runtime:

CMake variables and cache

Contains a name and value pair of CMake variables. Modified variables will be saved in CMakeSettings.json.
Save and generate CMake cache to load variables

☐ Show advanced variables | static |

Name	Value	Save to JSON
USE_STATIC_CRT	☑	☑

Figure 1.7: Linking the C runtime statically

- Remove the library suffix to create a file name without the compiler version:

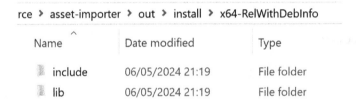

Figure 1.8: Removing the suffix of the created file

Next, select **Build** and then **Install** in the context menu of the `CMakeLists.txt` file.

After the installation is finished, the following folder structure will be generated:

rce › asset-importer › out › install › x64-RelWithDebInfo

Name	Date modified	Type
include	06/05/2024 21:19	File folder
lib	06/05/2024 21:19	File folder

Figure 1.9: Asset importer library and includes

We have to make all the files discussed in this section available for all examples in the book. To do this, two options are available – copy the files to a fixed path or add an environment variable.

Copying the Assimp files

First, create this folder on your computer:

```
C:\Program Files\assimp
```

Then, copy the two folders `lib` and `include` into it:

Share   View

› This PC › System (C:) › Program Files › assimp

Name	Date modified	Type	Size
include	06/05/2024 21:19	File folder	
lib	06/05/2024 21:23	File folder	

Figure 1.10: The two folders have been copied to the Program Files folder

The CMake search script for Assimp will try to find the static library and the header files in this folder.

Adding an environment variable to help CMake find the files

As an alternative solution, you can create a folder on your PC wherever you want, for instance, to D:\assimp. Then, copy the folders lib and include into the folder and set the environment variable **ASSIMP_ROOT** to the location of the created folder:

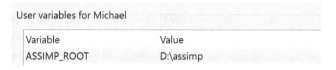

Figure 1.11: The environment variable ASSIMP_ROOT pointing to a folder on the PC

Please remember that you have to restart Visual Studio 2022 after setting the environment variable.

Installing the Vulkan SDK on Windows

For Vulkan support, you also need to have the Vulkan SDK installed. Get it here: https://vulkan.lunarg.com/sdk/home.

Do a default installation, and make sure to add **GLM headers.** and **Vulkan Memory Allocator header.**, as the CMake search scripts will use them if the Vulkan SDK is installed:

Figure 1.12: Adding GLM and VMA during Vulkan SDK installation

Make sure to restart Visual Studio 2022 after installing the Vulkan SDK to allow detecting the Vulkan SDK header files and environment variables.

Compiling and starting the example code

Running the examples can be done in two different ways: following the book example by example or compiling all the code at once to browse all the examples.

Compiling the code can be done using the following steps:

1. To open an example project, choose **Open a local folder** from the Visual Studio 2022 start screen or **Open CMake** from the **File** menu of Visual Studio 2022, then navigate to the folder with the example code you want to compile, or to the top-level folder of the example code if you want to compile all examples at once. Visual Studio will automatically detect and configure CMake in the selected folder for you. The last line of the output window should be as follows:

```
1> CMake generation finished.
```

2. This confirms the successful run of the CMake file generation.

3. Now, set the startup item by right-clicking on the CMakeLists.txt file – this step is required to build and run the project:

Figure 1.13: Configuring the startup item in Visual Studio 2022

4. After setting the startup item, we can build the current project. Right-click on the CMakeLists.txt file and choose **Build**:

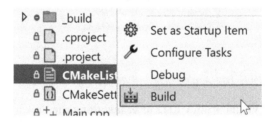

Figure 1.14: Build the project in Visual Studio 2022

5. After the compilation succeeds, start the program in a non-debug build by using the unfilled green arrow:

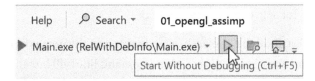

Figure 1.15: Start the compiled program without debugging in Visual Studio 2022

If you are a Linux user, you can follow the explanation in the following section to get all the tools and libraries onto your system.

Installing the required tools and libraries for Linux

Modern Linux distributions already contain most of the tools needed to compile the example code for the book.

Downloading Open Asset Import Library

For the common Linux distributions, Assimp should be available from the package manager. For Ubuntu, you need to install the Assimp development package:

```
sudo apt install libassimp-dev
```

Installing a C++ compiler and the required libraries on Linux

If you use Ubuntu Linux, all required dependencies can be installed by using the integrated package manager. Use this command to install the packages for the OpenGL-based examples:

```
sudo apt install git gcc g++ cmake ninja-build
    libglew-dev libglm-dev libglfw3-dev zlib1g-dev
```

To use Clang as a compiler, instead of GCC, you can use this command:

```
sudo apt install git llvm clang cmake ninja-build
    libglew-dev libglm-dev libglfw3-dev zlib1g-dev
```

If you plan to build the Vulkan examples, these additional packages are required and should be installed to get the most out of the Vulkan code:

```
sudo apt install glslang-tools glslc libvulkan-dev vulkan-validationlayers
```

If you want to use the latest Vulkan SDK instead of the Ubuntu version, you can download the package from the **LunarG** website:

`https://vulkan.lunarg.com/sdk/home#linux`

For other Linux distributions, the package manager and the names of the packages may differ. For instance, on an Arch-based system, this command line will install all required packages to build the OpenGL examples:

```
sudo pacman -S git cmake gcc ninja glew glm glfw assimp zlib
```

For the Vulkan examples, these additional packages are required on Arch-based installations:

```
sudo pacman -S vulkan-devel glslang
```

Compiling the examples via the command line on Linux

The examples can be compiled directly on the command line, without using an IDE or editor. To build a single example, change into the chapter and example subfolders of the folder containing the cloned repository, create a new subfolder named `build`, and change into the new subfolder:

```
$ cd chapter01/01_assimp_opengl
$ mkdir build && cd build
```

To compile all examples at once, create the `build` folder in the top-level folder of the example code and then change into the new subfolder.

Then, run CMake to create the files required to build the code with the `ninja` build tool:

```
$ cmake -G Ninja ..
```

The two dots at the end are needed; CMake needs the path to the `CMakeLists.txt` file.

If you build a single example, let `ninja` compile the code and run the generated executable file:

```
$ ninja && ./Main
```

If all the required tools and libraries are installed and the compilation is successful, an application window should open.

When building all examples at once, a new folder named `bin` will be created inside the top-level folder, containing a subfolder for every chapter and in every chapter's folder the two subfolders for the two examples of that chapter, similar to the source-code structures.

In case of build errors, you need to check the requirements again.

If you want to use an IDE, you can continue with the installation of Eclipse.

Installing Eclipse on Linux

If you want to compile the example code with the Eclipse IDE on Linux, some extra steps are required:

1. Download and install **Eclipse IDE for C/C++ Developers** from `https://www.eclipse.org/downloads/packages/`.

2. After installing Eclipse, head to the marketplace under **Help**:

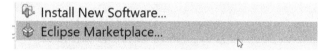

Figure 1.16: Accessing the Eclipse marketplace

3. Install the **cmake4eclipse** and **CMake Editor** packages. The first one enables CMake support in Eclipse, with all the features we need, and the second one adds syntax coloring to the CMake files. The extra colors make it more convenient to edit the files:

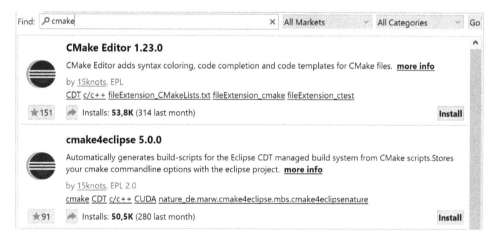

Figure 1.17: Installing the CMake Editor and cmake4eclipse

Compiling and starting the example code can be done in the following steps:

1. Select **Open Project from File System** from the **File** menu.

2. Choose **Directory...** and navigate to the folder with the source code:

    - If you want to build all examples at once, select the top-level source folder, press **Deselect All**, and select only the first project.

    - To build only a single example, you can either use **Deselect All** on the top-level folder and select only the example you want to build, or you can descend into the folder for the specific example.

3. Click on **Finish** to open the project.

4. Next, choose **Build Project** from the context of the project folder.

5. You may need to switch the console output to show the current build messages. Use the small arrow with the tooltip **Display Selected Console**:

Figure 1.18: Selecting the right output to see the build messages

6. If Eclipse does not refresh the project content after the build, choose **Refresh** from the context menu of the project folder, or press *F5*.

7. Choose **Run As**, and select the second option, **Local C/C++ application**.

8. Select the **Main** executable from the window to run the program.

Figure 1.19: Choosing the Main executable to run the compiled application

As the last step of the preparations, we look at the organization of the code in the GitHub repository of the book.

Code organization in this book

The code for every chapter is stored in the GitHub repository, in a separate folder with the relevant chapter number. The number uses two digits to get the ordering right. Inside each folder, one or more subfolders can be found. These subfolders contain the code of the chapter, depending on the progress of that specific chapter.

For all chapters, we put the Main.cpp class and the CMake configuration file, CMakeLists.txt, into the project root folder. Inside the cmake folder, helper scripts for CMake are stored. These files are required to find additional header and library files.

All C++ classes are located inside folders, collecting the classes of the objects we create. The Window class will be stored in the window subfolder to hold all files related to the class itself, and the same applies to tools – the logger, the model classes, and the renderer-related classes. After you have all the required code and tools installed, let's get a general idea of what game character animations are about.

Animating game characters — a primer

Moving a game character around in a virtual world with lots of different animations, changeable outfits, a collision detection system for other characters and the environment, and maybe even interaction with other characters looks nice and simple when playing a game.

But the mathematics and techniques behind the smoothly animated game characters are extensive and complex. Every movement, animation, action, or state change of the character involves a long journey until the final image is rendered to the screen.

Let's look at a high-level explanation of animations first. If you already know the details, you can skip to the next section.

About nodes, bones, skeletal animation, and skinning

The building blocks of an animated three-dimensional character model are the so-called **nodes**. A node can be compared to a joint in the virtual body of the character, like the shoulder or hip.

All nodes in the character model are connected in the form of a virtual skeleton, forming the **bones** of the model. By attaching child nodes to a node, modeling an arm with a hand and fingers, or a leg with a foot and toes – or even an entire human-like skeleton – is no problem. The starting point of the virtual skeleton is the so-called root node. The root node has no parent node and is used as the starting point for animations.

Usually, the level of detail does not reach the details of a skeleton in a real-world object since many of the real bones are static or play only a minor role in muscle or pose changes during animation.

The virtual skeleton of the character model can be animated by rotating nodes around their center point – and thus rotating the bone to all attached child nodes around the center point of this node. Just imagine raising your arm a bit: your upper arm will rotate around your shoulder joint, and the lower arm, hand, and finger follow the shoulder rotation. This kind of animation is called a **skeletal animation**.

A character needs to be stored in a more or less natural pose in the file, which is called the reference pose, or **bind pose**. You will find most models in a **T-pose** where both arms create a horizontal line, and sometimes see the **A-pose**, where the position of the arms of the skeleton resembles the uppercase letter A.

To animate a character, the transforms of each node between the position in the bind pose and the desired position in an animation pose need to be changed. Since the transformation of a node needs to be calculated in the local coordinates of that specific node, an **inverse bind matrix** per node exists to transform between local and world coordinates.

The animations themselves are stored in animation **clips**. An animation clip does not contain node transforms for every possible time of the animation but only for specific time points. Only the node transforms at so-called **key frames** are stored in the animation clip data, resulting in less data usage. Node positions between two key frames are interpolated using linear interpolation for translation and scaling, and spherical linear interpolation (SLERP) for rotations.

By using interpolation between two key frames, the skeleton can be brought into virtually any pose between the two stored poses. By interpolating between key frames or even interpolated poses of different animation clips, **blending** between the two poses can be achieved, Blending can be used to change the animation clip of a model without visual distortion, for instance, to create a smooth transition between a walking and a running animation clip.

The virtual skin of a character model is called a **mesh**, and applying a mesh to a skeleton in the vertex shader of the rendering pipeline is called **skinning**. To give the virtual skin a natural appearance, every vertex of the mesh uses **weights** to handle the influence of surrounding nodes.

These weights are used as a factor for node transforms: the higher the node weight, the more transforms of that node will be applied to the vertex, and vice versa. By using the node weights, the effects of expanding and compressing the skin and underlying muscles of the virtual body can be modeled with good precision.

In the glTF file format, four weights per vertex are used, but other file formats with more weights also exist.

There is a special kind of animation called a **morph animation**. In a morph animation, parts of a mesh are replaced, and the vertex positions can be interpolated between the different meshes. Morph animations are used to model facial expressions, updating only parts of a character model's face instead of the entire model. By replacing only parts of the mesh but keeping the skeletal information unchanged, morph animations can be easily added to skeletal animations.

Another form of animation is the so-called **additive animation**. Additive animations are some sort of mix between skeletal and morph animations: by adding the difference between the current pose and the bind pose to the skeletal animation clip, the animations of the additive clip are modeled on top of the skeletal animation, but only for the nodes that are changed in the additive animation clip.

Additive animations are used to move only specific parts of a character independently of the main skeletal animation. For instance, the skeletal animation contains only the walking or running part of the body, while the additive animation clip changes only the head or hands. Now the character can move the head to look around, without the need to create walking and running animations containing all possible head movements.

The combination of skeletal, morph, and additive animation enables us to build powerful and natural-looking characters for our virtual world, allowing the model to walk or run beside us, follow our movements with the head, and use facial morph animations to speak all at the same time.

Now let us look at the general workflow for creating character model animations. We can divide the animation workflow into two parts: preparation and updates. While the preparation part is needed only once while loading the model, updates are usually made for every frame drawn to the screen.

We will dive into the preparation process of the model first.

Preparing the data for efficient usage

Game character models are stored in single files, or as a collection of files, each for a specific purpose. For instance, model and texture data could reside in separate files, allowing artists to change the images independently of the model vertices.

The following steps must be done in the application before the file in the model data can be used for animation and rendering:

1. As the first step in the preparation phase, these files must be loaded into the memory of the computer. Depending on the implementation in the game, partial loading is possible, adding only the elements of the character model that are needed at a specific level, or in a specific part of the virtual world.

2. Then, the data needs to be pre-processed. The representation of the data in the files on disk may be optimized in terms of saving space, but for efficient manipulation and rendering, a different kind of optimization is required.

    For example, different rendering APIs, like OpenGL, Vulkan, and DirectX, may need slightly different representations of vertex or texture data, or shader code to be uploaded to the GPU. Instead of storing the different versions in the model file, a generic representation may be used. The required adjustments or conversions will be done after loading.

3. As the last step, static data like vertex data or textures will be uploaded to the GPU, and other static and variable data parts are stored in C++ classes and objects.

At this point, the model is ready to use. With the first appearance of that character on the screen, a continuously running task of data updates is needed. These per-frame tasks are required for states that change at runtime, such as positions or animation poses.

Updating character data

Since the data of the character is split between main memory and GPU memory, the game or animation program must sample, extract, convert, and upload data for every single frame the character is drawn to the screen.

For instance, the key-frame data of the animations needs to be updated according to the animation clip to be shown and the time since the last frame.

The following steps must be done in every frame to create the pixels of a single model instance for a specific time point of a selected animation clip:

1. Blending between different animation clips could be requested by the program flow, and additional animation parts may be needed, like additive blending for the head or the hands, or facial animations to allow a facial expression for the character. So, we extract rotation, translation, and scaling for all nodes at the specified replay time from all animation clips and combine the per-clip node transformsations into a final transformation matrix for every node.

2. After the animation data is sampled and combined, the skeleton of the character needs to be adjusted. According to the animation data, every virtual bone must be translated, rotated, and scaled to reach the desired destination.

3. Also, the world position of the character may need to be updated. World position changes can occur in different forms, like running around, jumping, or falling down. Knowing the exact position of all characters is an important part of the remaining steps.

4. Once bone positions and the world position of the character have been determined, collision detection can run. The collision detection checks if the character intersects with other characters or environmental objects like the floor and walls, or even if the character was hit by a projectile. As a reaction to the collision detection results, adjustments to the character properties, like position, or animation clip may be triggered.

5. Having the collision data at hand, inverse kinematics adjustments may run. Adjusting the skeleton data of the character could be needed to avoid character limbs intersecting with the wall or the floor, or to level the feet position on uneven ground.

6. Now, the pure CPU part of the character update is nearly over. As a final step from the CPU side, the updated animation data is uploaded to the GPU and the render commands are issued. By storing the dynamic character data in the GPU, the rendering itself can run without much additional workload from the CPU.

7. On the GPU, the vertex shader transforms the incoming vertex data according to the properties of the current view, like distances or perspective distortion. After other possible shader stages, the fragment shader receives the data from the rasterization stage of the GPU and draws the pixels to the output framebuffer.

8. After all pixels of the level data, characters, and the HUD, as well as maybe additional debug data, have been sent to the GPU, the visible and the drawing buffers are swapped – at this point, the character appears on the screen, at the position and in the animated pose we expect to see.

In between all these update steps, compute shaders may run on the GPU to calculate data. Running compute shaders allows the program to offload the calculations for multiple characters, freeing the CPU to work on other parts of the game.

As you can see, a lot of work is needed until you see a game character running around in the virtual world. Let's now start the journey into character animation with an overview of Open Asset Import Library.

What is Open Asset Import Library?

Open Asset Import Library, in short **Assimp**, is a cross-platform library to import and convert 3D model files. The different file formats are converted into a hierarchical data structure, enabling a programmer to support a wider range of model formats in a single, comprehensive way.

Figure 1.20 shows the key elements and their relationships:

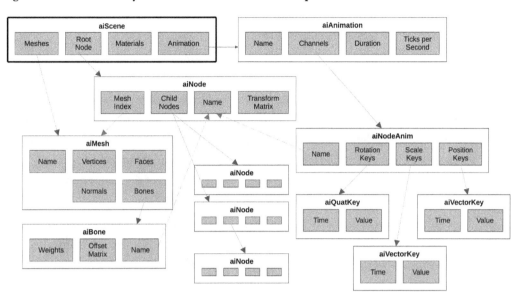

Figure 1.20: A simplified version of Assimp's data structures

Let us take a closer look at these data structures and their functions:

- aiScene is the central element of Assimp's data structure. The root node entry, all information about the polygonal meshes, the materials, and the animations are stored in the aiScene element.

- The root node of aiScene points to a structure called aiNode. In every aiNode, possible child nodes are stored, eventually creating a node tree. Also, a transform matrix resides in the aiNode structure, defining the local transformation, relative to the parent node. This matrix is called the TRS matrix for the three possible transformations: translation, rotation, and scale, in this order. By combining the TRS transforms from the root node down to every node of the skeleton, the final world position of a node can be calculated only by using the world position of the root node and the local transformations of every node in the skeleton hierarchy.

- The node name is used in other structs, like the bones or the animations, to refer back to this specific node. For the vertices of the node, an index to the corresponding aiMesh structure in aiScene is stored here.

- All data that will be drawn on the screen is stored in `aiMesh` structs. Every mesh consists of a number of so-called faces, usually triangles. For every vertex of every face, important data like the vertices, normals, and texture coordinates are stored directly in `aiMesh`. The drawing order of the vertices is stored separately as indices in the other structures, allowing features like space-saving reuse of vertices.

- For animations, the model "skeleton" consists of bones, stored in `aiBone` structs. Here, the offset matrix defines the offset between the position in mesh space and the bind pose in bone space (in the glTF file format, this is the "inverse bind matrix"). Additionally, ,several value pairs are stored for every vertex, each containing a node index and a weight value. In every pair, the weight value specifies the fraction of the nodes movement that is applied to the vertex.

- The position of every vertex in the `Assimp` meshes can be bound to up to four bones, and the influence of each of these four bones on the final vertex position can be controlled by a weight value between 0 and 1. The weight is used as a scaling factor for the transformations of the specified bone – a value of 1 means that the vertex makes the same transformations as the bone, and for a value of 0, the vertex ignores the transforms of the bone.

- On the right side of *Figure 1.20*, the data for animations is shown. The `aiAnimation` struct contains the animation channels for bones and meshes, the overall duration of the specific animation, and the number of frames per second for this animation.

- As an example for the animations, we will look at the `aiNodeAnim` struct. This struct consists of key frames with rotations, translations, or scales to apply to a specific node. The node name in the `aiNode` struct is used to find the corresponding bone to animate.

Currently, more than 50 different file formats are known to Assimp. Some notable examples are listed here:

- Autodesk 3D Studio (`.3ds`), AutoCAD (`.dxf`), and FBX (`.fbx`)
- Collada (`.dae`) and glTF (`.gltf` and `.glb`), managed by the Khronos Group
- Wavefront vertices (`.obj`) plus materials (`.mat`)
- STL files, mostly known from 3D printing (`.stl`)
- Game engine formats, i.e., from Quake (`.md3`/`.md5`), or Half-Life (`.mdl`)

Even though the number of formats is impressive, it needs to be stated that not all models you find can be imported into the application by using `Assimp`.

Several of these file formats are reverse-engineered from closed source applications, and only a subset of versions work. Other formats are open source, like Collada or glTF, but some of those formats are also constantly evolving. Also, not all new features have yet been implemented in Assimp. So, even with a versatile asset import library like Assimp, you may end up with a model that fails to be imported, produces "vertex garbage" on screen, or is missing some of its properties. Nevertheless, Assimp is currently the best open source solution to load many different game and non-game 3D models into your own application.

Loading a model file with Assimp boils down to importing the aiScene object of a file, checking for the existence of other data types, and importing that data into the application. In the next section, we will do a short walk-through of the steps to load a model file with Assimp.

The complete source code for the application can be found in the folder chapter01, the subfolder 01_opengl_assimp for OpenGL, and the subfolder 02_vulkan_assimp for Vulkan.

Loading a model file

To load a model file with Open Asset Import Library, we must include the following three headers in the implementation file of the AssimpModel model loading class in the model folder:

```
#include <assimp/scene.h>
#include <assimp/Importer.hpp>
#include <assimp/postprocess.h>
```

Next, we create an Assimp::Importer instance in the loadModel() method, and use the importer to load a file from disk:

```
Assimp::Importer importer;
const aiScene *scene = importer.ReadFile(modelFilename,
  aiProcess_Triangulate | aiProcess_GenNormals);
```

We hand over the file name of the asset file we want to load, plus the two values aiProcess_Triangulate and aiProcess_GenNormals as optional postprocessing flags.

The first flag, aiProcess_Triangulate, instructs Assimp to triangulate all polygons with more than three vertices, if those polygons exist in the file. Since our basic renderer only understands triangles, a polygon with more than three vertices would cause graphical errors.

Using aiProcess_GenNormals as the import flag ensures that all triangles have normal vectors. Default normal vectors pointing upward from the surface of the triangle will be created only if no normal vector is found. Existing normals are not changed by the flag.

Next, we must check if the import was successful:

```
if(!scene || scene->mFlags & AI_SCENE_FLAGS_INCOMPLETE ||
    !scene->mRootNode) {
  return false;
}
```

We assume a failed import if the scene pointer itself is a `nullptr`, the scene is marked as incomplete by the importer, or the scene has no root node defined.

After the model file has been loaded successfully, we will scan the model for embedded textures.

Loading embedded textures

Some model formats can embed the textures into the object file. If the function call to `HasTextures()` returns true, we loop over all textures of the model file.

```
if (scene->HasTextures()) {
  unsigned int numTextures = scene->mNumTextures;
  for (int i = 0; i < scene->mNumTextures; ++i) {
```

Inside the loop, we extract the texture name, height, and width, as well as the pixel data of the texture. The texture name is only for information purposes, since the data is embedded into the model file, but having the name is helpful while debugging problems:

```
std::string texName =
  scene->mTextures[i]->mFilename.C_Str();
int height = scene->mTextures[i]->mHeight;
int width = scene->mTextures[i]->mWidth;
aiTexel* data = scene->mTextures[i]->pcData;
```

Now, we create a shared pointer and try to import the texture data. If the import fails with an unexpected error, we stop loading the model:

```
std::shared_ptr<Texture> newTex =
  std::make_shared<Texture>();
if (!newTex->loadTexture(texName, data,
    width, height)) {
  return false;
}
```

Embedded textures are references in the format `*10` – a star plus the index number of the texture. So, we create the internal name and insert the shared pointer into a `std::unordered_map`, mapping the texture name to our data object containing the texture data:

```
    std::string internalTexName = "*" + std::to_string(i);
    mTextures.insert({internalTexName, newTex});
}
```

In addition to any embedded textures, a placeholder texture will be added:

```
mPlaceholderTexture = std::make_shared<Texture>();
std::string placeholderTex = "textures/missing_tex.png";
if (!mPlaceholderTexture->loadTexture(placeholderTex)) {
  return false;
}
```

Placeholder textures for objects are common in many game engines, showing objects with missing textures, instead of a black object or random data from the GPU memory.

Parsing the node hierarchy

After checking for embedded textures, we continue by processing all nodes. Due to the hierarchical organization, we take a recursive approach here. As the first step, we create an object for the root node:

```
std::string rootNodeName = rootNode->mName.C_Str();
mRootNode = AssimpNode::createNode(rootNodeName);
```

An `AssimpNode` object contains data about the position, rotation, and scaling of one of the model parts in the virtual world. This transformation data also includes the position, rotation, and scale of its parent node, moving all the nodes to their intended position.

Then, this new root node will be used as the basis to collect all child nodes, grandchild nodes, and so on:

```
processNode(mRootNode, rootNode, scene, assetDirectory);
```

Inside the `processNode()` method, four tasks are done for every node:

- Collecting the mesh data itself, like vertex positions, normals, or texture coordinates
- Collecting external textures from materials

- Collecting bones for skeletal animations
- Descending into the hierarchy to process the child nodes of this node

We start by iterating through all meshes of the node:

```
unsigned int numMeshes = aNode->mNumMeshes;
  for (unsigned int i = 0; i < numMeshes; ++i) {
    aiMesh* modelMesh = scene->mMeshes[aNode->mMeshes[i]];
```

The `AssimpMesh` class contains the logic to extract vertex data, textures, and bones. We simply create a local `mesh` instance and let the `processMesh()` method do all the extraction work for us:

```
    AssimpMesh mesh;
    mesh.processMesh(modelMesh, scene, assetDirectory);
```

After the Assimp mesh has been processed, we add the converted mesh data, the collected textures, and the bones to the data structures of the model itself:

```
    mModelMeshes.emplace_back(mesh.getMesh());
    mTextures.merge(mesh.getTextures());
    std::vector<std::shared_ptr<AssimpBone>> flatBones =
      mesh.getBoneList();
    mBoneList.insert(mBoneList.end(),
      flatBones.begin(), flatBones.end());
  }
}
```

Now, we store the current node in a node map and a node list:

```
    mNodeMap.insert({nodeName, node});
    mNodeList.emplace_back(node);
```

Saving the same node in two different data structures is needed to speed up the access during different phases of the program.

The `mNodeMap` contains the nodes in a `std::unordered_map`, allowing us to access any node by its node name in constant time. But a huge disadvantage is that a `std::unordered_map` does not preserve the insertion order by default. Using a `std::map` would not help either since all entries of a `std::map` will be sorted by the key in ascending order. We could solve the sorting issue by using a custom comparator function for the map, but since we are also accessing the nodes based on the index position, a second data structure will be used: the `mNodeList`.

In the mNodeList, all nodes are stored in a flat but hierarchical order, guaranteeing us to access any of the nodes before its child nodes. This way, the mNodeList is fast when it comes to updates that need to be done in all nodes. We can just iterate from start to end through the vector.

At the end of processNode(), we check for child nodes, and process any child nodes we find in a recursive manner:

```
unsigned int numChildren = aNode->mNumChildren;
for (unsigned int i = 0; i < numChildren; ++i) {
  std::string childName =
    aNode->mChildren[i]->mName.C_Str();
  std::shared_ptr<AssimpNode> childNode =
    node->addChild(childName);
  processNode(childNode, aNod->mChildren[i],
    scene, assetDirectory);
}
```

After processing all nodes in the hierarchy, we have collected all meshes, textures, and skeletal data from the model.

Adding vertex buffers for the meshes

Back in the loadModel() method, we create a combined vertex and index buffer object for every mesh, upload the extracted vertex data, and store the buffer in a std::vector called mVertexBuffers:

```
for (auto mesh : mModelMeshes) {
  VertexIndexBuffer buffer;
  buffer.init();
  buffer.uploadData(mesh.vertices, mesh.indices);
  mVertexBuffers.emplace_back(buffer);
}
```

To draw the imported model, we can now simply iterate over the mModelMeshes vector and use the drawIndirect() call of the VertexIndexBuffer class to draw all triangles of this specific mesh with only a single draw command. The method is called "indirect" because Assimp stores the model data internally as vertices plus indices, and we draw the triangles in the indirect mode, via the indices.

In addition, an instanced version of the draw call is available, named `drawIndirectInstanced()`. Instanced drawing allows us to draw several instances of the same mesh on different positions of the screen, but the workload of creating the extra triangles is done by the GPU, not the CPU.

Importing animations

As the last step of the model-loading process, we check for animations and iterate over the internal data structure of the animations in the model file:

```
unsigned int numAnims = scene->mNumAnimations;
for (unsigned int i = 0; i < numAnims; ++i) {
  const auto& animation = scene-> mAnimations[i];
```

For every animation we find, we create an object of the class `AssimpAnimClip`, and add all channels of the current animation clip:

```
std::shared_ptr<AssimpAnimClip> animClip =
    std::make_shared<AssimpAnimClip>();
animClip->addChannels(animation);
```

Some models do not specify a name for the animation clip, so we set the name to the number of the clip if the name is empty:

```
if (animClip->getClipName().empty()) {
  animClip->setClipName(std::to_string(i));
}
```

Having distinctive clip names is a requirement for the UI to select the animations by name.

Finally, we store the clips in the `mAnimClips` vector:

```
mAnimClips.emplace_back(animClip);
}
```

At this point, all relevant data of the model has been loaded, extracted, and converted. As stated at the end of the *What is Open Asset Import Library?* section, the quality of the imported data depends on various factors, particularly the compatibility with `Assimp`.

Checking the code for all the details

You should take a look at the implementation of the other classes prefixed with "Assimp" in the `model` folder, and the implementations of the extraction methods in these classes. In general, the methods simply read out the C-style data structures from `Assimp`, constructing custom C++

classes. The data for the mesh is converted into GLM types, allowing us to do a simple upload to the GPU, instead of a time-consuming change at every draw.

Now that we have the basics ready to open a model file, we run into a simple but essential problem: *The file name for the model file is hardcoded.*

Rather than hardcode the path to our model file for loading, let's add the ability to browse for a file. A simple way to load a specific model from a file into the application is with an "Open File" dialog, allowing us to choose the file we want to import. To achieve the seamless integration of such a dialog into the program, we will use an ImGui-based solution, instead of an OS-native dialog.

Extending the UI with an Open File dialog

ImGui can be used to create simple UIs like in our animation application, but the code can be also extended to build different kinds of tools. For our application, a dialog to choose a file on the system is helpful to load models at runtime, freeing us of hardcoding the model names in the code or using models as command-line parameters when starting the application.

Various ImGui-based file dialogs exist; a nice and easy-to-integrate file dialog can be found in the GitHub repository of Stephane Cuillerdier at `https://github.com/aiekick/ImGuiFileDialog`.

For a simple integration of the file dialog, we will use CMake's `FetchContent` to download and build the code.

Integrating the file dialog into CMakeLists.txt

First, we add a new `FetchContent` block into the `CMakeLists.txt` file, right below the end of the ImGui fetching:

```
FetchContent_Declare(
  filedialog
  GIT_REPOSITORY https://github.com/aiekick/ImGuiFileDialog
  GIT_TAG        v0.6.7
  CONFIGURE_COMMAND ""
  BUILD_COMMAND ""
)
```

We "short-cut" the configure and build commands here, since we only want to have the source code available, instead of building a standalone version of the file dialog.

Unfortunately, the initial configuration still needs the location of the ImGui headers. Since the FetchContent block does not allow setting additional compiler options, we need a small hack to alter the value of the CMake property COMPILE_OPTIONS during the fetch process.

To do so, we save the current state of COMPILE_OPTIONS in a new CMake variable called current_compile_options. Then, we adjust the compile options to include the headers from the ImGui source folder in the search list:

```
get_property(current_compile_options DIRECTORY
  PROPERTY COMPILE_OPTIONS)
set_property(DIRECTORY PROPERTY
  COMPILE_OPTIONS -I ${imgui_SOURCE_DIR})
```

Now, we can trigger the download and initialization of the file dialog source:

```
FetchContent_MakeAvailable(filedialog)
```

To avoid further confusion in the build system, we set the COMPILE_OPTIONS property back to its saved state, and also unset the variable we used to save the state:

```
set_property(DIRECTORY PROPERTY
  COMPILE_OPTIONS ${current_compile_options})
unset(current_compile_options)
```

In Visual Studio 2022, a new CMake configuration run is triggered automatically. In Eclipse, a new run of CMake must be triggered via the **Build Project** option in the right-click context menu of the project.

Including the functionality of the file dialog is easy; the UI class needs to be extended by only a couple of lines.

Using the ImGui file dialog

We can place the dialog code anywhere in the code of the createFrame() method of the UserInterface class in the UserInterface.cpp file within the folder opengl. First, we add an ImGui::Button named "Import Model". This button will open a modal version of the dialog:

```
    if (ImGui::Button("Import Model")) {
      IGFD::FileDialogConfig config;
      config.path = ".";
      config.countSelectionMax = 1;
      config.flags = ImGuiFileDialogFlags_Modal;
```

```
        ImGuiFileDialog::Instance()->OpenDialog(
          "ChooseModelFile", "Choose Model File", ".*",
          config);
    }
```

This button configures a special `FileDialogConfig` property of the file dialog. The `config.path` entry sets the path to open to the current path where the executable was started, while `countSelectionMax` tells the dialog to accept only a single file to be selected. Setting `flags` to `ImGuiFileDialogFlags_Modal` presents the file dialog on top of all other ImGui windows.

When the flags are set, `OpenDialog()` is called to open a dialog instance with the internal name `"ChooseModelFile"` as the first parameter; the window title `"Choose Model File"` as the second parameter; a filter to show all files, regardless of the file extensions, as the third parameter; and the configuration property as the last parameter.

Setting the internal name of the dialog to open in the `Display()` call allows us to define multiple open file dialogs, depending on the requirements of the program in the specific situation.

Right after the button, the file dialog itself is defined:

```
    if (ImGuiFileDialog::Instance()->Display(
        "ChooseModelFile")) {
      if (ImGuiFileDialog::Instance()->IsOk()) {
        ...
      }
      ImGuiFileDialog::Instance()->Close();
    }
```

The code for the file dialog follows the ImGui coding style. The first `if` around the `Display()` call returns `true` if the dialog is shown, that is, after the above `"Import Model"` button has been clicked. Then, the dialog code reacts by setting `IsOk()` to `true` after the `"OK"` button of the dialog has been clicked, allowing us to insert actions to take on the selected file. The final `Close()` call closes the dialog when a file has been selected.

Before we check the return value of the file dialog, we take a look at the file extension filter. Showing all files could make it difficult to find the file we want to load.

Adding a filter to show only supported file types

The `filter` field of the file dialog allows quite complex configurations, but we will check only three of them: a single filter, a group of extensions, and a regular expression-style filter.

Adding a single filter

The code in the *Using the ImGui file dialog* section already shows a single filter:

```
".*"
```

This filter simply means "anything after the last dot of the file name," so you will see all the visible files in the current folder.

You can also specify a single extension here, and only files with this one extension are shown:

```
".jpg"
```

Note on case sensitivity

In Linux, filtering is case sensitive.

So, the `.jpg` filter will *not* show a file named `IMAGE.JPG`!

Adding a group of filters

Grouping file extensions into a single filter works by separating them with a comma:

```
".jpg,.jpeg,.png"
```

However, this may not work as intended – you can still choose only one extension from the group, showing only files with the specific extension in the current folder. Allowing only one file extension from a group can be used for **Save File** dialogs, forcing the user to choose a specific file format from a list of available formats.

Adding a regular expression-style filter

The most useful variant for the filter is the regular expression style:

```
"Supported Types{.gltf,.glb,.obj,.fbx,.dae}"
```

Here, the string `"Supported Types"` will be shown as a filter in the dialog, and all files with the file extension named in the curly braces are shown.

You could also add multiple regular expression filters, separated by commas, to create a drop-down list of various file types. This line would enable you to choose between a couple of pictures, the textual and binary glTF formats, and all files:

```
"Pictures{.jpg,.png},Models{.gltf,.glb},All Files{.*}"
```

Since the filter field of the OpenDialog() call is a pointer to a character array, the filter list could even be created dynamically. Depending on the state of the program, the file types you want the user to select, and so on, you can present various filter options.

Having the file dialog open with a (possibly limited) amount of file types presented to the user, let's complete the code handling the file selected by the user.

Loading the model file

If a file was selected and the OK button was pressed, or the file name was double-clicked, the name including the full path of the chosen file is available by calling GetFilePathName():

```
std::string filePathName =
  ImGuiFileDialog::Instance()->GetFilePathName();
```

For a clear separation of concerns, the UI code does not handle the loading process itself. Instead, a simple lambda-based callback is created, and we call this callback with the name of the model:

```
if (modInstData.miModelAddCallbackFunction(
    filePathName)) {
  ...
}
```

The callback to add a new model is defined in the file ModelAndInstanceData.h in the model folder:

```
using modelAddCallback = std::function<bool(std::string)>;
```

During initialization of the renderer, the callback function is bound to the method addModel() of the renderer class via a lambda:

```
mModelInstData.miModelAddCallbackFunction =
  [this](std::string fileName) {
    return addModel(fileName);
  };
```

Now, when a file has been selected, the renderer is doing all the "dirty work" of importing the new model, signaling back if the model import was successful.

Right now, the return value of the callback only adjusts the position in the list of models. But it could be used to give feedback to the user – an error message popup can be presented if the model file could not be opened, or the same model file was already loaded.

Drawing the model to the screen

The process of drawing the model in the renderer is simple:

- Get the smart pointer that points to the Assimp model.
- If the model is animated, update the animation with the delta time between the last frame and this frame, and collect the new bone matrices.
- If the model is not animated, simply get the node matrices of the instances.
- Upload the matrix data to the shader storage buffer on the shader.
- Issue a draw call to the graphics API.

The custom classes handle all other steps required to draw the model, like uploading the vertex data or binding the correct texture for the mesh to draw next.

Loading and drawing a single file is already cool. But to use the full power of Assimp, we will allow adding and deleting different models and model instances at program runtime.

Adding and removing model instances dynamically

Supporting multiple instances from multiple models was done by creating the class AssimpInstance in the model folder. Every AssimpInstance contains a smart pointer to access its base model, including the nodes and bones. Adding multiple instances of the same model requires one of two options to handle nodes and bones: using a copy of the node data structures in every instance or sharing the model's nodes across all instances.

To avoid the duplication of all nodes in every instance, we will reuse the nodes of the model during the calculation of each final node position for the frame.

Reusing the bones for the sake of simplicity

To calculate the nodes during animation in the updateAnimation() method, we iterate the channels of the clip and use the model's corresponding node:

```
for (const auto& channel : animChannels) {
  std::string nodeNameToAnimate =
    channel->getTargetNodeName();
```

```
    std::shared_ptr<AssimpNode> node =
      mAssimpModel->getNodeMap().at(nodeNameToAnimate);
```

The position, rotation, or scale of every node change:

```
    node->setRotation(channel->getRotation(
      mInstanceSettings.isAnimPlayTimePos));
    node->setScaling(channel->getScaling(
      mInstanceSettings.isAnimPlayTimePos));
    node->setTranslation(channel->getTranslation(
      mInstanceSettings.isAnimPlayTimePos));
  }
```

For the root node, the local transformation of the instance is applied to the root transform matrix of the model:

```
  mAssimpMode->getNodeMap().at(
      mAssimpModel→getBoneList().at(0)->getBoneName()
    ->setRootTransformMatrix(
    mLocalTransformMatrix *
    mAssimpModel->getRootTranformationMatrix());
```

Then, the node properties are used to generate the final position of the bone, using the stored offset matrix from the corresponding bone and the local transformation matrix of the node.

First, we get the node corresponding to the bone of the model:

```
  mBoneMatrices.clear();
  for (auto& bone : mAssimpModel->getBoneList()) {
    std::string nodeName = bone->getBoneName();
    std::shared_ptr<AssimpNode> node =
      mAssimpModel->getNodeMap().at(nodeName);
```

Next, we update the matrix containing the translation, rotation, and scale properties of the node (hence the three letters **TRS** in the name):

```
    node->updateTRSMatrix();
```

Calling updateTRSMatrix() also retrieves the TRS matrix of the parent node and multiplies the local TRS matrix by the parent node's TRS matrix. Combining the local TRS matrix with its parent node matrix makes sure that all nodes will inherit the transformations from all previous nodes in the model's skeleton hierarchy.

Finally, we multiply the TRS matrix of the current node by the bone offset matrix for the node to compute the final world position for every node:

```
    if (mAssimpModel->getBoneOffsetMatrices().count(
        nodeName) > 0) {
      mBoneMatrices.emplace_back(
        mAssimpModel->getNodeMap().at(
        nodeName)->getTRSMatrix() *
        mAssimpModel
 ->getBoneOffsetMatrices().at(nodeName));
      }
    }
```

Reusing the model nodes works fine unless you plan to add a parallel (multi-threaded) calculation of instance animations: if more than one thread accesses the nodes of the model at the same time, at least one thread is modifying the node properties while other threads are reading the data, thus a so-called data race may occur, leading to a possible mix-up of the old and new data.

So, when using a multi-threading version of the code, a local copy of the node list will be required. The additional node map can be generated from the node list with a simple iteration over the list, adding the nodes by their names to a map.

Storing instance-specific settings

The remaining per-instance settings are stored in the struct InstanceSettings, defined in the file InstanceSettings.h in the model folder:

```
struct InstanceSettings {
  glm::vec3 isWorldPosition = glm::vec3(0.0f);
  glm::vec3 isWorldRotation = glm::vec3(0.0f);
  float isScale = 1.0f;
  bool isSwapYZAxis = false;

  unsigned int isAnimClipNr = 0;
  float isAnimPlayTimePos = 0.0f;
  float isAnimSpeedFactor = 1.0f;
};
```

In the first three variables, `isWorldPosition`, `isWorldRotation`, and `isScale`, the rotation, translation, and uniform scale of the instance are stored. The prefix `is` does not mean "it is" in this context but is the abbreviation of the struct name to have distinct variable names.

The fourth variable, `isSwapYZAxis`, has been added for tools using a different coordinate system. While we are using the Y axis as the vertical axis, several tools used (and still use) a coordinate system where the Z axis is vertical, and the Y axis is one of the horizontal axes. To change the coordinate systems, a simple rotation matrix will be applied if `isSwapYZAxis` is set to `true`.

The remaining three variables, `isAnimClipNr`, `isAnimPlayTimePos`, and `isAnimSpeedFactor`, are also quite self-explanatory. These variables are used to control the animation parameters of the instance.

Using the `AssimpModel` and `AsssimpInstance` classes will help us to develop a simple way to add and delete models and instances.

Dynamic model and instance management

The first building block of dynamic management is the struct `ModelAndInstanceData`, defined in the file `ModelAndInstanceData.h` in the `model` folder. A variable of this struct is maintained by the renderer, used during the `draw()` call, and also handed over to the UI:

```
struct ModelAndInstanceData {
  std::vector<std::shared_ptr<AssimpModel>> miModelList{};
  int miSelectedModel = 0;
```

The first vector, `miModelList`, contains all loaded models in the order of their addition. This list is shown in the UI as a list of currently loaded models. By using `miSelectedModel`, we keep track of which model is selected in the UI.

Next, we maintain two separate data structures for the instances:

```
  std::vector<std::shared_ptr<AssimpInstance>>
    miAssimpInstances{};
  std::unordered_map<std::string,
    std::vector<std::shared_ptr<AssimpInstance>>>
  miAssimpInstancesPerModel{};
  int miSelectedInstance = 0;
```

The instance is stored in two different kinds of structures for the same reasons as the node map and node list – depending on the requirements, accessing the instances in one or the other data structure will be faster and/or simpler.

The `miAssimpInstances` is a normal `std::vector`, where all instances of all models are stored. The instances vector is used to create the list of instances in the UI, retaining the order of addition. If instances or models are removed, the instances vector will be cleaned, still keeping the order of the remaining models.

For `miAssimpInstancesPerModel`, the reason is different. When we want to draw the models in the renderer, we need all instances of a specific model to collect the bone matrices for animated models, and the normal node matrices for non-animated models. Sorting or filtering the `miAssimpInstances` vector on every draw call would be quite expensive on the CPU side, so the separate structure helps us here.

At the end of the `ModelAndInstanceData` struct, some callback variables are defined:

```
    modelCheckCallback miModelCheckCallbackFunction;
    modelAddCallback miModelAddCallbackFunction;
    modelDeleteCallback miModelDeleteCallbackFunction;
    instanceAddCallback miInstanceAddCallbackFunction;
    instanceDeleteCallback miInstanceDeleteCallbackFunction;
};
```

These callbacks are used to move the job of creating or deleting models and instances from the UI back to the renderer. The UI is not the right place to adjust the data structures for models and instances, so these tasks will be forwarded to the renderer.

The callbacks themselves are C++-style function pointers, created with `std::function`:

```
using modelCheckCallback = std::function<bool(std::string)>;
using modelAddCallback = std::function<bool(std::string)>;
using modelDeleteCallback =
  std::function<void(std::string)>;
using instanceAddCallback =
 std::function<std::shared_ptr<
 AssimpInstance>(std::shared_ptr<AssimpModel>)>;
using instanceDeleteCallback =
  std::function<void(std::shared_ptr<AssimpInstance>)>;
```

Going back to the renderer, we look at the `addModel()` method that is called from the UI, as mentioned in the section *Loading the model file*.

The `addModel()` method for the OpenGL renderer looks like this:

```
bool OGLRenderer::addModel(std::string modelFileName) {
  if (hasModel(modelFileName)) {
    return false;
  }
```

First, we check if the model has been already loaded. To avoid confusion, a model file can be loaded only once. Having the exact same model file loaded twice (or more times) makes little sense.

Now, we try to load the specified model file:

```
std::shared_ptr<AssimpModel> model =
  std::make_shared<AssimpModel>();
if (!model->loadModel(modelFileName)) {
  return false;
}
```

When the loading fails, the model also returns `false` to the caller, even though the return value is not used currently.

If the model file can be loaded, it will be placed into a `std::vector` of models:

```
mModelInstData.miModelList.emplace_back(model);
```

From this list, the UI generates the combo box with the currently loaded model.

We also add an instance of the model and return the information about a successfully loaded model to the caller:

```
addInstance(model);
return true;
```

For a loaded model to be helpful, we need to create at least one instance, so we have something to render in the world. We use the already implemented way of creating a first instance, instead of having a separate solution.

The `addInstance()` method is also only a couple of lines long:

```
std::shared_ptr<AssimpInstance>
  OGLRenderer::addInstance(std::shared_ptr<AssimpModel>
    model) {
```

The signature of the method shows that we return the created instance to the caller. Even though the instance will be added to the internal data structures, getting the new instance from the method may be handy, i.e., when the instance should be further adjusted.

First, we create a new smart pointer of an `AssimpInstance` object:

```
std::shared_ptr<AssimpInstance> newInstance =
  std::make_shared<AssimpInstance>(model);
```

Here, the base model is given as the only parameter. The constructor of the `AssimpInstance` class has three additional parameters with default values set: the initial position, rotation, and scale. Setting these parameters may be useful in the future, but to create a single instance, they can be omitted.

Now, the new instance is inserted into two data structures, `miAssimpInstances` and `miAssimpInstancesPerModel`, of the struct `ModelAndInstanceData`:

```
mModelInstData.miAssimpInstances.emplace_back(newInstance);
mModelInstData.miAssimpInstancesPerModel[
  model->getModelFileName()
].emplace_back(newInstance);
```

As the last steps, we update the triangle count shown in the UI and return the newly created instance

```
updateTriangleCount();
return newInstance;
}
```

Deleting models and instances follows broadly the same path. The UI triggers the action via the callback; the renderer searches for the instance, or the model and all instances of that model, and removes them from the data structures.

Drawing all instances

The process of drawing the instances of the `Assimp` models has not changed much. We need to loop over all model instances, instead of just a single model. We use an "instanced" type of call to the graphics API that draws all instances of one `Assimp` model directly on the GPU:

1. Iterate over the `miAssimpInstancesPerModel` map to find all instances of a specific model.
2. If the model is animated, update the animation with the delta time between the last frame and this frame, and collect the new bone matrices.

3. If the model is not animated, simply get the node matrices of the instances.

4. Upload the matrix data to the shader storage buffer on the shader.

5. Issue an instanced draw call to the graphics API.

For *step 5* of the list, it is mandatory to have the exact count of the instances per model available as quickly as possible. The fastest way to get the number of instances is to measure the size of each vector in the `miAssimpInstancesPerModel` map.

If we use the unsorted `miAssimpInstances` vector to draw the instances instead, collecting all instances of the same model type would require extra work. Iterating over the `miAssimpInstances` vector to find all instances of the same model and adding these instances to temporary data structures costs precious time. This strategy would lower the maximum number of frames per second we could achieve. In order to use instanced draw calls, we need to process instances grouped by their associated model. So, we are drawing all instances by using the `miAssimpInstancesPerModel` vector.

Figure 1.21 shows the application after loading the example model from the `assets` folder and spawning a number of instances:

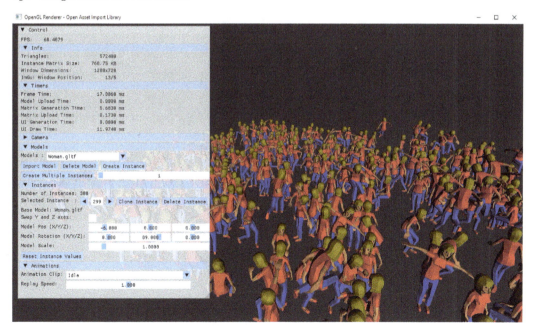

Figure 1.21: Multiple instances of the example animated character model

Summary

In this chapter, we took the first steps toward mastering C++ game animation programming by using **Open Asset Importer Library**, or `Assimp`. `Assimp` enables us to simplify and accelerate the path to animating and rendering model instances.

We started by looking at the general data structures of the `Assimp` library, how to parse the different parts of a file, and in which order. Next, we added a nice ImGui-based file dialog to the code, allowing us to select files in an interactive manner, instead of having to hardcode one or more model files we wish to open. At the end of the chapter, we explored how to add or remove models and instances at runtime, enabling us to create a more "crowded" virtual world.

In *Chapter 2*, we will move the computational load to calculate the model matrices from the CPU to the GPU, allowing us to have more CPU power left to do amazing things in our virtual world.

Practical sessions

You will see this section at the end of every chapter in the book. Here, I will add a bunch of suggestions and exercises that you can try out with the code on GitHub.

You could try to do the following:

- Add more controls to the animations, like the play direction, one/time vs. loop play, or even ping-pong replay, alternating between forward and backward replay of the chosen animation.

- Add an animation slider that lets you choose to show the frame at some point in time of an animation.

- Search for model files on the internet. Try out which models work, or to which extent they work. You do not have to limit this search to game character models; you can also search for game maps in compatible formats, or 3D-printable objects. Remember to adjust the file dialog filter to show the additional file formats.

Additional resources

For further reading, please take a look at the following resources:

- Microsoft on path length limit: `https://learn.microsoft.com/en-us/windows/win32/fileio/maximum-file-path-limitation?tabs=registry`

- Assimp GitHub repository: `https://github.com/assimp/assimp`

- Assimp documentation: `https://assimp-docs.readthedocs.io/en/latest/`

- Learn OpenGL section on Assimp: `https://learnopengl.com/Model-Loading/Assimp`

- Skeletal animation tutorial: `https://www.ogldev.org/www/tutorial38/tutorial38.html`

Get This Book's PDF Version and Exclusive Extras

UNLOCK NOW

Scan the QR code (or go to `packtpub.com/unlock`). Search for this book by name, confirm the edition, and then follow the steps on the page.

Note: Keep your invoice handy. Purchases made directly from Packt don't require an invoice.

2

Moving Animation Calculations from CPU to GPU

Welcome to *Chapter 2*! In the previous chapter, we explored the steps to load and animate a 3D model by using Open Assimp Import Library, or Assimp for short. The resulting application can render a large number of model instances. But, depending on your processor type and speed, the computational part for the model matrices becomes dominant quite fast. As a consequence, we are no longer able to reach 60 frames per second in the application.

In this chapter, we move the matrix calculations to compute shaders, running entirely on the GPU. We start with a short history of methods to do computations that are independent of the main code of the application, and the growth of parallelism in CPUs and GPUs. Next, we examine the current state of the matrix calculations. Then, we create a plan for what we should move to a compute shader, and how this relocation could be accomplished. As the last step, we check the results of the relocation and take a short look at which other parts of the application could possibly take advantage of offloading compute-intense work.

In this chapter, we will cover the following topics:

- What are compute shaders and why should we love them?
- Profiling animation performance
- Moving the node computations to the GPU
- Testing the implementation by scaling up
- How to debug a compute shader

Technical requirements

To use compute shaders, a GPU supporting at least OpenGL 4.3 and/or Vulkan 1.0 is required. Since the source code for the book is written for OpenGL 4.6 and Vulkan 1.1, we are safe here.

You can find the example code in the folder chapter02, subfolders 01_opengl_computeshader for OpenGL, and 02_vulkan_computeshader for Vulkan.

What are compute shaders and why should we love them?

Let's take a short look at the history of home computers to see how concurrency was handled. On servers, concurrent programs have been the norm since the mid-1960s but for home computers and game consoles, the evolution is a bit different.

The famous raster interrupt

While the general idea of interrupts has existed in computer systems since the beginning of computers, interrupts in home computers were normally used by the operating system to react to external events (though the first machines with interrupts were introduced in the 1950s). One of these interrupts signaled the beginning of a new picture to output to old "cathode-ray tube" TV sets: the raster interrupt.

The raster interrupt fired after the cathode ray was reset to the top left of the TV set. This steady event, occurring 50 times per second (in the EU; 60 times per second in the US), became a point of interest for programmers really quickly. By redirecting the interrupt handler to their own code, the machine could do work that needed to be done to a fixed time schedule, like playing music or graphic changes that should happen at a specific location on the screen. These programs embraced the capabilities of home computers even more than the architects of the machines could have imagined, like adding more sprites to the screen than the machine had available, drawing sprites inside of screen borders, raster bars, or even a simple form of multitasking on 8-bit CPUs.

Up to this day, retro coders do even more magic with old home computers. See the *Additional resources* section for links to demos plus tutorials on how the limitations of hardware were embraced over time.

Then, for a long time, nothing special happened. The era of 8- and 16-bit home computers ended, and x86 machines took over. However, the general system layout stayed the same – one processor core using time-sharing via interrupts to present the illusion of having multiple programs running at the same time.

The rise of multi-core machines

By the start of the year 2000, common desktop machines became capable of working with multiple CPU cores: Windows 2000 was introduced (Linux was able to utilize more than one CPU for a long time, but it was a niche system on desktops in 2000).

Five years later, the first processors with more than one computational core were available for desktop users: Pentium D and AMD 64 X2. These new CPUs were seen as the start of a new era in programming, since more than one process could run at the same time. That was also the start of an era of headaches for programmers – two threads could really run in parallel, requiring new thinking about synchronization.

Right now, the average CPU core count of a desktop machine is between 4 and 8. Taking into account the simultaneous multithreading of modern CPUs, many desktop machines can even handle between 28 and 32 threads in parallel. Sadly, the headaches for programmers are the same as 20 years ago – utilizing a large number of cores is still a complex and error-prone process.

Behind the scenes, another technology with an even more massive number of cores evolved: graphics processors.

Hidden multi-core champions

In the shadows of processor core upgrades, graphics cards also raised the number of parallel cores. They did this on even larger scales. Starting with only a couple of shader cores in 2009 and 2010, the growth in numbers is insane:

A NVIDIA GeForce RTX 4090 has a whopping 16,384 shader cores, and an AMD Radeon RX 7900 XTX has 6,144 shader cores.

These two numbers can't be compared directly due to internal differences between these two GPUs, but the raw numbers show one thing: If we were able to use some of the shader cores to calculate our model matrices for the animation frames, the computation would be a lot faster. At the same time, our CPU would have less work to do, enabling us to do other tasks while the GPU calculates the model matrices.

Thanks to graphics API designers and GPU vendors, using these shader cores is as easy as writing a small, C-like program: a compute shader.

Welcome to the wonderful world of compute shaders

Up to OpenGL 4.2, doing computations on the GPU was already possible by utilizing the other shader types, like vertex and fragment shaders. Similar to uploading arbitrary data to the GPU via texture buffer objects, shaders could be used to do massive parallel computations, saving the results into a texture buffer. The final texture could be read back to the CPU-accessible memory – et voila: the GPU helped us do some expensive calculations.

With the introduction of OpenGL 4.3, this process was simplified by officially adding compute shaders and **shader storage buffer objects (SSBOs)**. In Vulkan 1.0, the support for compute shaders and SSBOs was already mandatory, bringing the new graphics API to par with OpenGL 4.3+.

The advantages of SSBOs are great: shaders can read and write to an SSBO, unlike read-only uniform buffers. The general access to an SSBO is simplified too, as it has no hard-limited maximum size. Combined with slightly different padding for float and vec2 data types, getting or setting a value in an SSBO is simple, like using a C-style array:

```
layout (std430, binding = 0) readonly buffer Matrices {
  mat4 matrix[];
};
...
void main() {
  ...
  mat4 boneMat = matrix[index];
  ...
}
```

On the other hand, with compute shaders, you get full control of the number of shader instances you want to start. The overall number of shader invocations depends on the setting in the compute shader and the dispatch call.

Suppose we use the following compute shader settings:

```
layout(local_size_x = 16, local_size_y = 32,
  local_size_z = 1) in;
```

Then, run this OpenGL dispatch call:

```
glDispatchCompute(10, 10, 1);
```

It means we will send a request to start 51,200 instances of the shader to the GPU driver:

```
16*32*1*10*10*1 = 51200
```

For more details about compute shaders, links to tutorials for OpenGL and Vulkan are available in the *Additional resources* section.

While there are some additional limitations, like the number of shader cores used together for the sake of simplified internal management (called a wave on AMD GPUs, and a warp on NVIDIA GPUs), the number of invocations shows the user-friendly usage of compute shaders.

You, the programmer, don't need to care about spawning a massive number of threads in the code or joining them at the end of the program. Also, there is no need to create mutexes, or atomic variables, to control access to the data. All these steps are firmly hidden from your eyes in the depths of the graphics driver.

Though you are not free of obligations – you still have to make sure only a single shader invocation reads or writes a single buffer address. But, with the help of the control variables set by the GPU, like the global and local invocation IDs, this part is also easy – a lot easier compared to the efforts needed for manual multi-threading on the CPU.

So, how do we use the magic of the compute shaders in our program? The first step here is to analyze the hotspots in the code and to create a plan for how the same data could be computed on the GPU.

Profiling animation performance

To test the performance of the application on your system, you can import the test model named Woman.gltf in the woman subfolder of the assets folder, move the slider next to the **Create Multiple Instances** button to 100, and click the button **Create Multiple Instances** several times. Every click will add another 100 instances of the model, distributed randomly across the virtual world.

Or, you can change the code for the instance slider in the createFrame() method of the UserInterface class in the opengl folder. Adjust the fourth parameter of the call, controlling the maximum value of the slider:

```
ImGui::SliderInt("##MassInstanceCreation",
    &manyInstanceCreateNum, 1, 100, "%d", flags);
```

After you add a couple of hundreds of instances, you should see a picture similar to *Figure 2.1.*
The **Timers** section of the user interface has been zoomed into to show the values for the time it
takes to generate the model matrices:

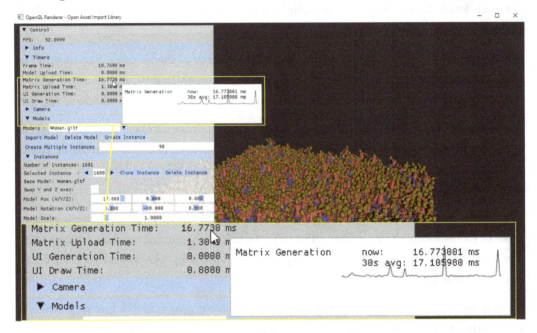

Figure 2.1: Model matrix generation time with 1,601 instances on the screen

Here, the 1,601 instances require more than 20 milliseconds to create the model matrices – which
is still a small value, if we calculate the raw numbers.

Each model has 41 animated bones. For each of the bones, two values for each of the **translation,
rotation, and scale (TRS)** are read in every frame. These values are mixed together by linear
interpolation for translation and scale, and **spherical linear interpolation (SLERP)** for rotation:

```
1601*41*3*2 = 393846
```

On top of these nearly 400,000 vector multiplications, every bone needs the resulting TRS
matrix created, multiplied by the parent matrix. Every matrix multiplication consists of 16 float
multiplications, so we have another ~100,000 multiplications:

```
1601*4*16 = 102464
```

That's quite a large amount of work to be done for the CPU in every single frame. These numbers are also reflected in the profiling outputs for Windows and Linux.

Let's verify the assumption about the workload of the CPU.

Locating the hotspots in the code

By using the built-in profiler of Visual Studio 2022, we see the function calls for the animations and the matrix multiplications among the functions with the most execution time spent inside a single function:

OGLRenderer::draw	159603 (95,78 %)	172 (0,10 %)	main
AssimpInstance::updateAnimation	134331 (80,62 %)	19475 (11,69 %)	main
std::operator<<char,std::char_traits<char>,std::all...	48740 (29,25 %)	23833 (14,30 %)	main
glm::operator*<float,0>	26069 (15,64 %)	25883 (15,53 %)	main
AssimpNode::updateTRSMatrix	24616 (14,77 %)	3689 (2,21 %)	main
AssimpAnimChannel::getRotation	16088 (9,65 %)	11828 (7,10 %)	main
ImGui_ImplOpenGL3_RenderDrawData	14959 (8,98 %)	3 (0,00 %)	main

Figure 2.2: Animation calls in Visual Studio 2022 profiling

After compiling the executable on Linux with the extra flag -pg, running the application, and starting gprof, the result is similar:

```
Flat profile:

Each sample counts as 0.01 seconds.
  %   cumulative   self              self     total
 time   seconds   seconds    calls   s/call   s/call  name
38.61     5.15      5.15     719798    0.00     0.00  AssimpInstance::updateAnimation(float)
19.23     7.72      2.57   24473132    0.00     0.00  AssimpAnimChannel::getRotation(float)
14.17     9.61      1.89   29511718    0.00     0.00  AssimpNode::updateTRSMatrix()
 8.92    10.80      1.19   24473132    0.00     0.00  AssimpAnimChannel::getScaling(float)
 6.26    11.63      0.84   24473132    0.00     0.00  AssimpAnimChannel::getTranslation(float)
 2.77    12.00      0.37     719798    0.00     0.00  AssimpAnimClip::getChannels()
```

Figure 2.3: Animation calls in Linux profiling

The vast amount of CPU time is needed to calculate the new translation, rotation, scaling, and model matrices for every node. So, let's check how to change the data representation to allow a simple upload to a compute shader.

Analyzing the current data representation

In the current implementation, the matrix work is done in the updateAnimation() method of the AssimpInstance class. For every frame the renderer draws to the screen, the following steps must be done:

1. First, we loop over all animation channels, getting the corresponding node of the model and updating the translation, scaling, and rotation of every node with the bone-local transforms from the animation data:

```
for (const auto& channel : animChannels) {
  std::string nodeNameToAnimate =
    channel->getTargetNodeName();
  std::shared_ptr<AssimpNode> node =
    mAssimpModel->getNodeMap().at(nodeNameToAnimate);
  node->setRotation(
    channel->getRotation(
    mInstanceSettings.isAnimPlayTimePos));
  node->setScaling(
    channel->getScaling(
    mInstanceSettings.isAnimPlayTimePos));
  node->setTranslation(
    channel->getTranslation(
    mInstanceSettings.isAnimPlayTimePos));
}
```

2. Then, we iterate over all bones, and update the TRS matrix of every node, calculating the node-local transforms:

```
mBoneMatrices.clear();
for (auto& bone : mAssimpModel->getBoneList()) {
  std::string nodeName = bone->getBoneName();
  std::shared_ptr<AssimpNode> node =
      mAssimpModel->getNodeMap().at(nodeName);
  node->updateTRSMatrix();
```

The TRS matrix update of a node includes the multiplication by the parent node TRS matrix.

3. At this point, we can collect the final TRS matrix for the nodes, and multiply it by the corresponding bone offset node, generating the mBoneMatrices vector containing the world position for every node:

```
if (mAssimpModel->getBoneOffsetMatrices().count(
    nodeName) > 0) {
  mBoneMatrices.emplace_back(
    mAssimpModel->getNodeMap().at(
    nodeName)->getTRSMatrix() *
  mAssimpModel->getBoneOffsetMatrices().at(nodeName));
  }
}
```

The extra .count() check for the bone offset matrices is done to avoid accessing an invalid matrix. The bone offset matrix should be valid for every node that is part of the animation, but it's better to be safe than sorry.

4. Then, in the draw() call of our renderer, i.e., in the OGLRenderer class, the animation is updated for every instance. After the animation update, the mBoneMatrices vector is retrieved and added to a local mBoneMatrices vector:

```
for (unsigned int i = 0; i < numberOfInstances; ++i) {
  modelType.second.at(i)->updateAnimation(
    deltaTime);
  std::vector<glm::mat4> instanceBoneMatrices =
    modelType.second.at(i)->getBoneMatrices();
  mModelBoneMatrices.insert(
    mModelBoneMatrices.end(),
    instanceBoneMatrices.begin(),
    instanceBoneMatrices.end());
}
```

5. As the next step, the local mBoneMatrices vector will be uploaded into the SSBO buffer:

```
mShaderBoneMatrixBuffer.uploadSsboData(
    mModelBoneMatrices, 1);
```

In the `assimp_skinning.vert` vertex shader in the `shader` folder, the bone matrices are visible as the `readonly` buffer:

```
layout (std430, binding = 1) readonly buffer BoneMatrices {
  mat4 boneMat[];
};
```

6. We use the values from the bone number of every vertex as an index into the bone matrices SSBO to calculate the final vertex skinning matrix named `skinMat`:

```
mat4 skinMat =
  aBoneWeight.x * boneMat[int(aBoneNum.x) +
    gl_InstanceID * aModelStride] +
  aBoneWeight.y * boneMat[int(aBoneNum.y) +
    gl_InstanceID * aModelStride] +
  aBoneWeight.z * boneMat[int(aBoneNum.z) +
    gl_InstanceID * aModelStride] +
  aBoneWeight.w * boneMat[int(aBoneNum.w) +
    gl_InstanceID * aModelStride];
```

7. As the last step, we use the `skinMat` matrix to move the vertex to the correct position for the specific animation frame:

```
gl_Position = projection * view * skinMat *
  vec4(aPos, 1.0);
```

As you can see, there are a lot of calculations needed for every single frame of the animation we render. Let's transfer the computational load to the graphics card.

Adjusting the data model

To move the calculations to the GPU, we create a new struct called `NodeTransformData` in the file `OGLRenderData.h` in the `opengl` folder:

```
struct NodeTransformData {
  glm::vec4 translation = glm::vec4(0.0f);
  glm::vec4 scale = glm::vec4(1.0f);
  glm::vec4 rotation = glm::vec4(1.0f, 0.0f, 0.0f, 0.0f);
}
```

For the Vulkan renderer, the struct needs to be created in the file `VkRenderData.h` in the `vulkan` folder.

In this new `struct`, we will save the transformation values on a per-node basis. We are using a `glm::vec4`, that's a vector type with four `float` elements for translation and scaling to avoid additional padding values for proper alignment and simply ignoring the last element in the shader.

GPU/CPU memory alignment may differ

Since GPUs are optimized for fast memory access, data in the buffers must be aligned in memory, in most cases to multiples of 16 bytes. This alignment will be automatically created when uploading data to the GPU. On the CPU side, a different alignment may be used, for instance for 3-element vector types like a `glm::vec3`, which is 12 bytes long. To use a `glm::vec3` vector, an additional `float` is needed as padding to match the 16-byte alignment because uploading misaligned data will end up in distorted images and incorrect results.

We also use a `glm::vec4` vector for the rotation, which is a `glm::quat` quaternion in the `AssimpChannel` class. The reason for this decision is simple: **GLSL**, the **OpenGL Shading Language**, does not know what a quaternion is, or how to handle a quaternion. We will have to implement the quaternion functions by ourselves in the compute shader. So, we utilize the normal 4-element vector to transport the four elements of the rotation quaternion to the shader.

Now, we can simplify the animation update. First, we add a local `std::vector` of our new type `NodeTransformData` to the class:

```
std::vector<NodeTransformData> mNodeTransformData{};
```

We iterate again over all channels, but instead of modifying the nodes of the model, we fill a local `NodeTransformData` variable with the transformation data:

```
for (const auto& channel : animChannels) {
  NodeTransformData nodeTransform;

  nodeTransform.translation =
    channel->getTranslation(
    mInstanceSettings.isAnimPlayTimePos);
  nodeTransform.rotation =
    channel->getRotation(
    mInstanceSettings.isAnimPlayTimePos);
  nodeTransform.scale =
    channel->getScaling(
    mInstanceSettings.isAnimPlayTimePos);
```

And, after a check to avoid accessing an invalid bone, we set the node transform of the corresponding bone with the collected transformation data:

```
    int boneId = channel->getBoneId();
    if (boneId >= 0) {
      mNodeTransformData.at(boneId) = nodeTransform;
    }
  }
}
```

During the `draw()` call of our renderer, we still need to update the animations in the same way:

```
  for (unsigned int i = 0; i < numberOfInstances; ++i) {
    modelType.second.at(i)->updateAnimation(deltaTime);
```

Then, we get the node transformation from the instance, and collect them in a local array:

```
    std::vector<NodeTransformData> instanceNodeTransform =
      modelType.second.at(i)->getNodeTransformData();
    std::copy(instanceNodeTransform.begin(),
      instanceNodeTransform.end(),
      mNodeTransFormData.begin() + i * numberOfBones);
  }
```

As the last step, we must upload the node transforms to an SSBO:

```
  mNodeTransformBuffer.uploadSsboData(mNodeTransFormData, 0);
```

The elements of the `NodeTransformData` struct are not 4x4 matrices, but only the three `glm::vec4` elements per node. So, we need to upload 25% less data to the SSBO in this step.

Having the node transformations available on the GPU is a cool first step. But, if we further analyze the data flow, we will find out we need much more data in our compute shaders to calculate the final model matrices. Let's see what else is required to calculate the world space positions from the bone-local transform data.

Adding missing data for the compute shader

The first, and most obvious missing data part is the array of bone offset matrices. In the CPU implementation, we multiply the final TRS matrix per node with the bone offset matrix for the same node:

```
  mBoneMatrices.emplace_back(
    mAssimpModel->getNodeMap().at(
```

```
          nodeName)->getTRSMatrix() *
      mAssimpModel->getBoneOffsetMatrices().at(nodeName));
```

Since the bone offset matrices are on a per-model base, we can add an SSBO to our AssimpModel class and upload the data during the model loading. We can simply add an SSBO to the AssimpModel.h header file in the model folder:

```
      ShaderStorageBuffer mShaderBoneMatrixOffsetBuffer{};
```

Then, in the loadModel() method, we fill a local vector with the offset matrices and upload the data to the SSBO:

```
    std::vector<glm::mat4> boneOffsetMatricesList{};
    for (const auto& bone : mBoneList) {
      boneOffsetMatricesList.emplace_back(
        bone->getOffsetMatrix());
    }
    mShaderBoneMatrixOffsetBuffer.uploadSsboData(
      boneOffsetMatricesList);
```

After we prepare the data for our compute shader, we bind the SSBO containing the bone offset matrices to the same binding point we configured in the matrix multiplication compute shader (binding = 2):

```
      modelType.second.at(0)->getModel()
        ->bindBoneMatrixOffsetBuffer(2);
```

A bit more hidden at first glance is the need for parent matrices. In the method updateTRSMatrix() of AssimpNode, we retrieve the TRS matrix from the parent node (if we have a parent node). Then, we use the parent node to calculate the TRS matrix of the node itself:

```
    if (std::shared_ptr<AssimpNode> parentNode =
        mParentNode.lock()) {
      mParentNodeMatrix = parentNode->getTRSMatrix();
    }
    mLocalTRSMatrix = mRootTransformMatrix *
      mParentNodeMatrix * mTranslationMatrix *
      mRotationMatrix * mScalingMatrix;
```

In the updateAnimation() method of the AssimpInstance class, we start with the update of the TRS matrix of the root node and descend into the child nodes, collecting the parent matrix node, which contains all transformation matrices up to the model root node.

For the compute shader, we need a different approach. Since all shader invocations run in parallel, we would need to cut down the number of invocations to one per model, allowing the known linear progression on the model matrices. To use a larger amount of shader invocations, we will create an int vector that contains the number of the parent node at each position. This "parent node vector" enables us to "walk" backward on the model skeleton in the shader, collecting all parent node matrices on the way.

We create the parent node vector in the loop with the bone offset matrices. First, we get the parent node of our current bone, then use a small lambda to get the position of the parent bone in the same bone list:

```
std::string parentNodeName = mNodeMap.at(
  bone->getBoneName())->getParentNodeName();
const auto boneIter = std::find_if(mBoneList.begin(),
  mBoneList.end(),
  [parentNodeName](std::shared_ptr<AssimpBone>& bone)
  { return bone->getBoneName() == parentNodeName; });
```

If we don't find a parent node in the bone list, we have found the root node of the model. In this case, we add a -1 to identify the root node. In all other cases, we add the index number of the parent bone:

```
if (boneIter == mBoneList.end()) {
  boneParentIndexList.emplace_back(-1);
} else {
  boneParentIndexList.emplace_back(
    std::distance(mBoneList.begin(), boneIter));
}
```

The boneParentIndexList now contains a flat list of the parent nodes for all the nodes in the model, with the special parent -1 for the root node. By a repeated lookup of the parent node, we can ascend the skeleton tree from every node, until we reach the root node with the special number -1 as parent.

To make the parent bone list available in the compute shader, we create another SSBO in the AssimpModel class, and upload the boneParentIndexList to the GPU:

```
mShaderBoneParentBuffer.uploadSsboData(boneParentIndexList);
```

Back in the renderer, the parent bone buffer will be bound to a binding point of our compute shader:

```
modelType.second.at(0)->getModel()
    ->bindBoneParentBuffer(1);
```

We haven't finished the workload transformation to the GPU yet. Some data needs to be handled in a different way when using a compute shader.

Relocating data to another shader

Also missing from the calculations now is the instance world position. The updateAnimation() method contains the following line to set the transformation matrix for the root node of the model:

```
mAssimpModel->getNodeMap().at(
    mAssimpModel->getBoneList().at(0)->getBoneName())
    ->setRootTransformMatrix(mLocalTransformMatrix *
    mAssimpModel->getRootTranformationMatrix());
```

The root transformation matrix of the model contains general transformations that will be applied to the entire model, like a global scaling of the model. The other matrix, mLocalTransformMatrix, is used to set the user-controlled parameters of the model instance. The local transformation matrix allows us to rotate and move the model instance in the virtual world.

In contrast to the bone offset matrices, the root node transformation will be moved to the assimp_skinning.vert vertex shader, not to a compute shader. It does not matter which of the two shaders does the matrix multiplication, but moving the root node transformation to the vertex shader may lower the load of the computer shaders a bit. Also, the vertex shader only runs for objects that are drawn to the screen, not for instances that are culled before the rendering itself, or invisible instances, potentially lowering the overall computational load of the GPU.

Doing the last preparations

And, at last, we can also decide how many distinct computer shaders we need:

We need – at least – two compute shaders.

To calculate the final TRS matrix for a node, we need to have all parent TRS matrices completed, with all matrices multiplied from the current node up to the model root. Since we can only control the amount of shader invocations we start, but not when or how long such a shader invocation runs, we need to set some sort of barrier between the calculation of the node TRS matrices, and the process of collecting the matrices along the skeleton.

The only way to create such a barrier is on the CPU side. A barrier will be added while submitting the compute shader to the graphics API, telling the GPU to wait for the first shaders to finish, before it starts the second batch.

So, we will have to start with the node transforms, wait until all node transform matrices are finished, and then start the calculation of the final node matrices.

After the theoretical part is done, we can start the shader-related implementation.

Moving the node computations to the GPU

The process of loading a compute shader differs only slightly from a vertex or fragment shader. For OpenGL, we have to set the shader type in the glCreateShader() call:

```
glCreateShader(GL_COMPUTE_SHADER);
```

For Vulkan, we must set the correct shader stage during the creation of the VkShaderModule:

```
VkPipelineShaderStageCreateInfo computeShaderStageInfo{};
computeShaderStageInfo.sType =
  VK_STRUCTURE_TYPE_PIPELINE_SHADER_STAGE_CREATE_INFO;
computeShaderStageInfo.stage =
  VK_SHADER_STAGE_COMPUTE_BIT;
```

All the other steps of loading the shader code, linking, or creating the shader module, stay the same. Because we have only a single shader file, additional methods have been added to the Shader class. Loading a compute shader in OpenGL can now be achieved by calling the loadComputeShader() method of the Shader class with the relative file name of the shader source:

```
if (!mAssimpTransformComputeShader.loadComputeShader(
    "shader/assimp_instance_transform.comp")) {
  return false;
}
```

Vulkan uses the **Standard Portable Intermediate Representation (SPIR-V)** format for shaders. Instead of the shader source, the precompiled shader code must be loaded into the Shader class for the Vulkan renderer.

As we compute new matrices in the compute shaders, and we have to move these matrices between different shaders, two additional SSBOs are required.

Adding more shader storage buffers

The first SSBO will store the TRS matrices that we create from the node transforms. This SSBO is a simple buffer, defined in the header file for the renderer:

```
ShaderStorageBuffer mShaderTRSMatrixBuffer{};
```

The second SSBO will contain the final bone matrices that will be used in the skinning vertex shader. The bone matrix buffer is also added as a normal SSBO declaration in the header file of the renderer:

```
ShaderStorageBuffer mShaderBoneMatrixBuffer{};
```

One important step to use the SSBO in the shaders is the have a correct size set. If the SSBO is too small, not all data will be stored in the compute shader, and instances or body parts of instances may be missing. A wrong buffer size may be hard to debug – you may not even get a warning that the shader writes beyond the end of the buffer. We must calculate the buffer size according to the number of bones, the number of instances, and the size of the 4x4 matrix, as shown here:

```
size_t trsMatrixSize = numberOfBones *
  numberOfInstances * sizeof(glm::mat4);
```

Then, we resize the two SSBOs to the final matrix size:

```
mShaderBoneMatrixBuffer.checkForResize(trsMatrixSize);
mShaderTRSMatrixBuffer.checkForResize(trsMatrixSize);
```

When drawing multiple models, both buffers will end up with the maximum size of all models. But this does not do any harm, as the buffers will be reused for the next model and filled only up to the real amount of data used in the new model.

Calculating the node transforms in a shader

For the first compute shader, we must upload the node transform data to the first compute shader. We bind the SSBO storing the new TRS matrices created from the node transform to the proper binding point of the compute shader:

```
mAssimpTransformComputeShader.use();
mNodeTransformBuffer.uploadSsboData(
  mNodeTransFormData, 0);
mShaderTRSMatrixBuffer.bind(1)
```

The compute shader itself is named `assimp_instance_transform.comp`, located in the shader folder. The first line of the compute shader is the usual version definition; the second line defines the local invocation sizes:

```
#version 460 core
layout(local_size_x = 1, local_size_y = 32,
  local_size_z = 1) in;
```

Here, we create 32 invocations of the shader by default. You may need to experiment with the local sizes to achieve maximum performance. Shaders are started in groups of fixed sizes to simplify the GPU-internal management. Common values are 32 (called "warps," for NVIDIA GPUs) or 64 (called "waves," for AMD GPUs). It's kind of useless to set all the local sizes to 1 for NVIDIA or AMD GPUs, since the remaining 31 warps or respective 63 waves will be unused.

Next, we must add the `NodeTransformData` with the same data types as we used while declaring the type in the `OGLRenderData.h`:

```
struct NodeTransformData {
  vec4 translation;
  vec4 scale;
  vec4 rotation;
};
```

As a reminder: The `rotation` element is a quaternion, disguised as `vec4`.

Now, we define the two SSBOs, using the same binding points as in the renderer code:

```
layout (std430, binding = 0) readonly restrict
    buffer TransformData {
  NodeTransformData data[];
};
layout (std430, binding = 1) writeonly restrict
    buffer TRSMatrix {
  mat4 trsMat[];
};
```

We mark the node transform data as readonly, and the TRS matrices as writeonly. The two modifiers could help the shader compiler to optimize the access of the buffers, since some operations could be left out. The other modifier, restrict, also helps the shader compiler to optimize the shader code. By adding restrict, we tell the shader compiler that we will never read a value with a variable that we wrote before from another variable. Eliminating read-after-write dependencies will make the life of the shader compiler much easier.

To read the data from the TransformData buffer, three methods have been added. Within these three methods, called getTranslationMatrix(), getScaleMatrix(), and getRotationMatrix(), we read the data elements of the buffer and create 4x4 matrices for the corresponding transformation.

As an example, see the implementation of the getTranslationMatrix() method:

```
mat4 getTranslationMatrix(uint index) {
   return mat4(1.0, 0.0, 0.0, 0.0,
               0.0, 1.0, 0.0, 0.0,
               0.0, 0.0, 1.0, 0.0,
               data[index].translation[0],
                  data[index].translation[1],
                     data[index].translation[2],
                        1.0);
}
```

The resulting 4x4 matrix is an identity matrix, enriched by the translation data for the specific index in the TransformData buffer. The getScaleMatrix() method creates a scaling matrix, having the first three elements of the main diagonal set to the scaling values. Finally, the getRotationMatrix() method resembles the spirit of the mat3_cast algorithm from GLM, converting a quaternion into a 4x4 rotation matrix.

In the main() method of the first compute shader, we get the x and y dimensions of the shader invocations:

```
void main() {
   uint node = gl_GlobalInvocationID.x;
   uint instance = gl_GlobalInvocationID.y;
```

We will use the number of bones in the model as x dimension, simplifying the remaining part of the shader code:

```
uint numberOfBones = gl_NumWorkGroups.x;
```

Locating the correct index in the buffer is done by combining the number of bones, the shader instance (invocation), and the node we will work on:

```
uint index = node + numberOfBones * instance;
```

The main logic for the compute shader multiplies the translation, rotation, and scaling matrix in the TRS order, and saves the result in the buffer for the TRS matrices, at the same index of the node transforms:

```
trsMat[index] = getTranslationMatrix(index) *
   getRotationMatrix(index) * getScaleMatrix(index);
}
```

In GLM, matrices are multiplied from right to left, a fact that may be confusing at first. So, despite the name of the matrix being "TRS," the multiplications are performed in reverse order of the name: The model scaling is applied first, then the rotation, and then the translation comes last. Other math libraries or different matrix packings may use a different order of multiplication. Two extensive matrix tutorials are listed in the *Additional resources* section.

Saving the TRS matrix on the same spot as the node transforms retains the order of nodes in a model and the order of nodes in all model instances.

To trigger the shader execution, we call glDispatchCompute() for the OpenGL renderer, adding a memory barrier that waits for the SSBO:

```
glDispatchCompute(numberOfBones,
   std::ceil(numberOfInstances / 32.0f), 1);
glMemoryBarrier(GL_SHADER_STORAGE_BARRIER_BIT);
```

The memory barrier makes sure the CPU waits for a specific state of the GPU. In this case, we must wait until all SSBO writes have finished, so we set the bit for the shader storage buffers. The call to glMemoryBarrier() simply blocks execution, returning only after the GPU has reached the desired state.

Before we go on, let's take a look at what happens inside the compute shader when `glDispatchCompute()` or `vkCmdDispatch()` is called. *Figure 2.4* shows the internal elements of the compute shader invocations:

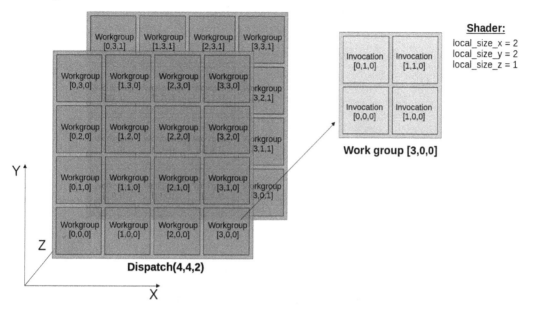

Figure 2.4: Global work groups and local invocation structure of a compute shader

When we call the dispatch command with the parameters 4,4,2, a total of number of 4*4*2 = 32 workgroups will be started, as shown on the left side of *Figure 2.4*. The total number of workgroups is simply the product of the three dimensions X, Y, and Z of the global compute space.

In each of the 32 workgroups, a total of four shader invocations are running, as seen for the workgroup [3,0,0] in the middle of *Figure 2.4*. The so-called local size is defined by the three shader layout values `local_size_x`, `local_size_y`, and `local_size_z`. The local size of a workgroup is calculated like the number of workgroups, by multiplying the three values for X, Y, and Z dimensions: 2*2*1 = 4.

A separation into workgroups is important if the shader instances need to communicate between each other since communication is only possible inside the same workgroup. Shader invocations from different workgroups are effectively isolated and unable to communicate.

As you can see, the total number of shader invocations can become huge quite quickly, since the local size of a single workgroup and the total number of workgroups are multiplied. This massive parallelism is the secret behind the raw power of a GPU.

So, for the x dimension, we use the numberOfBones, as stated before. By calculating the std::ceil of the numberOfInstances divided by 32 as the y dimension, we make sure to start groups of 32 shader invocations to calculate the matrices for up to 32 instances at once, as configured as the local y dimension in the shader code. If we have an instance count of less than a multiple of 32, the additional waves or warps are still running, but the results are ignored. Technically, we are reading and writing outside the buffer bounds, but the GPU driver should handle the situation, i.e., by discarding the writes.

For Vulkan, we must call VkCmdDispatch():

```
vkCmdDispatch(commandBuffer, numberOfBones,
    std::ceil(numberOfInstances / 32.0f), 1);
```

The size of the Shader Storage Buffer Object for the compute shaders in Vulkan should also be rounded to hold a multiple of 32 times the number of bones to avoid accidental overwrites of buffer data:

```
boneMatrixBufferSize +=
    numberOfBones * ((numberOfInstances - 1) / 32 + 1) * 32;
```

Barriers to synchronizing the shaders in Vulkan must be set to wait for the results of the queues. For synchronization between the compute shader and the vertex shader, we need to set the barrier between the writes of the compute shader and the first read operation of the vertex shader like this:

```
VkMemoryBarrier memoryBarrier {}
  ...
  memoryBarrier.srcAccessMask = VK_ACCESS_SHADER_WRITE_BIT:
  memoryBarrier.dstAccessMask = VK_ACCESS_SHADER_READ_BIT;

vkCmdPipelineBarrier(...
  VK_PIPELINE_STAGE_COMPUTE_SHADER_BIT,
  VK_PIPELINE_STAGE_VERTEX_INPUT_BIT,
  1, &memoryBarrier, ...);
```

Now, Vulkan waits for the compute shader to finish all calculations before starting the draw calls in the vertex shader.

The TRS matrix buffer now contains the matrices for every node, but without the parent nodes, the root node transform matrix, or any offset matrices.

Creating the final node matrices

Before we can start the next compute shader, we must bind all buffers that will be used during the shader run. We have a total of four SSBOs:

```
mAssimpMatrixComputeShader.use();
mShaderTRSMatrixBuffer.bind(0);
modelType.second.at(0)->getModel()
  ->bindBoneParentBuffer(1);
modelType.second.at(0)->getModel()
  ->bindBoneMatrixOffsetBuffer(2);
mShaderBoneMatrixBuffer.bind(3);
```

Since all data already resides on the GPU, we don't need any kind of upload here.

The second compute shader itself is called assimp_instance_matrix_mult.comp and can be found in the shader folder. The shader code starts – again – with a version and the local size definitions:

```
#version 460 core
layout(local_size_x = 1, local_size_y = 32,
  local_size_z = 1) in;
```

A local size of 32 is used since the code was developed on a machine with an NVIDIA GPU. For an AMD GPU, you should use a local size of 64, as explained in the section *Calculating the node transforms in a shader*.

Similar to the first compute shader, the SSBOs follow:

```
layout (std430, binding = 0) readonly restrict
    buffer TRSMatrix {
  mat4 trsMat[];
};
layout (std430, binding = 1) readonly restrict
    buffer ParentMatrixIndices {
  int parentIndex[];
};
layout (std430, binding = 2) readonly restrict
    buffer BoneOffsets {
  mat4 boneOffset[]
};
```

```
layout (std430, binding = 3) writeonly restrict
    buffer BoneMatrices {
  mat4 boneMat[];
};
```

The first buffer, TRSMatrix, contains the TRS matrices from the first compute shader. In the ParentMatrixIndices buffer, the shader can find the list containing the parent node for each of the nodes. The bone matrix offsets for every node are made available in the third buffer, BoneOffsets, and the final node matrices will be stored in the last buffer, BoneMatrices. The readonly and writeonly modifiers are set according to the usage of the buffers.

Since we use the same settings as the first compute shader, having virtually the same first lines in the main() method of the second compute shader should be no surprise:

```
void main() {
    uint node = gl_GlobalInvocationID.x;
    uint instance = gl_GlobalInvocationID.y;
    uint numberOfBones = gl_NumWorkGroups.x;
    uint index = node + numberOfBones * instance;
```

Now, we get the TRS matrix for the bone we will be working on:

```
    mat4 nodeMatrix = trsMat[index];
```

Next, we introduce a variable called parent, storing the index of the parent node:

```
    uint parent = 0;
```

We will need the parent node index to get the correct parent matrix while we walk the node skeleton up to the root node.

As the first step of the skeleton walk, we get the parent node of the node that we are working on:

```
    int parentNode = parentIndex[node];
```

In the following while loop, we get the parent matrix of the node and multiply both matrices. Then we look up the parent of the parent node, and so on:

```
    while (parentNode >= 0) {
        parent = parentNode + numberOfBones * instance;
        nodeMatrix = trsMat[parent] * nodeMatrix;
        parentNode = parentIndex[parentNode];
    }
```

The preceding lines of code may make you raise your eyebrows, since we apparently break one of the basic rules of GLSL shader code: the size of a loop must be known at compile time. Luckily, this rule does not apply to a `while` loop. We are free to alter the loop control variable inside the body of the loop, creating loops of various lengths.

However, this code could impact shader performance as GPUs are optimized to execute the same instructions on every thread. You may have to check the shader code on different GPUs to make sure you see the expected speedup.

Also be aware that the accidental creation of an infinite loop may end in a locked-up system since the shader code never returns the wave or warp to the pool. It's a good idea to ensure a valid exit condition for a while loop on the CPU side since a GPU lockup may only be resolved by a forced restart of your computer.

As long as we don't have errors or cycles in the parent node list, we will end at the last block for every node:

```
    if (parentNode == -1) {
      nodeMat[index] = nodeMatrix * boneOff[node];
    }
  }
```

Here, we multiply the resulting node matrix, containing all matrices up to the root node, by the bone offset matrix for the node, and store the result in the writable `NodeMatrices` buffer.

Starting the computation is done in exactly the same way as for the first shader. Run `glDispatchCompute()` for OpenGL, followed by a `glMemoryBarrier()`:

```
        glDispatchCompute(numberOfBones,
          std::ceil(numberOfInstances / 32.0f), 1);
        glMemoryBarrier(GL_SHADER_STORAGE_BARRIER_BIT);
```

And, for Vulkan, use `VkCmdDispatch()`:

```
        vkCmdDispatch(commandBuffer, numberOfBones,
          std::ceil(numberOfInstances / 32.0f), 1);
```

At this point, the `NodeMatrices` buffer contains the TRS matrices for all nodes, close to the result we had after the `updateAnimation()` call in the CPU-based version of the code in *Chapter 1* – with the exception of the model root matrix for the instance.

Finalizing the compute relocation

So, let's add the missing matrix calculation to the vertex skinning shader. First, we collect the matrices containing the world positions during the loop over all instances of the model:

```
mWorldPosMatrices.resize(numberOfInstances);
for (unsigned int i = 0; i < numberOfInstances; ++i) {
  ...
  mWorldPosMatrices.at(i) =
    modelType.second.at(i)->getWorldTransformMatrix();
}
```

Then, the world position matrices are uploaded into an SSBO, and bound to the vertex skinning shader:

```
mAssimpSkinningShader.use();
mAssimpSkinningShader.setUniformValue(
  numberOfBones);
mShaderBoneMatrixBuffer.bind(1);
mShaderModelRootMatrixBuffer.uploadSsboData(
  mWorldPosMatrices, 2);
```

In the vertex skinning shader itself, the new buffer is introduced:

```
layout (std430, binding = 2) readonly restrict
    buffer WorldPosMatrices {
  mat4 worldPos[];
};
```

Finally, we create a combined matrix from the world position and the vertex skin matrix, and use the new matrix to calculate the position of the vertex and the normal:

```
mat4 worldPosSkinMat = worldPos[gl_InstanceID] * skinMat;
gl_Position = projection * view * worldPosSkinMat *
  vec4(aPos.x, aPos.y, aPos.z, 1.0);
...
normal = transpose(inverse(worldPosSkinMat)) *
  vec4(aNormal.x, aNormal.y, aNormal.z, 1.0);
```

Compiling and running the example from *Chapter 2* should result in the same functionality as the example from *Chapter 1*. We can load models and create a large number of instances, but we are still able to control the parameters of every single instance of every model. The main difference should be the amount of time it takes to create the transform matrices – we should see a large drop, compared to the CPU-based version, and end up most probably below 10 milliseconds. Depending on your CPU and GPU types, the speed gain will differ. But in all cases, the GPU shader should be notably faster than pure CPU calculations.

Let's see the speedup we achieved by using compute shaders.

Testing the implementation by scaling up

All features and the user interface are identical to *Chapter 1*. But our changes can be made visible by adding more and more instances. If you add the same 1,600 instances as in *Figure 2.1*, you will see much smaller matrix generation times. The values may be similar to *Figure 2.5*:

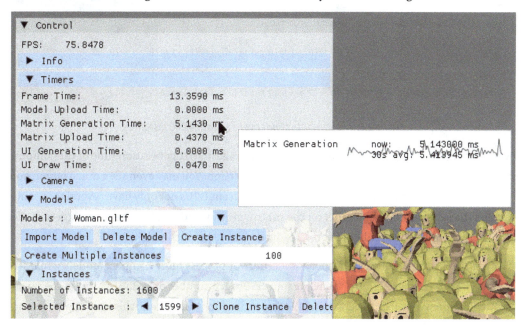

Figure 2.5: The compute shader version with 1,600 instances

The time for virtually the same matrix operations went down from ~24 milliseconds on the CPU to less than 6 milliseconds by using compute shaders. We won around 18 milliseconds of CPU time in every single frame!

Now let us add more models – many models. Let's say we add a total of 4,000 instances of the example model. The resulting matrix generation times on your machine may be similar to the number in *Figure 2.6*:

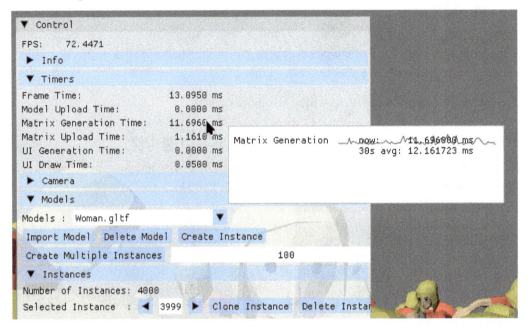

Figure 2.6: The compute shader version with 4,000 instances

Even with 2.5 times the number of instances, the average matrix generation time of the compute shader code is still at about half the time of the CPU version. You may even see a much larger, non-linear performance gain with more powerful GPUs. Recent GPUs not only have several thousands of cores that are working in parallel on the matrix multiplications, but the next biggest model also nearly doubles the number of cores, leading to more parallelization.

We can scale up the number of instances a lot more or process more complex models while still having a lower matrix generation time. At some arbitrary number of instances, the frame rate of the application will still drop below 60 FPS. Depending on your system, this may happen before reaching the 4,000 instances of *Figure 2.6*, or much later.

If you attach a profiler to the application, you will spot the new bottleneck of our calculation: The quaternion SLERP at the end of the method getRotation() in the AssimpAnimChannel class:

```
glm::quat rotation =
  glm::normalize(glm::slerp(mRotations.at(timeIndex),
  mRotations.at(timeIndex + 1), interpolatedTime));
```

Also, the two `mix()` calls of `getTranslation()` and `getScale()` in the `AssimpAnimChannel` class will be among the top findings of the profiler.

At this point, you could try to move even more operations to the compute shaders. But be aware that your mileage may vary. Some changes could raise the computational load of the GPU more than the CPU load will be lowered. That's the moment when you should grab a good book about shader programming, or watch some conference talks, if you want to continue your journey into the world of compute shaders. The best way to get into GPU computation is still "learning by doing" and not giving up if the shader does not give the expected results. But be warned: Here will be dragons around, eating your time...

Before we close this chapter, let's talk briefly about compute shader debugging.

How to debug a compute shader

Compute shaders are cool – at least, until you run into some kind of trouble.

While you can easily attach a debugger to the CPU code to see what's going on, the GPU side is harder to check. A mistake in a fragment shader may cause distorted graphics, providing some hint for where the bug lies, but in other cases, you might see just nothing. In addition to undoing the latest changes, you can always attach a debugging tool like **RenderDoc** and check out what's going wrong with the usual shader types.

But, while RenderDoc has experimental support for compute shader debugging, this support is still limited. So, in contrast to other shader types, a compute shader is mostly a "black box" for us with RenderDoc – a program receiving and outputting opaque data.

Depending on your GPU, you might want to try out NVIDIA Nsight (for NVIDIA GPUs) or the AMD Radeon GPU Profiler (for AMD GPUs). Links to all three tools are available in the *Additional resources* section.

In many cases though, the problems in a compute shader come from simple mistakes. Uploading wrong or incomplete data to an SSBO, stride or padding problems, getting the order of elements wrong, swapping the order of a (non-commutative) matrix multiplication by accident... simple, but annoying errors that can take ages to find.

A quite easy way to see what a compute shader stage does is by reading back the contents of the SSBOs. As an example for OpenGL, these lines read the data inside the SSBO `buffer` into the `std::vector` named `bufferVector`:

```
glBindBuffer(GL_SHADER_STORAGE_BUFFER, buffer);
glGetBufferSubData(GL_SHADER_STORAGE_BUFFER, 0,
```

```
    buffer, bufferVector.data());
  glBindBuffer(GL_SHADER_STORAGE_BUFFER, 0)
```

The contents of the SSBO could be compared to the results of the same calculations done on the CPU. Step by step and buffer by buffer, the problem may be narrowed down until the error has been found.

Reading back an SSBO may not be an obvious solution to do compute shader debugging, but every little bit of help is welcome here. But, depending on the complexity of the shader, you may be thrown back to a manual walk-through of the code. Also, try to use a simple dataset to simplify debugging.

Summary

In this chapter, we moved a large part of the computations from the CPU to compute shaders on the GPU. After a brief history of concurrent code execution, we created a plan on how to move the node transform calculation to the GPU, and we finally executed that plan. At the end of the chapter, we checked the resulting application for the speedup we achieved.

In the next chapter, we will take a look at solutions to add a visual selection to the model view application. Being able to create thousands of model instances is nice, but locating one special instance among all the others is nearly impossible right now. We will discuss two different approaches and implement one of them.

Practical sessions

There are some additions you could make to the code:

- Add "Programmable Vertex Pulling" to the code.

  With Programmable Vertex Pulling, the vertex data will no longer be pushed by using a vertex buffer. Instead, the vertex data will be uploaded to a UBO or SSBO to the GPU, and the vertex shader is used to extract all the data for every vertex from that buffer.

- Move `mix()` and `slerp()` from `AssimpAnimChannel` to the GPU.

  When the two data values for the timings of translation, rotation, and scaling have been extracted from the channel vector, a linear interpolation for translation and scaling and a SLERP for rotation are required. Both interpolation types are called thousands of items per frame – maybe the GPU is faster.

- Blend between two animations in a compute shader.

  This task is similar to the previous practical session. But, instead of doing the interpolation between the animation keys of a single animation clip on the GPU, do the interpolation between the transformations at the same time for two different animation clips.

  For extra difficulty: Combine both tasks and do interpolations between the 4 values for the node transformations of two animation clips in a compute shader.

- Use RenderDoc to view the buffer contents.

  Since the buffer data type is shown as RGB values in RenderDoc, you may see some interesting and recurring patterns in the buffers.

Additional resources

- C64 demo coding: `https://codebase64.org/doku.php?id=base:start`
- Atari ST demo scene: `https://democyclopedia.wordpress.com`
- pouët.net demo scene archive: `https://www.pouet.net`
- LearnOpenGL on compute shaders: `https://learnopengl.com/Guest-Articles/2022/Compute-Shaders/Introduction`
- Vulkan Tutorial on compute shaders: `https://vulkan-tutorial.com/Compute_Shader`
- *Vulkan Compute: High-Performance Compute Programming with Vulkan and Compute Shaders* by *Kenwright*, published by the author himself, ISBN: 979-8345148280
- GLSL Interface block restrictions: `https://www.khronos.org/opengl/wiki/Interface_Block_(GLSL)`
- Matrix multiplication guide: `https://blog.mecheye.net/2024/10/the-ultimate-guide-to-matrix-multiplication-and-ordering/`
- Tutorial on different matrix multiplications: `https://tomhultonharrop.com/mathematics/matrix/2022/12/26/column-row-major.html`
- OpenGL memory barriers: `https://registry.khronos.org/OpenGL-Refpages/gl4/html/glMemoryBarrier.xhtml`
- RenderDoc homepage: `https://renderdoc.org`
- NVIDIA Nsight: `https://developer.nvidia.com/tools-overview`
- AMD Radeon GPU Profiler: `https://gpuopen.com/rgp/`

Join our community on Discord

Join our community's Discord space for discussions with the author and other readers:

`https://packt.link/cppgameanimation`

3

Adding a Visual Selection

Welcome to *Chapter 3*! In the previous chapter, we offloaded the majority of matrix and vector calculations to the GPU. A modern graphics card has more (and also more specialized) computing cores than a desktop CPU, so, moving the compute load to the GPU will free the main CPU from most of the animation work.

In this chapter, we will add a couple of simplifications when working with a lot of model instances. After the changes in the previous chapter, we are able to display thousands of model instances on the screen, but selecting a specific instance is still hard. We will start by adding coordinate arrows to identify the currently selected instance. Next, we will add a function that allows us to center the specified instance in the middle of the screen. Then, a graphical highlight will be created, further helping us to find the selected instance among all instances. As the last step, we will add a model without triangles, and an instance from this empty model, allowing us to deselect the visible instances.

In this chapter, we will cover the following topics:

- Implementing a "move to instance" function
- Adding a highlight to the selected instance
- Selecting a model instance with point and click
- Implementing a null object to allow deselection

At first glance, these topics may look unrelated to animation programming. But proper tooling is an essential part of creating a user-friendly application. Good tools will help the user to simplify application handling.

Later in the book, when you have created dozens or even hundreds of instances that are happily jumping and running around randomly on the screen, selecting one instance by simply clicking on it with the mouse, using a UI button to center the instance on the screen, or moving and rotating the instance by using the mouse will make your life a lot easier. And you might even forget how cumbersome the first two chapters were when it came to selecting an instance or changing instance properties.

Technical requirements

We will need the application code from *Chapter 2*: `https://github.com/PacktPublishing/` `Mastering-Cpp-Game-Animation-Programming`.

The example source code for this chapter can be found in the folder `chapter03`, subfolder `01_opengl_selection` for OpenGL, and `02_vulkan_selection` for Vulkan.

Implementing a "move to instance" function

As the first change for the "move to instance" functionality, we will add a small set of coordinate arrows appearing at the origin of the drawn model to identify the currently selected instance. We will also add a button to center the currently selected instance. Let's start with the implementation of the coordinate arrows.

Adding coordinate arrows

Since we will use lines instead of triangles to draw coordinate arrows at the center of the selected instance, we need some extra data structures, objects and shaders. To store the vertex and color data, we add two new structs to the declarations in the file `OGLRenderData.h` in the opengl folder:

```
struct OGLLineVertex {
  glm::vec3 position = glm::vec3(0.0f);
  glm::vec3 color = glm::vec3(0.0f);
};
struct OGLLineMesh {
  std::vector<OGLLineVertex> vertices{};
};
```

For Vulkan, the new structs are named `VkLineVertex` and `VkLineMesh`, residing in the file `VkRenderData.h` in the vulkan folder.

Uploading the coordinate arrow data to the GPU, a new class, LineVertexBuffer, in the opengl folder, will be added. A simple way to get the new class files is to copy the two source files for the VertexIndexBuffer class (VertexIndexBuffer.h and VertexIndexBuffer.cpp) in the opengl folder, and then adjust the init() method to send position and color data to the graphics card:

```
glVertexAttribPointer(0, 3, GL_FLOAT,
  GL_FALSE, sizeof(OGLLineVertex),
  (void*) offsetof(OGLLineVertex, position));
glVertexAttribPointer(1, 3, GL_FLOAT,
  GL_FALSE, sizeof(OGLLineVertex),
  (void*) offsetof(OGLLineVertex, color));

glEnableVertexAttribArray(0);
glEnableVertexAttribArray(1);
```

We must also enable both the position and the color attributes by using glEnableVertexAttribArray() with the corresponding index values (the first parameter of glVertexAttribPointer) to send the vertex data for both attributes to the vertex shader.

On the GPU side, two simple pass-through shaders are needed – the vertex and fragment shader will only pass the data through without additional transformations, except the required view and projection matrix transformations. The vertex shader named line.vert, located in the shader folder, uses the view and projection matrices of the camera position to calculate the final vertex positions. Then, the position and the color of the line endpoints are handed over to the fragment shader named line.frag, also located in the shader folder.

The vertices for our coordinate arrows are taken from a static model file named CoordArrowsModel in the model folder. We can hard-code the vertex positions and colors to keep the initialization simple:

```
/* X axis - red */
mVertexData.vertices[0].position =
  glm::vec3(0.0f,0.0f, 0.0f);
mVertexData.vertices[1].position =
  glm::vec3(1.0f, 0.0f, 0.0f);
mVertexData.vertices[2].position =
  glm::vec3(1.0f, 0.0f, 0.0f);
...
mVertexData.vertices[0].color =
```

```
    glm::vec3(0.8f, 0.0f, 0.0f);
  mVertexData.vertices[1].color =
    glm::vec3(0.8f, 0.0f, 0.0f);
  mVertexData.vertices[2].color =
    glm::vec3(0.8f, 0.0f, 0.0f);
  ...
```

The final positions for the vertices of the coordinate arrows are set in the draw( ) call of the render. As the first step, the line counter will be zeroed, and the mLineMesh vector for the vertices of the coordinate arrows is cleared:

```
  mCoordArrowsLineIndexCount = 0;
  mLineMesh->vertices.clear();
```

Next, we retrieve the settings of the currently selected instance, containing the position and rotation of the instance:

```
  InstanceSettings instSettings =
    mModelInstData.miAssimpInstances.at(
    mModelInstData.miSelectedInstance)
    ->getInstanceSettings();
```

Then, we add the number of vertices to the line counter variable mCoordArrowsLineIndexCount and iterate over each vertex in a std::for_each:

```
mCoordArrowsLineIndexCount +=
    mCoordArrowsMesh.vertices.size();
std::for_each(mCoordArrowsMesh.vertices.begin(),
    mCoordArrowsMesh.vertices.end(),
      [=](auto &n){
      n.color /= 2.0f;
      n.position =
        glm::quat(glm::radians(
        instSettings.isWorldRotation)) * n.position;
        n.position += instSettings.isWorldPosition;
    });
```

By using a lambda function, the position data of the vertices is altered to match the position and rotation of the instance. In addition, we dim the color of the coordinate arrows by dividing the color vector by a value of two.

The resulting per-vertex data is collected in the mLineMesh vector:

```
mLineMesh->vertices.insert(mLineMesh->vertices.end(),
  mCoordArrowsMesh.vertices.begin(),
  mCoordArrowsMesh.vertices.end());
```

Then, we will upload the vertex data to the GPU, and draw the coordinate lines:

```
mLineVertexBuffer.uploadData(*mLineMesh);
if (mCoordArrowsLineIndexCount > 0) {
  mLineShader.use();
  mLineVertexBuffer.bindAndDraw(GL_LINES, 0,
    mCoordArrowsLineIndexCount);
}
```

Here, the mCoordArrowsLineIndexCount is used to check if coordinate lines exist at all, and as a parameter to draw the correct number of points for the lines. Using the line count as a check value and a counter helps us if we don't want to draw any coordinate lines at all: We can simply skip filling mLineMesh and counting coordinate lines, skipping the line drawing automatically. Or, we could draw multiple coordinate arrows in a multi-selection scenario.

Uploading vertex data in Vulkan is much more complex compared to OpenGL due to the explicit nature of the Vulkan API. The full process for creating a different shader and uploading vertex data requires the following steps in Vulkan:

1. Create a pair of passthrough shaders in GLSL or HLSL (High-Level Shader Language for DirectX). For GLSL shaders, the syntax has only small differences – mostly it's about being more explicit when using the layout statement.

2. Create a new pipeline with the new shaders and a corresponding attribute definition. Vulkan needs a new pipeline since the pipeline itself will become *immutable* after creation (except for a few explicit dynamically configurable sub-objects, like the viewport). Vulkan shaders *cannot* be swapped at runtime like in OpenGL; we need to bind another pipeline to draw vertices with a different shader.

3. Upload the vertex data to the GPU by using a staging buffer. To achieve the best performance in Vulkan, the vertex data should be stored in an optimized format in a memory area where only the GPU has access. Using a buffer shared between the CPU and GPU requires additional synchronization by the driver and the data may not be in the optimal format for the GPU to draw, resulting in performance losses.

4. While recording the render pass commands to send to the GPU, we must bind both the new pipeline by using the `vkCmdBindPipeline()` method and the vertex buffer by using `vkCmdBindVertexBuffers()`. After submitting the command buffer to the driver, the vertices are drawn with the new shader.

You can check out the classes `Shader`, `Pipeline`, and `VertexBuffer` in the `vulkan` folder of the example code for implementation details. Also, a link in the section *Additional resources* to a Vulkan tutorial is available. The tutorial has a separate section about vertex buffer creation and data uploading.

Now, three small arrows are added to the selected instance, as shown in *Figure 3.1*:

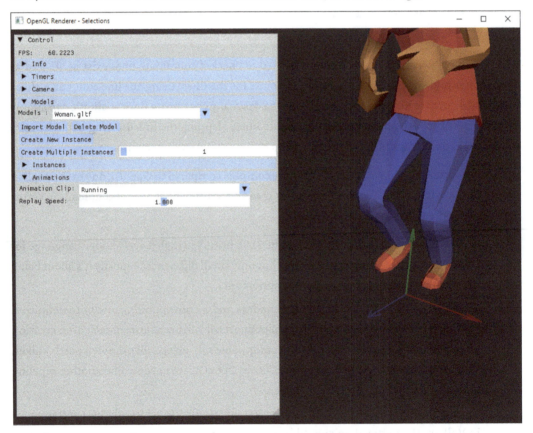

Figure 3.1: New coordinate arrows to identify the selected instance

The red arrow points to the direction of the positive x axis, the blue arrow points to the positive z axis, and the green arrow towards the positive y axis.

As the second step towards the "move to instance" function, the new UI button will be added.

Creating a button to center the selected instance

For the new button in the user interface, we will follow the previous implementations and add a callback for the UserInterface class. The callback calls a method in the renderer class, moving the camera calculations related from the user interface to the renderer.

In the UserInterface class, we add a new ImGui button, plus the new callback, using the current instance as parameter:

```
if (ImGui::Button("Center This Instance")) {
  std::shared_ptr<AssimpInstance> currentInstance =
    modInstData.miAssimpInstances.at(
      modInstData.miSelectedInstance);
  modInstData.miInstanceCenterCallbackFunction(
    currentInstance);
}
```

When the renderer is initialized, the callback miInstanceCenterCallbackFunction will be bound via a lambda function to the new centerInstance() method of the renderer:

```
mModelInstData.miInstanceCenterCallbackFunction =
  [this](std::shared_ptr<AssimpInstance> instance)
  { centerInstance(instance); };
```

The centerInstance() method extracts the position of the instance, adds a static offset of 5 units on all axes, and calls moveCameraTo() of the camera object:

```
void OGLRenderer::centerInstance(
    std::shared_ptr<AssimpInstance> instance) {
  InstanceSettings instSettings =
    instance->getInstanceSettings();
  mCamera.moveCameraTo(mRenderData,
    instSettings.isWorldPosition + glm::vec3(5.0f));
}
```

Finally, moveCameraTo() moves the camera to the instance position plus offset given in the renderer, and uses fixed values for azimuth and elevation to center the selected instance in the middle of the screen:

```
void Camera::moveCameraTo(OGLRenderData& renderData,
    glm::vec3 position) {
```

```
    renderData.rdCameraWorldPosition = position;
    renderData.rdViewAzimuth = 310.0f;
    renderData.rdViewElevation = -15.0f;
  }
```

Using hard-coded values for azimuth and elevation makes the process a bit easier, since the extraction of both values from a matrix generated by a method like glm::lookAt() is a bit more complex. You might try to set the camera angles from a transformation matrix by yourself – see the *Practical sessions* section.

You can add the new ImGui centering button anywhere in the collapsed header for the instances. In the example code, the button has been placed right below the arrows to select the current instance, as shown in *Figure 3.2*:

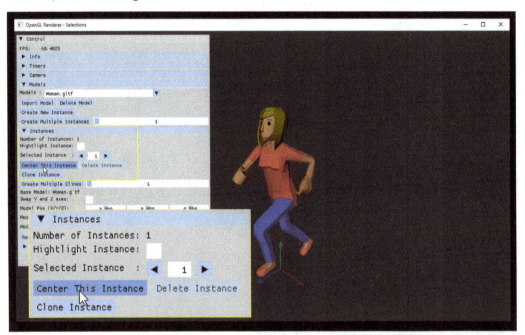

Figure 3.2: The currently selected instance has been centered

Centering the currently selected instance is a huge step towards a better *look & feel* for the application. We don't need to search for the blinking instance or the coordinate arrows to find the selected instance; now, we are literally only a mouse click away from reaching the instance.

Still, this solution has some drawbacks. What if we don't want to center the selected instance, maybe because we would like to keep the camera position fixed. So, let's add another function to the code that makes the currently selected instance even easier to find among all instances shown on the screen.

Adding a highlight to the selected instance

At first sight, adding some sort of highlight seems to be easy by adding some more fields to the vertices and the vertex buffer. Sadly, we are using instanced rendering for performance reasons. This means that all instances share the same vertex data. So, this approach does not work.

The next idea may be the instance placement and animations data. These matrices are calculated entirely by our compute shaders from *Chapter 2*, fed by the node transform data of the nodes. Adding model related data to every node seems to be a bit overkill, since the highlighted data is needed only once per instance, not once per node.

A better idea would be another SSBO, filled with the correct data in the draw() call of the renderer, right after the node transform data has been retrieved from the instance. In the instance loop, we have direct access to all instances of a model and can simply push a value to a std::vector, stating if this is the selected instance or not. After uploading the data of the vector to the SSBO, the shader instance can check the buffer data to see if the highlight should be added to the instance it is working on, or not.

Preparing the renderer to support highlights

As the first step for adding the highlight to the selected instance, we add a vector containing a float, and, for the OpenGL renderer, an SSBO to the renderer header file:

```
std::vector<float> mSelectedInstance{};
ShaderStorageBuffer mSelectedInstanceBuffer{};
```

Due to the different data logic, for Vulkan, a VkShaderStorageBufferData object in the VkRenderData struct in the file VkRenderData.h will be used instead.

In the draw() call of the renderer, we save the smart pointer of the currently selected instance, right before we start the loop across the models and instances:

```
std::shared_ptr<AssimpInstance> currentSelectedInstance =
  nullptr;
...
  currentSelectedInstance =
```

```
        mModelInstData.miAssimpInstances.at(
        mModelInstData.miSelectedInstance);
```

In addition to storing the instance, we alter a float value inside the `OGLRenderData` respective `VkRenderData` struct by adding a scaled `deltaTime`, and resetting the value once it reaches `2.0f`:

```
    mRenderData.rdSelectedInstanceHighlightValue +=
        deltaTime * 4.0f;
    if (mRenderData.rdSelectedInstanceHighlightValue > 2.0f) {
        mRenderData.rdSelectedInstanceHighlightValue = 0.1f
    }
```

The value of the variable `rdSelectedInstanceHighlightValue` will be used in the shader to scale up or down the color of the selected instance. By adding the value of `deltaTime` in every `draw()` call and resetting the highlight variable to `0.1f` when we reach `2.0f`, the selected install will blink from very dark to very bright. The blinking instance will be easier to spot on the screen, compared to just the coordinate arrows.

Inside the instance loop, we compare the smart pointer of the instance we are working on and the saved smart pointer of the selected instance. If they are identical, the alternating value of the variable `rdSelectedInstanceHighlightValue` will be set at the index of the current instance in the `mSelectedInstance` vector:

```
        if (currentSelectedInstance ==
            modelType.second.at(i)) {
            mSelectedInstance.at(i) =
                mRenderData.rdSelectedInstanceHighlightValue;
        } else {
            mSelectedInstance.at(i) = 1.0f;
        }
```

If we are working on any other instance in the loop, we simply set the x value to `1.0f`, resulting in an unchanged color of the instance in the shader.

The collected data of the `mSelectedInstance` vector is then uploaded to the SSBO. For example, the OpenGL renderer uses the `uploadSsboData()` method of the `ShaderStorageBuffer` class to upload the vector data to the GPU:

```
        mSelectedInstanceBuffer.uploadSsboData(
            mSelectedInstance, 3);
```

Adjusting logic to shaders and the UI

As the next step for adding the highlight to the selected instance, the shaders have to be adjusted. In the assimp_skinning.vert vertex shader in the shader folder, the new SSBO must be added:

```
layout (std430, binding = 3) readonly restrict
    buffer InstanceSelected {
  float selected[];
};
```

The same addition is needed in the assimp.vert shader in the shader folder, used for non-animated model instances.

Please check the binding number – due to the missing animation data, the number of SSBOs differs between the shaders for animated and non-animated instances: The shader for animated models binds the instance selection data on binding point 3 since binding point 2 is already used by the world position matrices:

```
mShaderBoneMatrixBuffer.bind(1);
mShaderModelRootMatrixBuffer.uploadSsboData(
    mWorldPosMatrices, 2);
mSelectedInstanceBuffer.uploadSsboData(
    mSelectedInstance, 3);
```

In contrast, the shader for non-animated models binds only two buffers:

```
mShaderModelRootMatrixBuffer.uploadSsboData(
    mWorldPosMatrices, 1);
mSelectedInstanceBuffer.uploadSsboData(
    mSelectedInstance, 2);
```

To adjust the color of the selected instance, we can now use the internal variable gl_InstanceID of the shader, retrieving the value of the data at the location of the instance in the selected buffer:

```
color = aColor * selected[gl_InstanceID];
```

As an optional change, we could also decrement the depth value of the selected instance by 1.0f:

```
if (selected[gl_InstanceID] != 1.0f) {
  gl_Position.z -= 1.0f;
}
```

Lowering the z element of the internal variable `gl_Position` will adjust the depth value of the triangle to the lowest possible value. This depth adjustment makes the highlighted instance visible even if other instances are closer to the camera position.

Finally, we add a `Boolean` variable named `rdHighlightSelectedInstance` in the `OGLRenderData` respective `VkRenderData` struct, allowing us to switch the highlight on and off. This new variable will be attached to an ImGui checkbox in the `UserInterface` class:

```
ImGui::Text("Hightlight Instance:");
ImGui::SameLine();
ImGui::Checkbox("##HighlightInstance",
    &renderData.rdHighlightSelectedInstance);
```

In *Figure 3.3*, the effect of combining highlighting and z position adjustment in the vertex shader is shown:

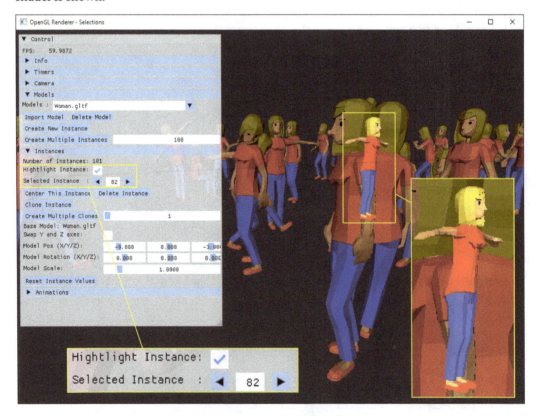

Figure 3.3: Highlighted instance drawn on top of instances closer to the camera

According to the relative size of the brighter instance, this instance would be at least partially hidden behind other instances closer to the camera. Yet, the adjustment of the z position draws the selected instance on top of all instances on the screen.

What cannot be shown in the picture is the alternating brightness of the selected instance. As set in the draw() call of the renderer, the colors of the selected instance go up from only 10% of the original color (start value of 0.1f) to 200% of the original colors (clamping at 2.0f).

The flashing colors of the instance will make it fairly easy to find the currently selected instance on the screen. But there is still a piece missing in the application: Being able to select the instance of choice by clicking into the window, instead of searching through all instances by using the instance number arrows. Let's tackle the visual selection now.

Selecting a model instance with point and click

Before we start with the implementation, we will look at the two different approaches to add visual selection to an application: by "shooting" a ray into the virtual scene, and by using a texture holding an index of the instances.

Pros and cons of shooting virtual rays

You may find the following idea of shooting a virtual ray into your scene appealing:

We already have the position of the camera in the virtual world as the first endpoint, and by mapping the mouse pointer positions back from screen positions to scene coordinates, you will get the second endpoint. Mapping coordinates back to the scene is only a couple of matrix inversions and multiplications away.

Sounds promising and easy, doesn't it?

Sadly, it is common to underestimate the final complexity at this point. As long as you only have a single model in the world, or two, everything is fine. You shoot the virtual ray into the scene, and loop over the triangles of each instance to find the closest intersection between the ray and the instance triangles.

But what happens when you have, say, 1,000 instances?

Every time you click the selection button on your mouse, you would have to iterate over all triangles of all instances, hoping to find at least one match. The test model of the book has roughly 2,000 triangles, so you will have to check for 2,000,000 possible intersections in a virtual world with 1,000 instances. Even with massive parallel computer shaders, this amount of calculation is a lot of wood to chuck for modern graphics cards.

There are several ways to exclude large areas of the virtual world from the hit tests. In combination with other hierarchical approaches on the node level, the number of intersection checks can be lowered by several orders of magnitude. We will cover optimizations of the process to find intersections when we handle instance collisions in *Chapter 8*.

What about the alternative idea – using a texture?

Advantages of drawing the instance index into a texture

The basic idea of an extra texture for the instance selection comes from **Deferred Rendering**. In deferred rendering, computations like lighting are not done in the fragment shader, but "deferred" after storing the required information in textures. The set of textures containing all information about the pixels on the screen is called the **G-Buffer**, short for **geometry buffer**.

By using the data of the textures in the G-Buffer, the complexity to apply lighting to a scene is lowered from `Number of triangles * Number of lights in the entire scene` to `Number of pixels of the G-Buffer * Number of nearby lights`.

Even for 4K or 8K graphic resolutions, the number of operations to create the lighting information is lowered drastically. And, by using other information from the rendering process, other effects are easily possible with deferred rendering, like shadow mapping, or indirect lighting.

For naive ray-shooting, the selection complexity grows with the number of instances in the virtual world, even if these instances are not visible on the screen. When we apply the deferred rendering approach to visual selection, we have a constant overhead of drawing some pixels into a separate texture. Our selection process no longer depends on a variable number of instances in the world. Also, the resolution of the buffers may affect the performance of the instance selection only marginally.

The amount of changes required to add visual selection with a separate texture is surprisingly low. Let's look at the steps we have to take.

Adjusting the framebuffer

We start with the `FrameBuffer` class and add a new color attachment. For the OpenGL version, the new color attachment is created as follows.

```
glGenTextures(1, &mSelectionTex);
glBindTexture(GL_TEXTURE_2D, mSelectionTex);
glTexImage2D(GL_TEXTURE_2D, 0, GL_R32F, width, height,
  0, GL_RED, GL_FLOAT, NULL);
```

```
glBindTexture(GL_TEXTURE_2D, 0);
glFramebufferTexture(GL_FRAMEBUFFER,
   GL_COLOR_ATTACHMENT1, mSelectionTex, 0);
```

For the selection texture, we add a texture containing only a single element, the red color. But we use a 32-bit wide red color, not only 8 bits, allowing us to store much more instance indices. The new texture is then added as a color attachment with the index 1 to the framebuffer.

A note on the texture data type (float)

It is possible to create a texture with the type of GL_R32UI, containing a 32-bit wide unsigned integer for every pixel. But all integer versions of the texture use a conversion factor for the components, raising the complexity of the selection process due to extra computations on reads and writes. In contrast, a GL_R32F buffer stores and retrieves an unaltered float value. By using a float on the GPU side, we are still able to store ~16.7 million instance indices (2^{24}), before the precision of a 32-bit float may lead to rounding errors during the conversion between integer and float values. See the section *Additional resources* for a link to a blog entry with more details of float precision.

Also, during framebuffer creation, we have to make sure our shader writes to both color attachments:

```
const GLenum buffers[] = { GL_COLOR_ATTACHMENT0,
 GL_COLOR_ATTACHMENT1 };
glDrawBuffers(2, buffers);
```

If we don't change the buffers to draw to, only the models will be drawn on the screen, and the selection texture will never be filled.

To clear the color buffer and the selection buffer with different values, a new method called clearTextures() has been added to the FrameBuffer class:

```
void Framebuffer::clearTextures() {
  static GLfloat colorClear[] =
    { 0.25f, 0.25f, 0.25f, 1.0f };
  glClearBufferfv(GL_COLOR, 0, colorClear);
  static GLfloat selectionClearColor = -1.0f;
  glClearBufferfv(GL_COLOR, 1, &selectionClearColor);
```

```
    static GLfloat depthValue = 1.0f;
    glClearBufferfv(GL_DEPTH, 0, &depthValue);
}
```

The selection texture can store arbitrary float values, using a -1.0f to clear the selection texture, which is a nice method to have a unique value for the empty background.

We also avoid creating yet another SSBO to store the instance index, and extend the mSelectedInstance vector from float to glm::vec2:

```
    std::vector<glm::vec2> mSelectedInstance{};
```

By moving the existing highlight color to the x element of the glm::vec2 vector, we have a free float type spot, and we can store the instance index in the y element.

Creating a selection shader

Adding a new color buffer to the framebuffer also requires two new pairs of vertex/fragment shaders: One pair for animated models, another pair for non-animated models. But since we already send the selection information for instance highlighting to the shader, only small additions to the existing shader code are needed.

Since we can reuse the shaders, the first step is to copy the existing files. For the non-animated models, copy the shader assimp.vert to assimp_selection.vert, and assimp.frag to assimp_selection.frag. The same name addition will be used for the animated model shader: Copy the file assimp_skinning.vert to assimp_skinning_selection.vert, and assimp_skinning.frag to assimp_skinning_selection.frag.

We also need two new shader objects in the renderer, so we add the private Shader member variables named mAssimpSelectionShader and mAssimpSkinningSelectionShader to the file OGLRenderer.h:

```
    Shader mAssimpSelectionShader{};
    Shader mAssimpSkinningSelectionShader{};
```

Like the existing shaders, the two new shaders are loaded in the init() method of the renderer.

Then, two lines must be added to the new vertex shaders. The first new line adds a new output variable named selectInfo to the vertex shader, allowing us to hand over the selection data for the current triangle to the fragment shader:

```
    ...
```

```
layout (location = 2) out vec2 texCoord;
```

```
layout (location = 3) out float selectInfo;
```

The second line at the end of the main() method does the actual forwarding to the fragment shader:

```
    selectInfo = selected[gl_InstanceID].y;
}
```

For the two new fragment shaders, similar changes are needed. On top of the shader code, we must add the new input variable selectInfo:

```
layout (location = 2) in vec2 texCoord;
layout (location = 3) flat in float selectInfo;
```

Also, the fragment shader output has to be adjusted. Replace the single FragColor output line with the following two lines:

```
layout (location = 0) out vec4 FragColor;
layout (location = 1) out float SelectedInstance;
```

We write two different outputs now, one for each color buffer: The color buffer of the frame buffer will be filled with the RGBA values for the on-screen color of each pixel as before, and at the end of the main() method, the instance index passed through from the vertex shader will be written to the second color buffer:

```
    SelectedInstance = selectInfo;
```

If we use the new selection shader now when drawing the instances, the index of the instance will be added to the selection buffer for every single pixel of that of the instances onscreen.

Reading a pixel from a texture

Reading out the color of the pixel at a given position will be done in the method readPixelFromPos() of the FrameBuffer class.

First, we initialize our designated return variable with a special value, making it easy to find errors when OpenGL refuses to read out the pixel color due to a configuration problem:

```
float Framebuffer::readPixelFromPos(unsigned int xPos,
    unsigned int yPos) {
  float pixelColor = -444.0f;
```

Next, we bind our framebuffer object as buffer to read from, and we select the color attachment 1 of the framebuffer, containing the selection texture:

```
glBindFramebuffer(GL_READ_FRAMEBUFFER, mBuffer);
glReadBuffer(GL_COLOR_ATTACHMENT1);
```

Then, we adjust the internal alignment used during the read process, and read out the color value of a single pixel at the given xPos and yPos position:

```
glPixelStorei(GL_UNPACK_ALIGNMENT, 1);
glReadPixels(xPos, yPos, 1, 1, GL_RED, GL_FLOAT,
    &pixelColor);
```

Finally, we switch the framebuffer back to color attachment 0, unbind the buffer and return the pixel color:

```
glReadBuffer(GL_COLOR_ATTACHMENT0);
glBindFramebuffer(GL_READ_FRAMEBUFFER, 0);
return pixelColor;
}
```

Adding mouse button handling

Selecting an instance will be added to the left mouse button. It feels natural to click on an instance to select it. To store the status of the selection, a Boolean member variable named mMousePick is added to the renderer.

Then, the following line must be added to the handleMouseButtonEvents() method of the renderer:

```
if (button == GLFW_MOUSE_BUTTON_LEFT &&
    action == GLFW_RELEASE) {
  mMousePick = true;
}
```

Using the GLFW_RELEASE action here, reacting when the left mouse button is released, matches the selection style of many applications. If you want to change the behavior, you can use the action GLFW_PRESS.

We use the mMousePick value to trigger different actions in the drawing process only when a selection event has been triggered by the user. Separating normal drawing and the extra operation for selection helps to retain the maximum speed of the application, avoiding operations that are only required during the selection.

As an example, the shader with the logic to draw into the selection texture will be only called if a selection event was triggered:

```
if (mMousePick) {
  mAssimpSkinningSelectionShader.use();
} else {
  mAssimpSkinningShader.use();
}
```

Assigning an index to each instance

To ensure we always maintain a unique index for every instance, any time an instance is added or removed, we assign its overall index. Using the unique index per instance also helps us in accessing the current instance in the miAssimpInstances vector.

We add a new variable isInstanceIndexPosition to the struct InstanceSettings, located in the file InstanceSettings.h in the model folder:

```
struct InstanceSettings {
  ...
  int isInstanceIndexPosition = -1;
};
```

The variable isInstanceIndexPosition will be set in the method assignInstanceIndices(), doing a loop over all the instances:

```
void OGLRenderer::assignInstanceIndices() {
  for (size_t i = 0;
      i < mModelInstData.miAssimpInstances.size(); ++i) {
    InstanceSettings instSettings =
      mModelInstData.miAssimpInstances.at(i)
      ->getInstanceSettings();
    instSettings.isInstanceIndexPosition = i;
    mModelInstData.miAssimpInstances.at(i)
```

```
    ->setInstanceSettings(instSettings);
  }
}
```

The method `assignInstanceIndices()` is called whenever instances are added or removed.

Having an easy to access instance number at hand helps us to fill the y element of the `mSelectedInstance` vector during the loop over all instances of a model:

```
if (mMousePick) {
  InstanceSettings instSettings =
      modelType.second.at(i)->getInstanceSettings();
  mSelectedInstance.at(i).y =
    static_cast<float>(
    instSettings.isInstanceIndexPosition);
}
```

Selecting the instance at mouse positions

As the final step for the visual selection, we trigger the pixel read at the end of the `draw()` call in the renderer:

```
if (mMousePick) {
  glFlush();
  glFinish();
```

By surrounding the pixel read with a check for the `mMousePick` variable, we make sure the functions to read back the pixel will be called only on the selection event.

This guarding check is especially important for the calls to `glFlush()` and `glFinish()`. Both commands are required to make sure all shader runs have ended, and the data in the selection texture is complete. While `glFlush()` empties the internal buffers and triggers the rendering itself, `glFinish()` blocks the renderer and waits for all previous OpenGL calls to have finished. Forcing these OpenGL commands on every frame decreases the number of frames per second in most implementations.

Next, we call `readPixelFromPos()` on the `FrameBuffer` instance:

```
float selectedInstanceId =
  mFramebuffer.readPixelFromPos(mMouseXPos,
  (mRenderData.rdHeight - mMouseYPos - 1));
```

Due to the different orientations of the y axis in OpenGL on the one hand and Windows and Linux on the other, we need to invert the y position when reading out the pixel.

After we retrieve the pixel color, we check if any instance was selected, or the mouse click was done on the background of the screen:

```
if (selectedInstanceId >= 0.0f) {
  mModelInstData.miSelectedInstance =
    static_cast<int>(selectedInstanceId);
}
mMousePick = false;
}
```

As the last step, we set `mMousePick` to `false`, stopping the selection mode immediately.

In *Figure 3.4*, the selection texture for a larger group of model instances is shown:

Figure 3.4: The selection texture

The background color in *Figure 3.4* has been changed to white. In the actual selection texture, the clear value of `-1.0f` will be clamped to zero, resulting in a black background. Also, the index values have been adjusted to enhance the visibility of the instances. If we render the selection texture with the real float values, all index values will be clamped to `1.0f`, resulting in a picture where all instances appear in bright red.

Selecting a single instance by using the mouse is working great now. As one of the ideas in the *Practical sessions* section, you could try to add more functionality, like selecting multiple instances at the same time. i.e., by keeping the *Ctrl* or *Shift* key down while selecting instances, newly selected instances are added, showing the coordinate arrows and the highlight on all selected instances.

But there is one thing left that may annoy you: There is no way to select no instance at all. We will add a solution for an empty selection in the last section of this chapter.

Implementing a null object to allow deselection

Adding a deselection by doing a click into the background of the application window comes with a bunch of interesting implications. For instance, the position 0 may be a valid index in the miAssimpInstance vector, stating that the first instance has been selected. So, simply using zero to signal that no instances are selected does not work. Even worse: Using zero as the first index may confuse users of the application, as it is not intentional to start counting numbers at zero, instead of one.

In addition, the default buffer background value of –1 is an invalid array index. Using the value of -1 as an index into the miAssimpInstance vector would simply crash the application. Since we will use the instance vector frequently in the code, adding a range check for every single access would be crucial because even missing a single check will lead to a crash.

So, we need another signalling mechanism to switch between the two selection variants and a simplification of the range checks. To catch both problems with a single solution, we will use an empty model as a **null object**.

What is a null object?

Using a null object is a well-known design pattern for object-oriented programming. Usually, you would use a nullptr to signal the absence of an object instance. But, using a nullptr requires creating an extra check before every usage of the instance for being valid or not. Dereferencing a non-existing instance leads to a runtime error, and the application crashes.

The null object is a valid object instance, delivering a well-defined, but neutral behavior. Function calls in the instance of the null object are valid, but may return nothing viable, like an empty list, or some default values. This behavior frees the code of extra checks, since the instance itself is valid.

For our selection problem, we simply create an instance of the AssimpModel class that returns no vertices, plus empty lists or vectors for nodes, meshes, and so on. Then, we add the special model as the first model to the miModelList vector and add one instance of the "null model" as the first instance to the miAssimpInstances vector and to the miAssimpInstancesPerModel map.

If we select the first model instance now, we have a valid object, just without any triangles drawn to the screen. Switching off the coordinate arrows or adjusting the user interface to disable controls if no instance is selected can be done without extra signalling variables. We just need to test `miSelectedInstance` for being 0.

We will alter the original pattern a bit, and don't use a derived class. Instead, we will provide an empty object of the `AssimpModel` class.

Creating and using the AssimpModel null object

Since we initialized the class members variables already in the header file `AssimpModel.h` with default values, creating a null object can be achieved by creating an empty instance. And the simplest way to create an instance of the `AssimpModel` class without setting any data is by using the implicitly created default constructor. We don't even need to define a custom constructor; the C++ compiler will handle everything we need in the background.

In the `init()` method of the renderer, we create a smart pointer to the null model, and add the model pointer to the `miModelList` vector:

```
std::shared_ptr<AssimpModel> nullModel =
  std::make_shared<AssimpModel>();
mModelInstData.miModelList.emplace_back(nullModel)
```

Then, we can create an `AssimpInstance` instance from the null model, and place it into the `miAssimpInstancesPerModel` map and the `miAssimpInstances` vector:

```
std::shared_ptr<AssimpInstance> nullInstance =
  std::make_shared<AssimpInstance>(nullModel);
mModelInstData.miAssimpInstancesPerModel[nullModel
  ->getModelFileName()].emplace_back(nullInstance);
mModelInstData.miAssimpInstances.emplace_back(
  nullInstance);
```

As the final initialization step, we update the index numbers of the instances:

```
assignInstanceIndices();
```

Now, the instance of the `nullModel` model has the index number 0. Any instance added in the application will now start at index 1. Matching numbers for the overall number of instances and the instance index will avoid confusion about differences in the instance numbering schema.

To skip the model during vertex processing in the `draw()` call of the renderer, a check for the triangle count has been added:

```
if (numberOfInstances > 0 &&
    modelType.second.at(0)->getModel()
    ->getTriangleCount() > 0) {
  ...
```

In case we have no triangles in a model, all instances of this specific model will be skipped.

In addition, we check for the instance number 0 before generating the final vertex position for the coordinate arrows:

```
if (mModelInstData.miSelectedInstance > 0) {
  ....
```

Whenever the very first instance is selected – the instance of the null model – no coordinate arrows will be drawn on the screen. We can even remove the `size()` check of the `miAssimpInstances` vector here, as we know we have at least one valid instance available.

Adjusting the user interface

In the user interface, we will cheat a bit to keep the instance selection fields disabled in case the null instance is selected:

```
bool modelListEmtpy =
    modInstData.miModelList.size() == 1;
bool nullInstanceSelected =
  modInstData.miSelectedInstance == 0;
size_t numberOfInstances =
  modInstData.miAssimpInstances.size() - 1;
```

By subtracting 1 from the size of the `miModelList` vector, we ignore the null model in that vector. We also ignore the null instance of the null model to count the instances in `numberOfInstances`. The additional Boolean `nullInstanceSelected` helps us to disable parts of the user interface when models and instances are available, but we have not selected any of the instances.

In *Figure 3.5*, the effect of the deselection by using the null object is shown:

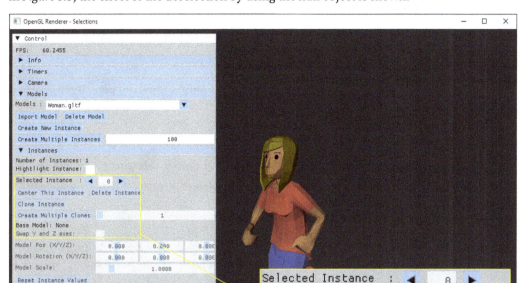

Figure 3.5: User interface is partially disabled when nothing is selected

No coordinate arrows are drawn at the feet of the model instance, as we hide the arrows when the null instance is selected. Also, the user interface is partially disabled, an effect of ignoring the null instance when counting the number of instances.

Summary

In this chapter, we enhanced the instance selection methods in the code for better handling of finding the selected instance on the screen. Plus, we added the ability to select an instance by using the mouse. First, we implemented a button to center our virtual camera on the selected instance. Next, we added the ability to highlight the selected model, making it easier to spot on the screen. Then, we implemented a visual selection, allowing the user to select an instance by clicking on any instance with the mouse. Finally, we created the possibility to select no instance at all, avoiding accidental changes.

In the next chapter, we will lay some groundwork to adapt more game engine features to the model viewer. As well as splitting the behavior of the viewer into an edit mode and a pure viewer functionality, we will add the ability to revert ongoing changes to an instance. At the end of the next chapter, we will implement undo/redo functionality, allowing the user to revert changes, or to reapply previous changes.

Practical sessions

There are some additions you could make to the code:

- Calculate azimuth and elevation when moving the camera.

  Right now, the values for azimuth and elevation are hard-coded. You could try to calculate both values from the transformation matrix.

- Implement a visual multi-selection.

  Enhance the selection so that holding *Ctrl* or *Shift* during selection clicks will add the newly selected instance to the other selected instances, instead of replacing the current selected instance.

- Extra difficulty: Implement instance moving via coordinate arrows.

  Since the coordinate arrows for the selection are drawn in a separate shader, you could try to add an extra set of selection indices to the arrows and adding the arrows to the selection texture. When the user clicks on one of the arrows instead of the mode, you could switch the application to a mode where the instance can be moved along the selected axis. This behavior is similar to moving an instance in any common 3D editor.

Additional resources

- OpenGL basics: `https://learnopengl.com/Getting-started/Hello-Triangle`
- OpenGL Shader programming: `https://learnopengl.com/Getting-started/Shaders`
- Vulkan Tutorial: `https://vulkan-tutorial.com`
- Demystifying Floating Point Precision: `https://blog.demofox.org/2017/11/21/floating-point-precision/`
- Null object pattern: `https://www.geeksforgeeks.org/null-object-design-pattern/`

Get This Book's PDF Version and Exclusive Extras

Scan the QR code (or go to packtpub.com/unlock). Search for this book by name, confirm the edition, and then follow the steps on the page.

Note: Keep your invoice handy. Purchases made directly from Packt don't require an invoice.

Part 2

Transforming the Model Viewer into an Animation Editor

In this part, you will build the foundation for the game character animation by enhancing the model viewer into an animation editor. You will learn how to add a separate viewing mode, allowing you to disable parts of the code that may not need or want to be active at some time, such as the user interface when recording videos. You will be also introduced to the general idea of the ability to revert changes made to model instances, ending up in a basic implementation of an undo/redo functionality. You will also learn how to store the currently loaded models and instances plus various settings to a YAML file, and how to load the data back into the application, allowing you to continue editing the models at any time, or to create multiple configurations. Finally, you will explore different camera types for the virtual world, giving you the chance to view the character animations from all angles and perspectives you may think of.

This part has the following chapters:

- *Chapter 4, Enhancing Application Handling*
- *Chapter 5, Saving and Loading the Configuration*
- *Chapter 6, Extending Camera Handling*

4

Enhancing Application Handling

Welcome to *Chapter 4*! In the previous chapter, we added capabilities for a better selection of a single instance among a possibly large number of models and instances. We started with a simple "move to" function and added a highlight to the current instance as the next step. Then, we implemented a visual selection by using the mouse. Finally, we created a null object to allow selecting no instance at all.

In this chapter, we will focus on the edit mode. First, we will add the capability to switch off all controls and menus by creating a separate view mode. The split between edit and view modes will help us in later chapters to stop all automatic actions when we configure instance settings. Next, we will implement a simplified version of the undo functionality, allowing us to reset the settings of a model instance after applying changes. As the last step, we will implement undo and redo of setting changes on the instance level.

In this chapter, we will cover the following topics:

- Switching between edit and view modes
- Reverting changes before applying
- Implementing undo and redo functionality

Technical requirements

The example source code for this chapter is in the chapter04 folder, in the 01_opengl_edit_view_ mode subfolder for OpenGL and 02_vulkan_edit_view_mode for Vulkan.

After making instance selection easy in *Chapter 3*, changing the settings of an instance will be the next topic to tackle. Right now, we have a Control menu on the screen, capturing the mouse input if the pointer is placed over the ImGui window. Any change we make will remain permanent in the current application session. Reverting any accidental rotation or scaling to the exact same value as before could be very difficult since we would have to memorize the previous values to undo the change.

We will now change the application to toggle to a mode without any controls or selection and add a rather simple but useful undo and redo functionality to roll changes to instances back or forward.

Switching between edit and view modes

If we start the current version of the application, we will see that a large part of the screen is blocked by the user interface whenever we want to make changes to instances.

Figure 4.1 shows what the user interface window looks like when all headers are expanded:

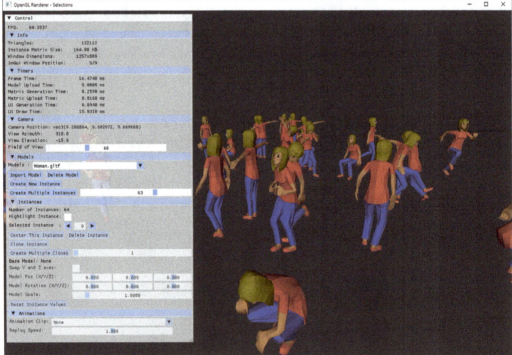

Figure 4.1: User interface blocking parts of the screen

As more and more options will be added later in the book, the user interface may fill up even more of the available window space. In addition, a selected instance will blink if the highlight is active and the coordinate arrows are placed below it.

To change the overall appearance, we must check which features should be disabled in a separate view mode.

Deciding what should be switched in view mode

Our main goal for this section is to remove the ImGui **Control** window to have the full application available for interacting with the model instances. We could just switch off the rendering of the user interface, but if we do not show the user interface window, there is no need to do any calculations like the timer and FPS updates. So, for the first decision, we will skip the user interface in the **View mode**.

We must also add a shortcut to avoid forwarding mouse button events to ImGui when the user interface is not active. ImGui saves the positions of all control elements, and we would still get unwanted side effects, like being unable to move the camera if we switch the user interface while the mouse pointer is above the ImGui window.

Even without a user interface, all parts related to the instance selection are still active. This means we do not need the instance selection in view mode, since there is no way to adjust instance parameters without a user interface. Our second decision here is to switch off everything connected to the instance selection. We will disable mouse picking, including the selection shaders, the coordinate arrows, and the highlight calculation.

We will also adjust the window title, reflecting the current view/edit state of the application. Changing the window properties from the renderer requires a bit of callback "magic" but helps to immediately see what mode the application is in.

The implementation of most of the switch of view and edit mode is simple. We just need a variable to save the current state, and some of the branches to enable or disable above specified operations for the two modes.

Adding the state variable plus code

As the first implementation step, we create a new enum class named appMode in the OGLRenderData.h file in the opengl folder:

```
enum class appMode {
  edit = 0,
```

```
    view
};
```

For the Vulkan renderer, the `appMode` enum class will reside in the `VkRenderData.h` file in the `vulkan` folder.

In addition, a variable named `rdApplicationMode` must be added to the `OGLRenderData` struct for the OpenGL renderer, and the respective `VkRenderData` struct for the Vulkan renderer:

```
appMode rdApplicationMode = appMode::edit;
```

We initialize `rdApplicationMode` with the value for the edit mode, avoiding visible changes to the application functionality at startup.

To enable or disable a feature in the renderer, depending on the mode, we can simply check the value of the `rdApplicationMode` variable:

```
if (mRenderData.rdApplicationMode == appMode::edit) {
    ...
}
```

For example, to switch between the animated shader with and without selection support, the following lines are used:

```
    if (mMousePick &&
        mRenderData.rdApplicationMode == appMode::edit) {
      mAssimpSkinningSelectionShader.use();
    } else {
      mAssimpSkinningShader.use();
    }
```

To disable rendering of the user interface in view mode, we surround the `render()` call to the user interface in the renderer with a check for the application mode:

```
if (mRenderData.rdApplicationMode == appMode::edit) {
  mUIDrawTimer.start();
  mUserInterface.render();
  mRenderData.rdUIDrawTime = mUIDrawTimer.stop();
}
```

We disable the timer calls in view mode too – without a user interface on screen, filling the timer values would be a waste of computing power.

Switching from edit to view mode and back will be done by pressing a hotkey. We cannot use an ImGui button here if we disable the user interface completely since we would need the button to toggle back to edit mode.

Toggling between the two modes and changing the title

For the mode switch, a simple check for the F10 key is done in the handleKeyEvents() method of the renderer:

```
if (glfwGetKey(mRenderData.rdWindow, GLFW_KEY_F10) ==
    GLFW_PRESS) {
  mRenderData.rdApplicationMode =
    mRenderData.rdApplicationMode == appMode::edit ?
    appMode::view : appMode::edit;
  setModeInWindowTitle();
}
```

Any other unused key can be achieved by placing the respective GLFW key name as the second parameter into the glfwGetKey() call.

The call to setModeInWindowTitle() needs further explanation, as we are using callback functions to change the title string of our application window. The function call itself is short and simple:

```
void OGLRenderer::setModeInWindowTitle() {
  if (mRenderData.rdApplicationMode == appMode::edit) {
    setWindowTitle(mOrigWindowTitle + " (Edit Mode)");
  } else {
    setWindowTitle(mOrigWindowTitle + " (View Mode)");
  }
}
```

We save the original window title in the init() method of the renderer, and append the default mode (**Edit mode**) to the window title:

```
mOrigWindowTitle = getWindowTitle();
setModeInWindowTitle();
```

Since the Window class initializes the renderer class, we have to move the window title change request backward, from the renderer to the application window.

First, two std::function aliases are created in the renderer header file, OGLRenderer.h for OpenGL and VkRenderer.h for Vulkan:

```
using GetWindowTitleCallback =
    std::function<std::string(void)>;
using SetWindowTitleCallback =
    std::function<void(std::string)>
```

We also add two public methods to the declaration of our renderer:

```
        SetWindowTitleCallback setWindowTitle;
        GetWindowTitleCallback getWindowTitle;
```

Using the aliases makes it easier to handle the calls to std::function.

Next, we create two methods matching the callback signatures in the Window class header file, window.h, in the window folder:

```
        std::string getWindowTitle();
        void setWindowTitle(std::string newTitle);
```

In addition, a private member variable named mWindowTitle is added, storing the current title of the window:

```
        std::string mWindowTitle;
```

Storing the window title in a variable may be handy for debugging log prints.

Then, right after initializing the renderer in the init() method of the Window class, two lambda functions are used to forward the Window class function calls to the renderer:

```
    mRenderer->getWindowTitle = [this]()
        { return getWindowTitle(); };
    mRenderer->setWindowTitle = [this](std::string
        windowTitle) { setWindowTitle(windowTitle); };
```

When we press F10 now, the renderer appends a mode string to the original window title and forwards the created string via callback to the Window class. This way, the current application mode is presented in the title text of the application window.

In *Figure 4.2*, the user interface and the selection have been disabled. Check the window title to see the current mode:

Figure 4.2: No user interface in view mode

Without the user interface window in view mode, the entire application window can be used to fly around in the virtual world. By pressing *F10*, we can go back to the edit mode to adjust the parameters of the model instances.

An outlook for future changes

For every new feature we add later in the book, we must decide how to handle the feature in edit and view mode. Some of the new features are only feasible in edit mode, like adding and configuring different cameras in *Chapter 6*. Using the cameras, on the other hand, is best done in view mode since we only need to switch between different cameras when roaming through the virtual world we created. We will have to think about the usage of a new feature every time.

After adding a separate view mode, let's go back to the basic application handling. Whenever we select an instance and change one of the settings, we are stuck with the new value, without a proper way to reset the instance state to a "last known good" setting. In the next section, we will add a basic mechanism to revert at least the last change to a model instance.

Reverting changes before applying

The main purpose of the current model viewer application is to view model instances. But, next to pure model viewing, adjusting instance properties and settings will become a larger part of the application throughout the book. And changing settings can go wrong in many ways. A solution to preview a change sounds like a good feature to add.

The basic idea

A simple rollback method would allow us to accept a change to the instance setting, or to revert the same settings to the previous values. We could experiment with the values, try to move the instance to the correct destination, or adjust other parameters to fit our needs. When we are happy with the result, we push the **Apply** button, and the instance settings are made permanent. The same workflow can be used for the next instance, and so on, until we have placed all instances in the way we imagined.

Adding code and User Interface elements

First, we add two new private members to the UserInterface.h header file of the UserInterface class:

```
std::shared_ptr<AssimpInstance> mCurrentInstance;
InstanceSettings mSavedInstanceSettings{};
```

In the mCurrentInstance smart pointer, we store the currently selected instance, and in the mSavedInstanceSettings variable, we will save the original settings of the currently selected instance.

Since we are retrieving the current instance several times in the user interface, we can simply remove the currentInstance declaration in all other places within the CollapsingHeader block.

Reading the settings of the currently selected instance stays the same:

```
if (numberOfInstances > 0) {
  settings = modInstData.miAssimpInstances.at(
    modInstData.miSelectedInstance)
    ->getInstanceSettings();
```

But, in addition, we also check if the currently selected instance is different compared to the new
mCurrentInstance pointer:

```
    if (mCurrentInstance !=
        modInstData.miAssimpInstances.at(
        modInstData.miSelectedInstance)) {
      mSavedInstanceSettings = settings;
      mCurrentInstance =
        modInstData.miAssimpInstances.at(
        modInstData.miSelectedInstance);
    }
  }
```

Whenever the current instance changes, we store the new selected instance in the mCurrentInstance
pointer, and we also save the instance settings we just retrieved in the mSavedInstanceSettings
variable.

The mSavedInstanceSetting variable enables us now to revert the settings of the instance,
undoing any changes. To toggle the setting revert, we add a new button named Reset Values
to Previous below the existing Reset Values to Zero button:

```
    ImGui::SameLine();
    if (ImGui::Button("Reset Values to Previous")) {
        settings = mSavedInstanceSettings;
    }
```

To undo any changes, we copy the saved instance settings back to the current settings variable.
At the end of the CollapsingHeader **Instances**, the values in settings are saved to the currently
selected instance. Et voilà, we have reverted the settings to the state when we selected the instance.

Applying the changes just does the copy operation the other way around:

```
    ImGui::SameLine();
    if (ImGui::Button("Apply Changes")) {
      mSavedInstanceSettings = settings;
    }
```

Here, the saved settings are overwritten by the current settings of the instance, making the current
settings the new default for an undo operation.

Figure 4.3 shows the location of the two new buttons:

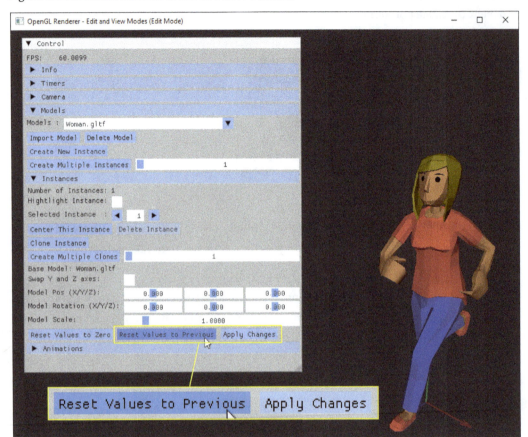

Figure 4.3: Button to revert instance settings, respectively doing a permanent apply

By using the **Apply Changes** button, the current changes to the model instance are made permanent. And with the **Reset Values to Previous** button, we can revert any changes to the instance to the state when we pressed **Apply Changes** before.

Drawbacks of the current solution

Using two buttons to apply or revert every instance setting change is time-consuming and cumbersome. A version that applies the changes automatically and more often would generate a much better workflow while editing instance properties. The general idea from this section will be kept; we just add some more automatic behavior.

Let's create a real-world undo and redo solution.

Implementing undo and redo functionality

Nearly every application has some way to undo one operation or more, and many applications also allow a redo of reverted steps. Accidents can happen in both ways; undoing an unwanted undo can save a lot of time and stress for the user.

What do we need to create undo and redo?

To be able to undo a simple operation that changes object properties, we need to save the previous values. Undoing that change could then be done by applying the "old" values to the same object, and restoring the state of that object before the change.

For more complex undo operations, storing the operation type is also required. If we delete something, the undo step must recreate the object with the same properties, and vice versa – undoing the creation of a new object will delete that object.

Other options could be also taken into account. Do we want to store the absolute previous values or just the difference to the new values? By storing relative values, redoing the changes that followed the reverted operation could use the adjusted values as a basis, while absolute values would overwrite intermitted adjustments. And do we store the complete settings for that object, or only the changed parameter(s)? The implication is similar to the absolute and relative values before.

From a technical side, our implementation will use two stacks: one for the possible undo operations and another for the possible redo operations. Every configuration change will push the new and the old settings to the undo stack, allowing the reversal of the changes by applying the old settings.

After the undo operation has been done, the very same setting combination will be taken from the undo stack and pushed to the redo stack. If we now do a redo of the same operation, the new settings will be applied, and the settings will be moved back to the undo stack.

This simple workflow will allow us a virtually endless undo and redo size, limited mostly by the amount of memory in the computer. And, since the settings are small, it would take a very long time to fill up the computer memory with the two stacks.

As the first step on the road to undo and redo, we will create a storage container class that encapsulates all the information we need to revert the settings in one or the other direction.

Creating a setting storage class

The new class is called `AssimpSettingsContainer`, and the header and implementation file are in the model folder. In the header file, a struct is declared to store all the settings we need for both undo and redo:

```
struct AssimpInstanceSettings {
  std::weak_ptr<AssimpInstance> aisInstance;
  InstanceSettings aisInstanceSettings{};
  InstanceSettings aisSavedInstanceSettings{};
};
```

The `AssimpInstanceSettings` struct saves the previous and current settings of an instance, along with a weak pointer to the instance. Using `std::weak_ptr` instead of `std::shared_ptr` here has two important reasons:

- A weak pointer breaks the dependency between the `miAssimpInstances` vector containing the instance `std::shared_ptr` and the settings stored for undo/redo because a weak pointer is not added to the reference counter of the smart pointer for the instance. If we use another shared pointer when storing the undo/redo information instead, the memory for a deleted instance may not be freed, since there could be another active reference to the instance stored somewhere in the undo or redo stack.

- When requesting the weak pointer to return the shared pointer by using the `lock()` call, we can easily find deleted instances and remove the saved settings. The `lock()` call returns a `nullptr` if the shared pointer is no longer available, and we simply use a `pop()` call on the respective stack to remove the dead settings.

If we want to save the settings instances of an instance, we call the `apply()` method of the `AssimpSettingsContainer` class. The `apply()` method creates a new `AssimpInstanceSettings` object and pushes the settings to the undo stack.

We also clear the redo stack while saving a new setting via `apply()`. It may be useless to use the redo operation after we reverted a couple of changes and applied recent changes since the redo operations could create conflicts with the latest changes, or even overwrite the latest change. Removing all settings from the redo stack is a quick and safe way to avoid side effects after the latest changes are applied.

The implementation of the undo() and redo() methods is short and simple:

1. Check for any deleted instances by requesting the shared pointer from the weak pointer, and remove the settings struct if the instance pointer is invalid. The check will be done in a while() loop to find all deleted instances.

2. If the stack is empty (i.e., because all instances that had settings saved for undo or redo are gone), we return from the operation immediately.

3. Get the top entry from the stack and apply the saved settings to the instance in case of an undo operation, or the new settings for a redo operation.

4. Push the top entry of a stack to the opposite stack and remove the top entry.

Now, all relevant instance changes can be saved to the undo stack. If we choose to undo a change to an instance, we can also immediately redo the very same change. In the background, the structs containing old and new settings and the instance pointer are just moved between the two stacks on undo and redo operations.

Adding the new operations to the renderer requires a bit of extra work.

Hooking up the storage class to the renderer

The renderer will be extended by two new methods for the undo/redo related code, called undoLastOperation() and redoLastOperation().

At the start of each of the methods, we call the respective operation on the settings container:

```
mModelInstData.miSettingsContainer->undo();
assignInstanceIndices();
```

In addition, a call to assignInstanceIndices() will be issued. Enumerating all instances after undo and redo operations is crucial. The settings taken from the stack could contain an invalid instance index in the isInstanceIndexPosition variable after other instances have been deleted, resulting in access outside the miAssimpInstance vector.

A side effect of the enumeration is a position change in the miAssimpInstances vector. So, we cannot just take the new isInstanceIndexPosition to select the instance that was changed by the undo or redo operation. Instead, we retrieve the instance pointer of the changed instance from AssimpInstanceSettings and use std::find_if to search the miAssimpInstance vector for a matching pointer. If we don't find the correct instance, the null instance will be selected, resulting in no instance to be selected.

Defining hotkeys for undo and redo

To use undo and redo functions by using known key combinations on the keyboard, we add the new keys to the `handleKeyEvents()` method in the renderer:

```
if (mRenderData.rdApplicationMode == appMode::edit) {
  if (glfwGetKey(mRenderData.rdWindow,
      GLFW_KEY_Z) == GLFW_PRESS &&
      (glfwGetKey(mRenderData.rdWindow,
      GLFW_KEY_LEFT_CONTROL) == GLFW_PRESS ||
      glfwGetKey(mRenderData.rdWindow,
      GLFW_KEY_RIGHT_CONTROL) == GLFW_PRESS)) {
    undoLastOperation();
  }
  ...
}
```

Here, only the undo part is shown, utilizing the key combination `CTRL` + `Z`, like many other applications. The redo function is called when `CTRL` + `Y` is pressed, which is also a well-known key combination to redo changes.

Undo and redo functionality will only be activated in edit mode. We cannot adjust instance settings in view mode, so we also do not need to revert or redo changes.

We are now able to call the undo and redo functions by key combinations. However, for easier access, reaching both operations via a menu bar would be great.

Adding an ImGui menu to allow direct access

Luckily, a menu bar can be added with a few ImGui calls:

```
if (ImGui::BeginMainMenuBar()) {
  if (ImGui::BeginMenu("Edit")) {
    if (ImGui::MenuItem("Undo", "CTRL+Z")) {
      modInstData.miUndoCallbackFunction();
    }
    if (ImGui::MenuItem("Redo", "CTRL+Y")) {
      modInstData.miRedoCallbackFunction();
    }
    ImGui::EndMenu();
```

```
        }
    ImGui::EndMainMenuBar();
    }
```

Like other ImGui widgets, the main menu bar itself, and all menus in the menu bar, start with an ImGui::Begin*() line and end with an ImGui::End*() line. As with other ImGui widgets, the ImGui menu commands return a Boolean value of true if they are activated (i.e., by clicking the left mouse button on the menu item).

Also, we are using – once again – callback functions in the ModelAndInstanceData struct to move the workload to do the undo and redo operations from the user interface to the renderer.

In *Figure 4.4*, the new ImGui menu bar of the application is shown:

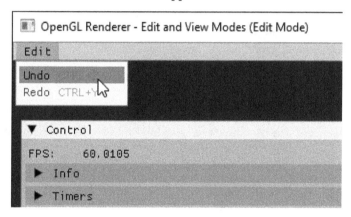

Figure 4.4: Main menu bar, containing the edit menu with undo and redo entries

The menu was created by the small code snippet in this section, and new menu entries and menu items can be added easily. Two new menu entries can be implemented when you solve the tasks in the *Practical sessions* section.

Limits and enhancements of our undo/redo implementation

One of the biggest shortcomings of the current undo/redo implementation is the limitation to react to configuration changes of single instances. We do not capture other features, like loading or deleting models, or the creation of multiple instances of a model at once.

Adding undo/redo support for multiple instances would need an extension of the AssimpSettingsContainer class to store all affected instances in a single group. In case of an undo or redo operation, we don't want to step through every single instance, but all instances should reappear or disappear at the same time.

Including model changes to the undo/redo stacks requires another rework of the settings container class. Now, we would have to check what kind of object we are working on and add the model change plus the affected instance changes. Deleting a model also removes all instances of that model; an undo operation would need to restore the model and all instances with their respective settings.

Extending the currently implemented undo/redo functionality to support multiple instances and model changes can be found as a task in the *Practical sessions* section at the end of this chapter. But be warned, building a mature undo/redo system is not trivial and will require a significant amount of time.

As you can see, keeping up a consistently working undo/redo feature adds a lot of overhead to an application, but the time spent on good undo and redo handling is well-invested. The future user of any application will thank the programmers for being able to recover from unwanted changes, like an accidental change, or even the deletion of elements.

Summary

In this chapter, we added a second application mode to disable all features that are not needed for a visit to the virtual world. The user interface, selection, and all parts belonging to such topics can be disabled by a hotkey now. Next, we tested a basic rollback operation for instance setting changes and enabling a simple undo. Finally, we enhanced the rollback to an undo/redo functionality for any setting changes on the instance level.

In the next chapter, we will implement the ability to save the current configuration of all models and instances to a file, plus restore all models and instances from a saved file. With a working save and load functionality, we can stop changing the virtual world at any time and continue in the exact same state at a later point in time.

Practical sessions

There are some additions you could make to the code:

- Move the **Import Model** button to the menu bar.

  The **Import Model** button may feel a bit misplaced since the start, but now we have the chance to change the functionality. Move the functionality of the button to a submenu of the menu bar, making it easier to understand how to import a model to the application.

- Add a confirmation dialog when the application is closed.

  If we use key combinations like ALT + F4 now or press the icon to close the window, the application ends immediately. Add a simple popup dialog with a yes/no question, allowing the user to stop another possibly accidental operation. Since we have a menu bar now, you can also create a File->Exit entry, calling the same logic to request confirmation before closing the application. Oh, and don't forget to switch back to edit mode when the application exit is requested. A hidden exit dialog is hardly usable.

- Enhanced difficulty: Add a full-featured undo/redo.

  Right now, we only store simple setting changes. Extend the AssimpSettingContainer class to also store the addition and deletion events of instances. You may need an enum to store the action because, during the undo and redo operations, you need to execute the opposite action. You may have to adjust the two stacks to also store vectors of instance settings. Doing a mass-adding of instances should be reverted in both directions by a single undo or redo call, not by acting on every single instance of the group.

Additional resources

- The Command pattern, used for undo/redo operations: https://gameprogrammingpatterns. com/command.html
- *Game Programming in C++* by *Sanjay Madhav*, published by *Pearson Addison-Wesley*, ISBN 978-0134597201

Join our community on Discord

Join our community's Discord space for discussions with the author and other readers: https://packt.link/cppgameanimation

5

Saving and Loading the Configuration

Welcome to *Chapter 5*! In the previous chapter, we added a separate view mode to the application. In this view-only mode, the user interface and selection functionality are disabled. Then, we added a simplified and, eventually, a full version of undo/redo for the instances. Setting changes to an instance can now be reverted, or reapplied.

In this chapter, we will add the ability to save the configuration of the application to a file. First, we will explore different file types to store the data. After considering the pros and cons of each type of file and determining a suitable file format, we will dive into the structure of the file format. Then, we'll implement a parser class that will allow us to load and save our configuration. Finally, we will load a default configuration at application startup, allowing the user to play around with the application.

For any bigger application, it is crucial to be able to save the current state of data that was created or changed, stop the application, and load the data again to continue working. It's also crucial to recover from a hanging or crashed application by restoring the latest saved version. You don't want to risk losing hours of your work because the application cannot save the data properly to local or remote storage.

In this chapter, we will cover the following topics:

- Textual or binary file formats – pros and cons
- Choosing a text format to save our data
- Exploring the structure of a YAML file

- Adding a YAML parser
- Saving and loading the configuration file
- Loading a default configuration file at startup

Technical requirements

The example source code for this chapter is in the `chapter05` folder, in the `01_opengl_load_sve` subfolder for OpenGL and `02_vulkan_load_save` for Vulkan.

Before we add save and load functionality to our application, let's take a look at some ways to save the data to a storage device.

Textual or binary file formats – pros and Cons

Whenever you play a game, cut a video, edit a photo, or write a piece of text or a book, you will make use of the integrated load and save functions integrated with the software you are using. Saving a game at a safe spot, storing a video sequence after making a large number of edits, or pressing *Ctrl + S* every now and then in the text editor has become normal to us.

But have you ever thought about the data that is saved and loaded? You might have some questions regarding the following functions, like:

- What needs to be stored to fully restore your latest state?
- What format should be used to save the data?
- What happens if a program is updated? Will I be able to load the saved data?
- Can I read or change the saved file without the original program?

For all programs you only use, the decision about the format and amount of data lies in the hands of their developers. But, for our application, we must decide which data needs to be saved, and how to save the data to the storage.

All types of data formats have pros and cons; here is a short round-up.

Saving and loading binary data

In the early times of the computer era, storage space and computation time were expensive, precious, and scarce. To minimize space and time during the save and restore process, the data was more or less only a memory dump.

The data to save was stored in internal data types, into a memory area of the computer and then literally copied byte by byte to a floppy disk or a hard drive.

Loading the same data was as easy and fast as saving it: read the data from the storage device to the computer's memory (again, byte by byte) and interpret it as the same internal data types that were used while saving.

Let's take a look at some of the advantages and disadvantages of binary data:

- **Advantages:**

    - Files are small.

    - Saving and loading the data can be done by just copying the data, leading to a higher speed for save and load operations.

- **Disadvantages:**

    - To change the data outside the application, special knowledge is needed.

    - Corrupted data could cause unpredictable side effects or crashes.

    - Updates to the save file format may be hard. *Magic bytes* are needed to find the actual version and to map the loaded data to the correct internal data types.

Binary data may not be portable across architectures due to different endianness. For this reason, it is generally good advice to avoid binary save files unless absolutely necessary. We can still read CONFIG.SYS and AUTOEXEC.BAT files created on MS-DOS systems 30 years ago, but the binary save files from spreadsheet calculators or word processors of the same time are unusable, at least without the correct tools or hard work to reverse-engineer the file format. Outside of well-documented and standardized formats, like pictures or sound files, saving binary data **will** cause trouble, as you may not be able to open the binary files on a different operating system, or even just a newer version of the same system. Also, loading the file on a different CPU architecture, bit width, or endianness will most probably fail due to a different memory layout of the data types.

Since CPU time and storage space are no longer limited, the advantages of text formats now clearly outweigh those of binary saves.

Saving and loading textual data

After more and more CPU power, network bandwidth, and storage space became available, textual formats started to become the first choice to save data. Developing code is much easier when you can create or adjust the saved files with a simple text editor, or when you can find errors by printing the text lines to log files.

For a text-based save file, the conditions differ from those for a binary save:

- Files are larger, except when they are compressed into a .zip file or similar. Then, another transformation step (pack/unpack) is needed.

- Data must be transformed from binary representation to text and back, every time the data is loaded and saved.

- Domain-specific knowledge of the file format may be required for larger changes, or to create a save file *from scratch*. But for simple value changes, a text editor is the only tool we need.

- Corrupted data can be fixed, or the corrupt data elements may be simply deleted from the text file. Better to lose only some data than all of it.

- File format updates can be detected by advancing a version number in the file, helping the application to use the correct transformations.

- Loading the same file on a computer with a different architecture or operating system is no problem at all. The textual representation is the same, and due to the transformation from text to binary data types, endianness or data type lengths do not matter.

- Some caveats still exist for cross-platform usage, like different path separators in Windows and Linux, or the different interpretation of points and commas in the locale settings of the system.

- If the configuration needs to be split into multiple files, packing all files into a compressed file is the most common way. By adding all configuration files in a `.zip` or `.tar.gz` file, you end up with only a single file, and save some disk space due to the compression.

Using a textual representation for our save file is the way to go. And, by defining a simple file format, it is even possible to create a configuration file by hand.

But, before we start creating a file format on our own, let's check some available file formats. By using a well-known file format, we can save a lot of time since we don't have to create the functions to parse and write a file.

Choosing a text format to save our data

We will look at three popular configuration file formats in this section:

- INI
- JSON
- YAML

All three formats find applications in certain fields but may not be suitable in others.

The INI file format

One of the oldest formats to store configuration data is the so-called INI format. The name comes from the file extension `.ini`, which is a three-letter abbreviation for initialization. An INI file is mostly used to configure programs.

In the INI file, simple key/value pairs are stored and organized in optional sections. A section name is enclosed in square brackets, and the section scope runs from the start of the section to the start of another section, or the end of the file.

Here is an example of a section and some key/value pairs for a database connection:

```
[database-config]
type = mysql
host = mysql
port = 3306
user = app1
password = ASafePassWord1#
```

Sections can be nested to create some sort of hierarchy by separating sections and subsections by special characters, like a dot (.) or a backslash (\). It's crucial for the parser to recognize these section divisions; otherwise, each section will be treated independently, without considering their hierarchical relationship.

The lack of duplicate key names makes it hard to store hierarchical or non-trivial data where the same key may occur more than once, like a model file or an instance configuration.

The JSON file format

JSON, short for JavaScript Object Notation, made its debut in the early 2000s. As in the INI file, key/value pairs are stored in a JSON file. Sections similar to the INI file sections do not exist; instead, a JSON file allows the creation of complex, tree-like hierarchies. Also, arrays of the same data type can be defined.

The main usage for JSON files is electronic data interchange, for instance, between web applications and backend servers. Good readability of the file format by humans is only a side effect; JSON files are mostly read and written by applications.

This is an example of a JSON file, containing the same data as the INI file example:

```
{
  "database-config": {
    "type": "mysql",
    "host": "mysql",
    "port": 3306,
    "user": "app1",
    "password": "ASafePassWord1#"
  }
}
```

Sadly, due to the large number of braces, the file format is hard to write correctly on the first try. Also, no comments are allowed, so testing different options *on the fly* can only be done by saving a copy of the original file and adjusting the content.

The YAML file format

The name YAML was originally an acronym for *Yet Another Markup Language*. At the start of the 2000s, the *yet another* prefix for a product name was used as computer-related humor, stating the ever-growing repetition of unoriginal ideas. But, since YAML is not a markup language like HTML or XML, the meaning of the name was changed to the recursive acronym *YAML Ain't Markup Language*.

YAML and JSON are closely related. A JSON file can be transformed into a YAML file, and vice versa. The main difference between the two formats is that instead of using curly braces, the hierarchy in YAML is created by indents.

YAML's main goal was to be readable by humans. The YAML format is widely used to create and maintain structured and hierarchical configuration files (i.e., in configuration management systems and cloud environments).

Here is an example of the YAML file format, again with the same data as INI and JSON:

```
database-config:
  type: mysql
  host: mysql
  port: 3306
  user: app1
  password: ASafePassWord1#
```

Since the YAML format is simple and powerful, has all the features we need, and can be read and written without stumbling over missing braces, like in JSON, we will use a YAML file to store the configuration data for our application.

Exploring the structure of a YAML file

Let's look at the three main components of a YAML file:

- **Nodes**
- **Maps**
- **Sequences**

Let's start with the node.

The YAML node

The main object of a YAML file is a so-called node. A node represents the data structure below it, which can be a scalar value, a map, or a sequence.

We use this snippet of a configuration file as an example:

```
database-config:
  type: mysql
```

Both `database-config` and `type` are YAML nodes. While the `database-config` node holds a map containing the key `type` and the value `mysql`, the node type just has the scalar value `mysql` in it.

The YAML map

A YAML map contains between zero and an arbitrary number of key/value pairs. Plus, there is an interesting correlation between nodes and maps: the key and the value may be another node, creating the hierarchy in the file.

Let's extend the configuration snippet from the node section before:

```
database-config:
  type: mysql
  host: mysql
  port: 3306
```

As stated before, database-config is both a node and a map. The key of the map named database-config is the name database-config, and the value is another map, containing the three key/value pairs.

The YAML sequence

To enumerate similar elements, a YAML sequence is used. A sequence can be seen as a C++ std::vector, where all elements must be of the same kind. Like the C++ vector, you iterate over the sequence, reading the data elements one by one.

Sequences come in two different flavors: the *block style* and the *flow style*.

In the block style, an indented dash (-) is used as an indicator of the elements:

```
colors:
  - red
  - green
  - blue
```

In contrast, the flow style uses square brackets, and the elements are separated by commas:

```
colors: [red, green, blue]
```

Both styles represent the same data. It is a matter of personal preference and readability.

By combining maps and sequences, complex data structures can be created.

Combinations of maps and sequences

A powerful way to represent data can be achieved by mixing maps and sequences. For instance, we could store the position and rotation of all our model instances like this:

```
instances:
  - position: [0, 0, 0]
    rotation: [0, 0, 0]
  - position: [1, 0, -3]
    rotation: [0, 90, 0]
  - position: [3, 0, 3]
    rotation: [0, -90, 0]
```

Here, both combinations of maps and sequences are used.

First, we create a map out of the keys position and rotation; the values are flow-style sequences of numbers, representing a glm::vec3. YAML always stores the shortest possible representation of a scalar number. So, as long as values have no fractional part, an integer value will be used, even for float and double types. Then, the map of position and rotation is used in a block sequence to create an array-style representation of the model instances.

To read the data of the instances into our application, we must first iterate over the model instance sequence, and for every instance, we can extract the position and rotation values.

After the basic excurse into the YAML file format, we will now implement a YAML parser and writer class for our application to save and load its configuration. Having the configuration stored on disk is like saving a text document – we can quit the application and continue to work in the virtual world later. We can also use the saved files to return to the previous state of the virtual world.

Adding a YAML parser

Like other tools we are already using (the Open Asset Import Library, GLFW, or ImGui), we will use a freely available open source solution: yaml-cpp.

By integrating yaml-cpp, we can read and write YAML files from C++ with minimal effort. The biggest step is to make sure our custom data types are known to yaml-cpp. Plus, we have to think about a proper structure for the data file.

Let's start by exploring how to integrate yaml-cpp into our project.

Getting yaml-cpp

For Linux systems, getting yaml-cpp is easy. Similar to the other tools, most distributions already contain the yaml-cpp library and header files. For instance, in Ubuntu 22.04 or later, yaml-cpp and its development files can be installed with the following command:

```
sudo apt install libyaml-cpp-dev
```

If you are using an Arch based Linux distribution, you can install yaml-cpp with the following command:

```
sudo pacman -S yaml-cpp
```

For Windows, we are also in luck. yaml-cpp uses CMake, and by using the CMake FetchContent commands, downloading yaml-cpp can be added to the project with only a couple of lines. First, we add the FetchContent declaration to the CMakeLists.txt file in the project root. We are using version 0.8.0 of yaml-cpp:

```
FetchContent_Declare(
  yaml-cpp
  GIT_REPOSITORY https://github.com/jbeder/yaml-cpp
  GIT_TAG 0.8.0
)
```

Make sure we are inside a WIN32 section in the CMakeLists.txt file. We do not need to download the library on Linux.

Then, we trigger the download of yaml-cpp and add the variables for the directories:

```
FetchContent_MakeAvailable(yaml-cpp)
FetchContent_GetProperties(yaml-cpp)
if(NOT yaml-cpp_POPULATED)
  FetchContent_Populate(yaml-cpp)
  add_subdirectory(${yaml-cpp_SOURCE_DIR}
    ${yaml-cpp_BINARY_DIR} EXCLUDE_FROM_ALL)
endif()
```

Windows also needs a script to detect the downloaded dependency. The detection script must be named Findyaml-cpp.cmake and placed into the cmake folder.

The main function of the script boils down to these two CMake functions:

```
find_path(YAML-CPP_INCLUDE_DIR yaml-cpp/yaml.h
          PATHS ${YAML-CPP_DIR}/include/)
find_library(YAML-CPP_LIBRARY
             NAMES ${YAML-CPP_STATIC} yaml-cpp
             PATHS  ${YAML-CPP_DIR}/lib)
```

Thanks to CMake's FetchContent, the YAML-CPP_DIR variable is populated with the path to the downloaded yaml-cpp code. So, the script only checks if the header and library can be found.

Integrating yaml-cpp into the CMake build

For Linux and Windows, we must set the proper include path for the compiler, and we must add the yaml-cpp libraries to the list of linked libraries.

To update the include path, add the YAML_CPP_INCLUDE_DIR variable to the include_directories directive:

```
include_directories(... ${YAML_CPP_INCLUDE_DIR})
```

And for the linker, add yaml-cpp::yaml-cpp to target_link_libraries in Windows:

```
target_link_libraries(... yaml-cpp::yaml-cpp)
```

For Linux, only the name yaml-cpp of the shared library is needed:

```
target_link_libraries(... yaml-cpp)
```

After running CMake again, yaml-cpp will be downloaded and made available to the rest of the code.

Adding the parser class

Parsing the YAML file for loading and creating the content for writing will be done in a new class called YamlParser, located in the tools directory. We can use yaml-cpp in our code after including the header file:

```
#include <yaml-cpp/yaml.h>
```

To store the intermediate data while loading or creating a data structure to save to disk, two additional private members are needed:

```
    YAML::Node mYamlNode{};
    YAML::Emitter mYamlEmit{};
```

YAML::Node transforms the nodes of a YAML file from the disk into a C++ data structure, simplifying the access to the data that has been loaded. YAML::Emitter is used to create a YAML file in memory by appending data elements, eventually writing the structured data to a file.

Using the node type of yaml-cpp

Accessing the structured or scalar data of a yaml-cpp node is done by using the node name as the index to the C++ map stored in the YAML::Node class:

```
    mYamlNode = YAML::LoadFile(fileName);
    YAML::Node settingsNode = mYamlNode["settings"];
```

To retrieve the scalar value of a simple key/value map, the special operator as exists:

```
int value = dataNode.as<int>();
```

Since a YAML file has no knowledge of the data types stored in the value, we have to explicitly tell yaml-cpp how to interpret the incoming data. Here, yaml-cpp will try to get the value of the dataNode node as int.

After defining a transformation template, custom data types like structs can also be read directly into a variable of the same type:

```
InstanceSetting instSet = instNode.as<InstanceSettings>();
```

We will handle transformation templates in the *Saving and loading the configuration file* section.

Accessing sequences and maps

In yaml-cpp, sequences can be read by iterating over them using a for loop, and accessing the element by the index:

```
for (size_t i = 0; i < instNode.size(); ++i) {
  instSettings.emplace_back(
    instNode[i].as<InstanceSettings>());
}
```

The elements of the sequence are made available in the same order as they appear in the YAML file.

For maps, an iterator-style for loop is needed:

```
for(auto it = settingsNode.begin();
    it != settingsNode.end(); ++it) {
  if (it->first.as<std::string>() == "selected-model") {
    ....
  }
}
```

The key of the map element can be read via the first accessor of the C++ map container. Again, we must tell yaml-cpp which data type the map key is. Then, the value can be retrieved with the second accessor of the C++ map container.

If reading a value fails, for instance, because the type is wrong or no such node exists, an exception will be thrown. To avoid our program being terminated, we must handle all thrown exceptions.

Handling exceptions thrown by yaml-cpp

Instead of returning an error code, yaml-cpp throws exceptions whenever something goes wrong. By default, any unhandled exception terminates the program. Handling an exception in C++ is done like in other languages:

```
try {
  mYamlNode = YAML::LoadFile(fileName);
} catch(...) {
  return false;
}
```

The call that may cause an exception will be enclosed in a try block, and in case of an exception, the catch block will be executed.

We can simply catch all exceptions since any parsing failure may result in an empty or incomplete configuration file. If you want to have more detailed exception handling, you can explore the yaml-cpp source code.

Armed with the basics of yaml-cpp, we can start implementing the code to save and load a YAML file. We will start with the save functionality because after we have created a file on disk, loading the data elements back into the application will be much easier compared to hand-crafting a configuration file first.

Saving and loading the configuration file

Building our configuration file starts with the decision of what needs to be stored and how we want to store the elements. By reusing our custom data types like the InstanceSettings, creating the functions to save and load a file can be simplified. Now we no longer have to read each value individually, but we can use calls like getInstanceSettings() and setInstanceSettings() from the AssimpInstance class to transfer the values directly between the parser and the instance.

We will start by exploring what we want to save, and after adding the code to write our custom data to the file, a user interface dialog will be added, allowing a simple way to save the file to disk. Finally, we will step through the process of loading the configuration back into the application.

Deciding what to store in the configuration file

As mentioned in the *Saving and loading textual data* section, adding a version number can help a lot during the development of an application. If we need to change the data format, even slightly, raising the version number can help us to simplify branching between the old and new format(s) when reading a file.

Next, we should store the information about the selection. Restoring the selected model and instance, we can continue exactly from the same spot where we saved the configuration file.

Also, we should store the camera information. When working with more complex scenes later in the book, restoring the camera to the default position and angles may confuse the application user.

As the most important parts, we must store all information about the models and all instances on the screen required to restore the application to the same state as at the time of saving the configuration.

For the model, the file name and path are sufficient, as we use the file name as the model's name. The path to the model file will be saved relative to the application executable, and not as an absolute path, at least as long as the model resides on the same partition as the executable (Windows only). Both methods have their pros and cons:

- A relative path allows the user to check out the code from the book anywhere on their system, being able to use the example configuration file and example models *out of the box*. However, moving the executable to another directory or partition requires all configuration data and models to be moved too, or the configuration files must be manually adjusted.
- Using an absolute path may become handy to store a new configuration at a fixed location on the PC (i.e., in the home directory of the user). This way, the application could be started from any place on the PC and still find the configuration files and models.

To restore all instances, we need all information stored in the InstanceSettings struct plus the model name. To simplify restoring the instance via the model name, we add the model name as a std::string to the InstanceSettings struct. Having the model name in the struct allows us to hand over a std::vector of InstanceSettings values from the YAML parser to the renderer class; we don't need more complex data structures.

Let's start the implementation by creating custom element writer overloads.

Overloading the output operator of the emitter

The creators of yaml-cpp added a nice method to output the contents of complex structures to the YAML::Emitter. We only have to overload the operator<< in the YamlParser.cpp file in the tools folder:

```
YAML::Emitter& operator<<(YAML::Emitter& out,
    const glm::vec3& vec) {
  out << YAML::Flow;
  out << YAML::BeginSeq;
  out << vec.x << vec.y << vec.z;
  out << YAML::EndSeq;
  return out;
}
```

For the glm::vec3 data type, we add a flow type sequence, and then the three elements of the vector will be added to the stream. In the final file, a default YAML sequence will appear, containing the values of the glm::vec3 vector as in this example:

```
[1, 2, 3]
```

Our InstanceSettings struct must be added as the key/value pairs of a YAML map. The start and end of the map are set in the function storing the InstanceSettings:

```
YAML::Emitter& operator<<(YAML::Emitter& out,
    const InstanceSettings& settings) {
  out << YAML::Key << "model-file";
  out << YAML::Value << settings.isModelFile;
  out << YAML::Key << "position";
  out << YAML::Value << settings.isWorldPosition;
  out << YAML::Key << "rotation";
  out << YAML::Value << settings.isWorldRotation
  ...
}
```

The resulting maps will be added as the value of a YAML sequence, storing all relevant instance data in the configuration file.

Creating and writing the configuration file

To create a configuration file, the renderer will instantiate a local object of our YamlParser class, and call createConfigFile() on it:

```
YamlParser parser;
if (!parser.createConfigFile(mRenderData, mModelInstData)) {
    return false;
}
```

In the createConfigFile() method, the YAML::Emitter will be filled with the structures of our data. As an example, we will add a comment at the top of the file, and save the version number in the second line:

```
mYamlEmit << YAML::Comment("Application viewer
  config file");
mYamlEmit << YAML::BeginMap;
mYamlEmit << YAML::Key << "version";
mYamlEmit << YAML::Value << 1.0f;
mYamlEmit << YAML::EndMap;
...
```

In the final YAML file, the following first lines will appear:

```
# Application viewer config file
version: 1
```

Aa another example, to store the instance settings, we create a map named instances, and start creating a sequence as the value:

```
mYamlEmit << YAML::BeginMap;
mYamlEmit << YAML::Key << "instances";
mYamlEmit << YAML::Value;
mYamlEmit << YAML::BeginSeq;
```

Then, we can create a for loop over the instances and use the getInstanceSettings() call of the instance to directly store the instance settings to the emitter stream:

```
for (const auto& instance : modInstData.miAssimpInstances) {
  mYamlEmit << YAML::BeginMap;
  mYamlEmit << instance->getInstanceSettings();
```

```
    mYamlEmit << YAML::EndMap;
}
```

Thanks to the operator<< overload, no complex handling inside the loop is required.

As the last step, we close the sequence of instance settings, and close the map for the instances key:

```
    mYamlEmit << YAML::EndSeq;
    mYamlEmit << YAML::EndMap
```

The final YAML file will contain a sequence of all instances, including the newly added model file name:

```
instances:
  - model-file: Woman.gltf
    position: [0, 0, 0]
    rotation: [0, 0, 0]
    scale: 1
    swap-axes: false
    anim-clip-number: 0
    anim-clip-speed: 1
```

If we want to view the contents of the created configuration file before doing any disk writes, we can create a C string and output the string via the logger class:

```
    Logger::log(1, "%s\n", mYamlEmit.c_str());
```

Writing the file to disk will be done with a std::ostream. The error handling for the stream has been excluded for brevity in the following listing, but saving the file to disk is essentially done in just three lines:

```
bool YamlParser::writeYamlFile(std::string fileName) {
  std::ofstream fileToWrite(fileName);
  fileToWrite << mYamlEmit.c_str();
  fileToWrite.close();
  return true;
}
```

First, we create the output stream with the given file name. Then, we convert the std::string of the YAML::Emitter to a C string and write the string to the output stream. By closing the stream, the file will be flushed to the storage device.

Adding a file dialog to the user interface

To allow the user to store the configuration file in an arbitrary location and with a custom name, we will add a file dialog in the user interface. We are already using the ImGui-based file dialog to load a model file, and we can reuse the same dialog instance to present a **Save File** dialog to the user.

To create a dialog that lets the user choose a file name and location, three changes to the `IGFD::FileDialogConfig` variable named `config` must be made.

First, by selecting an existing file, we need an extra dialog to confirm an overwriting of the file. Luckily, the file dialog has such a confirmation dialog already built in. All we must do is add the flag `ImGuiFileDialogFlags_ConfirmOverwrite`:

```
config.flags = ImGuiFileDialogFlags_Modal |
  ImGuiFileDialogFlags_ConfirmOverwrite;
```

If we select an existing file, a new dialog will be shown, asking the user to confirm whether to replace the existing file or not.

Next, we will present a default path and file name for the configuration:

```
const std::string defaultFileName = "config/conf.acfg";
config.filePathName = defaultFileName.c_str();
```

Here, we are using the `config` folder and a file named `config.acfg` to present a default file to the user. The file dialog code will automatically enter the `config` folder and fill out the file name and extension.

As a last step, we add `.acfg` as the only file extension to the dialog:

```
ImGuiFileDialog::Instance()->OpenDialog(
  "SaveConfigFile", "Save Configuration File",
  ".acfg", config);
```

By using a new extension for the configuration file, we avoid trouble, like attempts to load a different file format or overwriting other files on the system.

The **OK** button of the file dialog retrieves the selected file name, and calls the callback function responsible for saving the configuration to disk:

```
if (ImGuiFileDialog::Instance()->IsOk()) {
  std::string filePathName =
```

```
        ImGuiFileDialog::Instance()->GetFilePathName();
      saveSuccessful =
        modInstData.miSaveConfigCallbackFunction(
        filePathName);
    }
```

We store the result of the callback function in the Boolean saveSuccessful. This way, we can check for any errors and present the user a dialog in case saving the configuration was not successful.

To inform the user about save errors, only a simple dialog is implemented, notifying the user to check the output messages of the application for details about the cause of the write error.

If you load some models now, create instances or clones, and save the configuration, you can inspect the created configuration file. All data from the *Deciding what to store in the configuration file* section should be in the configuration file.

Saving the data to disk is only half the job. To continue working from the same spot where we saved the file, we need to load the configuration file back into the application.

Loading the configuration file back and parsing the nodes

To support parsing custom data types in a YAML file, yaml-cpp allows us to define a C++ template for a struct named convert, located in the YAML namespace. The convert struct must implement two methods called encode and decode, doing the process of serializing the C++ types to YAML (encode) and deserializing from YAML back to C++ (decode). By using these two methods, yaml-cpp allows a seamless transformation between C++ types and YAML entries. The encode method creates a new YAML node from a primitive or custom data type, while the decode method reads the YAML node data and returns the primitive or custom data type.

For writing a glm::vec3 element to a YAML node and reading back a YAML node to a glm::vec3, the following template code must be implemented in a header file:

```
namespace YAML {
  template<>
  struct convert<glm::vec3> {
    static Node encode(const glm::vec3& rhs) {
      Node node;
      node.push_back(rhs.x);
      node.push_back(rhs.y);
      node.push_back(rhs.z);
```

```
        return node;
    }
```

To save the data from the glm::vec3, we create a new YAML node called node and add the three elements x, y, and z of the glm::vec3 to the node. The node is then returned to the caller of the encode() method.

Reading back the data from a node into a glm::vec3 variable is done with the decode() method:

```
    static bool decode(const Node& node, glm::vec3& rhs) {
      if(!node.IsSequence() || node.size() != 3) {
        return false;
      }
```

Checking the node type for the right type and size is optional, but it is a good style assuring we have the correct data for the custom data type to prevent runtime errors. Skipping this check and trying to parse the wrong data type will lead to an exception, terminating the entire program if unhandled.

Then, we read the data from a node by the sequence index, and set the three elements x, y, and z of the glm::vec3 to the float values from the node:

```
      rhs.x = node[0].as<float>();
      rhs.y = node[1].as<float>();
      rhs.z = node[2].as<float>();
      return true;
    }
  };
```

After defining the encode() and decode() methods, we can exchange data between a YAML node and a glm::vec3 by a normal assignment:

```
  glm::vec3 data;
  node["rotation"] = data.isWorldRotation;
  data.isWorldRotation = node["rotation"].as<glm::vec3>();
```

The same two methods are implemented for the InstanceSettings struct, helping us to read the settings of the instance directly back into a variable of the type InstanceSettings. To avoid polluting the header for our parser class, a new header called YamlParserTypes.h has been created in the tools folder. The YamlParserTypes.h header will be included in the header of the YamlParser class to make the new conversions available.

Once the configuration file is successfully parsed, all settings, model paths, and instance settings are extracted. But before we can load the models and create new instances, we must first clear the current list of models and instances.

Cleaning up and recreating the scene from the saved values

Removing all models and instances is a simple and straightforward process. In the renderer, we must do the following steps to have a fresh environment:

1. Set `miSelectedInstance` and `miSelectedModel` containing the currently selected instance and model to zero. The variables from this step and from *steps 2 and 3* were introduced in the *Dynamic model and instance management* section of *Chapter 1*. Then, at index zero, the new null model and null instance will be created.

2. Erase the `miAssimpInstances` vector and clear the `miAssimpInstancesPerModel` map. Now, all models are unused.

3. Erase the `miModelList` vector. Since all instances were already deleted, the shared pointers of the models will be no longer referenced, and the models will be deleted.

4. Add a new null model and a null instance. Both the null model and the null instance must be the first elements of the model list and the instances vector and map.

5. Clear the undo and redo stacks. In the stacks, we used only weak pointers, so this step can be done at any time.

6. Update the triangle count. After all models and instances were removed, the triangle count should be zero.

The entire procedure of cleaning up all models and instances has been added to the new `removeAllModelsAndInstances()` method of the renderer class, simplifying the usage whenever we need a clean and fresh environment.

Now, we can load the model files from disk, but without creating the default instance. After all models are loaded, we search the model from the `InstanceSettings` in the model list, create a new instance, and apply the settings from the configuration file.

Next, we should enumerate the instances as the instance index number is not stored in the `InstanceSettings`. But the instance should remain at the same index they had at save time, due to the linear reading of the `miAssimpInstances` vector when the YAML emitter is created and the same linear reading of the nodes when parsing the YAML file.

Finally, we restore the camera settings, selected model, and instance plus the status of the selection highlight from the parser.

At this point, the configuration should be fully loaded, and the application should contain the same models, instances, and settings as at the time of the save operation.

One question remains for the load process: What should we do if parsing the configuration file fails only partially? Maybe a model file was renamed or deleted, or the file was truncated or corrupted and the settings of the last instance are incomplete.

Strict or relaxed configuration file loading

One option to overcome parsing errors is to discard the entire configuration prior to deleting all current content of the application. This strict loading type is easy to implement; any kind of parsing error invalidates the configuration file at parsing time. We ignore the loading request and present just an error message to the user.

The other option is relaxed parsing. We try our best to load the valid models and fill in the missing configuration parts with default values but also tell the user that parts of the configuration file cannot be loaded.

In both cases, the error message should give detailed hints at which point the parsing failed. Therefore, the exception handling could be extended to know exactly what went wrong, and where. For relaxed handling, as much additional information about affected models, instances, or settings as possible should be presented to the user.

It is up to the creator of an application to decide which strategy fits best. Usually, an attempt to recover as much data as possible should be made. Losing only a small part of the created work is better than losing all data.

Common errors leading to corrupted files

A couple of factors can render your saved configuration file corrupt. Some common causes are listed here:

- Disk or partition is filled up to 100% while writing the file: Even with the large amount of storage we have today, this may happen, and you have only parts of your data saved.
- Permission problems: Sometimes, you might have permission to create files but not to write file content. So, your files seem to be saved, but the file has a length of zero bytes.
- Connection errors when saving to remote places: Your connection may be interrupted while writing a larger file, resulting in a partially written file.

- Conversion errors, for instance, by sending files per email: A mail program or a mail server may convert the file in an incorrect manner, leading to a partially corrupt file with some replaced characters.

- Incompatible locale setting: The machine where the file was saved could have used the comma as a decimal separator while your computer uses a point as the decimal separator. The numbers in the file will be misinterpreted or even set to zero if parsing fails. This problem is tricky to find and gets overlooked easily.

- Coding errors, like wrong version handling, wrong conversions, or incomplete error/ exception handling: You might save not all data, convert the data by accident to a wrong format, or miss parsing some of the data in the file. You should test the code reading and writing files for as many possible data types and object combinations as possible to find such errors.

- You should be aware that your save files could get corrupted on your machine or on the way from or to you. So, save your work often, use a versioning system like Git to store different versions of the files, and back up all your configuration files on a regular basis.

Now that we have the code to save and load the state of the application, we can provide a predefined default configuration at application startup.

Loading a default configuration file at startup

To help a user explore a new application, next to an extensive tutorial, a simple example of the content created with the application can be loaded at the first start, or maybe at any start of the application. Tinkering around with the available options helps us understand how the application works, and what kind of content manipulations are possible.

Loading a default configuration at startup can be achieved in different ways. A configuration file could be added at compile time (*baked* into the application), or one or more example files could be placed in a reachable folder, and the example file loaded at startup. Often, a separate configuration setting for the application is available to disable the automated loading of an example file.

As an example, we will load the configuration file `config/conf.acfg` from the load and save dialogs at application startup. Thanks to the already implemented YAML parser and file-loading code, the changes to the renderer class can be done with only a couple of lines.

First, we define the default configuration file as a new `private` member variable `mDefaultConfigFileName` of the renderer class:

```
const std::string mDefaultConfigFileName =
    "config/conf.acfg";
```

Hard-coding file paths or file names should be avoided in general, but for the first configuration file, we end up in a chicken/egg problem. If we want to store the name of the default configuration in another configuration file, instead of hard-coding the file name in the code, we will need another hard-coded file name. Such a bootstrapping problem can only be solved by hard-coding the first value.

Then, in the `init()` method of the renderer, we try to load the default configuration file:

```
if (!loadConfigFile(mDefaultConfigFileName)) {
  addNullModelAndInstance();
}
```

If the file cannot be found or fails to load, we only create the null model and the null instance. Since all other values are set as defaults at the first start, we end up with the same application as if we would have no default configuration at all.

Implementing load and save functionality to an application requires a bit of research for the right type of save file, and some more work to actually implement the features into the existing code. All changes and new features should be reflected in the save file of the application, thus requiring more work to keep the load and save code up to date as application features change. By adding a versioning schema to the configuration file, we are even able to load configurations from different development stages of the application.

Summary

In this chapter, we added the ability to save the current configuration of the application to a file and load the same configuration back into the application. First, we evaluated the advantages and disadvantages of binary and textual save files and checked three common text file types to find a fitting format for our save files. Next, we explored the chosen YAML file format and implemented the save and load functionalities. Finally, we added a default file to load at application startup to help the user with the first steps of the application handling.

In the next chapter, will take care of custom cameras in the application. Currently, we use only the *internal* camera to fly around in the virtual world. By adding custom camera types, more visualization options for the virtual world are possible. We will add a third-person-style camera, following one of the instances similar to an action game, and a stationary camera that follows one instance. Additionally, a simple camera manager will be added, and the configuration of the cameras will be also saved in the configuration file.

Practical sessions

There are some additions you could make to the code:

- Add a menu entry to create a new, empty scene.

  Right now, we can only load and save a configuration file. Removing all models and instances must still be done by hand. Add a menu entry plus code to remove all models and instances at once, giving the user a simple way to start from nothing.

- Add a flag and confirmation dialogs if a setting is changed.

  If the settings of one model are altered, set a `dirty` flag to remember that the user of the application changed the loaded model instance or a saved state. Then, if the user wants to load another configuration file, start over with an empty configuration or exit the application and show a confirmation dialog to make sure a chance is given to save the current settings.

- Add a `dirty` marker to the title.

  Several other applications are presenting some kind of notice to the user, stating that changes have been made since the last save. The title of the application window gets adjusted to show whether we are in edit or view mode, so adding a star (*) to the window title, or some words like "Not saved" should be easy.

Additional resource

Here is the GitHub repository for `yaml-cpp`: `https://github.com/jbeder/yaml-cpp`.

Get This Book's PDF Version and Exclusive Extras

UNLOCK NOW

Scan the QR code (or go to packtpub.com/unlock). Search for this book by name, confirm the edition, and then follow the steps on the page.

Note: Keep your invoice handy. Purchases made directly from Packt don't require an invoice.

6

Extending Camera Handling

Welcome to *Chapter 6*! In *Chapter 5*, we added the functionality to save and load the application configuration. First, we explored data types, file formats, and which data to save to a file. Then, we implemented a parser class to write and read configuration files in the YAML file format. At the end of the chapter, all models and instances plus the global settings were stored in a YAML file by using the yaml-cpp library, and all data could be read back into the application, enabling us to resume building the virtual world.

In this chapter, we will enhance the camera configuration. As the first two steps, we will extend the application to handle more than one camera and add multiple camera types. Then, we'll implement camera types for a first-person and third-person view, following a selected instance like in real games. Next, we will add stationary cameras, allowing a surveillance-style view of the virtual scenery. As the last step, we will add a hotkey to switch between cameras, along with orthogonal projection and mouse-wheel-based field of view adjustment.

In this chapter, we will cover the following topics:

- Adding multiple cameras
- Creating different camera types
- Implementing first- and third-person cameras
- Adding stationary cameras
- Switching between cameras and configurations

Technical requirements

The example code is in the chapter06 folder, in the subfolders 01_opengl_cameras for OpenGL and 02_vulkan_cameras for Vulkan.

Adding multiple cameras

In *Chapter 3*, we added a button in the user interface to jump to any instance. But we still land at the same angle and distance for every instance we choose, and returning to a great composition of different models on a map is close to impossible. You may write down the camera values or take a screenshot, but that is far from perfect.

Being able to add a virtually unlimited number of cameras to our scene allows us to create stunning map and model combinations and return to that view whenever we want. By adding different camera types, we can even go several steps further – a camera chasing one instance in the third person; another camera presenting the entire map in an isometric view; and yet another camera to see the virtual world through the virtual eyes of an instance – all reachable by pressing a hotkey or selecting a menu.

All those points will be implemented at the end of the chapter. So, let's start with the first step, and add multiple camera objects to the application.

From a single camera to an array of cameras

Right now, we have only a single camera in the application, defined in the Camera class in the tools folder. This camera provides a free view of the virtual world. We can move in all three axes and rotate around two of the three axes. Rotating the view around the axis pointing *into* the screen (roll) is less useful at this point for the model and animation viewer application since we would just see the effect of tilting our head to the side. In addition, navigating a camera in three dimensions without a fixed reference like the horizon could be quite difficult. So, we only implement up and down (Elevation) and rotation around the vertical axis (Azimuth). Upgrading the camera rotation and adding mouse or keyboard controls for a rotation around the third axis is left as an exercise for you.

The values for the camera position and the two rotation angles are stored in the OGLRenderData struct for OpenGL and in the VkRenderData struct for Vulkan:

```
float rdViewAzimuth = 330.0f;
float rdViewElevation = -20.0f;
glm::vec3 rdCameraWorldPosition =
  glm::vec3(2.0f, 5.0f, 7.0f);
```

To support multiple cameras, we need a simple `std::vector` of the `Camera` class elements and an `int` value, stating which of the cameras is currently selected. Since these settings are closer to the models and model instances than the rendering, we will store the new camera vector in the `ModelAndInstanceData` struct. To match the new contents, we will rename the `ModelAndInstanceData` struct to `ModelInstanceCamData`:

```
struct ModelInstanceCamData {
    ...
    std::vector<std::shared_ptr<Camera>> micCameras{};
    int micSelectedCamera = 0;
    ...
```

By using the refactoring function of your IDE, renaming the `ModelAndInstanceData` struct, along with the variables in classes and functions, is only a matter of some mouse clicks and a text edit.

In addition to the new struct name, we will also rename the file from `ModelAndInstanceData.h` to `ModelInstanceCamData.h` and move the file from the `model` folder to the `opengl` folder (the `vulkan` folder for Vulkan). In the end, it is a matter of personal preference where to store the header file, but using a central location as the folder containing the renderer makes a lot of sense since we access the struct mostly from the renderer.

In the `UserInterface` class, we add a combo box containing the names of the available cameras inside the definition of `ImGui::CollapsingHeader` named `Cameras`. The code for the combo box can be taken and adjusted from the model or animation clip selection.

Extracting the camera settings

Similar to the instance settings, we will extract the main camera settings to a separate struct called `CameraSettings`. A separate struct containing the camera variables makes it easier to read out or to apply all camera-related settings at once, instead of accessing all settings by setters and getters.

The `CameraSettings` struct resides in a header file, `CameraSettings.h`, residing in the `tools` folder:

```
struct CameraSettings{
    std::string csCamName = "Camera";
    glm::vec3 csWorldPosition = glm::vec3(0.0f);
    float csViewAzimuth = 0.0f;
    float csViewElevation = 0.0f
};
```

Next to a name for the camera, we start with the world position and the two view angles of the camera: Azimuth and elevation.

In the Camera class, the new CameraSettings.h header must be included, and a new private member variable called mCamSettings will be added. The three old variables containing position, azimuth, and elevation can be removed. All methods accessing the three variables for position and the view angles must be changed to store and retrieve the values inside the new mCamSettings variable.

We have to add a getter and a setter method for the new CameraSettings. The getter and setter will allow us to handle the cameras like the model instances, manipulating the camera settings by simple variable assignments.

Adjusting the renderer

As the renderer needs to update the position and view of the camera, we also need to upgrade some methods to use the selected camera.

The first step is always to get a pointer to the current camera and read the CameraSettings for easier access and changes:

```
std::shared_ptr<Camera> cam =
  mModelInstCamData.micCameras.at(
    mModelInstCamData.micSelectedCamera);
CameraSettings camSettings = cam->getCameraSettings();
```

If we changed any values, we must store the settings back to the camera:

```
cam->setCameraSettings(camSettings);
```

Then, in the handleMousePositionEvents() method, we change all variables from the old mRenderData variable, as highlighted in the following code:

```
mRenderData.rdViewAzimuth += mouseMoveRelX / 10.0;
```

The new camSettings variable, containing the new camera settings, looks like this:

```
camSettings.csViewAzimuth += mouseMoveRelX / 10.0f;
```

A similar change needs to be made in the draw() method of the renderer.

First, we remove the private mCamera member variable from the renderer class, as we will never use the single camera again. Then, we get the pointer to the camera and read the current camera settings.

Now, the update of the camera will be switched away from the old mCamera variable:

```
mCamera.updateCamera(mRenderData, deltaTime);
```

Instead, we update the currently selected camera via the cam pointer:

```
cam->updateCamera(mRenderData, deltaTime);
```

For the projection matrix, we use the new camSettings variable to read the currently configured field of view:

```
mProjectionMatrix = glm::perspective(
  glm::radians(static_cast<float>(
    camSettings.csFieldOfView)),
  static_cast<float>(mRenderData.rdWidth) /
  static_cast<float>(mRenderData.rdHeight),
0.01f, 500.0f);
```

We read the updated view matrix also by accessing the cam pointer:

```
mViewMatrix = cam->getViewMatrix();
```

Finally, in the centerInstance() method of the renderer, the call to the moveCameraTo() method of the camera must be adjusted, too. We no longer use the old mCamera variable, highlighted in the following code:

```
mCamera.moveCameraTo(...);
```

Now, we access the current camera directly in the micCameras vector:

```
mModelInstCamData.micCameras.at(
  mModelInstCamData.micSelectedCamera)->moveCameraTo(...);
```

Extracting the pointer to the current camera makes no sense here since this is only a single operation on the camera instance.

Defining a free camera as the default camera

Like the null model and the null instance, we should make sure to always have at least one
camera in the micCameras vector. Avoiding an empty array frees us from a lot of boundary
checks, and the always-available free camera is a nice feature on a new configuration or after
all existing cameras are removed.

To simplify the default free camera, a new method called loadDefaultFreeCam() will be added
to the renderer class:

```
void OGLRenderer::loadDefaultFreeCam() {
  mModelInstCamData.micCameras.clear();
```

First, we clear the vector containing all the cameras. Then, we create a new camera settings
object with some default values, apply the settings to the camera, and add the camera as the
first instance:

```
    std::shared_ptr<Camera> freeCam =
      std::make_shared<Camera>();

    CameraSettings freeCamSettings{};
    freeCamSettings.csCamName = "FreeCam";
    freeCamSettings.csWorldPosition = glm::vec3(5.0f);
    freeCamSettings.csViewAzimuth = 310.0f;
    freeCamSettings.csViewElevation = -15.0f;
    freeCam->setCameraSettings(freeCamSettings);
    mModelInstCamData.micCameras.emplace_back(freeCam);
    mModelInstCamData.micSelectedCamera = 0;
}
```

You can adjust the settings for the default free camera to your needs. The settings shown in the
previous code snippet just center the origin of the world, making the first instance of a loaded
model appear in the center of the screen.

Finally, we set the selected camera to zero, the index of our newly added camera.

Whenever we need to remove all cameras and add the default camera (i.e., when creating a new
configuration), we can just call loadDefaultFreeCam().

For the user interface, we should disable name changes to the default free camera by surrounding the name field with calls to `ImGui::BeginDisabled()` and `ImGui::EndDisabled()` when the camera instance 0 is selected.

Figure 6.1 shows the resulting user interface for the camera section:

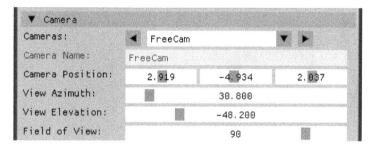

Figure 6.1: The new camera settings

Switching between cameras is now as simple as selecting a new base model or a new animation clip, for instance. In addition to the combo box, two arrows have been added, allowing us to directly select the previous and the next camera.

For real camera management, two functions are missing: creating a new camera and deleting an existing camera, with the exception of the default camera.

Adding and deleting cameras

To create a camera, two paths can be taken:

- Adding a camera at the origin, using default values
- Cloning the currently selected camera and all settings except the name

Forcing the user to return to the origin and move the new camera to the desired place in the virtual world feels a bit off. A much better solution is to be able to clone the currently selected camera since the user most probably wants to make the current view of the virtual world persistent.

Both cloning and deleting functions are handled by new callbacks, moving the burden of checks and all work to the renderer instead of the user interface. The new renderer methods, called `cloneCamera()` and `deleteCamera()`, are short and simple, so we skip the listing here.

However, handling camera names needs some extra attention. Duplicate names in the combo box will be confusing, so we have to find a solution to create unique names when cloning a camera. A simple way to create new names is to append a number to the name and raise the number by one on further clones.

The method handling the new names is called generateUniqueCameraName(), defined in the renderer class. The method has a camera base name as the only parameter.

First, we copy the base name, since we will adjust the name during the while loop if the camera name is already in use, and define a string named matches containing all numbers from zero to nine:

```
std::string camName = camBaseName;
std::string matches("01234567890");


while (checkCameraNameUsed(camName)) {
```

In the loop, we check if the camera name already has a number as a suffix. If not, we simply append a 1:

```
const auto iter = std::find_first_of(camName.begin(),
    camName.end(), matches.begin(), matches.end());
if (iter == camName.end()) {


    camName.append("1");
} else {
```

If we find a number, then we save the camera name without the trailing number into cameraNameString, convert the existing camera number to an int, increment the number by one, convert the new number back to a string, and combine the original camera name and the new number:

```
std::string cameraNameString = camName.substr(0,
    std::distance(camName.begin(), iter));
std::string cameraNumString = camName.substr(
    std::distance(camName.begin(), iter));
int cameraNumber = std::stoi(cameraNumString);
camName = cameraNameString +
    std::to_string(++cameraNumber);
    }
}
```

This way, we can create unique but still understandable camera names when we clone an existing camera.

The while loop in generateUniqueCameraName() uses another new method called checkCameraNameUsed(). Checking if the camera name is already in use is done by iterating over the existing cameras and comparing the camera names with the proposed new name:

```
bool OGLRenderer::checkCameraNameUsed(std::string
    cameraName) {
  for (const auto& cam : mModelInstCamData.micCameras) {
    if (cam->getCameraSettings().csCamName == cameraName) {
      return true;
    }
  }
  return false;
}
```

The same checkCameraNameUsed() method will be used in the user interface to detect a duplicate name when a camera is renamed. As in most places in the user interface, a callback to the renderer is used for the name check, moving the work to the renderer class.

In *Figure 6.2*, the new buttons to clone and delete the camera are shown, together with the result of pressing the **Clone Current Camera** button several times:

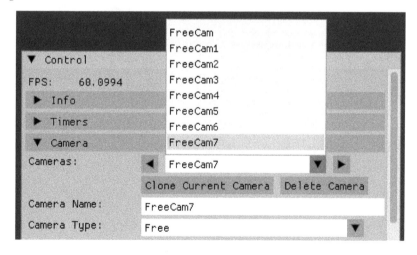

Figure 6.2: New buttons to clone and delete, plus some new cameras

As the last step for the transition away from a single camera, we must change the YAML-based configuration file to reflect the new camera configuration.

Adjusting camera configuration load and save

To load and save the new camera settings, we have to change the YAML parsing and emitting in the YamlParser class in the tools folder.

Decoding a YAML camera node can be achieved similarly to decoding glm::vec3 or InstanceSettings:, by adding a new decode method in a new convert template block in the header file YamlParserTypes.h:

```
Template<>
  struct convert<CameraSettings> {

  static bool decode(const Node& node,

      CameraSettings& rhs) {

    CameraSettings defaultSettings = CameraSettings{};

    rhs.csCamName =
        node["camera-name"].as<std::string>();

     try {

      rhs.csWorldPosition =

          node["position"].as<glm::vec3>();

    } catch (...) {

       rhs.csWorldPosition =

        defaultSettings.csWorldPosition;

    }

     try {

      rhs.csViewAzimuth =
          node["view-azimuth"].as<float>();
```

```
        } catch (...) {
            rhs.csViewAzimuth = defaultSettings.csViewAzimuth;


        }


    try {
        rhs.csViewElevation =
            node["view-elevation"].as<float>();


    } catch (...) {
        rhs.csViewElevation =
            defaultSettings.csViewElevation;
    }
```

Handling exceptions thrown while parsing nodes ensures recovering as much of the camera configuration as possible in case of malformed or missing keys. Being unable to parse the camera name still skips the entire camera to avoid naming trouble.

We also add the encode method to make a full implementation of the template. With the decode function available, we can read a node containing camera settings simply by passing the CameraSettings type to the .as<>() call:

```
... camNode.as<CameraSettings>();
```

For emitting camera configurations to a save file, we create a sequence and add a map for each of the cameras available:

```
    ...
    mYamlEmit << YAML::BeginMap;
    mYamlEmit << YAML::Key << "cameras";
    mYamlEmit << YAML::Value;
    mYamlEmit << YAML::BeginSeq;
    for (const auto& cam : modInstCamData.micCameras) {
        CameraSettings settings = cam->getCameraSettings();
        mYamlEmit << YAML::BeginMap;
        mYamlEmit << YAML::Key << "camera-name";
        mYamlEmit << YAML::Value << settings.csCamName;
        ...
    }
```

```
    mYamlEmit << YAML::EndSeq;
    mYamlEmit << YAML::EndMap;
```

In the saved YAML configuration file, a new sequence will appear for each camera, storing all camera settings as key/value pairs:

```
cameras:
  - camera-name: FreeCam
    position: [2.9061296, 11.1587305, 64.1114578]
    view-azimuth: 289.300262
    view-elevation: -34.4999695
```

Since we made essential changes to the configuration file, we should reflect the new on-disk format with a new version number.

Bumping the configuration file version

Adjusting the configuration file version number in the emitter is easy; we just have to raise the version number string from 1.0 to something like 1.1 or 2.0. From now on, all saved configuration files will have the new version number.

Loading a configuration file gets a bit more complex now. If we want to support the old file format, we must retain all methods that were used to parse the previous file version contents. After reading the version number of the file to parse, we must decide if we want to parse the new sequence style for multiple cameras, or get the settings for the single camera and apply those settings to the always-available default free camera. Saving the configuration could be done in the new version, resulting in a migration of a configuration file from the old to the new version.

Updating the configuration by supporting the reading of an older version is one of the tasks in the *Practical sessions* section.

We can create a bunch of free-floating cameras now, position the cameras in our virtual world, and switch between the cameras via the user interface. Still sounds a bit boring, doesn't it? Let's enhance the application more by adding different camera types.

Creating different camera types

Having the ability to add more than one camera in the virtual world is a good basis for adding a couple of predefined camera settings. The different camera types behave in different ways regarding the movement of the view and the movement of the camera itself.

We define a new enum class named `cameraType` in the `Enums.h` file:

```
enum class cameraType {
  free = 0,
  firstPerson,
  thirdPerson,
  stationary,
  stationaryFollowing
};
```

In the `CameraSettings` struct, a new variable of the `cameraType` type must be added:

```
cameraType csCamType = cameraType::free;
```

The names already tell a lot about the purpose of the camera types. Here is what all the types are about:

- The `free` camera is already known from previous code examples. We can freely move around the world in five degrees of freedom: three directions and two rotations. There are no movement restrictions for the camera or view.

- The `firstPerson` camera does what cameras in first-person games do: it allows you to see the virtual world through the eyes of the protagonist. In our application, we will attach the camera to the head of an instance and move both camera and view just as the instance does. However, there will be an option to unlock the view to avoid weird angles or motion sickness.

- The `thirdPerson` camera follows the selected instance like another person or a drone, showing the same angle of the virtual world as the instance sees but from the *outside* of the instance body. Some view adjustments are possible, like the distance from the instance, but both camera motion and view are controlled by the instance.

- The `stationary` camera can be compared to a fixed surveillance camera. The stationary camera can be placed anywhere in the world and at any angle, but once the camera is locked, no movement or view adjustment except the field of view is possible. The field of view setting is kept unlocked to allow zooming in and out, just like with a normal surveillance camera.

- Finally, the `stationaryFollowing` camera is a special type of surveillance camera. While both movement and view are not controllable by the user (again, with the exception of the field of view setting), this camera type will automatically center the selected instance, regardless of whether the instance is directly visible or not. And if the instance moves around, the camera will track that instance within the virtual world.

Depending on the camera type, we must restrict parts of the camera settings in the renderer. Whenever we are unable to change specific camera settings, like the position, we will also disable the user interface control for the same settings.

We will start with the first- and third-person cameras because both camera types have large parts of behavior changes and data retrieval in common.

Implementing first- and third-person cameras

For a first-person camera, the CameraSettings struct in the CameraSettings.h header in the tools folder needs some additional variables:

```
bool csFirstPersonLockView = true;
int csFirstPersonBoneToFollow = 0;
std::vector<std::string> csFirstPersonBoneNames{};
glm::mat4 csFirstPersonBoneMatrix = glm::mat4(1.0f);
glm::vec3 csFirstPersonOffsets = glm::vec3(0.0f);
```

The new variable csFirstPersonLockView is used to control if the first-person view follows the motion of the instance bone or if we relax that restriction and enable a free view, but still at a fixed position. We need a bone of the model skeleton to attach the camera to; the variable csFirstPersonBoneToFollow lets us set the bone we will follow. In the user interface, the contents of the csFirstPersonBoneNames vector are used to present a combo box with all bone names, and the selected bone will be saved in csFirstPersonBoneToFollow. The last variable, csFirstPersonOffsets, can be used to slightly move the camera position around, preventing the camera from being placed at a strange point inside the head of the instance or suchlike.

As we are doing skeletal animations, we need to access the matrix containing translation, rotation, and scaling of the bone where the camera is virtually attached. We could get the matrix by re-implementing the animation code from the first chapter, or we can extract the bone matrix from the Shader Storage Buffer Object after the compute shader from *Chapter 2* has finished calculating the final matrix data.

For a real-world application, you should use a profiler to check the costs of both versions. In the example application, we will use the compute shader results to avoid making the same animation calculations again.

Note on first-person models

For many first-person-style games, the first-person model will differ from the third-person model of the same character.

Sometimes, the head elements are removed or rotated away. This generates the *feeling* of having a virtual body if the player sees the arms, hands, and legs while having the head removed from interfering with the view. In other games, the body is removed entirely, and only a partial model like the lower arms or the arms up to the shoulder is drawn. The resulting view gives a simple but still *good enough* representation of the virtual body for a player.

We are using the same model for all camera types here, simply because swapping the model on the fly during camera switches will cause a lot of additional overhead. If you are interested in how much effort is needed to use another model in first-person, you are encouraged to add the logic to switch the models in parallel to the camera type.

Another addition to the CameraSettings struct is a weak pointer to the instance we want to follow:

```
std::weak_ptr<AssimpInstance> csInstanceToFollow{};
```

Similar to the undo/redo settings, we use a std::weak_ptr instead of a std::shared_ptr to avoid trouble if the instance we follow gets removed.

Capturing the instance in the user interface can be done by adding a button that stores the currently selected instance in the csInstanceToFollow variable of the camera settings. But be aware to check for the null instance or you will get unwanted results and have the camera centered at the origin.

Retrieving the bone matrix for the first-person view

The first part of the first-person magic is the retrieval of the final TRS of the bone we want to have our camera attached to. In the draw() call of the renderer, right after the second computer shader, we extract the bone matrix from the mShaderBoneMatrixBuffer SSBO:

```
glm::mat4 boneMatrix =
  mShaderBoneMatrixBuffer.getSsboDataMat4(
  selectedInstance * numberOfBones + selectedBone, 1).at(0);
```

We are using an overloaded getSsboDataMat4() method to read a single glm::mat4 at the position of the selected bone of the selected instance. To be able to read more than one matrix from an SSBO, getSsboDataMat4() returns a std::vector of glm::mat4. But since we only need a single matrix, we extract the first matrix of the vector by using .at(0).

The camera offset matrix is calculated with a simple glm::translate() call:

```
glm::mat4 offsetMatrix = glm::translate(glm::mat4(1.0f),
    camSettings.csFirstPersonOffsets);
```

Finally, a slightly monstrous call is used to calculate the position of the bone:

```
cam->setBoneMatrix(
  mWorldPosMatrices.at(selectedInstance) *
  boneMatrix * offsetMatrix *
  glm::inverse(modelType.second.at(0)
    ->getModel()->getBoneList().at(selectedBone)
    ->getOffsetMatrix()));
```

By using the correct matrix multiplication order (depending on the library, GLM uses right to left), the following operations are done:

1. Get the offset matrix of the selected bone from the model and calculate the inverse of the offset matrix. The offset matrix of a bone contains the offset of that bone between the skinning position and the default **T-pose**.

2. Multiply the inverse of the bone offset matrix by the camera position offset matrix, moving the camera slightly away from the bone offset.

3. Multiply the final bone TRS matrix by the previous product of the bone offset and camera matrices, moving the camera to the correct position of that bone relative to the model root.

4. Multiply the world position offset of the selected instance, moving the camera to the selected bone of our selected instance.

After the bone matrix has been calculated, we need to update the camera and re-upload the view and projection matrix to the GPU:

```
cam->updateCamera(mRenderData, deltaTime);
mViewMatrix = cam->getViewMatrix();
std::vector<glm::mat4> matrixData;
matrixData.emplace_back(mViewMatrix);
```

```
matrixData.emplace_back(mProjectionMatrix);
mUniformBuffer.uploadUboData(matrixData, 0);
```

Now, part two of the magic follows: calculating position, azimuth, and elevation.

Computing first-person camera parameters

To get the world position and the azimuth and elevation view angles from the rotation matrix of the bone, some tricks are required:

1. First, we set the camera position from the matrix:

    ```
    mCamSettings.csWorldPosition = mFirstPersonBoneMatrix[3];
    ```

    In a row-major rotation matrix, the translation is stored in the first three columns of the last row. By extracting the entire row and discarding the fourth value, we instantly get the translation of the bone.

2. For the elevation view angle, we rotate a vector pointing upward by doing multiplication with the bone TRS matrix:

    ```
    glm::vec3 elevationVector =
        glm::mat3(mFirstPersonBoneMatrix) * mSideVector;
    ```

    The matrix-vector multiplication rotates the reference vector mSideVector by the angles stored on the bone TRS matrix. In theory, we can use any vector as a reference; we are using a unit vector pointing to the positive Z axis here.

    The resulting vector points to the direction that was applied to the selected bone during animation calculation.

3. Next, we calculate the elevation angle:

    ```
    mCamSettings.csViewElevation =
        glm::degrees(std::atan2(glm::length(
        glm::cross(elevationVector, mWorldUpVector)),
        glm::dot(elevationVector, -mWorldUpVector))) - 90.0f
    ```

    By using the two-element arctangent, we can calculate the angle between two given vectors. We are using the upward-pointing mWorldUpVector here as the second parameter since we are interested in the rotation angle relative to the vertical axis. Arctangent calculation combines the cosine and the sine angle calculation between the two angles. For details about the formula, a link is available in the *Additional resources* section.

After converting the resulting angle from radians to degrees, we subtract 90 degrees to get the angle relative to the horizon (`mWorldUpVector` points upward). This method is numerically more stable for angles close to the reference vectors compared to the arccosine + dot product method that is usually used to calculate the angle between two vectors.

Elevation angle limits

Be aware of an important limitation to the elevation angle: The total range for the elevation angle is only 180 degrees (from -90 degrees to 90 degrees). You cannot look more up than directly upward, or more down than directly downward. Trying to adjust the elevation angle outside the limits results in a rotation of 180 degrees around the X axis – the azimuth angle will be adjusted, and the elevation angle will be still inside the limiting range.

At this point, the camera has the same up/down angle as our selected bone.

We can calculate the Azimuth in a similar way:

1. First, we rotate a vector by doing a multiplication with the bone TRS matrix. We again use the vector `mSideVector`, pointing toward the positive Z axis:

```
glm::vec3 azimuthVector =
  glm::mat3(mFirstPersonBoneMatrix) * mSideVector;
```

2. Then, we compute the angle between the rotated vector and another unit vector:

```
mCamSettings.csViewAzimuth =
  glm::degrees(
    glm::acos(
      glm::dot(
        glm::normalize(
          glm::vec3(
            azimuthVector.x, 0.0f, azimuthVector.z)),
          -mSideVector
      )
    )
  );
```

Two major differences are needed here, compared to the elevation angle:

- The dot product is not calculated from the entire rotated angle but mapped to two dimensions by setting the Y coordinate to zero. The reason for this mapping may not be obvious – when using all three dimensions, the elevation part (up/down) may be smaller than the azimuth part (rotate around the vertical axis) and the dot product calculates the wrong angle. By eliminating the elevation part, we get the correct result.

- We calculate the dot product against a vector pointing in the opposite direction. This sign change is needed to get the correct value of the azimuth angle. Alternatively, we can negate the result of the dot product to get the same effect.

3. As the last step, we check if the x component of the initially computed `azimuthVector` vector is less than zero and adjust the rotation angle accordingly:

```
if (azimuthVector.x < 0.0f) {
  mCamSettings.csViewAzimuth =
    360.0f - mCamSettings.csViewAzimuth;
}
```

Normally, we only get an angle between 0 and 180 degrees as the result of calling the inverse cosine function `std::acos()`. By taking the direction of the resulting rotated vector into account, we can modify the calculations to retrieve the full angle between 0 and 360 degrees.

If we create the view direction from the computed elevation and azimuth values now, the camera looks in exactly the same direction as the selected bone:

```
updateCameraView(renderData, deltaTime);
```

Figure 6.3 shows the first-person view of a model doing the **Pickup** animation:

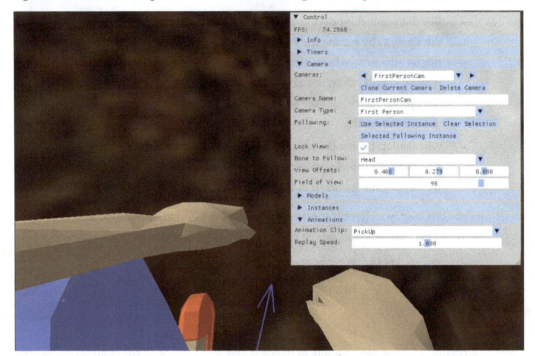

Figure 6.3: First-person view during the "pickup" animation

You can see that the instance squats and tries to get something on the ground, but you see the animation directly with the eyes of the instance, not from the outside. Be aware that the camera might end up somewhere inside the model, resulting in graphical artifacts since we draw only the outside faces of the triangles. For the third-person view, a different approach is needed.

Moving the camera in a third-person view

In a third-person view, we don't need to follow any bone of the model. We just need to follow the model's location. The location can be retrieved via the `InstanceSettings` of the instance. But there is a catch: we must set the position of the camera to a place behind the instance.

First, we have to calculate the azimuth angle by using the rotation of the instance:

```
float rotationAngle = 180.0f -
    instSettings.isWorldRotation.y;
```

The offset of 180 degrees is needed due to the different angle ranges of instances and cameras. While the instance has a range of -180 to 180 degrees, the camera uses a range of 0 to 360 degrees. We also invert the direction of the instance rotation.

Next, we calculate the offset of the camera from the instance by using simple trigonometry:

```
glm::vec3 offset = glm::vec3(
  -glm::sin(glm::radians(rotationAngle)),
  1.0f,
  glm::cos(glm::radians(rotationAngle))
) * mCamSettings.csThirdPersonDistance;
```

Using sine and cosine rotates the camera around the center of an imaginary unit circle. A unit circle has a radius of one, so using 1.0f for the Y axis of the offset leads to the same height distance from the ground as the radius of the imaginary circle. By using a uniform scaling with the csThirdPersonDistance variable, we can control the distance of the camera from the instance. And with the csThirdPersonHeightOffset variable, we can separately adjust the height of the camera.

Next, we add the separate camera height offset and set the world position of the camera to the instance world position plus the offset:

```
offset.y += mCamSettings.csThirdPersonHeightOffset;
mCamSettings.csWorldPosition =
  instSettings.isWorldPosition + offset;
```

Now, the camera is always placed behind the instance, and we can control the view distance and an additional camera height offset.

For the elevation angle of the view, we utilize the dot product again, this time between the vector from the camera to the instance and the upward-pointing mWorldUpVector:

```
glm::vec3 viewDirection =
  instSettings.isWorldPosition -
  mCamSettings.csWorldPosition;

mCamSettings.csViewElevation = (90.0f -
  glm::degrees(
    glm::acos(
      glm::dot(
        glm::normalize(viewDirection), mWorldUpVector
      )
```

```
    )
)) / 2.0f;
```

As a result, we get half the angle in degrees between the `mWorldUpVector` and the view direction. The camera points slightly down to the world position of the instance, but still upward enough to look over the shoulders of the instance.

Figure 6.4 shows the third-person view behind the selected model:

Figure 6.4: Third-person view

In addition to the calculation of camera position and view angles, we should disable the user-based camera movement. Ignoring the request to control the camera gives better feedback to the user than visibly resetting the camera changes in every frame.

Disabling manual camera movement

Ignoring the request to change the camera angle can be achieved by a simple addition. We only need to get the camera settings and surround the block, changing the `mMouseLock` variable in `handleMouseButtonEvents()` with the following condition:

```
if (!(camSettings.csCamType ==
    cameraType::thirdPerson ||
```

```
    (camSettings.csCamType == cameraType::firstPerson &&
    camSettings.csFirstPersonLockView)) &&
    camSettings.csInstanceToFollow.lock()) {
  ...
```

This complex condition can be broken down into the following rules: Only allow locking the mouse and moving the camera manually if:

- The camera type is not first-person or third-person.
- For a first-person camera, the view is unlocked.
- For both camera types, a target instance to follow is set.

This means the camera can be freely moved on a free camera type, as long as no instance has been set as a target in first- and third-person, and the view of a first-person camera is not set to locked.

The condition line may look a bit scary, but creating the same conditions with opposite logic elements to avoid the initial exclamation mark negation creates a Boolean expression of similar complexity. So, we could happily stick with this expression.

Since we haven't implemented the *roll* rotation, a rotation around the axis pointing toward the screen, the two new cameras may behave unexpectedly.

Limits of current first-/third-person cameras

If you rotate the currently locked instance about the X and/or Z axes on a first-person camera, the view will be rotated around wildly, only following the position of the selected bone and not the rotation. This behavior could be fixed by adding the third rotation to the camera and doing a **roll** around the axis pointing into the screen. After adding the sixth degree of freedom, all calculations have to be adjusted to include the new angle.

Also, the third-person camera may be placed incorrectly on models that are rotated in a different angle, or models that may need to have the Z and Y axes swapped.

Although adding the last rotation is possible, the use inside the application is limited to cases like the first-person view, since you can get the same results by reversing the roll rotation and rotating the map instead of the model. For the *wrong* rotated third-person models, additional fixed rotation checkboxes would be needed, or more offset rotations.

You are encouraged to extend the current code base and add instance settings that honor the edge cases mentioned in this section.

After adding cameras directly related to the instance position, let's continue with the stationary cameras.

Adding stationary cameras

A stationary camera can be used in several situations. You made a great-looking composition of character models and props. Or, you want to have a top-down view of the entire game map you loaded and see where every character is placed. Maybe you even want to follow one of the instances wandering around the map. A perfect fit for stationary cameras.

For the pure stationary camera, the configuration is simple. Just add the camera type to the activation of the mMouseLock Boolean in the handleMouseButtonEvents() method of the renderer:

```
... && camSettings.csCamType != cameraType::stationary ...
```

And in updateCamera() of the Camera class, add the following line, right after checking for the zero deltaTime:

```
if (mCamSettings.csCamType == cameraType::stationary) {
   return;
}
```

That's it! As soon as you select a stationary camera, the right-click of the mouse will be ignored, and the camera will also never receive any updates.

If a stationary camera should follow an instance, a bit more code is needed.

Creating a stationary follow camera

The first step for creating a stationary instance-follow camera is the same as for the pure stationary camera – add the camera type to the handleMouseButtonEvents() method of the renderer class:

```
if (!((camSettings.csCamType ==
   cameraType::stationaryFollowing)
```

We must add the camera type to the brackets for first- and third-person type checks since we only want to disable the camera manual movement if an instance to follow has been configured.

For the update of the camera position and view, a mix of the algorithms from first and third person will be created. You will recognize the code samples from the previous sections.

First, we get the instance and calculate the view direction from the camera to the instance position:

```
std::shared_ptr<AssimpInstance> instance =
  mCamSettings.csInstanceToFollow.lock();
glm::vec3 viewDirection = instance->getWorldPosition() -
  mCamSettings.csWorldPosition;
```

Next, we set the elevation angle of the view to the cosine of the angle between the view direction to the instance and the upward-pointing mWorldUpVector:

```
mCamSettings.csViewElevation = 90.0f -
  glm::degrees(
    glm::acos(
      glm::dot(
        glm::normalize(viewDirection), mWorldUpVector
      )
    )
  );
```

Using the dot product between the view direction and the upward-pointing vector has been used in first- and third-person cameras in a very similar way.

Then, we map the same view direction vector to two dimensions and calculate the angle between the *flattened* view direction vector and a vector pointing toward the negative z axis:

```
float rotateAngle =
glm::degrees(
  glm::acos(
    glm::dot(
      glm::normalize(
        glm::vec3(viewDirection.x, 0.0f, viewDirection.z)),
      glm::vec3(0.0f, 0.0f, -1.0f)
    )
  )
);
```

Finally, we extend the azimuth angle to a full 360 degrees:

```
if (viewDirection.x < 0.0f) {
  rotateAngle = 360.0f - rotateAngle;
```

```
    }
  mCamSettings.csViewAzimuth = rotateAngle
```

The 2D-mapped vector, the dot product, and the extension of the azimuth angle to 360 degrees instead of only the 180 degrees of the dot product are exactly the same as for the first-person camera.

When we now use the `stationaryFollowing` type for a camera and select an instance as a target, the camera view will automatically follow the instance wherever we move it. But manual movement of both the camera and the camera view is prohibited.

Handling the new camera types already works well, but there is still room for improvement. So, let's add some more features to the application.

Switching between cameras and configurations

For faster movement between the available cameras in the `micCameras` vector, keyboard shortcuts are handy.

Configuring keyboard shortcuts for camera selection

All we have to do to add keyboard shortcuts is add a small piece of code to the `handleKeyEvents()` method of the renderer:

```
    if (glfwGetKey(mRenderData.rdWindow,
        GLFW_KEY_LEFT_BRACKET) == GLFW_PRESS) {
      if (mModelInstCamData.micSelectedCamera > 0) {
        mModelInstCamData.micSelectedCamera--;
      }
    }
    if (glfwGetKey(mRenderData.rdWindow,
        GLFW_KEY_RIGHT_BRACKET) == GLFW_PRESS) {
      if (mModelInstCamData.micSelectedCamera <
          mModelInstCamData.micCameras.size() - 1) {
        mModelInstCamData.micSelectedCamera++;
      }
    }
```

In the previous code snippet, the square bracket keys are set as hotkeys to select the previous or next camera. An extended version could also be added (i.e., by directly selecting the first nine cameras by pressing the number keys *1* to *9*).

We also don't limit the camera changes to edit mode to allow switching between cameras in the view mode.

Another cool addition is the orthogonal projection. While perspective projection tries to mimic the size reduction of objects farther away from the camera, orthogonal projection will retain the dimension of the objects.

Adding orthogonal projection

You may recognize a game similar to the picture in *Figure 6.5*:

Figure 6.5: A small level in orthogonal projection

This version of the Stalkyard map from Half-Life was created by the user pancakesbassoondonut on Sketchfab. The map is available at `https://skfb.ly/6ACOx` and licensed under the Creative Commons Attribution license CC BY 4.0 (`https://creativecommons.org/licenses/by/4.0/`).

Older games used orthogonal projection only for aesthetic reasons. Without scaling the textures or changing the angle of the faces, very little computational power was required to create stunning-looking games.

To support orthogonal projection, we create a new enum class named `cameraProjection` in the `Enums.h` file:

```
enum class cameraProjection {
  perspective = 0,
  orthogonal
};
```

In the `CameraSettings` struct, we add two new variables named `csCamProjection` and `csOrthoScale`:

```
cameraProjection csCamProjection =
  cameraProjection::perspective;
float csOrthoScale = 20.0f;
```

While `csCamProjection` is used to swap between perspective and orthogonal projection, the `csOrthoScale` variable will define a zoom-level style setting of the orthogonal projection, similar to the field of view setting for perspective projection.

The current code to create the projection matrix in `mProjectionMatrix` will be moved into a check for the new projection setting:

```
if (camSettings.csCamProjection ==
  cameraProjection::perspective) {
...
} else {
```

And, if the orthogonal projection has been selected, we will use `glm::ortho()` instead of `glm::perspective()` to create the projection matrix. First, we read `csOrthoScale` and use the value to scale the aspect ratio and the left and right plus near and far plane distances:

```
float orthoScaling = camSettings.csOrthoScale;
float aspect = static_cast<float>(mRenderData.rdWidth)/
  static_cast<float>(mRenderData.rdHeight) *
  orthoScaling;
float leftRight = 1.0f * orthoScaling;
float nearFar = 75.0f * orthoScaling;
```

The call to `glm::ortho()` creates the orthogonal projection matrix, moving the origin of the virtual world to the origin of the screen:

```
mProjectionMatrix = glm::ortho(-aspect, aspect,
    -leftRight, leftRight, -nearFar, nearFar);
```

By using the center of the virtual world as the center for the projection matrix, we get a nicely scaled result on the screen. Due to the camera position in the view matrix, we are even able to move the camera in the orthogonally drawn virtual world.

The only restriction here is the movement *into* the screen: While moving the camera left and right or up and down adjusts the view as expected, a forward and backward movement will show no changes in the first place. This missing reaction to a camera movement in the direction of the z axis is caused by the basic principle of the orthogonal projection. We don't have a view frustum like in the perspective projection: the projection matrix creates a huge rectangular box instead, and every triangle inside that box is drawn.

Reaching a point with the camera where some triangles are behind the far z plane of the rectangular box requires us to move the camera far away from the origin of the virtual world. You can try to reach such a point by yourself, but it will take a lot of time, even with the faster camera movement.

Despite the cool-looking effect of an orthogonal projection, be aware that depth perception can be tricky in such a case. Our brain has learned that the size of an object will decrease if the distance to it grows, and objects with the same apparent sizes but different distances do not have the same sizes in real life. With all instances on the screen being the same size, you may be completely off when guessing which instances are closer to the camera.

User interface controls for the projection settings

To control which projection will be used, two radio buttons are added to the `UserInterface` class. The first radio button is used to activate the perspective projection:

```
ImGui::Text("Projection:        ");
ImGui::SameLine();
if (ImGui::RadioButton("Perspective",
    settings.csCamProjection ==
    cameraProjection::perspective)) {
  settings.csCamProjection =
    cameraProjection::perspective;
}
```

The second radio button activates the orthogonal projection:

```
ImGui::SameLine();
if (ImGui::RadioButton("Orthogonal",
    settings.csCamProjection ==
    cameraProjection::orthogonal)) {
  settings.csCamProjection =
    cameraProjection::orthogonal;
}
```

Right below the field of view slider, a slider for the orthogonal scaling will be created:

```
ImGui::Text("Ortho Scaling:    ");
ImGui::SameLine();
ImGui::SliderFloat("##CamOrthoScale",
    &settings.csOrthoScale, 1.0f, 50.0f, "%.3f", flags);
```

The checkboxes and sliders are also surrounded by checks for camera types or conflicting settings. Disabling or even hiding controls that could confuse a user is better than trying to explain why changing settings does not give the expected result.

By having multiple cameras and an extended camera handling available, exploring the virtual world and the model instances got a level-up. We can now place cameras in different areas of the world, and by using a first- or third-person camera, instances and instance animations can be viewed like in a real game.

A note on cameras and large models

When working with large models or models with a high scaling factor, clipping issues may occur for different camera types because some parts of the model are outside of the near and far clipping planes for the scene depth. Model parts too close to the camera position appear to have holes in them and model parts too far away may just vanish from the screen. In these cases, you need to adjust the scaling of the model or the configuration of the near and far plane for the projection matrices in the renderer.

Summary

In this chapter, new camera functionality was implemented. First, we extended the current camera handling to support more than one camera object. Next, several camera types were defined and implemented, like first-person and third-person cameras. Finally, handy additions for handling cameras were made. Switching between the list of defined cameras by using keyboard shortcuts helps to simplify access, and the orthogonal projection creates interesting results for viewing the instances.

In the next chapter, we will add more life to our virtual world by enhancing the instance animations. By adding animations to different internal states of an instance, like walking, running, or jumping, we will be able to move the instance within the virtual world. And by blending animations between these states, the transition between the different states will be made smooth.

Practical sessions

There are some additions you could make to the code:

- Extend the YAML loader to migrate the configuration file.

  As mentioned in the section *Bumping the configuration file version*, add the functionality to load both the old and new versions of the configuration file. Saving the file could be done in the newest version.

- Add oscillation to the stationary camera.

  Like in real life, a security camera could have the additional ability to automatically move left and right, or up and down. Possible controls are the extent and speed of the movement.

- Add a rotation around the vertical axis of the third-person camera.

  Instead of just being able to view the instances from behind, add another property containing the rotation around the vertical axis. By rotating the camera 90 degrees, you would be able to create a three-dimensional side-scroller, and by rotating the camera 180 degrees, the instance would face you while walking or running.

- Add the roll rotation to the camera.

  Currently, the camera supports only elevation (look up and down) and azimuth (rotation around the vertical axis). Implement the third rotational axis to allow the camera to be moved to any arbitrary angle.

- Extend the third-person camera to be more action-like.

  You could try to add more features to the third-person camera. What about a camera mounted on a spring, only loosely following the motion of the instance? Or effects like zooming a bit more out on moving forward, following with a small delay on rotations, or even tilting a bit when walking sideways? Or you could add a small shake on collisions, like the instance running into an obstacle. Also, presets for those different types would be handy.

- Change camera implementation to quaternions.

  Adding the third dimension in the previous task will most probably lead to rotations resulting in a gimbal lock, thus losing one degree of freedom again because one axis is rotated or close to another axis. Changing the entire camera rotation to use quaternions instead of Euler angles should solve gimbal lock situations.

- Add spline-based camera and target paths.

  To create fly-by scenes, you could add splines for the camera position to follow along, including configurable speed and ping-pong movement. By adding splines as targets, you could create camera shots of the virtual worlds.

- Show the cameras as separate objects in edit mode.

  Similar to the arrows for the model manipulation, you could add a view frustum and a small box to depict the position and orientation of the cameras in the virtual world. Different camera types could be shown by different line colors.

- Make the camera symbols selectable with the mouse.

  After you finish the previous task, you could also add the camera symbols to the selection texture. Just reserve a range of values exclusively for the cameras, draw the boxes and/ or frustum lines to the selection texture, and switch between instances and cameras, depending on the value you get back from the graphics card buffer.

- Expert difficulty: Add a **picture-in-picture** window.

  Most game engines have the ability to show a minimized version of another camera in a small window of the application screen. Creating a separate camera display requires some low-level additions to the renderer class since the entire scene has to be drawn twice by using the view and projection matrices of both cameras.

ImGui has the ability to draw a texture to the screen – you could render the second camera view to a texture and show the image in an ImGui window. Adding additional information like the camera name and type to the window title would enhance the picture-in-picture mode even more.

To avoid confusion when two different camera types are active, limiting the type-based restrictions to be only active in edit mode may be a good idea.

Additional resources

- 3D Math Primer for Graphics and Game Development: `https://gamemath.com/book/`
- How to calculate the angle between two vectors in 3D: `https://www.quora.com/How-do-I-calculate-the-angle-between-two-vectors-in-3D-space-using-atan2`

Join our community on Discord

Join our community's Discord space for discussions with the author and other readers:

`https://packt.link/cppgameanimation`

Part 3

Tuning Character Animations

In this part, you will dive into the depths of character animations. You will start by computing lookup tables for animation frames and storing the results in GPU memory, enabling you to access any animation frame without uploading it to the GPU first. You will also learn how to blend between the animation clips to create better transitions. Then, you will be introduced to collision detection between instances and add collision detection and reaction to a collision based on axis-aligned bounding boxes and spheres. You will also explore the idea of a graphical, node-based extension to the model editor, allowing you to control the behavior of the instances by adding and connecting predefined execution blocks. Finally, you will learn how facial animation and additive blending work, and implement the two new animation types into the animation editor.

This part has the following chapters:

- *Chapter 7, Enhancing Animation Controls*
- *Chapter 8, An Introduction to Collision Detection*
- *Chapter 9, Adding Behavior and Interaction*
- *Chapter 10, Advanced Animation Blending*

7

Enhancing Animation Controls

Welcome to *Chapter 7*! In the previous chapter, we added some camera functions. We started by implementing support for multiple camera objects and added new camera types. We also set keyboard shortcuts to allow the simple selection of the existing cameras. As the last step, we added an orthogonal camera configuration, which enabled us to create entirely different views of the model instances and the virtual worlds.

In this chapter, we will update animation blending and controls to a new level. First, we will implement blending between two animations in the existing transformation compute shader. Also, we will move the calculation of translation, scaling, and rotation for each node to lookup tables onto the GPU. Next, we will add new instance states to the code, storing the kind of actions the instance could do, like walking, running, and jumping, plus the direction of movement. Then, we will create UI controls, allowing us to map the existing animation clips to instance actions. Finally, we will add the logic for the mapping between animations and actions.

In this chapter, we will cover the following topics:

- Blending between animations with style
- Adding new states to the code
- Linking states and animations
- Saving and loading the states

Technical requirements

The example code in the chapter07 folder, in the 01_opengl_animations folder for OpenGL and the 02_vulkan_animations folder for Vulkan.

Blending between animations with style

If you solved the second and third tasks in the *Practical sessions* section in *Chapter 2* and moved more parts of the animation blending to the GPU, parts of this section may be familiar to you. But do not worry if you skipped the tasks, as the process of moving the transformation data to lookup tables and doing the interpolation calculations on the GPU is straightforward.

Let's start with the lookup table data.

The power of lookup tables

Currently, the data for the animation keyframes and the corresponding node transformations is extracted during model loading, and all the data is stored in arrays inside `AssimpAnimChannel` objects.

For every node in every frame, six lookups are needed to extract the translation, scaling, and rotation for the previous and current keyframe time. Then, the values are interpolated pairwise to calculate the final transformation for the specified node.

However, doing the same calculations repeatedly is time-consuming. A better solution is to generate all the interpolated transforms when the model is loaded, and only do a lookup of the final transform value when playing the animation.

The trade-off here is clear: GPU memory versus CPU computing power. Setting the size of the lookup tables too small will cause visible artifacts, while setting the size of the lookup table data too large will waste precious GPU memory without having any visual benefits. You can experiment with the lookup table size, but ~1,000 elements for the transform values should be a good balance between visuals and memory size.

An alternative lookup solution

A more memory-friendly version of the lookup table can be achieved by creating a table for the keyframe times and using the extracted data as the index into the original transformation data. You may use this variation if you have a lot of nodes and animation clips to save GPU memory. Or you could use these sparser lookups if there are only a few keyframes per animation. On the downside of this version, you need to calculate the pair-wise interpolations between the values per keyframe again, adding more computing load to the GPU.

In addition to the new transform data storage, we will scale all animation clips to have the same time length. Without the need to scale the length of two animation clips, blending between two clips becomes much simpler.

Creating the lookup tables

As preparation for the lookup tables, we must find the maximum length of all animation clips. Before adding the animation clips to the loadModel() method of the AssimpModel class, we iterate over all animations and store the maximum length in a new private member variable called mMaxClipDuration:

```
unsigned int numAnims = scene->mNumAnimations;
for (unsigned int i = 0; i < numAnims; ++i) {
  const auto& animation = scene->Animations[i];
  mMaxClipDuration =
    std::max(mMaxClipDuration,
    static_cast<float>(animation->mDuration));
}
```

Then, the maximum value is used as an additional parameter to the addChannels() call:

```
for (unsigned int i = 0; i < numAnims; ++i) {
  ...
  animClip->addChannels(animation, mMaxClipDuration,
    mBoneList);
  ...
}
```

Finally, inside the addChannels() method, we hand over the maximum duration to every channel we are extracting:

```
for (unsigned int i = 0; i < animation->mNumChannels; ++i) {
  ...
  channel->loadChannelData(animation->Channels[i],
    maxClipDuration);
  ...
}
```

Creating the lookup table data itself will be shown in the following code snippets by using the code to create the translation data as an example. For scaling and rotation, the same principle applies.

The first step for every lookup table is the extraction of the minimum and the maximum keyframe times:

```
mMinTranslateTime =
   static_cast<float>(nodeAnim->mPositionKeys[0].mTime);
mMaxTranslateTime =
  static_cast<float>(
  nodeAnim->mPositionKeys[mNumTranslations - 1].mTime);
```

Then, we calculate three scaling factors:

```
float translateScaleFactor = maxClipDuration /
   mMaxTranslateTime;
mTranslateTimeScaleFactor = maxClipDuration /
   static_cast<float>(LOOKUP_TABLE_WIDTH);
mInvTranslateTimeScaleFactor = 1.0f /
   mTranslateTimeScaleFactor;
```

These include:

- The first variable, translateScaleFactor, stores the ratio between the maximum clip duration and the maximum keyframe time. We need the first scaling factor when we advance the time in the lookup table data creation.

- In mTranslateTimeScaleFactor, we calculate the ratio between the maximum clip duration and the size of our lookup table. The second scaling factor is simply the keyframe time step width of the lookup table entries.

- As the last scaling factor, mInvTranslateTimeScaleFactor stores the inverse of the mTranslateTimeScaleFactor value. We will use the third scaling factor in the compute shader to calculate the right index position in the lookup table from the keyframe time.

Next, we set a helper variable named timeIndex to 0 and iterate over our lookup table entries:

```
int timeIndex = 0;
for (int i = 0; i < LOOKUP_TABLE_WIDTH; ++i) {
```

For every lookup table entry, we extract the translation data from the mPositionKeys array of the aNodeAnim object for the current and next keyframe times into a glm::vec4:

```
glm::vec4 currentTranslate = glm::vec4(
    nodeAnim->mPositionKeys[timeIndex].mValue.x,
    nodeAnim->mPositionKeys[timeIndex].mValue.y,
```

```
            nodeAnim->mPositionKeys[timeIndex].mValue.z, 1.0f);
        glm::vec4 nextTranslate = glm::vec4(
          nodeAnim->mPositionKeys[timeIndex + 1].mValue.x,
          nodeAnim->mPositionKeys[timeIndex + 1].mValue.y,
          nodeAnim->mPositionKeys[timeIndex + 1].mValue.z,
          1.0f);
```

Even though we only need the first three values for the translation, a four-element vector is used for proper data alignment in the Shader Storage Buffer Object.

Now, we extract the time values for the current and next keyframes, plus the current time of the animation:

```
        float currentKey = static_cast<float>(
          nodeAnim->mPositionKeys[timeIndex].mTime);
        float nextKey = static_cast<float>(
          nodeAnim->mPositionKeys[timeIndex + 1].mTime);
        float currentTime = i * mTranslateTimeScaleFactor /
          translateScaleFactor;
```

For the current time, two scaling factors are used.

By using the two translation vectors and the time values, we can create an interpolated glm::vec4 of the two translations at the time stamp of the lookup table entry:

```
        mTranslations.emplace_back(glm::mix(
          currentTranslate,
          nextTranslate,
          (currentTime - currentKey) / (nextKey - currentKey)));
```

Finally, we check whether the current time of the lookup table entry is longer than the time of the next keyframe. If it is, we increment our time index:

```
        if (currentTime > nextKey) {
          if (timeIndex < mNumTranslations - 1) {
            ++timeIndex;
          }
        }
      }
```

The mTranslations vector now contains interpolated translation values for every time point of the animation clip in a step width defined by mTranslateTimeScaleFactor, and by using the inverse value, mInvTranslateTimeScaleFactor, we can access the corresponding lookup table entry if we know the replay time of the clip.

Uploading the data tables to the GPU

Once all animation clips have been converted to lookup tables, we can upload the array data to an SSBO. The buffer preparation part is longer as we must ensure all nodes are initialized properly, even the non-animated nodes. We will only explore the translation steps here since the logic for scaling and rotation is mostly identical. The biggest difference is the already known utilization of a four-element vector to transport the quaternion data of the rotations to the compute shader.

As the first step, we create a std::vector of glm::vec4 to hold the data for all node transformations:

```
std::vector<glm::vec4> animLookupData{};
```

Then, we define the size of the lookup table data:

```
const int LOOKUP_SIZE = 1023 + 1;
```

The addition of 1023 and 1 instead of the number 1024 is a hint of what happens next:

```
std::vector<glm::vec4> emptyTranslateVector(
    LOOKUP_SIZE, glm::vec4(0.0f));
emptyTranslateVector.at(0) = glm::vec4(0.0f);
```

We create an empty vector of LOOKUP_SIZE length and initialize the vector with a zeroed four-element vector. Using zeroes for the translation makes sure non-animated nodes will have no translational transformations.

At the first position of the vector, we do another explicit setting to zero for documentation purposes because we will use the x component of the first position in every lookup table to store the mTranslateTimeScaleFactor. It may look a bit redundant to store the inverse scale factor in every vector, but because we integrated the value directly into the lookup data, the compute shader will find all the data in one place.

After creating appropriate empty vectors for scaling and rotation, we create a triplet of translation, rotation, and scaling for every bone in the bone list:

```
for (int i = 0; i < mBoneList.size() *
    mAnimClips.at(0)->getNumChannels(); ++i) {
```

```
        animLookupData.insert(animLookupData.end(),
          emptyTranslateVector.begin(),
          emptyTranslateVector.end());
      animLookupData.insert(animLookupData.end(),
          emptyRotateVector.begin(),
          emptyRotateVector.end());
      animLookupData.insert(animLookupData.end(),
          emptyScaleVector.begin(),
          emptyScaleVector.end());
    }
```

By using the full number of bones in the array we may waste a couple of kilobytes, but we don't need to add extra logic inside the compute shader to choose between animated and non-animated logic.

Now we loop over all animation clips, and for every clip, over all channels. Since we have already initialized all the data with default values, we only need to upload the data for the animated bones:

```
    int boneId = channel->getBoneId();
    if (boneId >= 0) {
```

The offset value is calculated by using the bone list size and LOOKUP_SIZE to find the position of the translation data for the channel's bone in the current animation clip:

```
      int offset = clipId * mBoneList.size() *
        LOOKUP_SIZE * 3 + boneId * LOOKUP_SIZE * 3;
```

Next, we set the mTranslateTimeScaleFactor value of the channel at the x component of the first position, get the translation data for the channel, and copy the data into the lookup data vector:

```
      animLookupData.at(offset) =
        glm::vec4(channel->getInvTranslationScaling(),
        0.0f, 0.0f, 0.0f);
      const std::vector<glm::vec4>& translations =
        channel->getTranslationData();
      std::copy(translations.begin(),
        translations.end(),
        animLookupData.begin() + offset + 1);
```

Then, the offset value is advanced to the next lookup data position before storing the next transformation data:

```
offset += LOOKUP_SIZE;
```

After all the translation, scaling, and rotation data is stored in the animLookupData vector, we can upload the data to the SSBO:

```
mAnimLookupBuffer.uploadSsboData(animLookupData);
```

Now, the animation lookup data for the loaded model is available on the GPU. When we need to access the transformation data in the compute shader, we can simply bind the SSBO.

Adjusting the renderer code and the compute shader

To be able to tell the compute shader which animation to play and/or blend, we define a new struct called PerInstanceAnimData in the OGLRenderData.h file in the opengl folder for OpenGL:

```
struct PerInstanceAnimData {
  uint32_t firstAnimClipNum;
  uint32_t secondAnimClipNum;
  float firstClipReplayTimestamp;
  float secondClipReplayTimestamp;
  float blendFactor;
};
```

For Vulkan, the file is named VkRenderData.h and resides in the vulkan folder.

Here, we simply store the first clip number plus the timestamp of the current frame we want to render from the first clip. Also, a possible second animation clip, the time stamp for the second clip, and the blending factor between the two clips can be sent to the compute shader.

In the renderer, we define two new private data members:

```
std::vector<PerInstanceAnimData> mPerInstanceAnimData{};
ShaderStorageBuffer mPerInstanceAnimDataBuffer{};
```

The mPerInstanceAnimData variable stores the clip numbers, time stamp, and blending factor for every instance, and mPerInstanceAnimDataBuffer is the CPU-side handle for the animation data SSBO.

Then, in the instance loop in the draw() call of the renderer, we update the per-instance animation data with the values of the instances:

```
PerInstanceAnimData animData{};
animData.firstAnimClipNum =
  instSettings.isFirstAnimClipNr;
animData.secondAnimClipNum =
  instSettings.isSecondAnimClipNr;
animData.firstClipReplayTimestamp =
  instSettings.isFirstClipAnimPlayTimePos;
animData.secondClipReplayTimestamp =
  instSettings.isSecondClipAnimPlayTimePos;
animData.blendFactor =
  instSettings.isAnimBlendFactor;
mPerInstanceAnimData.at(i) = animData;
```

When preparing the first compute shader, we bind the animation lookup data and upload the instance animation data:

```
mAssimpTransformComputeShader.use();
mUploadToUBOTimer.start();
modelType.second.at(0->getModel()
  ->bindAnimLookupBuffer(0);
mPerInstanceAnimDataBuffer.uploadSsboData(
  mPerInstanceAnimData, 1);
mShaderTRSMatrixBuffer.bind(2);
```

Now, all the data we need for the compute shader is ready to be computed.

In the assimp_instance_transform.comp compute shader, in the shader folder, we also need to define the PerInstanceAnimData struct to be able to access the SSBO:

```
struct PerInstanceAnimData {
  uint firstAnimClipNum;
  uint secondAnimClipNum;
  float firstClipReplayTimestamp;
  float secondClipReplayTimestamp;
  float blendFactor;
};
```

And we declare the two buffer bindings using the same binding points as in the renderer code:

```
layout (std430, binding = 0) readonly restrict
    buffer AnimLookup {
  vec4 lookupData[];
};
layout (std430, binding = 1) readonly restrict
    buffer InstanceAnimData {
  PerInstanceAnimData instAnimData[];
};
```

In the `main()` method of the compute shader, we define the same lookup table size and offset calculation as in the `AssimpModel` class:

```
int lookupWidth = 1023 + 1;
uint node = gl_GlobalInvocationID.x;
uint instance = gl_GlobalInvocationID.y;
uint numberOfBones = gl_NumWorkGroups.x;
uint boneOffset = lookupWidth * 3;
uint clipOffset = numberOfBones * boneOffset;
```

We can now access all the animation settings for each instance by using the `instance` variable as the index in the `InstanceAnimData` SSBO:

```
uint firstClip = instAnimData[instance].firstAnimClipNum;
uint secondClip =
  instAnimData[instance].secondAnimClipNum;
float blendFactor = instAnimData[instance].blendFactor;
```

For instance, to get the `mTranslateTimeScaleFactor` value for the translation data, we must use the same formula as in C++ to access the first element of the translation lookup data for the clip:

```
float firstTransInvScaleFactor = lookupData[firstClip *
  clipOffset + node * boneOffset].x;
```

Even slight differences between C++ and shader formulae or data types could lead to discrepancies in the transferred data, so we need to be strict here to do exactly the same operations and use the same data types.

Then, we use the inverse time scale factor to calculate the correctly scaled index in the translation lookup data:

```
int firstTransLookupIndex =
  int(instAnimData[instance].firstClipReplayTimestamp *
  transInvScaleFactor) + 1;
```

The per-node translation data for the first and second animation clip can also be calculated as in C++:

```
vec4 firstTranslation = lookupData[firstClip *
  clipOffset + node * boneOffset +
  firstTransLookupIndex];
...
vec4 secondTanslation = lookupData[secondClip *
  clipOffset + node * boneOffset +
  secondTransLookupIndex];
```

Now we can interpolate between the two animation clip translations:

```
vec4 finalTranslation = mix(firstTanslation,
  secondTanslation, blendFactor);
```

We do the same lookup and interpolation for the scaling values. For rotation, the same code as the GLM implementation for SLERP is used.

Finally, the product of all three transformation matrices is stored in the SSBO containing the resulting TRS matrices of all instances:

```
uint index = node + numberOfBones * instance;
trsMat[index] =
  createTranslationMatrix(finalTranslation) *
  createRotationMatrix(finalRotation) *
  createScaleMatrix(finalScale);
```

At this point, the mShaderTRSMatrixBuffer SSBO in the renderer contains the same data as we had with the CPU-based transformation calculations.

But all we need to upload to the compute shader is the data of the animations we want to draw. So, the transformation calculation in the updateAnimation() method of the AssimpInstance class can be removed, leaving the following three lines to be executed when we update the animation of the instance:

```
mInstanceSettings.isFirstClipAnimPlayTimePos +=
  deltaTime *
  mInstanceSettings.isAnimSpeedFactor * 1000.0f;
mInstanceSettings.isAnimPlayTimePos =
  std::fmod(mInstanceSettings.isFirstClipAnimPlayTimePos,
  mAssimpMode->getMaxClipDuration());
mModelRootMatrix = mLocalTransformMatrix *
  mAssimpModel->getRootTranformationMatrix();
```

We simply advance the clip time by the delta time and update the instance root matrix.

If you compile and run the code now, the only visible difference is a much lower matrix generation time when the number of instances goes up. For a recent computer model, reaching 10,000 or even 20,000 animated instances of the basic model should be no problem. We don't need so many instances in the virtual world, but the lower CPU usage for animations and animation blending gives us more freedom to implement more features in the remaining chapters of the book.

Now that we have a fast and easy-to-use animation calculation, we can implement a state-based system to organize the behavior of each instance. By defining different states, like a movement direction or an action the instance will do, we create the first steps on the path to an animation system where we can control the instance as we would do in a simple game.

So, let's continue by adding new instance states.

Adding new states to the code

Our future game character should be able to perform typical actions for a character in a game: wait idle for player input, walk in all four main directions, run forward, plus a bunch of other actions. Depending on the available animations, we could add a state for jumping or rolling, punching, or waving.

For maximum flexibility, we will allow characters of all models to perform all the configured actions. Then we can use the UI to map an animation clip to each action we want to use for a specific model. Without a mapped animation clip, the requested action will be simply ignored.

Using bit fields and plain enums

We will add two different enum class definitions to the Enums.h file. The first enum called
moveDirection is a bit field:

```
enum class moveDirection : uint8_t {
  none = 0x00,
  forward = 0x01,
  back = 0x02,
  right = 0x04,
  left = 0x08,
  any = 0xff
};
```

For every direction, a different bit can be set in a variable. A bit field is needed when multiple
values can appear at the same time. In our case, it would be normal to have the character running
forward and to the left at the same time.

The two additional enum values, none and any, are special placeholders. If the character is just
idling, forcing a direction for the idle state would be strange since the character cannot "idle
forward" or "idle to the left." So, the separate enum value none for not moving at all will help us to
keep the code a bit simpler. The value any can be used as a wildcard or fallback for walking states.
For example, we could set a generic walk animation for all directions, and instead of configuring
all four directions with identical animation clips, we use the any direction to use this one clip for
all walk movements.

To be able to work with the values of the moveDirection enum in a real bit field manner, we have
to define the bitwise Boolean operators OR and AND for the new data type. The declaration is short
and simple, as the following code for the logical AND operator between two movement directions
shows:

```
inline moveDirection operator | (moveDirection lhs,
    moveDirection rhs) {
  using T = std::underlying_type_t <moveDirection>;
  return static_cast<moveDirection>(static_cast<T>(lhs) |
    static_cast<T>(rhs));
}
```

A second enum class named moveState takes care of the possible character actions:

```
enum class moveState  {
  idle = 0,
  walk,
  run,
  hop,
  jump,
  ...
  wave,
  NUM
};
```

Here, no bit field is needed. We may be able to run and jump at the same time and will handle these cases in the code. But most of the actions cannot be executed at the same time.

We simply list all possible movement states in the moveState enum class. The final value, NUM, can be utilized to iterate over all the enum values in a for loop, i.e., starting from the first action with the value zero (idle) and ending at the last valid action wave.

Having not just numbers for movement directions and state will become handy in the UI and for debug messages, so we add two new maps from the enum class values to strings in the ModelInstanceCamData struct in the ModelInstanceCamData.h file:

```
std::unordered_map<moveDirection, std::string>
  micMoveDirectionMap{};
std::unordered_map<moveState, std::string>
  micMoveStateMap{};
```

We will fill the two state maps in the init() method of the renderer with appropriate string values. Next, we must extend the settings structs for instances and models.

Extending model and instance settings

The special handling of the idle, walk, and run animation clips requires a new struct called IdleWalkRunBlending in a new ModelSettings.h file in the model folder:

```
struct IdleWalkRunBlending {
  int iwrbIdleClipNr = 0;
  float iwrbIdleClipSpeed = 1.0f;
  int iwrbWalkClipNr = 0;
```

```
   float iwrbWalkClipSpeed = 1.0f;
   int iwrbRunClipNr = 0;
   float iwrbRunClipSpeed = 1.0f;
};
```

Here, we simply store the clip numbers and replay speeds for the three movements.

The new `IdleWalkRunBlending` struct will be added to another new `struct` called `ModelSettings`, along with the model's name and file name:

```
struct ModelSettings {
  std::string msModelFilenamePath;
  std::string msModelFilename;
  std::map<moveDirection, IdleWalkRunBlending>
    msIWRBlendings;
};
```

The `AssimpModel` class needs a new `private` data member of type `ModelSettings`:

```
    ModelSettings mModelSettings;
```

Both the model's file name and name will be relocated from the `AssimpModel` class to the new `ModelSettings` struct to have all the "variable" parts of a model accessible with simple getter and setter calls, similar to the instances.

Before we can use the new states and animation features in an instance, we must add variables of the two new enum `class` types to the `InstanceSettings` struct in the `InstanceSettings.h` file in the `model` folder:

```
    moveDirection isMoveDirection = moveDirection::none;
    moveState isMoveState = moveState::idle;
```

In addition, we must adjust the instance settings for the animation clips. Since we can have two different animations plus animation blending, we need two clip variables instead of only one, and the blending factor as a per-instance setting:

```
    unsigned int isFirstAnimClipNr = 0;
    unsigned int isSecondAnimClipNr = 0;
    float isAnimBlendFactor = 0.0f;
```

We also store the values for the speed and acceleration of the instance:

```
glm::vec3 isAccel = glm::vec3(0.0f);
glm::vec3 isSpeed = glm::vec3(0.0f);
```

The speed of the specific instance will be used to select the correct idle, walk, or run animation clip. By using an acceleration-based movement, we achieve a more natural appearance of the character instances. In real life, we also accelerate and decelerate while moving, instead of jumping directly from idle to run speed.

Adding the idle/walk/run logic

The blending logic for idle/walk/run animation clips is defined in the method called playIdleWalkRunAnimation() in the AssimpInstance class.

After a sanity check for the model of the instance, we calculate the absolute speed of the instance, read the model settings containing a map with the blending settings, and create a new, empty variable blend of type IdleWalkRunBlending:

```
float instanceSpeed =
    glm::length(mInstanceSettings.isSpeed);
ModelSettings modSettings =
    mAssimpMode->getModelSettings();
IdleWalkRunBlending blend;
```

Next, we check whether we have configured direction-specific animation clips:

```
if (modSettings.msIWRBlendings.count(
    mInstanceSettings.isMoveDirection) > 0 ) {
  blend = modSettings.msIWRBlendings[
    mInstanceSettings.isMoveDirection];
} else if (modSettings.msIWRBlendings.count(
    moveDirection::any) > 0) {
  blend = modSettings.msIWRBlendings[moveDirection::any];
} else if (modSettings.msIWRBlendings.count(
    moveDirection::none) > 0) {
  blend = modSettings.msIWRBlendings[moveDirection::none];
} else {
  return;
}
```

If such a direction clip is found, the blend variable is filled with the appropriate settings. If no direction-specific clip was found, we check for the special any and none directions too, trying to use a generic animation for all directions. And if we don't find the generic animation clips, we return from the method. Without a configured clip for idle/walk/run, it makes no sense to play any animation.

Controlling whether to blend between idle and walk or between walk and run animations is done by using the instanceSpeed variable:

```
if (instanceSpeed <= 1.0f) {
  mInstanceSettings.isFirstAnimClipNr =
    blend.iwrbIdleClipNr;
  mInstanceSettings.isSecondAnimClipNr =
    blend.iwrbWalkClipNr;
  mInstanceSettings.isAnimSpeedFactor = glm::mix(
    blend.iwrbIdleClipSpeed,
    blend.iwrbWalkClipSpeed, instanceSpeed);
  mInstanceSettings.isAnimBlendFactor = instanceSpeed;
} else {
```

Here, we scale speed factors and blend between the idle and walk animations based on the instanceSpeed value. By using a value of 0.0f for idle and 1.0f (inclusive) for full walk speed, the animation will be blended smoothly between the instance standing still and walking around.

To blend the instance animations from walking to running, we use an instanceSpeed range between 1.0f (exclusive) and 2.0f. The logic stays the same; we must only subtract 1.0f from the speed factor and the blending for the linear interpolation between the walk and run clips:

```
  mInstanceSettings.isFirstAnimClipNr =
    blend.iwrbWalkClipNr;
  mInstanceSettings.isSecondAnimClipNr =
    blend.iwrbRunClipNr;
  mInstanceSettings.isAnimSpeedFactor = glm::mix(
    blend.iwrbWalkClipSpeed,
    blend.iwrbRunClipSpeed, instanceSpeed - 1.0f);
  mInstanceSettings.isAnimBlendFactor =
    instanceSpeed - 1.0f;
}
```

The `instanceSpeed` values of `1.0f` for walk speed and `2.0f` for run speed were chosen because they work best for linear interpolation between the clips. Any other ranges are possible; you just must adjust the scaling for the animation blending accordingly.

Using acceleration and deceleration

As our instances should move in the virtual world, we need to control the speed of the instance we control. But instead of using the speed directly, we will go for an acceleration-based speed model. Using a separate acceleration value to speed up or slow down the instance gives more natural results. Like real physical bodies, our model instances in the virtual world have their inertia working against speed changes.

First, the `AssimpInstance` class needs three new `private float` variables named `MAX_ACCEL`, `MAX_ABS_SPEED`, and `MIN_STOP_SPEED`:

```
const float MAX_ACCEL = 4.0f;
const float MAX_ABS_SPEED = 1.0f;
const float MIN_STOP_SPEED = 0.01f;
```

In `MAX_ACCEL`, we store the maximum acceleration our model can achieve, and `MAX_ABS_SPEED` limits the speed of the instance. Acceleration and speed are three-component vectors, and moving in different directions may add up to larger values. Limiting both values helps to prevent instances from moving too fast in the virtual world.

An acceleration-based model has a major drawback: stopping an instance can become difficult. Since we only add and subtract the acceleration values from the speed, reaching the exact value of zero is hard. To achieve a full stop, we define a minimal speed in the `MIN_STOP_SPEED` variable. If the current speed of the instance is lower than the value of `MIN_STOP_SPEED`, we set acceleration and speed to zero, eventually stopping the instance.

Instance acceleration is controlled in the `updateInstanceState()` method of `AssimpInstance` class. Basically, we check for a movement direction and set the corresponding x or z components of `isAccel`:

```
if (state == moveState::walk || state == moveState::run) {
  if ((dir & moveDirection::forward) ==
      moveDirection::forward) {
    mInstanceSettings.isMoveKeyPressed = true;
    mInstanceSettings.isAccel.x = 5.0f;
```

```
    }
    ...
```

If a direction key is pressed, we set isMoveKeyPressed to true and apply the acceleration.

When we release all movement keys, the deceleration of the instance kicks in. The slowdown logic happens in the updateInstanceSpeed() method of the AssimpInstance class:

```
float currentSpeed =
  glm::length(mInstanceSettings.isSpeed);
static float maxSpeed = MAX_ABS_SPEED;
```

We also save the maximum speed of the instance locally. Using a static variable helps to keep track of accelerating and slowing down the instance between walk and run speed.

First, we calculate the length of the 3-component isSpeed vector. The resulting length is then used to check whether we are still moving when no movement key is being pressed:

```
if (!mInstanceSettings.isMoveKeyPressed) {
  if (currentSpeed > 0.0f) {
    if (mInstanceSettings.isSpeed.x > 0.0f) {
      mInstanceSettings.isAccel.x = -2.5f;
    }
    ...
```

For the possible move directions of the instance, we check whether any speed is left and use an acceleration in the opposite direction of the speed to slow down the instance.

And if we are slower than MIN_STOP_SPEED, we forcibly set speed and acceleration to zero, movement state to idle, and move direction to none:

```
    if (currentSpeed < MIN_STOP_SPEED) {
      currentSpeed = 0.0f;
      mInstanceSettings.isAccel = glm::vec3(0.0f);
      mInstanceSettings.isSpeed = glm::vec3(0.0f);
      mInstanceSettings.isMoveState = moveState::idle;
      mInstanceSettings.isMoveDirection =
        moveDirection::none;
    }
  }
```

Limiting speed and acceleration to the maximum values is a two-step process. If we exceed the maximum value, we normalize the vector:

```
float currentAccel =
  glm::length(mInstanceSettings.isAccel);
if (currentAccel > MAX_ACCEL) {
  mInstanceSettings.isAccel =
    glm::normalize(mInstanceSettings.isAccel);
```

Now the length of the isAccel vector equals 1.0f. Then, we scale the vector to the maximum length:

```
    mInstanceSettings.isAccel *= MAX_ACCEL;
```

After the multiplication, all three components of isAccel are scaled down to a resulting length of MAX_ACCEL.

Updating the instance speed is done by adding the deltaTime fraction of the acceleration in isAccel to isSpeed:

```
mInstanceSettings.isSpeed +=
  mInstanceSettings.isAccel * deltaTime;
```

To reach run speed, we double the maxSpeed value:

```
  if (mInstanceSettings.isMoveState == moveState::run) {
    maxSpeed = MAX_ABS_SPEED * 2.0f;
  }
```

If we no longer run but are over maxSpeed, we slow down to walk speed:

```
  if (currentSpeed > maxSpeed) {
    if (mInstanceSettings.isMoveState != moveState::run) {
      maxSpeed -=
        glm::length(mInstanceSettings.isAccel) * deltaTime;
      if (maxSpeed <= MAX_ABS_SPEED) {
        maxSpeed = MAX_ABS_SPEED;
      }
    }
```

The example code uses a simple linear interpolation to reach the desired instance speed. You might want to experiment with other techniques like ease-in/ease-out curves, or cubic curves to adjust the interpolation between different instance speeds.

And if we are faster than maxSpeed while accelerating to walk or run speed, we limit the instance speed isSpeed to maxSpeed:

```
mInstanceSettings.isSpeed =
    glm::normalize(mInstanceSettings.isSpeed);
mInstanceSettings.isSpeed *= maxSpeed;
```

At this point, the currently selected instance would move smoothly from the idle animation clip to the walk animation clip, and even get a speedup to the run animation if we switch to the run state. Sadly, we cannot see anything yet since there is no mapping between movement states, directions, and animation clips.

So, let's link the animation clips to existing states.

Linking states and animations

We start with the connections between the three states (idle, walk, and run), and map the corresponding model animation clips to these three states. The IdleWalkRunBlending struct and the msIWRBlendings member variable in the ModelSettings struct are already in place, so we only have to take care of the UI.

Mapping idle/walk/run animations

Figure 7.1 shows the mapping section of the **Control** window for the three states: idle, walk, and run:

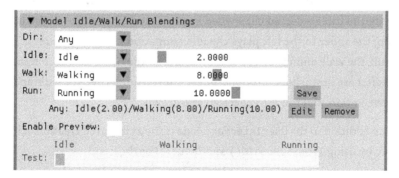

Figure 7.1: Mapping between move direction, move state, and animation clip

We will step through the control elements from top to bottom and explore the new code in the `createSettingsWindow()` method of the `UserInterface` class:

- The **Dir** combo box shows the names of the available entries of the `moveDirection` `enum class`. The combo box is filled by using the `micMoveDirectionMap` map from the `ModelInstanceCamData` struct. We store the selected entry in a `static moveDirection` type variable to retain the value.

- For the three combo boxes named **Idle**, **Walk**, and **Run**, we extract the animation clips from the model of the instance and store the selected clip in a `static int` for each state. The replay speed slider allows us to set individual replay speeds for every clip. We had the same combo box/float slider combination in the (now removed) **Animations** part of the **Control** window.

- To store the current combination of direction, clips, and speeds, press the **Save** button. The `UserInterface` code simply creates or updates the `msIWRBlendings` entry for the selected direction.

- Below the combo boxes, all saved mappings are listed. If you press the **Edit** button on one of the entries, the corresponding line will be loaded into the combo boxes and speed sliders. By pressing **Remove**, the entry will be deleted.

- To enable a preview for the current mappings, check the **Enable Preview** checkbox. In testing mode, the active mapping settings are used to animate the currently selected instance and blend between the three states. Make sure to disable preview mode once you have found good settings for the mappings.

- Above the **Test** slider, the names of the three animation clips for the three states, idle/walk/run, are shown. You can see the names changing if you select a different animation clip in any of the combo boxes. The **Test** slider allows you to preview the animation blending between the three selected clips when the test mode is enabled in the **Model** section. Moving the slider to the left plays the idle animation clip; if the slider is in the middle position, the walk animation clip is shown; and on the right, the run animation is played. Between these three slider positions, linear interpolations between idle and walk as well as between walk and run are generated and drawn.

One interesting addition to the `UserInterface` code is the automated creation of button IDs for every mapping by using `ImGui::PushID()` and `ImGui::PopID()`:

```
ImGui::PushID(buttonId++);
if (ImGui::Button("Edit##Blending")) {
    ...
```

```
        }
        ImGui::PopID();
```

ImGui needs a unique identifier for every control element. Failing to provide a unique ID leads to unwanted results, since triggering one control element also triggers the other element(s) containing the same ID.

By using an incrementing integer value as an identifier, every mapping line will have unique **Edit** and **Remove** buttons, and the buttons will only affect *their* mapping line.

Another nice ImGui feature is the ability to close a `CollapsingHeader` element from another part of the code:

```
        ImGui::GetStateStorage()->SetInt(
            ImGui::GetID("Model Animation Mappings"), 0);
```

The internal state storage of ImGui saves information about the elements of the current ImGui window. With the `SetInt()` call and the `CollapsingHeader` name, we can control the open/close state of any header in the current ImGui window.

This way, we forcibly close the other two mapping `CollapsingHeader` elements. We are changing the animation clip settings in all three mapping headers, and ImGui applies the settings multiple times, leading to unwanted results.

After all idle/walk/run animation clips have been set, we continue with the actions.

Mapping actions to animation clips

In the `moveState` enum `class`, we have defined several actions for the instances, next to the already configured `idle`, `walk`, and `run` states. Depending on the animations in a model file, not all actions may be available for all models. But there is no need to worry: the code will ignore actions without a configured animation. Pressing the action key will result in no animation or action.

All configured action mappings are saved to the `ModelSettings` struct in the `ModelSettings.h` file in a new map called `msActionClipMappings`:

```
    std::map<moveState, ActionAnimation>
      msActionClipMappings;
```

The new `ActionAnimation` struct contains the clip number and the replay speed:

```
struct ActionAnimation {
  int aaClipNr = 0;
  float aaClipSpeed = 1.0f;
};
```

We will start again with the UI part. In *Figure 7.2*, the `CollapsingHeader` for the action mapping is shown:

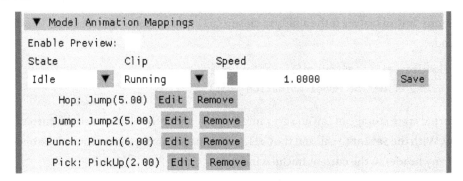

Figure 7.2: Mapping movement states to animation clips and speeds

The `UserInterface` code for this mapping type is similar to the idle/walk/run mapping as we do essentially the same kind of mapping. We have the following elements:

- A combo box for the elements of the `moveState` enum `class`, filled with the values of the `micMoveStateMap` map
- A second combo box for the clips, generated from the animation clips of the model
- A speed slider defining the replay speed of the clip
- A **Save** button to add the current mapping to the `msActionClipMappings` map
- A list of saved mappings, and every mapping line has two buttons to **Edit** or **Remove** the current line

The note from the idle/walk/run mapping also applies here. When a mapping for the none movement direction exists in the **Model Idle/Walk/Run Blendings** section, the currently selected clip is *not* playing. To see a preview of the animation clip, you need to temporarily remove the none direction.

To blend between the idle/walk/run state and any action in the `AssimpInstance` class, we can use the clip number and replay speed from the `msActionClipMappings` map and use the clip as the destination clip for a blending operation:

```
mInstanceSettings.isSecondAnimClipNr =
  modSettings.msActionClipMappings[mActionMoveState]
  .aaClipNr;
float animSpeed =
  modSettings.msActionClipMappings[mActionMoveState]
  .aaClipSpeed;
```

If we want our model to change to an action, we call the `setNextInstanceState()` method of the `AssimpInstance` class. The renderer uses this call in the `handleMovementKeys()` method to request a state change of the selected instance:

```
moveState nextState = moveState::idle;
..
if (glfwGetKey(mRenderData.rdWindow, GLFW_KEY_E) ==
    GLFW_PRESS) {
  nextState = moveState::punch;
}
...
currentInstance->setNextInstanceState(nextState);
```

Before we dive into the animation blending logic, let's finish the UI part by looking at how to set allowed clip sequences.

Defining allowed state changes

While previewing the different animation clips of the models, you will notice that some clips only work when the instance stands still, while other animations are only usable if the instance is walking or running.

To prevent unwanted and unnatural transitions between clips, for instance, from an idle model to a full-speed jump animation, we define which action state changes are allowed. The **Destination** state can only be triggered when the **Source** state is the current active state.

Figure 7.3 shows some allowed state changes:

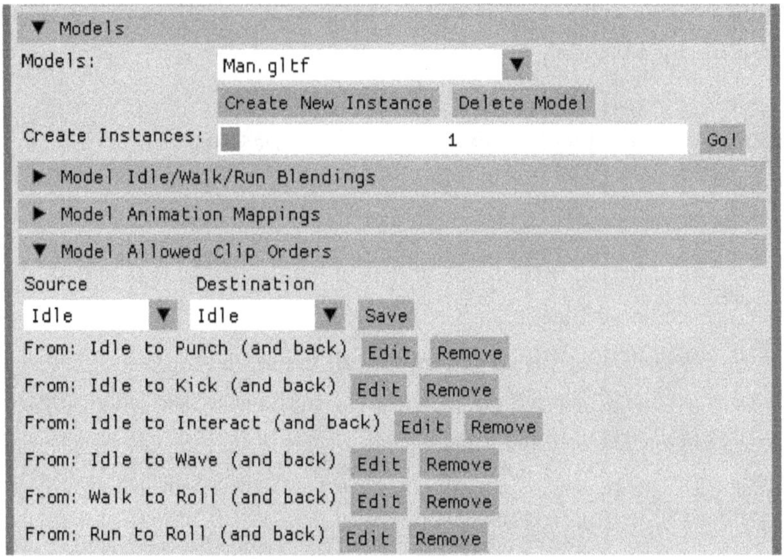

Figure 7.3: Allowed state changes of a model

The state order is saved in the `ModelSettings` struct using a `std::set` containing `std::pair` elements of `moveState` entries:

```
std::set<std::pair<moveState, moveState>>
  msAllowedStateOrder;
```

A `std::map` would not work here as we need to configure multiple destination states for the same source state.

After all the states are mapped to animation clips and the dependencies between states have been configured, we will explore the way the model actions are concatenated to give (mostly) smooth blending and transition effects.

Using a finite state machine to control the animation flow

The task of maintaining states over time and transitions from one state to another state after an event can be solved best by using a **finite state machine**. And in C++, such a state machine can be modeled with a simple `switch`/`case` statement.

Before we start the implementation, let's look at the states and transitions of the state machine in *Figure 7.4*:

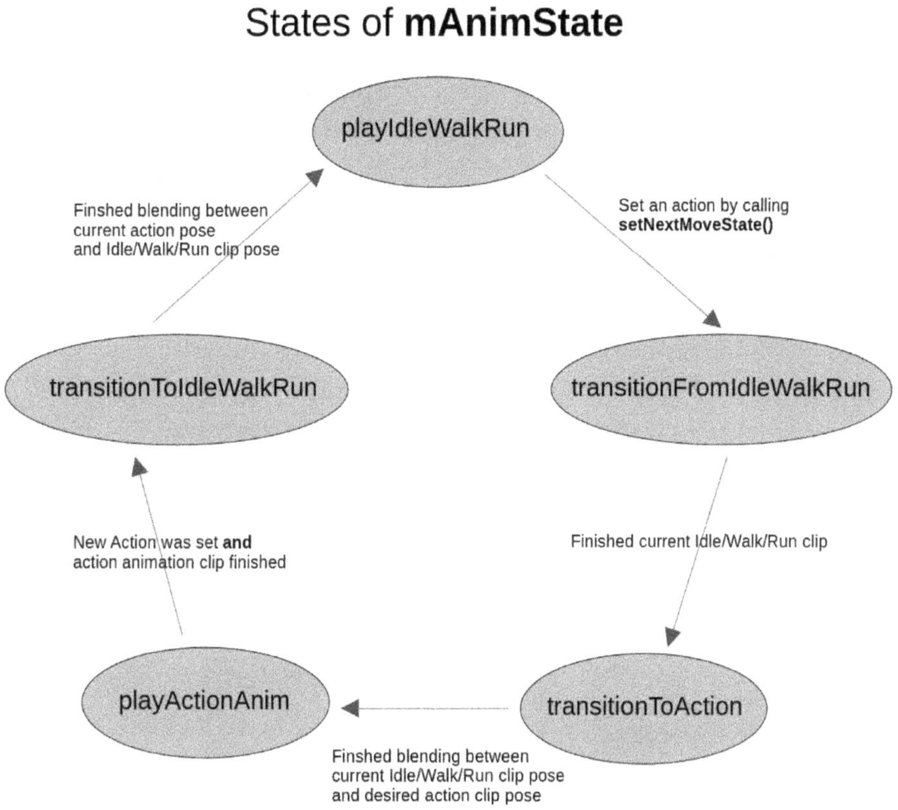

States of **mAnimState**

Figure 7.4: State machine of the mAnimState *variable in the* AssimpInstance *class*

These five states and the transitions between the states can be explained as follows:

1. We start at the state machine at playIdleWalkRun. Here, the default, instance-speed-based blending between the movement states, idle, walk, and run, is played.

2. Once an action is requested, we check whether source (current state) and destination (action state) are in the msAllowedStateOrder map. If yes, we prepare the directional clips and change to the transitionFromIdleWalkRun state.

3. The transitionFromIdleWalkRun state is needed to smooth the transition from idle/walk/run to the requested action. Most animation clips start from a similar pose of body, arms, and legs. By blending the current idle, walk, or run animation to the starting point of the same animation clip, the instance is adjusted back to its starting pose. After reaching the starting pose, we advance to the transitionToAction state.

4. In transitionToAction, we blend from the initial pose of the idle, walk, or run animation clip to the action state animation clip. This transition is only a few frames long and adds a smooth blending to the action clip. Once the transition to the action clip is done, we change to playActionAnim.

5. Once we are in playActionAnim, the animation for the requested action state is played at the configured replay speed until the end of the clip is reached. When the action animation clip is played, keyboard requests to switch to other animation clips or to return to the idle/walk/run cycle are ignored. Once the action animation clip is finished and no new requests for an action have been issued, the state is changed to transitionToIdleWalkRun.

Similar to transitionToAction, the transitionToIdleWalkRun state is used to blend between the action clip and the idle/walk/run clip. The destination clip (idle, walk, or run) is chosen via the instance speed. For a smooth animation cycle, the positions of the body, arms, and legs are the same as the start and end of the clip. By blending the end of the action clip with the start of an idle/walk/run clip, we have a smooth transition back to the initial state. After the blending is finished, we change the state back to playIdleWalkRun.

For the animation clip transitions, we create a new enum struct called animationState in the Enums.h file containing the states of the finite state machine:

```
enum class animationState : uint8_t {
  playIdleWalkRun = 0,
  transitionFromIdleWalkRun,
  transitionToAction,
  playActionAnim,
  transitionToIdleWalkRun
};
```

The state machine is defined in the updateAimStateMachine() method of the AssimpInstance class. The states are built as switch/case statements moving forward on the conditions outlined in *Figure 7.4*:

```
switch (mAnimState) {
  case animationState::playIdleWalkRun:
    playIdleWalkRunAnimation();
    ...
    break;
  case animationState::transitionFromIdleWalkRun:
    blendIdleWalkRunAnimation(deltaTime);
```

```
      break;
    case animationState::transitionToAction:
      blendActionAnimation(deltaTime);
      break;
    case animationState::playActionAnim:
      playActionAnimation();

      ...

      break;
    case animationState::transitionToIdleWalkRun:
      blendActionAnimation(deltaTime, true);
      break;
  }
```

You can check the details of the finite state machine in the updateAnimStateMachine() method of the AssimpInstance class. The code is simple and straightforward: we just replay and blend between various animation clips.

With the blending code and the finite state machine in place, you can change to the view mode of the application by pressing F10. If you press a key for an action while you are at an allowed source state, the action clip will be played. Right after the action clip, the instance goes back to the previous idle/walk/run state.

To complete this chapter's features, we need to make the state and clip mappings permanent by adding the contents of the ModelSettings struct and all related custom data types to the configuration file.

Saving and loading the states

We can reuse some of the save and load code we created in the previous chapters when saving and loading the current state of custom data types. The moveState and moveDirection enum class types will be stored as integer values in the YAML configuration file of the application. The three new struct types, IdleWalkRunBlending, ActionAnimation, and ModelSettings, are deconstructed into their elements when saving them to the configuration file and reassembled when reading the values. The C++ maps and sets are created by using the known combination of YAML sequences and YAML maps.

Storing the new data types

For the moveState and moveDirection structs, we create a new convert template in the
YamlParserTypes.h file in the tools folder that will simply cast to int and back:

```
template<>
struct convert<moveState> {
  static Node encode(const moveState& rhs) {
    Node node;
    node = static_cast<int>(rhs);
    return node;
  }
  static bool decode(const Node& node, moveState& rhs) {
    rhs = static_cast<moveState>(node.as<int>());
    return true;
  }
};
```

The YAML emitter overloads for moveState and moveDirection in the YamlParser.cpp file in
the tools folder are also casting the values to int:

```
YAML::Emitter& operator<<(YAML::Emitter& out,
    const moveState& state) {
  out << YAML::Flow;
  out << static_cast<int>(state);
  return out;
}
```

Now we can read and write the new data types like every other type when we generate or parse
our YAML configuration file.

Both struct types, IdleWalkRunBlending and ActionAnimation, only use int and float values, so
the main task here is to find good names for the YAML nodes. For example, the ActionAnimation
values are stored as clip and clip-speed in the YAML file:

```
static bool decode(const Node& node, ActionAnimation& rhs) {
  rhs.aaClipNr = node["clip"].as<int>();
  rhs.aaClipSpeed = node["clip-speed"].as<float>();
  return true;
}
```

Saving the contents of the ModelSettings struct is also straightforward. We simply output all the values and iterate over the msIWRBlendings and msActionClipMappings maps and the msAllowedStateOrder set by using for loops:

```
    ...
    if (settings.msActionClipMappings.size() > 0) {
      out << YAML::Key << "action-clips";
      out << YAML::Value;
      out << YAML::BeginSeq;;
      for (auto& setting : settings.msActionClipMappings) {
        out << YAML::BeginMap;
        out << YAML::Key << setting.first;
        out << YAML::Value << setting.second;
        out << YAML::EndMap;
      }
      out << YAML::EndSeq;
    }
    ...
```

Reading back the ModelSettings is done in the getModelConfigs() method of the YamlParser class. The YAML parsing inside getModelConfigs() method is identical to the parsing of the InstanceSettings or CameraSettings struct. By using the convert template, all we must do is instruct yaml-cpp to use the correct data type when filling the temporary modeSettings vector:

```
modSettings.emplace_back(modelsNode[i].
  as<ModelSettings>());
```

Parsing the C++ maps and sets is a bit tricky. We need to iterate over the node containing the sequence, get every entry as a std::map, and add the map to the corresponding map of the ModelSettings type:

```
    if (Node clipNode = node["idle-walk-run-clips"]) {
      for (size_t i = 0; i < clipNode.size(); ++i) {
        std::map<moveDirection, IdleWalkRunBlending> entry =
          clipNode[i].as<std::map<moveDirection,
          IdleWalkRunBlending>>();
        rhs.msIWRBlendings.insert(entry.begin(),
          entry.end());
      }
    }
```

Reading back the model settings in the renderer

Saving the model settings is entirely done by the YAML emitter; no changes to the
saveConfigFile() method of the renderer are needed. To get the model settings back into the
application in the loadConfigFile() method, we use the getModelConfigs() method of the
YAML parser:

```
std::vector<ModelSettings> savedModelSettings =
  parser.getModelConfigs();
```

Then, we loop over the contents of the vector and we try to add the models using the file name
and path found in the loaded model settings:

```
for (const auto& modSetting : savedModelSettings) {
  if (!addModel(modSetting.msModelFilenamePath,
      false, false)) {
    return false;
  }
}
```

If the model cannot be loaded, we stop the loading process. If we want to have more relaxed file
handling in case of errors, we can store the models that failed to load, skip the instances of the
failed models, and inform the user in a dialog that an error has occurred.

Next, we get the model by the file name again and restore the model settings:

```
std::shared_ptr<AssimpModel> model =
  getModel(modSetting.msModelFilenamePath);
model->setModelSettings(modSetting);
```

Finally, we restore the model that was selected when the configuration was saved:

```
mModelInstCamData.micSelectedModel =
  parser.getSelectedModelNum();
```

Now, all animation clip mappings and the state sequences are restored. The application user can
take a break from creating a virtual world at any time without losing progress.

With the additions from this chapter, we can bring the instances on the screen to life. Depending
on the available animations in the model file, the instance can not only walk and run, but also
do additional actions like jumping up or forward, rolling around, punching targets, waving,
or interacting with the environment. The animations are also blended between the different
movements and actions, creating a game-like feeling.

Summary

In this chapter, we improved animation processing efficiency and added gameplay-like controls to map animation clips to the current animation state. We started by moving the computational work of animation blending from the CPU to the GPU and created lookup tables to reduce the amount of work for the GPU (at the cost of memory usage). Then, we added the different movement states to the code, including a UI-based mapping between states and animation clips. As the last step, we added the new mappings to the YAML configuration file, allowing us to save and restore the mappings.

In the next chapter, we will take a closer look at collision detection. After we can move the instance in the virtual world, we need to avoid just *running through* other instances on the screen. As the first step, we will explore the theoretical background of collision detection and discuss the problems of a naive implementation. Then, we will add spatial partitioning to the virtual world and instance simplifications to reduce the complexity of the collision detection checks. Finally, we will implement multi-level collision detection, allowing us to detect collisions between instances with minimal costs.

Practical sessions

There are some additions you could make to the code:

- Use root motion to control instance movement.

    Instead of moving the position of the instances around the virtual world and playing the animation at a specific rate, so-called **Root Motion** can be used to let the animation clips control the movement of the character. In root motion, the movement of the model's root bone is coordinated by the animation and not by us, allowing a better sync of the feet on the ground. However, root motion data must be baked into model animations to work. Updating the animations is beyond the scope of the book.

- Add a second direction for the idle/walk/run mapping.

    Right now, only animations for the four main directions (forward, backward, left, and right) plus the special wildcards none and any can be configured. Moving diagonally may look a bit awkward when the feet are not synchronized with the instance movement.

- Add animation blending for diagonal movement.

  Similarly to the previous task, instead of adding multiple directions, you can try to blend between the forward/backward and left/right animation clips when the instance is moving in a diagonal direction.

- Add a preview for the state order configuration.

  To preview the transition from **Source** to **Destination** state, the finite state machine would need to be adjusted with some sort of testing mode. The source state must be set and played for a while, i.e., until the animation clip is restarted. Then, the transition to the destination state must be triggered. Plus, we need to forbid the instance from moving; all transitions must happen without changing the world position of the instance.

- Allow animation clips to be played in the reverse direction.

  The woman model has a clip with a **sit-down** animation. To make the instance stand up again, you could add a Boolean to play the clip either forward or in reverse direction.

- Add more speed interpolation functions and make them selectable.

  As mentioned in the *Using acceleration and deceleration* section, the interpolation between different speeds is done by a simple linear interpolation. Try to add more advanced interpolation variants here, like separate ease-in and ease-out functions based on curves. You could also add an extra field to the model settings that stores the interpolation function and make additional fields in the UI to choose an interpolation to use.

- Use a graphical tool to draw nodes and connections.

  The **Graph Editor** from ImGuizmo (see the link in the *Addition resources* section) adds nodes and connections to ImGui. You could change the mapping configurations to have nodes for states and animation clips and use the connections to define mappings.

Additional resources

ImGuizmo GitHub repo: `https://github.com/CedricGuillemet/ImGuizmo`

Get This Book's PDF Version and Exclusive Extras

Scan the QR code (or go to packtpub.com/unlock). Search for this book by name, confirm the edition, and then follow the steps on the page.

Note: Keep your invoice handy. Purchases made directly from Packt don't require an invoice.

8

An Introduction to Collision Detection

Welcome to *Chapter 8*! In the previous chapter, we extended the instance animation system. We started by adding lookup tables for the animation transforms and moved the computations to the GPU. Next, we added movement states and UI controls to the application to create mappings between states and animation clips. As the last step, we updated the YAML parser to save and restore the animation clip mappings.

In this chapter, we will implement a two-tier collision detection for the instances. We will start with an exploration of the complexity of collision detection, and how to lower the complexity by removing instances based on their distance and by simplifying the representation of the instances. Then, we will discuss methods to simplify the instances to minimize the number of intersection checks even more. Next, we will implement a quadtree to limit the number of instances to check, and finally, we will add bounding spheres to the instances to create the two tiers of collision detection.

In this chapter, we will cover the following topics:

- The complexities of collision detection
- Using spatial partitioning to reduce complexity
- Simplifying the instances for faster collision checks
- Adding a quadtree to store nearby model instances
- Implementing bounding spheres

Technical requirements

The example code is in the chapter08 folder, in the subfolders 01_opengl_collisions for OpenGL and 02_vulkan_collisions for Vulkan.

The complexities of collision detection

We already talked about the complexity of finding a collision in *Chapter 3* when deciding how to implement a visual selection, either using ray shooting or buffer drawing. We've chosen to draw the instances into a separate buffer, avoiding collision detection entirely.

Now is the right time to do a short reprise of the complex topic and to present solutions to accelerate finding collisions between instances.

Avoiding the naive way

If we would check every triangle of every instance against all triangles of all other instances for collisions in the virtual world, this would come with immense processing costs. These simple, brute-force collision checks would grow exponentially, making it impossible to keep up a reasonable frame time when adding more and more instances.

Instead of using the naive solution, we should take a step back and think about possible types of simplification before implementing any kind of collision detection.

One idea is to reduce the number of instances we have to check against. Why bother with instances in distant parts of the virtual world? Even if our object is some kind of bullet, rocket, or other flying entity, all we can possibly hit needs to be "less than an arm's length" away from us. All other objects can be safely ignored.

To achieve this reduction, we can split the world into different areas. And suddenly, we only have to check the area we are in. Maybe we have to check adjacent areas too, depending on the algorithm we use, but the total number of instances we have to check against can be reduced by a large amount.

On the other hand, we can lower the computational work for collision detection by reducing the amount of surface elements to test if we are even close to any of the triangles of the instance. Any kind of simplification will become handy; the fewer intersections to test, the better.

Representing an instance as a box or sphere may produce a lot of false results, but if the collision check against the box or sphere around the instance already fails, we can immediately sort out this instance from our list of possible collision targets.

Both ideas combined – reducing the number of instances to check and lowering the complexity of the instance checks – help to do collision checks in real time, even with larger numbers of detailed models.

Let's start with the spatial partitioning of the virtual world.

Using spatial partitioning to reduce complexity

In this section, we will take a look at some methods to split our world space into different parts, lowering the number of instances in each of the parts. We start with the simplest variant of spatial partitioning in two or three dimensions, the grid.

Grid

In a **grid**, the virtual lines divide the virtual world into equally sized squares or rectangles, or equally sized cubes and cuboids.

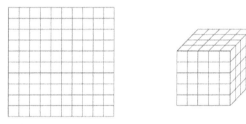

Figure 8.1: 2D and 3D grids

While grids are easy to create, *Figure 8.1* already shows some of the problems. Objects larger than the grid spacing must be placed into all overlapping grid fields, requiring checking all affected fields for other instances.

And while the vast majority of the grid will remain empty, "crowded places" inside the virtual world can lead to many instances inside a single field of the grid. Many instances mean many checks, and an uneven distribution of instances may cause slowdowns due to the number of calculations.

A sort of successor to the grid is the quadtree. A quadtree addresses the uneven distribution problem of the grid.

Quadtree

The basic element of a **quadtree** is a single cell, being either a square or a rectangle. We will only use square cells for the description, but all holds true for rectangle-shaped cells, too. Objects are inserted with their position and sizes into the root cell, usually by using a two-dimensional bounding box covering the extents of the object.

The magic part of a quadtree starts when a configurable threshold of objects per cell has been hit. The affected cell is subdivided into four equally sized child cells. Any object overlapping one or more children could be either kept in the parent cell or added to all affected child cells, depending on the implementation. All other objects are moved into the respective child cell. See *Figure 8.2* for an example of a quadtree:

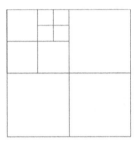

Figure 8.2: A quadtree with different subdivisions

Dividing the squares into four child cells and moving the objects from the parent cell into the child cells reduces the number of objects per cell to be less than the configured threshold, minimizing the number of objects to test for collisions.

If the sum of all objects inside the four child cells falls below the threshold, all objects are moved to the parent cell again, and the now empty child cells are deleted. This dynamic behavior helps to keep the number of objects in each cell between zero and the threshold, independent of the size, number of parents, or location of a cell.

A quadtree can hold only two-dimensional information about the object's position and size. To extend the same logic into three dimensions, an octree can be used.

Octree

The basic functionality of a quadtree and an **octree** is identical. The only difference is the number of dimensions used for the element of the tree itself. While a quadtree uses squares or rectangles as cells, an octree is made of cubes or cuboids. In *Figure 8.3*, a simple octree is shown:

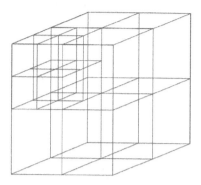

Figure 8.3: An octree with subdivisions

The inserted objects are internally maintained as three-dimensional axis-aligned bounding boxes, representing the extents of the object. A split operation when reaching the threshold results in creating eight sub-cubes as child cells (or eight sub-cuboids).

An octree is an effective way to remove large parts of the three-dimensional space when checking for possible collisions. Another data structure to handle two- and three-dimensional space partitioning is **binary space partitioning (BSP)**.

Binary space partitioning

You may have heard of the three letters BSP from older games. One of the first games using BSP trees to maintain level data was the 1993 game **Doom** from **Id Software**.

Although the level data in Doom was only two-dimensional, the game engine created the illusion of a fully three-dimensional game.

A BSP tree is created by recursively dividing the world space by using lines (2D) or planes (3D) as hyperplanes, creating a front side and a back side. The division into front and back sides continues until the remaining partition fulfills some exit condition; for games, this condition is usually when the partition is either completely filled or empty.

If any other lines or planes are hit by the subdivision, these lines or planes are split into two parts, one residing on the front side and the other on the back side.

Figure 8.4 shows the subdivision of a space and the resulting BSP tree:

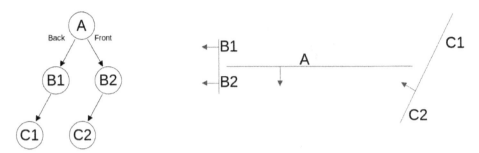

Figure 8.4: An example object and the resulting BSP tree

In *Figure 8.4*, line A is used as the starting point, with the front side pointing downward. Splitting the space into two halves also splits lines B and C, resulting in lines B1, B2, C1, and C2. Line B1 lies on the back side of A and will be added as the left child to A, and B2, on the back of A, as the right child of A. Both lines C1 and C3 are on the back sides of B1 and B2, so they are added as the left children to B1 respective to B2.

While parsing a BSP tree to find a partition is really fast, generating the same BSP tree is a time-consuming task. The tree generation is done offline in most cases, and the precalculated tree is shipped with the game or application. Checking all lines or planes against all other lines or planes is the same type of problem we have with collision detection.

The inability to quickly change or update the elements of a BSP tree makes such a tree only suitable for static data (i.e., for level data of a game). Dynamic game elements, like doors or players, require using a different data structure, for instance, an octree.

Similar to BSP trees, a k-d tree is fast for searching elements but slow for creation or updates.

K-d tree

A **k-d tree** stores information about objects in a k-dimensional space. The algorithm is a bit more complex compared to the previous trees. At every data point insertion, the remaining space gets split into two parts, and after the split, the affected dimension is changed.

For a two-dimensional k-d tree, the split dimensions alternate between the X and Y axes; for a three-dimensional k-d tree, it alternates in the order X, Y, and Z; and so on. *Figure 8.5* shows what a k-d tree in two and three dimensions looks like:

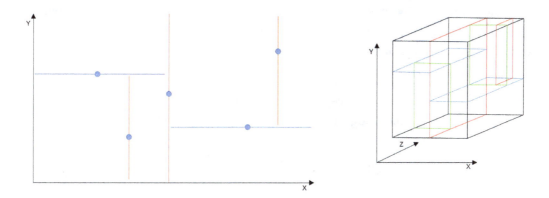

Figure 8.5: A two- and a three-dimensional k-d tree

The red lines and the respective blue lines are for the split dimension in 2D: red stands for an X split and blue for a Y split. In three dimensions, the same pattern applies, and we use the "next" dimension upon consecutive splits. Due to the removal of parts of the remaining space, searching in a k-d tree for an element is fast. The main uses for k-d trees are point clouds and searching for the nearest neighbors of a given point.

A slightly different method for space partitioning is by using a bounding volume hierarchy.

Bounding volume hierarchy

In contrast to the previous tree variants, a **bounding volume hierarchy** can be achieved by different types of geometrical representations. As an example, we are using two-dimensional bounding circles, as shown in *Figure 8.6*:

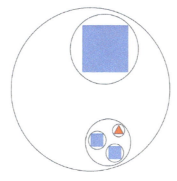

Figure 8.6: A bounding volume hierarchy made of circles

By enclosing two or more bounding circles into a larger bounding circle, the number of collision tests can be lowered. If the possible colliding object does not hit the outer circle, there is no need to check any of the inner circles for possible collisions. The inner circles are impossible to reach for the colliding object.

Only if we hit the outer circle is a deeper check required. Similar to the other trees, a bounding volume hierarchy can remove larger parts of the world space from further collision checks.

Before we start the implementation of a spatial partitioning algorithm, we need to explore the second way of accelerating collision detection: using simplified representations of the instances for faster checks.

Simplifying the instances for faster collision checks

Instead of checking every triangle of the instances after reducing the overall number, we can greatly improve the performance of collision checks if we use **model abstractions**. These abstractions are made of only a few geometrical elements, like boxes, cuboids, or circles, enclosing the instance. If these abstractions don't intersect, the instances cannot have a collision, and we can remove the instance already from our list of candidates.

One of the fastest abstractions for an object is the axis-aligned bounding box.

Axis-aligned bounding box

An **axis-aligned bounding box** (AABB) is a rectangle or cuboid, just large enough to contain the object, and all lines of the rectangle or planes of the cuboid are aligned with the axes of the Cartesian coordinate system. We will use the two-dimensional variant of an AABB during the implementation of the quadtree, the bounding box. *Figure 8.7* shows a two-dimensional bounding box:

Figure 8.7: A two-dimensional bounding box

AABBs are best suited for objects shaped close to squares, rectangles, cubes, or cuboids. For round objects, AABBs will produce a lot of space between the object and the box extents, leading to more "false positives" when checking for a possible collision.

Checking intersections between AABBs is a quick and easy task. Since all four lines or six sides are aligned to axes, only one dimension per line or plane needs to be checked against the opposite line or plane of the second instance.

For instance, the bottom plane of instance one and the top plane of instance two can be checked by just comparing the Y values (if the Y axis points upward). If this check signals that the instances are not colliding (namely, the top plane of the second instance is not above the bottom plane of instance one), the collision check can be ended immediately – these two instances cannot intersect at all. So, we can do a fast preflight check by using AABBs.

When we rotate an AABB with the object, an **oriented bounding box (OBB)** will be created.

Oriented bounding box

Just rotating the AABB with the object may be tempting, since we still have a good ratio between the object data and the extra space of the box. See *Figure 8.8* for an example:

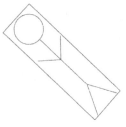

Figure 8.8: An oriented bounding box

But be aware that OBBs are not just AABBs in disguise! Rotating the planes will no longer allow us to do simple coordinate checks, and we now need to solve a lot of plane equations or use advanced methods like the so-called **Separating Axis Theorem** to check if the side planes of the two OBBs intersect. Plus, the creation and rotation of OOBs can be complex and ambiguous. So, the tip here is to stay away from OBBs; in most cases, they are not worth the additional complexity.

For round(ish) objects, bounding circles and spheres are a good simplification type.

Bounding circles and spheres

A bounding circle in two dimensions, or a bounding sphere in three dimensions, is rather simple. We just need a center point and a radius, and we are done. *Figure 8.9* shows a bounding circle around an object:

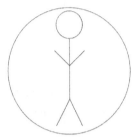

Figure 8.9: A bounding circle around an object

Checking against a bounding circle or sphere is also fast and simple. The Pythagorean theorem helps us to calculate the distance to the center of the sphere from any point in the world. Only if the calculated distance is smaller than the radius will a collision hit occur.

Please keep in mind that the Pythagorean theorem includes calculating a square root, a quite expensive operation if you don't use modern **Single Instruction, Multiple Data (SIMD)** CPU extensions like **Streaming SIMD Extensions (SSE)** or **Advanced Vector Extensions (AVX)**. One possible optimization here is using the square of the radius and skipping the square root when calculating the distance. Since both results are squared now, the outcome of the comparison is identical to the square root version.

An interesting adaptation of the bounding circle or bounding sphere is a capsule.

Capsule

Capsules look like a stretched version of a circle or a sphere, where the middle part is shaped like a rectangle or cylinder. Capsules are used for human bodies since the overall form of a capsule comes closer to the body shape compared to spheres or rectangular bounding boxes. *Figure 8.10* shows an example of a capsule:

Figure 8.10: A capsule around a simple character

When using the same values for the radius of the ending circles or spheres, and the central rectangle or cylinder, we need to store only the central line of the capsule and the radius. Calculating the distances of a possible collision point is not much more expensive than the calculations for bounding circles or spheres.

On the high end of the costs for collision checks comes the convex hull.

Convex hull

A **convex hull** is defined as the smallest **convex** volume containing the object. Emphasizing the convex property of the hull is done on purpose since this property allows algorithmic optimizations to some extent. However, the number of planes for the complex hull can become high, and the construction may be not trivial. See *Figure 8.11* for a convex hull:

Figure 8.11: A convex hull around an object

Checking a convex hull for collisions needs a lot of tests, possibly lowering the effect we wanted to achieve with our model simplification. As long as you don't have models with lots of triangles, a convex hull may be out of scope.

On the other hand, if small collision errors can be tolerated, the convex hull can be used as a replacement for a high-poly model, and all collision checks can be done only against the convex hull.

As the last method, the bounding volume hierarchy can be used. The hierarchy model is not just suitable for space partitioning but also for model simplification.

Bounding volume hierarchy

The general idea of the **bounding volume hierarchy** for space partitioning also holds true to simplify the instances. But here, the model parts are enclosed in larger and larger volumes. *Figure 8.12* shows a simplified example of the bounding volume hierarchy around a character model:

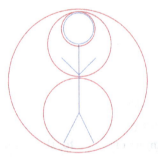

Figure 8.12: Bounding spheres in a hierarchy around an object

A failing check on one of the larger volumes allows us to discard the body part(s) inside the volume completely. By using a carefully crafted configuration, only a small number of tests are needed to decide if the instance should stay on the list for deeper checks, or if it can be ignored.

For details about collision checking between convex objects, you can look at the **Gilbert–Johnson–Keerthi (GJK)** distance algorithm. The GJK algorithm reduces the collision detection complexity by using the so-called Minkowski difference. A link to a web page explaining the principle of the GJK algorithm is available in the *Additional resources* section.

For the sake of simplicity, because of the fast updates, and also based on setting a limit to the number of instances to check, we will implement a quadtree into the application and bounding spheres for the instances. The quadtree will allow us to do the first step of collision detection much faster than the "brute-force" pairwise comparisons of all models in the naive approach. The bounding spheres are great for a balance between the number of collision checks and the number of false positives due to the free space between the sphere and the instance triangles.

Next, let's jump into the implementation of the quadtree.

Adding a quadtree to store nearby model instances

Getting complex code right is hard, so using an open-source implementation of a quadtree is a viable option. The best fitting version of a quadtree I've found is from **Pierre Vigier** and can be found on GitHub here: https://github.com/pvigier/Quadtree.

The code from Pierre is based on C++ templating to have great flexibility on the data one stores in the quadtree. Also, he uses a custom-templated two-dimensional vector type for storing positions and sizes.

We don't need this kind of flexibility as we will store only an int containing the instance index position in the quadtree. And since we are using GLM for all other cases where we need a two-dimensional vector type, we will change the bounding box implementation to use glm::vec2 to store box position and size.

Adjusting the bounding box code

As the first step for the new and shiny quadtree, we need to adjust the code for the bounding box. Instead of storing the top and left positions and width plus height as single values, we use a vec2 for position and size. Transforming the templated C++ code from the Box.h file in the include folder of the GitHub repository is done fairly easily, and we end up with constructors, a couple of getters, and the two methods contains() and intersects() in the BoundingBox2D.h and BoundingBox2D.cpp files in the newly created quadtree folder.

The most complex method is intersects() to check if two bounding boxes intersect each other:

```
bool BoundingBox2D::intersects(BoundingBox2D otherBox) {
  return !(
    mPosition.x >= otherBox.getRight() ||
    otherBox.getTopLeft().x >= getRight() ||
    mPosition.y >= otherBox.getBottom() ||
    otherBox.getTopLeft().y >= getBottom()
  );
}
```

In the `AssimpInstance` class, a new `private` member named `mBoundingBox` will be added, storing the bounding box of the instance:

```
BoundingBox2D mBoundingBox{};
```

We don't need to load or save the bounding box, so it can be stored directly in the `AssimpClass`, outside of the `InstanceSettings` struct.

We need two trivial `public` methods to store and retrieve the bounding box:

```
BoundingBox2D getBoundingBox();
void setBoundingBox(BoundingBox2D box);
```

As the last step for the bounding box implementation, we must add the new `quadtree` folder to the `CMakeLists.txt` file in the `project root` folder in two places, to be able to use the bounding box and the quadtree in other classes. First, add the folder with a wildcard for all `.cpp` files to the `SOURCES` file search:

```
file(GLOB SOURCES
  ...
  quadtree/*.cpp
  ...
)
```

Then, append the `quadtree` folder to the include directory list:

```
target_include_directories(${PROJECT_NAME} ... quadtree)
```

After recreating the CMake files, which should be done automatically by Visual Studio and other IDEs after saving the changes in `CMakeLists.txt`, we can continue with the implementation of the quadtree.

Rewriting the quadtree code to fit our needs

We will store the new `Quadtree` class in the `Quadtree.h` and `Quadtree.cpp` files in the quadtree folder. The transformation from the quadtree C++ template to a C++ class needs some extra steps compared to the bounding box code.

We will need to make the following adjustments while translating the C++ template code:

- Replace the custom `Vector2` type with `glm::vec2`.
- Replace the custom `Box` type with the `BoundingBox2D` type and change the parameters to `glm::vec2`.

- Replace the `assert()` checks with log outputs.
- Add a `clear()` method that removes all contents of the quadtree.
- Add code to clean up the pairs of colliding instances with swapped IDs.
- Use return values for results instead of output parameters.
- Use a callback function instead of the `GetBox` function parameter.

For the callback function, we add another callback to the `Callbacks.h` file, taking an `int` as the only parameter and returning a `BoundingBox2D`:

```
using instanceGetBoundingBox2D =
    std::function<BoundingBox2D(int)>;
```

The quadtree will be added to the renderer as a `private` member variable named `mQuadtree`:

```
    std::shared_ptr<QuadTree> mQuadtree = nullptr;
```

During the initialization in the `initQuadTree()` method, we will bind the callback function to the `getBoundingBox()` method, using the instance index as the parameter:

```
    mQuadtree->instanceGetBoundingBox2DCallback =
      [this](int instanceId) {
       return mModelInstCamData.micAssimpInstances.at(
         instanceId)->getBoundingBox();
    };
```

Filling the quadtree will happen in the `draw()` call of the renderer while iterating over the instances of the models. For each instance, we create the bounding box and add the instance to the quadtree:

```
    BoundingBox2D box{position, size};
    instances.at(i)->setBoundingBox(box);
    mQuadtree->add(instSettings.isInstanceIndexPosition);
```

Creating the bounding box for every instance will be handled in the section *Calculating the instance bounding boxes*.

One important question for the quadtree usage remains: Should we update the instance positions in the tree in every frame, or should we clear the entire quadtree and add all instances again?

Updating an object inside a quadtree needs to be done by deleting and re-adding. So, if we have mostly static objects in the quadtree, updates would be fine. But since our plan is to have many instances moving around and/or playing animations, the position and/or bounding box will change in almost every frame. In such an environment, instance removal and addition will be more expensive than clearing the quadtree and adding all instances with fresh data.

Starting over with a fresh quadtree in the draw() call of the renderer is easy. Right before going into the instance loop, clear the contents of the quadtree:

```
mQuadtree->clear();
```

After the quadtree is ready, we have to solve the question of how to generate the bounding boxes for the instances. The answer may be surprising: We need to split the work between the GPU and the CPU.

Calculating the instance bounding boxes

The first idea when it comes to a large number of calculations for all instances will most probably be "I will use a compute shader!", especially after we have solved some compute-intense problems by offloading the work to the GPU. But in this case, the CPU must do a part of the job.

While compute shaders are great for calculating independent results in a massively parallel way, they aren't well suited for simple tasks like creating a bounding box. To calculate the bounding box of an instance, we need to store the minimum and maximum coordinates of all nodes for every instance in the virtual world, combining the intermediate results to create the final bounding box. On the CPU, we can easily grab the vertex positions from the data structures one by one, do the required calculations, and store the final AABB back in memory.

But if we would like to compute the AABB coordinates inside a shader, we may end up overwriting the results of other shader invocations if the AABB results use the same buffer positions. Or we will have a huge list of coordinates that must be sorted afterward. Sorting the coordinates could be done in another computer shader too, but parallel sorting algorithms tend to be complex because they face the same constraints of not being able to write data to the same buffer positions.

So, instead of worrying about data synchronization issues in compute shaders, we use them for what they can do very fast: creating lookup tables.

Adding a three-dimensional bounding cube class

To store the generated lookup data, we will add a C++ class for a three-dimensional AABB. Using AABBs here has the advantage of having data to draw debug lines in the renderer, but the third set of coordinates adds only a little overhead to storage and generation time. Also, a possible upgrade to an octree for a fast collision check in all three dimensions will be simple.

The new class is called AABB and will reside in the tools folder. Next to the constructor, some public getters and setters, and the two private floats mMinPos and mMaxPos, the AABB class has two public methods called create() and addPoint().

By using the create() method, we add a point at the position given as the glm::vec3 parameter as the minimum and maximum extents for the bounding box. And with addPoint(), we extend the bounding box to include the new point:

```
void AABB::addPoint(glm::vec3 point) {
    mMinPos.x = std::min(mMinPos.x, point.x);
    mMinPos.y = std::min(mMinPos.y, point.y);
    mMinPos.z = std::min(mMinPos.z, point.z);
    mMaxPos.x = std::max(mMaxPos.x, point.x);
    mMaxPos.y = std::max(mMaxPos.y, point.y);
    mMaxPos.z = std::max(mMaxPos.z, point.z);
}
```

If the new point is inside the bounding box, nothing happens. But if the point is outside of the bounding box, the box will be expanded in one, two, or three dimensions to include the new point. In the end, we will have a box around all the points we added, defined by the minimum and maximum values of the three dimensions.

For generating debug lines to draw in the renderer, the public method getAABBlines() is used. In getAABBLines(), we create the 12 lines between the 8 possible combinations of the minimum and maximum positions of the x, y, and z elements of mMinPos and mMaxPos:

```
mAabbMesh->vertices.at(0) =
    {{mMinPos.x, mMinPos.y, mMinPos.z}, color};
mAabbMesh->vertices.at(1) =
    {{mMaxPos.x, mMinPos.y, mMinPos.z}, color};
...
mAabbMesh->vertices.at(22) =
    {{mMaxPos.x, mMaxPos.y, mMinPos.z}, color};
mAabbMesh->vertices.at(23) =
    {{mMaxPos.x, mMaxPos.y, mMaxPos.z}, color};
```

Creating the AABB lookup tables

The general idea of the AABB lookup tables is to precalculate the AABB for a fixed number of frames of every animation clip for every model. Having the bounding boxes in a lookup table allows us to retrieve a good approximation of the model's AABB in a frame of an animation clip.

By blending between AABB coordinates of the same frame number in two different clips plus transforming the final AABB according to the model's transformations, we can calculate a well-fitting AABB for the instance at low computing costs, even if the instance is in the middle of an animation blending.

Creating the lookup table is a mix of a compute shader and CPU work, done in the `createAABBLookup()` method of the renderer. The lookup table is generated in the renderer class for two reasons:

- The main method to load the models is placed in the renderer, and we also expose the model loading method to the user interface via callback.

- The renderer already has the compute shaders loaded. We can use the shaders directly, instead of using another set of the same shaders in the `AssimpModel` class.

For the compute shader part, we can reuse the code from the instance loop of the `draw()` call of the renderer we made back in *Chapter 2*.

To find the maximum extents of the model, we will use the nodes. To calculate the nodes per instance, the two compute shaders `assimp_instance_transform.comp` and `assimp_instance_matrix_mult.comp` can be used. In the translation part of the calculated matrices containing translation, rotation, and scale of the node, the location of each node is stored. The only difference here is the node offset matrices.

While these offset matrices are required for vertex skinning, they would give the wrong results for node positions. We can remove the offset matrices in the calculations by binding an SSBO full of identity matrices, giving us only the node's TRS matrices.

By extracting the node positions per instance and creating a per-node AABB from the positions, we have an easy way to calculate the data we need for the quadtree and the debug display. For the 2D bounding box, we simply extract the x and z elements of the AABB, generating a "top-down" view of the AABB.

The AABB calculations are done per animation clip and per node of the model. The resulting std::vector will be stored in the AssimpModel data of the model we just loaded. To retrieve the correct AABB data for a time position in an animation clip, we use the same logic we already have for generating the vertex skinning matrices and take the scaled time position as an index into the lookup data. If we blend between two animations, we can even blend between the AABBs of the two animations.

Using the AABB in the model and renderer

When iterating over the instances in the draw() call of the renderer, we can now retrieve the AABB data for the animation clip and time position by calling getAABB():

```
AABB instanceAABB = model->getAABB(instSettings);
```

Inside getAABB(), the data from animation and instance translation, rotation, and scale are used to create an AABB fitting the instance. In detail, getAABB() will:

- Look up the AABBs of the first and second animation clip
- Blend between the two AABBs according to the animation blend factor
- Scale the resulting AABB by the instance scale factor
- Rotate the AABB in case the axis swap of the model is activated
- Rotate the AABB according to the instance rotation (which is an OBB now)
- Generate a new AABB from the rotated ABB
- Translate the AABB to the instance position

At this point, the AABB encloses the instance.

Since blending and rotations are still expensive operations that may harm performance in scenes with many instances, a speed-up can be achieved by parallelizing the computations with SIMD operations of modern processors, like SSE or AVX. But even keeping the AABB lookup data on the GPU may be beneficial. Calculating the bounding boxes of all instances with a compute shader and downloading the results could be still faster than pure CPU calculation, despite the additional download of the results.

To achieve the best possible performance, you might want to implement different versions of the getAABB() method and profile the application with various scene sizes and complexities.

After the AABB is adjusted for the instance, we calculate the position and size of the two-dimensional bounding box for the quadtree:

```
glm::vec2 position =
  glm::vec2(instanceAABB.getMinPos().x,
  instanceAABB.getMinPos().z);
glm::vec2 size =
  glm::vec2(std::fabs(instanceAABB.getMaxPos().x -
  instanceAABB.getMinPos().x),
  std::fabs(instanceAABB.getMaxPos().z -
  instanceAABB.getMinPos().z));
```

Now, we have all the data to insert the instance into the quadtree:

```
BoundingBox2D box{position, size};
instances.at(i)->setBoundingBox(box);
mQuadtree->add(instSettings.isInstanceIndexPosition);
```

To make sure we create a working quadtree, we will add a new ImGui window containing the quadtree, including all subdivisions and instances. Seeing the quadtree in action helps a lot to find any implementation bugs.

Creating a window to show the quadtree plus contents

For the ImGui window, we create a new method called `createPositionsWindow()` in the `UserInterface` class. Inside this method, we create a new window by using `ImGui::Begin()`. Next, we retrieve the world boundaries to have the origin, size, and center point to draw.

Then, we iterate over all instances, using the position and size of the bounding box to draw ImGui rectangles at the 2D world positions of the instances. We also use the pairs of the `micInstanceCollisions` variable to draw non-colliding and colliding instances in different colors.

Finally, we retrieve the bounding boxes of the quadtree and all the subdivisions. To get the bounding boxes of all levels of the quadtree, we add a pair of `public` and `private` methods to the `Quadtree` class called `getTreeBoxes()`. The `getTreeBoxes()` method recursively iterates over the quadtree nodes and child nodes, storing the bounding boxes in a `std::vector` of `BoundingBox2D` elements. We draw all quadtree boxes by using white lines.

Figure 8.13 shows an example of the quadtree window:

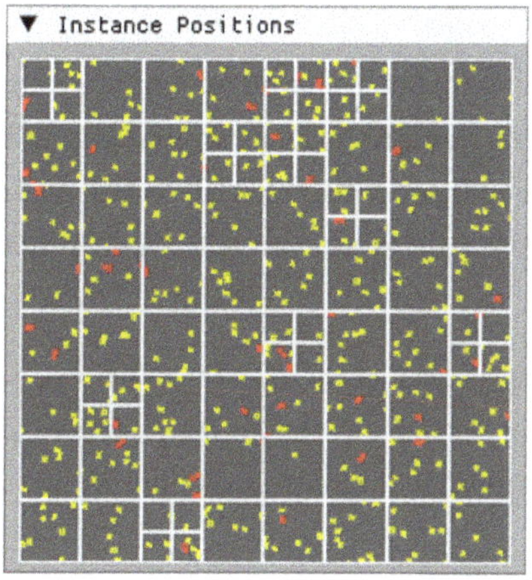

Figure 8.13: A quadtree with subdivisions, instances, and detected collisions

In *Figure 8.13*, the quadtree and all its subdivisions are drawn in white. The bounding boxes of a normal instance are drawn as yellow lines and colliding instances are drawn as red lines.

Filling the quadtree and drawing the result on the screen is only the first half of the collision detection; we also need to do something with the information of instances colliding in the virtual world.

Retrieving the colliding instances and reacting to collisions

Getting the list of all colliding instances out of the quadtree is done by calling findAllIntersections() of the mQuadtree object:

```
mModelInstCamData.micInstanceCollisions =
    mQuadtree->findAllIntersections();
```

We store the result in the new variable micInstanceCollisions in the ModelInstanceCamData struct to make the instance collisions available for other parts of the code (i.e., for debug drawing lines). The colliding instances are given to us as pairs of instances.

To see the results of a collision in the screen, we can iterate over the pairs of instances and rotate one or both instances:

```
for (const auto& instPairs :
    mModelInstCamData.micInstanceCollisions) {
  instances.at(instPairs.first)->rotateInstance(6.5f);
```

```
    instances.at(instPairs.second)->rotateInstance(-5.3f);
}
```

Walking or running into another instance should now rotate your instance, or your instance and the colliding instance. Even though the angle is small, it will be incremented for every frame where a collision between those instances is detected. At a normal frame rate of 60 or 75 FPS, you will see yourself instantly rotated away from the other instance, suddenly running in a different direction.

If you don't like having the instances just rotating on collisions, you can try to implement more complex reactions to collisions. Check out the *Practical sessions* section for a task about adding collision resolution and the *Additional resources* section for links to resources about collision avoidance.

Drawing the AABB debug lines

In the case that your instance or the other instance does not rotate and you can still walk right through other instances, drawing the AABB lines to the screen will become helpful.

To draw the debug lines in the renderer, we can use the pairs in `micInstanceCollisions`, retrieve the AABB lines from both affected instances, and add the vertices of the lines to a `private` variable called `mAABBMesh`. Then, we upload the vertex data to the line vertex buffer, and by using the line shader, we draw the AABBs to the screen:

```
mLineVertexBuffer.uploadData(*mAABBMesh);
mLineShader.use();
mLineVertexBuffer.bindAndDraw(GL_LINES, 0,
  mAABBMesh->vertices.size());
```

As an alternative solution, we can iterate over all instances and use the instance indices in the pairs in `micInstanceCollisions` to switch the color of the AABB to draw.

For more control over the AABB lines, a separate section in the ImGui **Control** window will be created. Combined with a new enum class called `collisionDebugDraws` and a bit more code in the `drawAABBs()` method in the renderer, you can switch between three different drawing modes:

- No AABBs
- Only the colliding AABBs in red
- All colliding AABBs in red and all other AABBs in yellow

Figure 8.14 shows an example of a detected collision, using yellow lines around non-colliding instances and red lines around the two colliding instances:

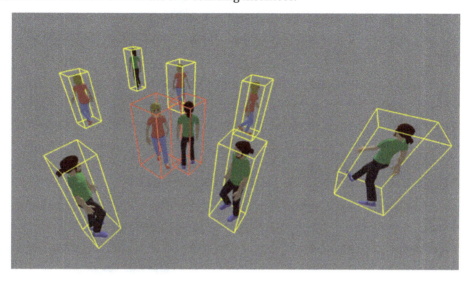

Figure 8.14: Two colliding instances among other non-colliding instances

Don't be alarmed if some of the instances behave strangely, like constantly rotating around themselves. The reaction to collisions with other instances and the world boundaries is still very basic (just a rotation). We will enhance the collision handling in *Chapter 9*.

After the quadtree is working and reduces the number of instances to check to a configurable minimum, we will start the implementation of one of the listed simplifications: By utilizing the nodes of the game character models as anchor points, bounding spheres have a good trade-off between creation and checking complexity.

So, let's go and add some spheres to the models.

Implementing bounding spheres

Bounding spheres as abstractions of higher detailed models can be used in different ways. One possible way is shown in *Figure 8.9*, where the sphere encloses the entire model. But as you can see in *Figure 8.9*, we would have a lot of empty space around the model, resulting in more false positives. Plus, we already have a method to do a broader check for possible collisions: the bounding boxes.

Instead, we will use the spheres to simplify the instances at a more detailed level by adding configurable bounding spheres to the model's nodes. Even though we would have to now check several dozens of spheres against the spheres of another instance, we are still way below the computational power we would need to check every single triangle of both models against each other.

The number of false positives will also remain at an acceptable level. As stated broadly in the *Simplifying the instances for faster collision checks* section, choosing between a higher detailed simplification and more computations or simpler abstractions and more false positive collision detections is a tradeoff we have to live with, but we can make the decision strategically.

Creating the data for the bounding spheres

To create the sphere data, we use the same first step as in the bounding box calculations. We use the compute shaders `assimp_instance_transform.comp` and `assimp_instance_matrix_mult.comp`, combined with replacing the bone offset matrices with identity matrices. The result of this shader run is an SSBO containing the node positions of all instances we want to equip with bounding spheres.

But, in contrast to the bounding boxes, we can use another compute shader to calculate the bounding spheres for the nodes. The third compute shader, called `assimp_instance_bounding_spheres.comp`, uses the TRS matrices of the nodes created by the previous compute shaders, the world position matrices from the instances, and the parent node indices to create a bounding sphere for every node of every instance.

Another SSBO called `SphereAdjustment` is used, containing a `vec4` for every node. These sphere adjustments can be set by a UI extension that maps the node names of the model to one `SliderFloat` and one `SliderFloat3`, allowing us to resize and move around the bounding spheres created by the shader. By carefully placing the bounding spheres, we can make sure to have as little empty space around the model that would be detected as collision.

Figure 8.15 shows the new UI section:

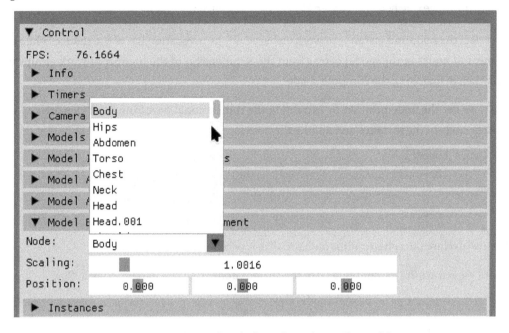

Figure 8.15: Fine-tuning the bounding spheres of a model

The SphereAdjustments SSBO is backed by a std::vector of glm::vec4 elements called msBoundingSphereAdjustments, placed in the ModelSettings struct. In the adjustments vector, each vec4 is split, using the first three elements for the position and the last element for the radius of each sphere.

And since it's a good idea to not have to tune the bounding spheres on every application restart, the contents of the msBoundingSphereAdjustments buffer are added to the YamlParser class to be able to save and restore the adjustments.

Both the addition to the user interface and to the YAML parser are more or less trivial, copied from already existing ImGui and YAML parsing code parts. You can explore the UserInterface and YamlParser classes to check out the code changes.

Our third compute shader, assimp_instance_bounding_spheres.comp, also reuses parts of other shaders. The top of the main() method is identical to the matrix multiplication compute shader:

```
void main() {
    uint node = gl_GlobalInvocationID.x;
    uint instance = gl_GlobalInvocationID.y;
```

```
uint numberOfBones = gl_NumWorkGroups.x;
uint index = node + numberOfBones * instance;
```

We select the node and instance to work on based on the invocation IDs of the shader, while the number of nodes in the model comes from the X dimension of the number of work groups we use when dispatching the compute shader.

Next, we get the node position by extracting the translational part from the TRS matrix of the specific node of the instance and adding the position from the sphere adjustment buffer:

```
vec3 nodePos =
  (worldPosMat[instance] * trsMat[index])[3].xyz;
nodePos += sphereAdjustment[node].xyz;
float radius = 1.0;
```

We also declare the sphere radius and initialize it with a default value.

Then, we extract the parent node ID of the current node from the parent index buffer:

```
int parentNode = parentIndex[node];
```

The parent node is used to switch between nodes that have a parent and the parent or unconnected, standalone nodes. If we find a valid parent, we calculate the world position of the parent node, including the position adjustment:

```
if (parentNode >= 0) {
  uint parentIndex = parentNode +
    numberOfBones * instance;
  vec3 parentPos =
    (worldPosMat[instance] * trsMat[parentIndex])[3].xyz;
  parentPos += sphereAdjustment[parentNode].xyz;
```

By using the node and parent position, we calculate the middle point between the node and its parent. We calculate the radius of the sphere – again, adjustable by the sphere adjustment value:

```
    vec3 center = mix(nodePos, parentPos, 0.5);
    radius = length(center - nodePos) *
      sphereAdjustment[node].w;
```

For the root node, we set the radius of the sphere to the adjustable value:

```
    } else {
      radius = sphereAdjustment[node].w;
    }
```

At the end of the main() method, we add a small check to disable small spheres already in the shader:

```
    if (radius < 0.05) {
      sphereData[index] = vec4(0.0);
    } else {
      sphereData[index] = vec4(nodePos, radius);
    }
  }
```

As we need to run the three compute shaders from several different places in the renderer code, we make our lives easier by adding the code to fill and run the shaders to a new method called runBoundingSphereComputeShaders.

Drawing bounding spheres

The second usage of the compute shaders for the bounding spheres is a debug display, similar to the AABBs. After running the compute shaders, we can use another new vertex and fragment shader pair to draw the spheres to the screen.

In the main() method of the new sphere-drawing vertex shader called sphere_instanced.vert, we extract the center and radius of the sphere:

```
  void main() {
    vec3 boneCenter = sphereData[gl_InstanceID].xyz;
    float radius = sphereData[gl_InstanceID].w;
```

To speed up the drawing, we will use an instanced drawing call for the rendering API, so we can use the special variable gl_InstanceID here (the variable gl_InstanceID was renamed to gl_InstanceIndex in Vulkan). Both OpenGL and Vulkan are internally incrementing the values of the variable gl_InstanceID respective gl_InstanceIndex for every instance, allowing us to draw thousands of bounding spheres from a single set of vertices.

Resizing the spheres to the correct radius is done by a small GLSL function called `createScaleMatrix()` in the shader, essentially creating a scaling matrix with the radius value in the main diagonal elements:

```
mat3 scaleMat = createScaleMatrix(radius);
```

Then, we scale the original position of the sphere vertex by the scaling matrix, add the sphere adjustment, create the final shader matrix by multiplication with `view` and `projection` matrices, and set the line color:

```
gl_Position = projection * view *
   vec4(scaleMat * aPos + boneCenter, 1.0);
lineColor = vec4(aColor, 1.0);
}
```

Running the sphere shader is done by calling an instanced version of the `Shader` class drawing command:

```
mLineVertexBuffer.uploadData(mSphereMesh);
mSphereShader.use();
mBoundingSphereBuffer.bind(1);
mLineVertexBuffer.bindAndDrawInstanced(GL_LINES, 0,
   mSphereMesh.vertices.size(), numberOfSpheres);
```

For the Vulkan renderer, the equivalent drawing calls are used (`vkCmdBindPipeline()`, `vkCmdBindVertexBuffers()`, `vkCmdBindDescriptorSets()`, and `VkCmdDraw()`).

Since the bounding spheres for collision detection may not be identical to the bounding spheres we want to draw on the screen, we use separate methods for drawing debug spheres. The main difference between our debug draw methods is the creation of the list of instances to feed the compute shaders with.

We could draw bounding spheres only on the selected instance by calling `drawSelectedBoundingSpheres()`, show the bounding boxes for instances with collisions by calling `drawCollidingBoundingSpheres()`, or create "fluffy white snowballs" around all instances in the screen, as in *Figure 8.16*, by calling `drawAllBoundingSpheres()`.

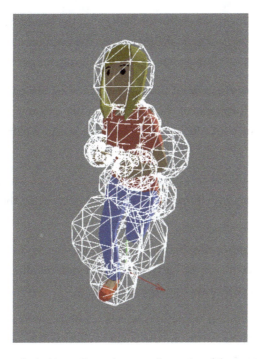

Figure 8.16: Adjusted bounding spheres on the nodes of the woman's model

Now that we are able to calculate and draw bounding spheres for the models, let's add the spheres as a second tier to the collision detection code.

Using the bounding spheres for collision detection

The colliding instances from the quadtree are collected in the renderer by calling findAllIntersections() and saved to micInstanceCollisions, as already stated in the *Retrieving the colliding instances and reacting to the collision* section:

```
mModelInstCamData.micInstanceCollisions =
  mQuadtree->findAllIntersections();
```

To make the collision detection code easier to maintain, we move the intersection extraction call to a new method called checkForInstanceCollisions(). This new method will be the starting point for all code related to collision detection and handling.

Our first step to extend collision detection is done by calling the above findAllIntersections() method to get all colliding instances from the quadtree. Then, we split up the instances by model into separate sets of int. Using separate lists of colliding instances per model is needed because different models may have a different number of nodes.

Then, for every set of instances, we create the SSBO with the bounding spheres and extract the sphere data to a map of `glm::ve4` vectors. We will use the instance index position as the key for the map, splitting up the SSBO into a map containing all spheres per instance as values.

The real collision check for the bounding spheres is done by comparing all spheres from one colliding instance with all spheres of the second colliding instance. We already reduced the number of these checks by a lot, since we only have the instance pairs left that were delivered by the quadtree.

But even if checking the spheres for collisions is an easy task and we just have to compare the distance between the centers with the sum of the radii of both spheres, the number of comparisons will make this check slow.

Even with a shortcut to remove all spheres with a radius of zero and stopping to compare when a collision has been detected, a check between two just-not-colliding instances with 30 active spheres per model will need 900 such comparisons.

Speeding up the sphere compare operations with a compute shader is possible, but problems like different node counts for each instance in a pair to check will raise the complexity and lower the efficiency of a compute shader.

While the parallel computation on the GPU may be fast, uploading and downloading the data and running the shader for a single pair of instances may add a significant delay, nullifying the acceleration of the compute shader.

So, we stick with the CPU-based solution to calculate the second tier of the collisions between bounding boxes. Unless we have thousands of instances in a very small virtual world or many instances in a small part of the world, the overall number of collision checks will remain low.

Figure 8.17 shows an example of a collision detected by the bounding boxes (drawn with red lines), and an additional collision of any of the bounding spheres (also in red):

Figure 8.17: A collision was detected by the bounding spheres of the instances

Handling collision remains identical to the reaction of collisions with bounding boxes in the *Retrieving the colliding instances and reacting to collisions* section – we simply rotate the colliding instances about a fixed angle in every frame. We will enhance the reaction to collisions in *Chapter 9* and *Chapter 12*.

Collision detection is a complex topic with many algorithms and choices based on your application's specific needs. We need to know what kind of objects we need to check to select a good shape of an abstraction, and depending on the complexity of the abstraction, we may need to adjust the algorithm (or algorithms) to use when trying to find collisions. We did not even touch the collision resolution part that resolves the collision by moving the instances apart after an intersection was detected. If you want to dive deeper into the world of game physics, collision detection, and collision resolution, check out the books in the *Additional resources* section.

Summary

In this chapter, we explored collision detection and created a two-tier collision detection for the application. We started by discussing the shortcomings of a naive solution, then we explored spatial partitioning methods and model simplifications to lower the number of checks we have to do until we are quite sure which instances really have some collisions. Finally, we implemented a quadtree with bounding boxes and bounding spheres to find out which instances collide.

In the next chapter, we will create "real" **non-player characters (NPCs)** and let the instances come to life by adding configurable behavior. We will start by exploring the nature of behavior trees and their relation to the decision-making of NPCs, and we will implement code to support behavior trees for our instances. As the last step, we will look at the interaction between models as a specialized set of the general behavior.

Practical sessions

Here are some additions you could make to the code:

- Add UI controls for the quadtree configuration.

  Currently, the quadtree is statically initialized during the renderer `init()` call. Add UI controls and a setter callback function to adjust the maximum number of instances before splitting up the box and the maximum depth of the tree.

- Add UI controls to configure the world borders.

  The instances are running around in the virtual world, and if one instance reaches the virtual border set in `mWorldBoundaries`, it will be rotated to stay inside the boundaries. Add some sliders and callbacks to control the origin and size of the virtual world, and make sure the **Instance Positions** window will be updated, too.

- Implement an octree plus three-dimensional AABB checks.

  Right now, we are using only two-dimensional bounding boxes for the instances, just as if the instances were seen top-down. Extend the quadtree to become an octree and add three-dimensional intersection checks between the AABBs of the instances.

- Speed up the bounding sphere collision check.

  Due to the general complexity of the checks – we have to check every sphere of the first instance against every sphere of the second instance – the collision check is quite slow. Maybe a compute shader can help here. In contrast to the bounding box generation, we need only a single yes/no answer per instance to signal if a collision occurred. Using an atomic counter per sphere or instance could help avoid lengthy post-processing work after the computer shader has done its job.

- Add a simple bounding volume hierarchy.

  Instead of checking all spheres of both instances, you could add some unused nodes to the models and add bigger bounding spheres to these nodes, enclosing some of the smaller spheres. Check the spheres by starting with the largest spheres for both instances. If these large spheres don't collide, all spheres inside the larger sphere can never have a collision, and the entire part of the body could be skipped for the next collision checks.

- Enhanced difficulty: Do a real triangle-to-triangle check between the instances.

  This is the ultimate goal in collision detection. By checking the instances for real intersections, not just some AABBs or bounding spheres, natural-looking collision behavior could be achieved. Also, make note of the benefits of this method and see whether the extra precision benefits the runtime behavior.

- Enhanced difficulty: Add collision resolution.

  When the collision check signals a collision between two instances, it's already too late – the instances are partially intersected. Good collision detection comes with collision resolution where the instances are moved apart when a collision is found. Several books have been written about collision detection and collision resolution; see the *Additional resources* section for some well-known titles. There are still many caveats on the path to "making it right."

Additional resources

- Separating Axis Theorem: `https://dyn4j.org/2010/01/sat/`
- Gilbert–Johnson–Keerthi distance algorithm: `https://cse442-17f.github.io/Gilbert-Johnson-Keerthi-Distance-Algorithm/`
- Template-based quadtree implementation: `https://github.com/pvigier/Quadtree`
- Collision Detection in Interactive 3D Environments: ISBN 978-1558608016
- Real-Time Collision Detection: ISBN 978-1558607323
- Game Physics Engine Development: ISBN 978-0123819765
- Game Physics: ISBN 978-0123749031
- Collision Avoidance: `https://code.tutsplus.com/understanding-steering-behaviors-collision-avoidance--gamedev-7777t`
- More about Collision Avoidance: `https://www.gameaipro.com/GameAIPro2/GameAIPro2_Chapter19_Guide_to_Anticipatory_Collision_Avoidance.pdf`

Join our community on Discord

Join our community's Discord space for discussions with the author and other readers:

`https://packt.link/cppgameanimation`

9

Adding Behavior and Interaction

Welcome to *Chapter 9*! In the previous chapter, we took a deeper look into collision detection. After a discussion about the complexity of finding colliding instances in the virtual world, we explored ways to speed up the collision search by adding world partitioning and model simplifications. Then, we implemented a quadtree to split up the world into smaller areas, and we added bounding boxes and bounding spheres for the instances. Finally, we used both the quadtree and the instance boundaries to detect a collision between instances.

In this chapter, we will add some sort of "real-life" behavior to the instances, giving them the ability to walk around the virtual world by themselves and react to events like the collisions we added in the previous chapter. First, we will take a brief look at behavior trees and state machines and how both works. Then, we will add a visual editor to visually represent the state machines of the instances themselves. At the end of the chapter, we will extend the code to execute the behavior changes from the created node trees, and we will add interaction as an additional form of behavior.

In this chapter, we will cover the following topics:

- Structures to control instance behavior
- Adding a visual node editor
- Extending the code to support behavior changes
- Adding interaction between instances

Technical requirements

The example code can be found in the folder chapter09, in the subfolder 01_opengl_behavior for OpenGL and 02_vulkan_behavior for Vulkan.

Structures to control instance behavior

In the early days of computer games, the behavior of enemies and other **non-player characters** (**NPCs**) was rather simple. Based on only the game state or a few properties, like *The player has eaten a large dot, I must stay away from them!* (Pac-Man) or *I saw the player, so I will attack them!* (many first-person shooters), the computer counterparts were acting only with a small set of rules.

Later, control structures like "plain" state machines, hierarchical state machines, and behavior trees changed the **artificial intelligence** (**AI**) in games a lot, since it became easy to model complex tasks for enemies and NPCs. Now, it is possible to not only create more alternatives for behavior choices but also let computer-controlled world inhabitants act more like intelligent beings. Spotting the player may lead to a handful of different outcomes from NPCs, based on world factors, their own properties, and a bit of randomness.

A behavior tree simplifies creating behaviors for NPCs and helps reasoning about the states the NPC will be in at any given time. Still, a behavior tree is only an enhanced finite state machine with nodes and links between nodes. The current state of the tree is memorized by the behavior subsystem, and based on configured factors in the nodes, state changes to subsequent nodes in the tree are executed. Without huge complexity, behavior trees are easy to implement but still powerful in games.

A common way to create a behavior tree is by using specialized nodes, for instance:

- Selectors, choosing one among a set of options
- Sequences, running tasks in a specific order
- Conditions, using the outcome of previous nodes to choose the next node
- Loops, which repeat a part of the tree several times until a condition is met
- Actions, which affect the character state or perform an action, like attacking
- World perception, changing behavior based on events or world properties

Using special nodes helps a lot in building a flexible behavior tree. The enemy or NPC can gather information about the world and other objects in it and choose a different path on the next tree execution if the world around it changes, leading to a more reactive, believable, and less robotic behavior by not doing the same moves and actions repeatedly.

Figure 9.1 shows a simple idea for an NPC behavior:

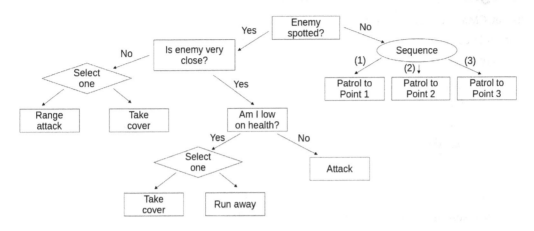

Figure 9.1: A simple behavior plan

Even though the plan looks straightforward, it encapsulates sophisticated behavior. Considering the enemy's distance and health status while scanning the plan for the desired behavior should result in fairly impressive NPC actions. By switching, with random variations, between taking cover and a range attack, directly attacking approaching enemies, or just trying to hide or run away as the last option, watching a group of these NPCs fighting incoming enemies would be entertaining.

We will add a simple state machine to control the behavior of the instances in this chapter. Also, to simplify creating and controlling the behavior with the state machine, we will add a tool to create nodes and links. So, let's go on a short detour and add a visual node editor to the application.

Adding a visual node editor

Like in the previous chapters, we will use an open-source tool to build our visual node editor instead of building our own solutions by hand. There are several ImGui-based node editors available. You can find a curated list in the *Additional resources* section.

In this chapter, we will use the extension called **imnodes** by Johann "Nelarius" Muszynski. The source code for imnodes is available on GitHub:

```
https://github.com/Nelarius/imnodes
```

Like in the previous chapters, we will use CMake to fetch imnodes for us.

Integrating imnodes by using CMake

To let CMake manage imnodes as a dependency, add a new `FetchContent` block to the file `CMakeLists.txt` in the project root between the `FetchContent` block for `stbi` and the `WIN32`-only area:

```
FetchContent_Declare(
  imnodes
  GIT_REPOSITORY https://github.com/Nelarius/imnodes
  GIT_TAG v0.5
)
```

We will use the Git tag `v0.5` here to avoid problems introduced by new commits to the `master` branch, resulting in not finding the ImGui source code.

Next, we make the imnodes code available and let CMake populate the variable for the source folder:

```
FetchContent_MakeAvailable(imnodes)
FetchContent_GetProperties(imnodes)
if(NOT imnodes_POPULATED)
  FetchContent_Populate(imnodes)
  add_subdirectory(${imnodes_SOURCE_DIR} EXCLUDE_FROM_ALL)
endif()
```

Then, we append the source directory variable for imnodes to the list of already existing external source files and include directories:

```
file(GLOB SOURCES
  ...
  ${imnodes_SOURCE_DIR}/imnodes.cpp
)
...
target_include_directories(... ${imnodes_SOURCE_DIR})
```

As a last step, we add a compiler definition to the existing `add_definitions` line:

```
add_definitions(... -DIMGUI_DEFINE_MATH_OPERATORS)
```

By setting `IMGUI_DEFINE_MATH_OPERATORS`, ImGui exposes some of the internal mathematical operations to external modules like imnodes.

After running CMake, which most IDEs will perform automatically after saving the `CMakeLists.txt` file, imnodes is available and can be included in the user interface. Now, let us learn how to work with imnodes.

Using imnodes to create UI elements

Since imnodes is based on ImGui, imnodes function calls are like ImGui calls, with imnodes acting as a container to enclose the UI elements in a graphical node representation. A graphical node, like the wait node shown in *Figure 9.2*, can be added and removed dynamically to a node editor window, and links between input and output pins can be created.

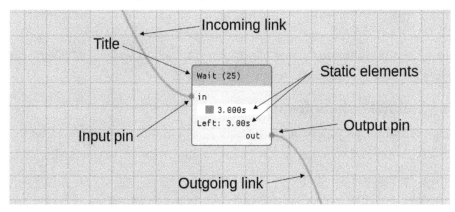

Figure 9.2: The elements of a simple imnodes wait node

Elements of a node are the title bar and an arbitrary number of input pins, output pins, and static elements. In the title bar, a descriptive name to identify the node type is shown, like the word **Wait** in *Figure 9.2*. The input pin of the wait node is used to connect parent node(s) to this specific node, and on the output pin, one or more child nodes can be connected. All user controls are built using static elements, such as the slider for the time to wait, or the text field showing the time running toward 0 if the wait node was activated.

But imnodes only maintains the nodes and links. We must implement the logic behind the node editor according to our needs. To get a better impression of how much – or how little – effort is needed to create such a node editor, we will walk through the steps needed to draw a node like in *Figure 9.2* to the screen.

Creating the imnodes context

Like ImGui, imnodes needs a basic set of data about the current session, that is, the context. The imnodes context must be created after ImGui's context, as imnodes relies on data from ImGui. So, the init() method of the UserInterface class will be extended by the CreateContext() call of imnodes:

```
ImGui::CreateContext();
ImNodes::CreateContext();
```

imnodes' context needs to be destroyed before ImGui's context. To do that, we call DestroyContext() of imnodes before ImGui's DestroyContext() in the cleanup() method of the UserInterface class:

```
ImNodes::DestroyContext();
ImGui::DestroyContext();
```

With the context ready, we can start to use the function calls to imnodes. Similar to the ImGui namespace, the ImNodes namespace will be used as a prefix.

Setting default values for imnodes

Choosing a global color style can be done exactly like in ImGui. For instance, to set the "light" color style for ImGui and imnodes, use the following lines in the init() method:

```
ImGui::StyleColorsLight();
ImNodes::StyleColorsLight();
```

Another call in the init() method of the UserInterface class can be made to set the modifier key used to detach links from a node. By default, imnodes uses the Alt key to detach a link. With the following two lines, we can set the key binding to use the Control key instead:

```
ImNodesIO& io = ImNodes::GetIO();
io.LinkDetachWithModifierClick.Modifier =
  &ImGui::GetIO().KeyCtrl;
```

After we change the defaults (or not), the node editor window itself will be created.

Creating the node editor

Like any other ImGui element, the node editor must be created inside an ImGui window. We call BeginNodeEditor() right after the start of a new ImGui window:

```
ImGui::Begin("Node editor");
ImNodes::BeginNodeEditor();
```

Now you should see a window with a visible grid – the node editor. All imnodes and ImGui calls are available in this context, although it is not possible to draw ImGui elements directly onto the node editor as they will overlay the node editor elements.

To end the node editor and the ImGui window, we call `EndNodeEditor()` just before ending the ImGui window. If we want to have a transparent mini map of the entire node editor window shown on the top left of the window, we can call `MiniMap()` before ending the editor:

```
ImNodes::MiniMap();
ImNodes::EndNodeEditor();
ImGui::End();
```

At this point, the node editor window will look like *Figure 9.3*:

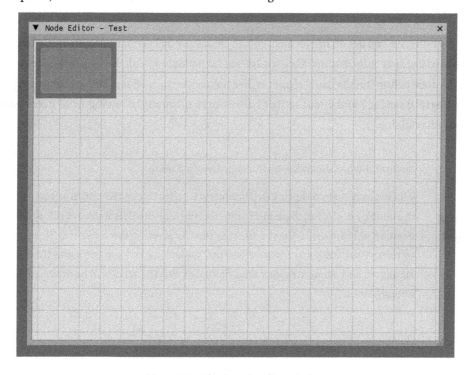

Figure 9.3: A fresh node editor window

Inside the node editor window, new nodes can be created. For a small example, we will hardcode all properties into the node. In the section *Extending the node editor*, a context menu will be added, allowing us to create and delete nodes at runtime.

Adding a simple node

A new node can be started by calling `BeginNode()`, using an `int` value as the unique identification for the node:

```
const int nodeId = 1;
ImNodes::BeginNode(nodeId);
ImGui::Text("Sample Node");
ImNodes::EndNode();
```

Like in ImGui itself, all imnodes UI elements must have a unique ID set to be distinguishable by ImGui. Internally, imnodes uses the `ImGui::PushID()` call to set the ID for the group containing the node data. We only need to take care that all elements in the node editor have unique identifications set.

Inside the node, we can use all ImGui elements to create control elements. Some ImGui elements may behave unexpectedly. For instance, an `ImGui::Separator()` call draws a line up to the right end of the node editor. But the usual elements, like text, buttons, or sliders, are working as expected. Calling `BeginDisable()` and `EndDisable()` also works normally, allowing us to make parts of the node unavailable.

Be careful when disabling ImGui elements in a node

While it may seem tempting to completely remove unneeded ImGui elements from the node by enclosing them in `if` statements, be aware that imnodes calculates the position of input and output pins from the IDs given to the attributes. If you want to remove attributes or ImGui elements, make sure to keep the same IDs for the attributes and elements remaining visible, or else the links will be attached at the wrong places.

Figure 9.4 shows the result of the previously found lines of code:

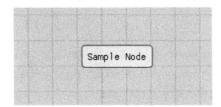

Figure 9.4: The sample node

Besides being movable by holding the left mouse button, our new node is not useful. So, let us add some elements to the node, called "attributes" in imnodes.

Creating imnodes attributes and ImGui elements in a node

All attributes for a node must be defined between `BeginNode()` and `EndNode()`. Make sure to skip the `ImGui::Text()` line from the section *Adding a simple node* as it will destroy the layout of the node.

The first imnodes attribute we add is a node title, by using `BeginNodeTitleBar()`:

```
ImNodes::BeginNodeTitleBar();
ImGui::TextUnformatted("A cool node title");
ImNodes::EndNodeTitleBar();
```

The title is shown in a separate area at the top of the node and shows if it is unselected, hovered over, or selected.

Next, we create an input pin by calling `BeginInputAttribute()`:

```
const int inputId = 2;
ImNodes::BeginInputAttribute(inputId);
ImGui::Text("in");
ImNodes::EndInputAttribute();
```

An input node definition creates a "magnetic" dot on the left side of the node, allowing us later to connect links. A node can have from zero to virtually unlimited input pins, but most probably, only a few pins will be used.

After the input pin, we use `BeginStaticAttribute()` to create a static attribute:

```
const int staticId = 3;
static bool checkboxState = false;
ImNodes::BeginStaticAttribute(staticId);
ImGui::Checkbox("A fancy checkbox", &checkboxState);
ImNodes::EndStaticAttribute();
```

Static attributes have no input or output connectors on the sides of the node. You can use a static attribute just like every other control element in an ImGui window.

Finally, we add an output pin with `BeginOutputAttribute()`:

```
const int outId = 4;
ImNodes::BeginOutputAttribute(outId);
ImGui::Text("                   out");
ImNodes::EndOutputAttribute();
```

Like input pins, output pins create a connector to dock links. But for output pins, this connector is on the right side of the node.

In *Figure 9.5*, the resulting node created by the code lines in this section is shown:

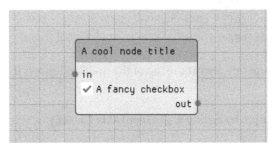

Figure 9.5: The updated example node

The updated node already looks great. We have a title, input and output pins, and a checkbox controlled by a stateful variable – all in just about twenty lines of code.

Connecting nodes with links is also simple, as we will see now.

Maintaining links between nodes

Links in imnodes have three properties: a unique link ID, a start pin ID, and an end pin ID. The unique link ID is needed to identify and draw the link itself, and the pin IDs are taken from the output pin of the parent (or source) node respective to the input pin of the child (or destination) node.

By combining these three IDs, links in imnodes are best managed as pairs of pin IDs in a map of link IDs:

```
std::map<int, std::pair<int, int>> links;
```

The inner `std::pair` stores the IDs of the start pin (output) and the end pin (input) of a link, in that order. With the outer `std::map`, we create a connection between the link ID and the pair of pin IDs.

Output first, input second

It is noteworthy to say that imnodes strictly follows this order. The first reported pin is always the output pin of the parent node, and the second pin is the input pin of the child node. Following this rule makes it easy to use nodes and links to create a finite state machine, maintaining the state of the node tree with a bunch of simple rules.

Drawing the existing nodes can be done by calling `Link()` with exactly the three link properties mentioned earlier in the section:

```
for (const auto& link : links) {
  ImNodes::Link(link.first,
    link.second.first, link.second.second);
}
```

All links in the map are now drawn as lines with curves at both ends, connecting the output pin of the parent node (first element of the pair) and the input pin of the child node (second element of the pair).

New nodes are signaled from imnodes *after* the editor has been ended by calling `EndNodeEditor()`. Then, two imnodes calls can be used to create or delete links.

Whether or not a new link was created in the editor in the current frame can be requested by calling `IsLinkCreated()`:

```
int startId, endId;
if (ImNodes::IsLinkCreated(&startId, &endId)) {
  linkId = findNextFreeLinkId();
  links[linkId] = (std::make_pair(startId, endId));
}
```

If `IsLinkCreated()` returns true, the user made a new link between two nodes, and we can save the new link to the map. How `findNextFreeLinkId()` searches for a new link ID depends on the needs of the application. You can check out the example code, a simple implementation that reuses IDs from deleted links.

If an existing link was disconnected and then dropped, `IsLinkDestroyed()` returns true, giving back the ID of the dropped link as an output parameter:

```
int linkId;
if (ImNodes::IsLinkDestroyed(&linkId)) {
   links.erase(linkId);
}
```

imnodes has some other functions enabling custom link management, but for our node editor, `IsLinkCreated()` and `IsLinkDestroyed()` will be sufficient.

Duplicating the code for our example node (remember to use unique IDs for every attribute) and adding a link between the output pin ID of the first node and the input ID of the second node will result in something similar to *Figure 9.6*:

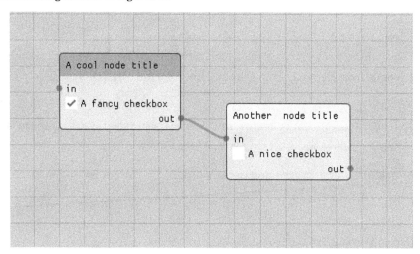

Figure 9.6: Two example nodes connected by a link

You will have to move the nodes apart since all new nodes are created in the same spot by default. Next to setting the initial position when creating a node, imnodes allows us to store the positions of all nodes in the current editor session by using `SaveCurrentEditorStateToIn iString()`. Restoring the positions can be achieved later by calling `LoadCurrentEditorStateF romIniString()`.

Having the nodes in the same place when reopening the editor helps to create a great user experience.

Now that we have explored how to manage the graphical part of the node editor using imnodes, we need to create a class to store state information and the imnodes draw calls. These new classes are the building blocks for the finite state machine driving the instance behavior.

Creating graph node classes

The basic element of node tree classes is an abstract class called GraphNodeBase, located in the new folder graphnodes. All other node classes will inherit from the base class, adding attributes and logic for specific tasks that the node has to take care of.

In contrast to a *full-featured* behavior tree, our simplified version will store the state of nodes in the nodes itself. Maintaining the node state in a separate part of the code would make the implementation more complex and harder to understand. The only drawback of using an integrated state is to make a copy of the entire node tree for every instance, as the node tree itself is used as the finite state machine. But node objects are small; adding a few nodes per instance creates a negligible overhead in memory space and compute time.

Before we dive into more details, here is a list of all the node types created in the example code for this chapter:

- **Root Node**

  The root node is the starting point of every node tree, created by default. It is not possible to remove the root node as it's the starting point of the entire tree. At the start of the execution of the finite state machine, the root node is activated first. Also, when no other nodes are active, the root node is triggered again to start over. Since there is no need to trigger the root node by some other node, the root node has only an output pin but no input pin.

- **Test Node**

  The test node helps develop and debug node trees. Like the root node, only an output pin is available, plus a button to activate the output pin.

- **DebugLog Node**

  This is another node to help build a node tree. Currently, node trees attached to an instance cannot be loaded into the editor for a live-debugging session. A task for implementing the ability to load an existing node tree into the editor window is available in the *Practical sessions* section. To watch specific actions, a debug log node can be added, printing a line to the system console when activated.

- **Wait Node**

  The wait node was already shown as an example in *Figure 9.2*. The node will delay the execution between two other nodes by a configurable time.

- **RandomWait Node**

  This is like the wait node, but an upper and lower limit can be set to the delay time, enabling a bit more random behavior.

- **Selector Node**

  The selector node also has a fixed delay, and after the delay time is up, a random output pin is activated.

- **Sequence Node**

  A sequence node activates the output pins one after the other, starting with pin number one. As an extra feature, the sequence node will wait for the child node on the active output to finish. Waiting for a child is currently only implemented for the two wait node types; more types or a cascade with grandchild nodes can be added. See the section *Practical sessions* for ideas.

- **Action Node**

  We added actions in *Chapter 7*. An action node allows us to trigger actions just like we did in *Chapter 7* while controlling the instance with a keyboard and mouse, enabling the instances to not just walk around but jump, roll, punch, or wave, based on the state of the node tree.

- **Event Node**

  An event node is triggered by an external event sent to the instance, for instance, when a collision happens. The event node also has a cooldown timer to ignore the same event for a small amount of time, avoiding erratic behavior by doing the same action on every update of the tree again if the event keeps being sent to the instance.

- **Instance Movement Node**

  The instance node allows us to control movement state and movement direction, instance speed, and instance rotation within the node tree. Using an instance node is required to change between the main movement states, like idle, walking, and running. In addition, both speed and rotation can be randomized within the upper and lower limits to enable a more nondeterministic behavior.

In *Figure 9.7*, all these nodes are shown:

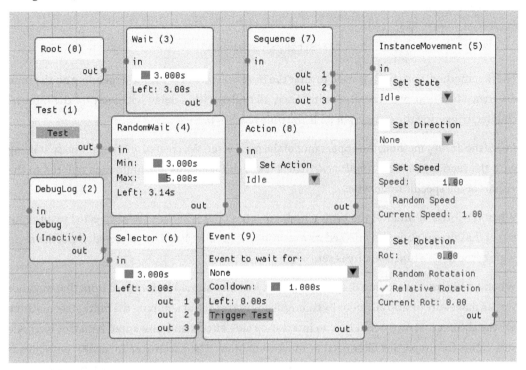

Figure 9.7: An overview of all nodes created for the example code

The number next to the node type is the numerical node ID. In case of errors, or when using a DebugLog node, having the node ID at hand may be beneficial.

Now let's check the most important parts of the GraphNodeBase class.

Exploring the base class for graph nodes

To ensure derived node classes are implementing a minimum set of functionalities, the GraphNodeBase class has several pure virtual methods declared in the header file GraphNodeBase.h in the folder graphnodes:

```
virtual void update(float deltaTime) = 0;
virtual void draw(ModelInstanceCamData modInstCamData) = 0;
virtual void activate() = 0;
virtual void deactivate(bool informParentNodes = true) = 0;
virtual bool isActive() = 0;
virtual std::shared_ptr<GraphNodeBase> clone() = 0;
```

```
virtual std::optional<std::map<std::string, std::string>>
  exportData() = 0;
virtual void importData(
  std::map<std::string, std::string> data) = 0;
```

The first method, update(), is used to alter the internal state of the node depending on the time difference between two frames. For instance, all nodes with a delay will decrease the internal counter, triggering the output pin once the time reaches 0.

Inside the draw() method, the appearance of the node is set. We created an example node starting with the section *Adding a simple node*. The draw() call contains all commands tailored to the visuals of the specific node type.

When the internal timer of the timing nodes reaches 0, or when a node connected to an input pin of the current node has finished its execution, activate() will be triggered. Here, the main logic of the node's functionality is set.

When a node tree controlling the behavior of an instance should be removed from that instance, we can make sure to stop all nodes by calling deactivate(). Not stopping the finite state machine for the current instance could lead to interesting side effects and unwanted behavior if a node sets values for properties like speed or movement state. The parameter informParentNodes is used to distinguish between an ordered shutdown of a node, i.e., notifying a parent node of type Sequence that the child node has finished execution, and a *full stop*, when all further actions should be avoided.

By using isActive(), the controlling code of the finite state machine can check if at least one node is still actively doing something, like waiting for a timer to reach 0. As soon as no active node is left, the root node will be triggered.

The clone() method is needed to create a copy of the current instance of a node, containing all settings. Since we are using inheritance, using a copy constructor to achieve the same result would be hard due to missing access to private members. A virtual cloning method makes our lives much easier, resulting in a 1:1 copy.

Finally, exportData() and importData() are used to get and set the current state of any node instance with any values set that are worth saving and restoring. Internally, the values of a node type are stored in a std::string map, avoiding more than one data type in the map. Also, using simple strings inside the YAML parser removes any conversion when interacting with the raw text data on disk. The graph node types know how to encode and decode the data, moving the node-specific save and load logic away from the YAML parser.

In addition to the pure virtual methods, a small number of non-pure virtual functions are declared and defined in the GraphNodeBase.h header. These methods are only useful for a small subset of node types. So, forcing all node types to implement the functionality makes no sense.

The first three methods, addOutputPin, delOutputPin, and getNumOutputPins, are used to handle the dynamic number of output pins on the Sequence and Selector nodes:

```
virtual void addOutputPin() {};
virtual int delOutputPin() { return 0; };
virtual int getNumOutputPins() { return 0; };
```

All three method names speak for themselves. Only the return value of delOutputPin() may need an explanation: when removing an output pin from a node, we must check if any links were connected to that pin. By returning the pin ID of the just-deleted output pin, all connected links can be removed by searching the map of links for the specific output node and deleting all affected links from the link map.

The other three virtual methods, childFinishedExecution, listensToEvent, and handleEvent, are even more special:

```
virtual void childFinishedExecution() {};
virtual bool listensToEvent(nodeEvent event)
  { return false; };
virtual void handleEvent() { };
```

The Sequence node type waits for the child node(s) connected to its output pins to report that they have finished execution. Both the Wait and RandomWait nodes will inform their parent node about a status change by calling childFinishedExecution().

Only the event node implements the last two methods, listensToEvent() and handleEvent(). Both method names should be self-explanatory. The split into two separate methods can be useful if some preparations need to be done between checking if a node would handle an event and the real event execution.

As an example for a derived class, we will check some implementation details of the wait node.

Creating the wait node

When constructing a new wait node, some defaults are set:

```
WaitNode::WaitNode(int nodeId, float waitTime) :
    GraphNodeBase(nodeId) {
```

```
    int id = nodeId * 1000;
    mInId = id;
    mStaticIdStart = id + 100;
    mOutId = id + 200;
    mWaitTime = waitTime;
    mCurrentTime = mWaitTime;
}
```

We are using a predefined range of attribute IDs here to simplify further coding and help debug issues. By multiplying the node ID by 1000, each node creates space for up to 1000 IDs per node, usable for input and output pins, or static elements like sliders and buttons. The number of nodes per tree is only limited by the storage capacity of an int, and we also recycle deleted node IDs – that's more than enough for nodes and pins, even for very large node trees. In addition, by simply doing an integer division of any pin ID by 1000, we get the node ID containing that specific pin. This is the perfect solution to identify the node when sending signals to the pins.

Cloning the wait node requires only a single line of code:

```
std::shared_ptr<GraphNodeBase> WaitNode::clone() {
    return std::make_shared<WaitNode>(*this);
}
```

This kind of virtual cloning is widely used and enables us to make an exact copy of that wait node, including all node-specific settings.

The draw() method code can be skipped since we just use a slider as the control element instead of the checkbox. Most of the draw() code is identical to the code in the sections *Adding a simple node* and *Creating imnodes attributes and ImGui elements in a node*, so we can skip the details here.

A call to activate() starts the wait timer. The private Boolean member variable mActive is set to true, and another private Boolean called mFired is set to false:

```
void WaitNode::activate() {
    if (mActive) {
        return;
    }
    mActive = true;
    mFired = false;
}
```

We use mFired only to change the color of the output pin from white to green, signaling in the editor window that the wait node has notified any node connected to the output pin.

Once mAcive is set to true, the update() method starts decrementing the wait time in mCurrentTime:

```
void WaitNode::update(float deltaTime) {
  if (!mActive) {
    return;
  }
  mCurrentTime -= deltaTime;
```

After the wait time is below 0, trigger signals for both the input and the output pin are sent out, the wait time is reset, the node is deactivated, and the color of the output pin changes:

```
  if (mCurrentTime <= 0.0f)
      fireNodeOutputTriggerCallback(mOutId);
      fireNodeOutputTriggerCallback(mInId);
      mCurrentTime = mWaitTime;
      mActive = false;
      mFired = true;
  }
}
```

The reason for triggering the input pin was discussed in the section *Creating graph node classes*: if the wait node is a child of a sequence node, the parent sequence node needs to know that the wait node is no longer active.

Finally, exporting and importing data is done by the two methods, exportData() and importData():

```
std::optional<std::map<std::string, std::string>>
    WaitNode::exportData() {
  std::map<std::string, std::string> data{};
  data["wait-time"] = std::to_string(mWaitTime);
  return data;
}
void WaitNode::importData(
    std::map<std::string, std::string> data) {
  mWaitTime = std::stof(data["wait-time"]);
  mCurrentTime = mWaitTime;
}
```

Both methods are straightforward. We just store the float in a std::string on exporting and read back the float value on importing.

All other specialized nodes are created in a similar way, implementing the required methods and enhancing the other virtual methods if needed.

Another well-known coding style from the application is using callbacks to call methods in other classes. GraphNodeBase uses two callbacks to handle events.

Using callbacks to propagate changes

By activating the first callback, a node informs the finite state machine that it has finished its execution, and the control should be given to the nodes connected to the output pin(s):

```
fireNodeOutputCallback mNodeCallbackFunction;
```

The method that handles this callback is the main part of the state management when advancing the status of the nodes.

Real behavior changes happen in the method executed by the second callback:

```
nodeActionCallback mNodeActionCallbackFunction;
```

This callback is used by the instance and action node types, informing, after quite a long callback cascade, the renderer class to manipulate a single property of the instance owning the node tree that started the callback.

Here is where all the magic happens, letting the instance mode change the movement state to walk or run, or start an action like jumping or waving the hand.

We will now take a closer look at more code that will make use of both callbacks.

Creating a behavior struct and a storage class for the instances

To store nodes, links, and the action callback, the new struct BehaviorData will be used, residing in the file BehaviorData.h in the model folder:

```
struct BehaviorData {
  std::vector<std::shared_ptr<GraphNodeBase>>
    bdGraphNodes{};
  std::unordered_map<int, std::pair<int, int>>
    bdGraphLinks{};
```

```
    std::string bdEditorSettings;
    nodeActionCallback bdNodeActionCallbackFunction{};
};
```

Nodes and links are stored in basic STL containers, and we also store the editor setting string in the struct, enabling us to save and restore the node positions in the node editor window. The nodeActionCallback callback is only needed in an intermediate fashion to create a link chain between the callbacks in the nodes and the class storing the behavior data struct itself.

The new class SingleInstanceBehavior is used to collect all data and methods for the behavior control of a single instance. Here, we create the chain for the nodeActionCallback callback by setting the callback function of the BehaviorData struct to the local method nodeActionCallback():

```
mBehaviorData->bdNodeActionCallbackFunction = [this]
    (graphNodeType nodeType, instanceUpdateType updateType,
    nodeCallbackVariant data, bool extraSetting) {
  nodeActionCallback(nodeType, updateType, data,
    extraSetting);
};
```

Whenever nodes of types are created that need to change instance data, the nodeActionCallback of the BehaviorData struct is set in the new node:

```
newNode->setNodeActionCallback(
    newBehavior.bdNodeActionCallbackFunction);
```

Finally, in the nodeActionCallback() method, the incoming data is transformed to include the instance ID, and another callback function is executed:

```
    mInstanceNodeActionCallback(mInstanceId, nodeType,
        updateType, data, extraSetting);
```

The callback chain decouples the internal instance and animation state from the state machine controlling it. By decoupling the states, it is possible for a node of the instance movement or action type to request a property change for the instance where this node resides in one of the behaviors without any knowledge of which instance the node is.

The remaining parts of the node actions will be implemented in the section *Extending the code to support behavior changes*, completing the chain from a single node in a node tree all the way up to the renderer.

For the second callback function, a lambda in the `SingleInstanceBehavior` class is used to connect the state update request to a local method:

```
mFireNodeOutputCallback = [this](int pinId)
  { updateNodeStatus(pinId); };
```

Inside `updateNodeStatus()`, some simple logic changes the active state of the nodes by using the `pinId` given as a parameter. Following the rule "output first, input second" for the link IDs of imnodes and the integer division of the pin ID, we could detect if the signal came from an input or output pin and even find the node that called `updateNodeStatus()`.

If `updateNodeStatus()` receives a call with an output pin ID as a parameter, all connected child nodes will be activated. If no connected child node is found on the output pin, we inform the parent node about a finished execution. This special handling is only relevant for a sequence node right now, enabling us to skip output pins without a connection.

For an input pin as a parameter, the corresponding node connected to that input pin will be informed. This is only needed at the end of the execution of a child node of a sequence node right now, but the functionality can be extended for new node types.

Without logging calls and comments, the entire `updateNodeStatus()` method is just about forty lines short, but it still does the main job of the entire behavior tree implementation.

To simplify the creation of new nodes, we will use the factory pattern. A node factory encloses all the logic needed to create a new node of a specified type in one place. Plus, we will enhance the editor with a context menu and the ability to switch between different node trees.

Adding a node factory

The factory pattern is a nice solution to create objects of classes derived from a single base class, keeping all parts of the creation logic in a single place.

The factory class `GraphNodeFactory` in the graphnodes folder is small and simple, similar to other factory classes. At the creation time of a factory object, the appropriate `fireNodeOutputCallback` is injected into the constructor, helping us to add the right callback destination to all new nodes. The constructor also adds a mapping between all node types and the names in the title area of the nodes. This name mapping frees us from adding the node name at node creation time; we only need the node type and a unique node ID to build a new node.

The `makeNode()` method does all the work by creating a new derived class according to the given node type, adding the callback, the mapped node name, and the node type of the chosen derived class. Like in all factories, the returned smart pointer is of the base class type, allowing us to store all new nodes in STL containers of the base class.

Extending the node editor

For better node handling, we create a context menu in the editor. The context menu can be opened by pressing the right mouse button in the node editor window:

```
const bool openPopup = ImGui::IsWindowFocused(
  ImGuiFocusedFlags_RootAndChildWindows) &&
  ImNodes::IsEditorHovered() &&
  ImGui::IsMouseClicked(ImGuiMouseButton_Right);
```

In fact, we create two different context menus. Which menu is shown depends on if we are hovering over a node or not:

```
if (openPopup) {
  if (ImNodes::IsNodeHovered(&mHoveredNodeId)) {
    ImGui::OpenPopup("change node");
  } else {
    ImGui::OpenPopup("add node")
  }
}
```

If no existing node is hovered over when pressing the right mouse button, an ImGui pop-up window to add a new node will be created, listing all available node types (all but the root node, which only exists once). If a node is hovered over, a different ImGui pop-up window is shown, containing actions that could be executed on the hovered-over node.

Figure 9.8 shows both context menus next to each other:

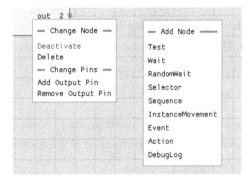

Figure 9.8: The two context menus of the editor

Which options in the **Change Node** menu are shown depends on the node type. For sequence and selector nodes, the number of output pins can be changed dynamically, so these two options appear, while for all other nodes, only **Deactivate** and **Delete** are shown. The availability to deactivate and delete a node is based on the active state of the node. For instance, you cannot delete an active wait node until the wait time has expired.

To edit an existing node tree into the existing editor window, a new method called `loadData()` is added:

```
void loadData(std::shared_ptr<BehaviorData> data);
```

Inside `loadData()`, both a new `SingleInstanceBehavior` and a new `GraphNodeFactory` object are created to allow editing the node tree the same way as a fresh node tree.

The editor also has an `update()` method to behave like a running node tree, updating the properties of all nodes depending on their state:

```
void updateGraphNodes(float deltaTime);
```

Finally, we add a flag called `mShowEditor` to control the visibility of the editor. When a new node tree is created, or an existing tree is edited, the window appears on screen. By clicking on the close button of the editor, or when the currently edited node tree is deleted, we hide the editor window.

The last step to complete the implementation of the imnodes-based visual node editor is adding all required data to the `YamlParser` class. We do not want to start over with an empty editor every time the application is started.

Saving and loading a node tree

Creating the required templates and overloads for the new behavior data is not much different from what we did in the previous chapters.

To add behavior data to the YAML file, an overload of the output stream operator in the file `YamlParser.cpp` is needed. The file can be found in the `tools` folder:

```
YAML::Emitter& operator<<(YAML::Emitter& out,
  const BehaviorData& behavior) {
```

Most of the code can be copied from the previously defined overloads. Having a map of strings created by `exportData()` makes it easy to save the state of the nodes:

```
if (node->exportData().has_value()) {
  std::map<std::string, std::string> exportData =
```

```
                node->exportData().value();
        ...
    }
```

By using `std::optional` in the return value for `exportData()`, we can easily skip the entire section in the YAML file if the node has no state to save. Without the `optional` keyword, we would need an additional check to determine if the node state needs to be saved or not.

For the loading part of the new behavior data, we must add a new convert template in the file `YamlParserTypes.h`:

```
    template<>
    struct convert<ExtendedBehaviorData> {
      static Node encode(const ExtendedBehaviorData& rhs) {
        ...
      }
      static bool decode(const Node& node,
        ExtendedBehaviorData& rhs) {
        ...
      }
    }
```

We are using the extended version of the `BehaviorData` struct since we only store the type of a node, and the YAML parser is the wrong place to create new nodes:

```
struct PerNodeImportData {
  int nodeId;
  graphNodeType nodeType;
  std::map<std::string, std::string> nodeProperties{};
};
struct ExtendedBehaviorData : BehaviorData {
  std::vector<PerNodeImportData> nodeImportData;
};
```

Node recreation will happen in the renderer class when loading a saved file, like the creation of models, instances, and cameras.

Most of the convert code can be taken from previously implemented templates. But there is one caveat to the decode() method. Instead of the data type of the node data, a std::map of strings, the yaml-cpp library requires us to use a vector of maps, containing a single entry for every line in the node data. The following code shows how the parsing is done:

```
std::vector<std::map<std::string, std::string>> entry =
    nodeDataNode.as<std::vector<std::map<std::string,
        std::string>>>();
```

All vector entries will be added to the nodeProperties variable of the intermediate PerNodeImportData struct:

```
if (entry.size() > 0) {
    for (const auto& mapEntry : entry) {
        nodeData.nodeProperties.insert(mapEntry.begin(),
            mapEntry.end());
    }
}
```

In the renderer, we restore the behavior node tree by creating a new SingleInstanceBehavior instance, a new BehaviorData struct, and new nodes of the saved type and ID, as well as loading back the saved properties. After the links are recreated and links and editor settings are imported to the new BehaviorData, the node tree is in the same state as when it was saved.

Restore order: Behavior before instances

We must restore the behavior node tree data before restoring the instances, since the behavior data will be copied to an instance if we had set a behavior before saving the configuration data.

Once the node editor itself is ready, we need to connect the node trees and instances. So, let's add the missing pieces to have the instances come alive.

Extending the code to support behavior changes

A few steps are left to fully support computer-controlled behavior in the instances. First, we need a copy of a node tree in every instance.

Creating a node tree copy for every instance

We cannot just copy the nodes since the original and copy would access the same node behind the shared pointer. Reusing the same nodes for multiple instances would lead to chaos, since collision events from all instances would be triggered, resulting in the same steps executed for all instances sharing the nodes.

To create a copy of the node tree for one of the instances, a custom copy constructor for the SingleInstanceBehavior class has been created. The copy constructor sets the required callbacks, copies the links, and loops through the vector of existing nodes to create a clone of every node. For nodes that change instance behavior, the additional node action callback will be set.

Next, the callback chain to the renderer must be completed. Right now, only the SingleInstanceBehavior class objects are informed that a node wants to send a property change request to an instance.

Connecting SingleInstanceBehavior and the renderer

Managing the copies of the instance behaviors will be done by the new BehaviorManager class, located in the model folder. The BehaviorManager class maintains a mapping between the instance IDs and the copy of the node tree the specific instance uses. Also, we have a new callback to keep the renderer in the loop to update instance properties of a node of the node tree:

```
std::map<int, SingleInstanceBehavior>
  mInstanceToBehaviorMap{};
instanceNodeActionCallback mInstanceNodeActionCallback;
```

To update the state of all node trees for the instances, an update() method exists in the BehaviorManager class:

```
void BehaviorManager::update(float deltaTime) {
  for (auto& instance : mInstanceToBehaviorMap) {
    instance.second.update(deltaTime);
  }
}
```

We just loop over all instances and call the update() method of the SingleInstanceBehavior object, which updates all nodes of the node tree.

In the renderer, a private member named mBehaviorManager is added and initialized during the init() method of the renderer:

```
mBehaviorManager = std::make_shared<BehaviorManager>();
mInstanceNodeActionCallback = [this](int instanceId,
    graphNodeType nodeType, instanceUpdateType updateType,
    nodeCallbackVariant data, bool extraSetting) {
  updateInstanceSettings(instanceId, nodeType, updateType,
    data, extraSetting);
};
mBehaviorManager->setNodeActionCallback(
  mInstanceNodeActionCallback);
```

A model instance can be added by handing over the instance ID and the node tree to the addInstance() method of the BehaviorManager class:

```
void addInstance(int instanceId,
    std::shared_ptr<SingleInstanceBehavior> behavior);
```

In the addInstance() method, we copy all nodes in the tree, set the callback to the renderer, and add the instance ID to the SingleInstanceBehavior object.

Now, any instance or action node inside the node tree of that instance can call the function bound to its nodeActionCallback member. The request goes up the callback chain and ends in the updateInstanceSettings() method of the renderer, containing all information for the renderer to change the instance property.

Finally, we must define all events we want to send to instances, plus where to place the code firing these events.

Adding events

To support events, a new enum class called nodeEvent is created in the file Enums.h located in the opengl folder (or the vulkan folder for Vulkan):

```
enum class nodeEvent : uint8_t {
  none = 0,
```

```
    instanceToInstanceCollision,
    instanceToEdgeCollision,
    NUM
};
```

To start, we define two values called instanceToInstanceCollision and instanceToEdgeCollision, used to inform an instance that a collision with another instance or a collision to the world boundaries has occurred. The first value, none, is used to ignore events in an event node, and the NUM value is needed to loop over all values in a for loop.

In the ModelInstanceCamData struct, a mapping called micNodeUpdateMap is added to translate a nodeEvent value to a readable string for the events:

```
    std::unordered_map<nodeEvent, std::string>
      micNodeUpdateMap{};
```

The renderer not only adds the strings during the init() method but also, all calls firing an event are sent from the renderer to the node trees:

```
    mModelInstCamData.micNodeEventCallbackFunction(
      instSettings.isInstanceIndexPosition,
      nodeEvent::instanceToEdgeCollision);
```

This new micNodeEventCallbackFunction callback is bound to the addBehaviorEvent() method of the renderer, and after chaining the request to existing objects, the call ends in the SingleInstanceBehavior class. There, all requested events are added to a vector:

```
      std::vector<nodeEvent> mPendingNodeEvents;
```

Events are handled in the update() call of the SingleInstanceBehavior class, calling the handleEvent() method of the node. The handleEvent() method was introduced in the section *Exploring the base class for graph nodes*. It simply activates all event nodes in the graph of the specified instance that are listening to this event type.

An example node tree containing events is shown here:

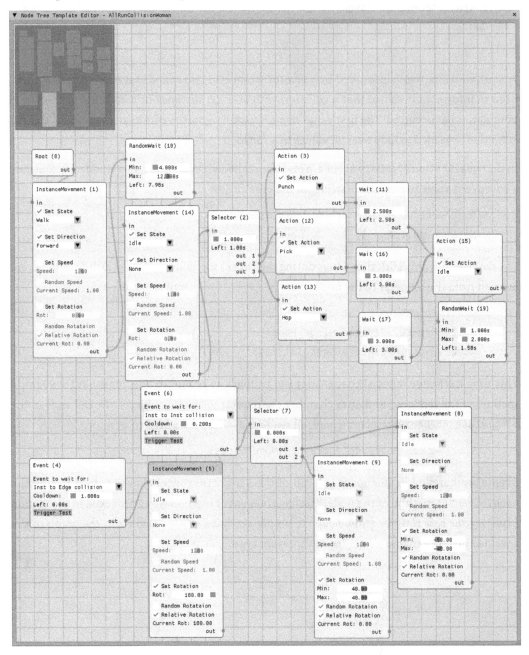

Figure 9.9: An overview of the node tree for the woman's model

We have split this image of the node tree into two parts, in *Figures 9.10 and 9.11*, for better understanding.

Figure 9.10 shows the default path in the node tree, beginning with the root node.

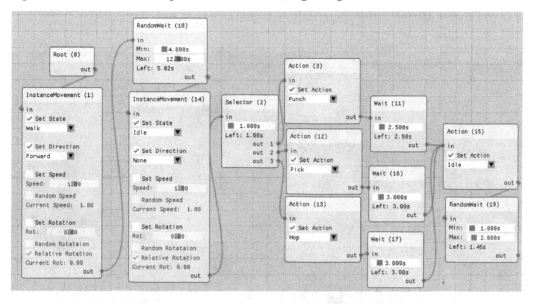

Figure 9.10: Default path in the node tree for the woman's model

Figure 9.11 shows the event nodes plus the reaction to events.

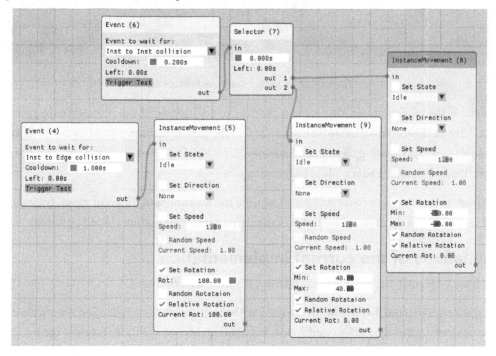

Figure 9.11: Events in the node tree for the woman's model

In *Figure 9.12*, the resulting behavior of the tree in *Figure 9.9* for the woman's model and a similar tree for the man's model is shown:

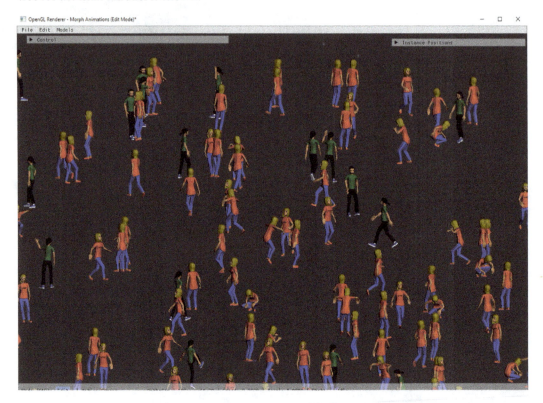

Figure 9.12: Instances living their virtual life

By default, the models are walking around, reacting to collisions with other instances by rotating a bit. After a collision with the world boundaries, the instances turn around. After a random time, the instances stop moving, and a random animation clip is played. At this point, the normal execution ends, and the root node is triggered again.

Although the node editor looks really cool, and we can add nodes of different types, create links, and save and load the state, some limits of the current implementation should be noted.

Limitations of the current implementation

Our basic implementation lacks some features of other behavior trees.

First, states are stored directly in the nodes. For the use case of the application we are creating, storing state data in the nodes is sufficient. But for larger trees, separate state storage becomes handy, mostly because we no longer need to copy the node data to the instances.

Also, changes to the node tree in the editor session are not automatically copied to the instances. You need to select an instance or model and apply the current state after every change.

Since only the original node tree data of the editor session is saved to the YAML file and not the tree data of the individual instances, restarting the application or reloading the configuration applies the editor state to all instances that use the specific node tree.

Finally, the nodes cannot access data from their instance or other data of the virtual world. Reacting to properties like position or rotation, or seeing if you are the primary or secondary candidate of a collision to adjust the rotation angle, is not possible.

Many of these limits can be removed with some effort and additional coding. See the *Practical sessions* section for ideas.

In the last section of this chapter, we will use the code we have added up until now to create a new feature: interaction between instances.

Adding interaction between instances

We already have an action called **Interaction**, starting the interaction animation clip for the man's model (and doing nothing visible for the woman's model, as the model does not have an animation clip to show some kind of interaction).

This *interaction* action will be extended to send an event to a nearby instance, stating that we want to interact with the instance. A possible reaction to the interaction request could be the replay of the waving animation clip for the man's model on the nearby instance, visually confirming that the event has been processed.

Creating interaction control properties

The renderer needs some variables and a bit of code to support interaction. We add these new variables in the `OGLRenderData` struct in the `OGLRenderData.h` in the opengl folder:

```
bool rdInteraction = false;
float rdInteractionMaxRange = 10.0f;
float rdInteractionMinRange = 1.5f;
float rdInteractionFOV = 45.0f;
std::set<int> rdInteractionCandidates{};
int rdInteractWithInstanceId = 0;
```

As always, for Vulkan, the variables have to be added to the VkRenderData struct in the VkRenderData.h file.

With these new variables, we can switch interaction on and off, as well as set a minimum and maximum scan range for other instances and a field-of-view angle that the peer instances need to be in. The field of view allows us to select only instances we are looking at, and instances that are looking toward us.

In the std::set of int values, we store all instances in the configured range and with the correct view angle. Finally, we store the instance we have chosen to interact with.

The interaction candidate selection is handled in findInteractionInstances() in the renderer. Like collision detection, we drill down from all instances to a single instance by narrowing down the selection properties.

A simple algorithm is used to find the instance suitable for interaction:

1. A BoundingBox2D object with the max size is used, and the query() method of the quadtree is called. Now we have all instances in that area.

2. All instances within the minimum range are sorted out, including ourselves.

3. By using the dot product between our own rotation angle and the distance vector between us and the remaining instances from step 2, all instances with the incorrect facing are removed.

4. The distances between us and all instances left in step 3 are sorted in ascending order, and the nearest instance is set to be the interaction instance.

If any step returns no valid candidates, the interaction request will be ignored.

Extending the handling code

Thanks to all our preparations, adding a new event is now extremely simple. First, we extend the nodeEvent enum by the new interaction value:

```
enum class nodeEvent : uint8_t {
    ...
    interaction,
    NUM
};
```

Then, we send the interaction event to the central behavior class when the interaction key is pressed, and our model plays the interaction animation clip:

```
if (glfwGetKey(mRenderData.rdWindow, GLFW_KEY_U) ==
    GLFW_PRESS) {
  if (mRenderData.rdInteractWithInstanceId > 0) {
    mBehaviorManager->addEvent(
      mRenderData.rdInteractWithInstanceId,
      nodeEvent::interaction);
  }
}
```

Finally, we create a new event node in the node tree for the man's model, setting the wave action. The new wave action is surrounded by two other actions setting the idle state for the instance to have a smooth animation blending, and two wait nodes allowing us to finish the animations (we have no feedback yet from the instance to the node tree).

The resulting part of the node tree can be seen in *Figure 9.13*:

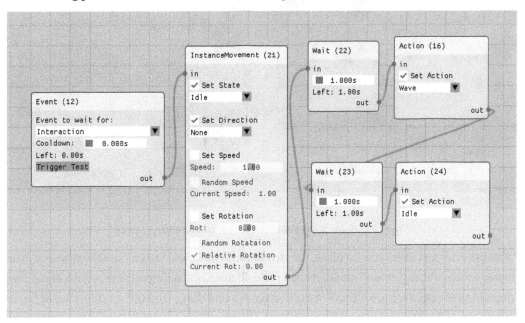

Figure 9.13: Reacting to an interaction event by playing the waving animation

That's all! Switching to view mode and pressing the *U* key near another man's instance will instruct that instance to stop and wave its hand back to us. After the wave animation, the portion of the node tree will end, resuming the normal behavior.

Drawing debug information

As with all previous additions, getting a new feature to work without proper debug information could be exhausting. For the interaction, we can utilize the AABB drawing code to draw a bounding box around the instance candidates, and we can use the line mesh to draw a square on the ground, showing the dimensions of the minimum and maximum search area.

Figure 9.14 shows an example of the debug lines, captured with a first-person camera:

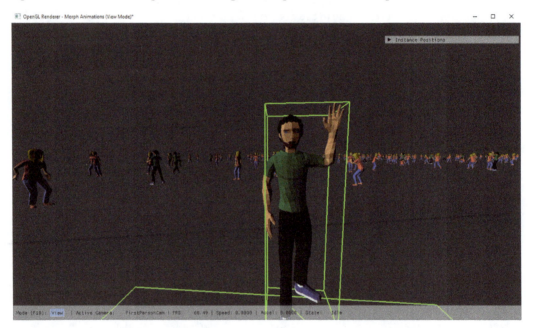

Figure 9.14: Interaction between the user and another instance

With behavior and interaction in place, the virtual world looks and feels more alive than ever. The instances are walking around alone, reacting to collisions, and doing various actions at random times. And we can even greet some of the instances – and they greet us back. It is a lot of fun to just fly around in the virtual world, watching the instances.

Summary

In this chapter, we created a simple form of NPCs in our virtual world. We started by exploring the basic nature of behavior trees and state machines, and to have a tool for creating the state machine controlling the behavior available, we added an ImGui-based visual node editor. Then, we added classes for different node types and integrated these new classes into the existing code, including a node factory and node editor extensions. Finally, we added interactions with other instances in the virtual world.

In the next chapter, we will go back to the animation side of things: we will add additive blending in the form of morph animations to create facial animations. First, we will discuss what morph animations are, and which constraints we must take care of. Then, we will import existing morph animations in the glTF models and offload the animation work to the GPU, similar to the other animations. As the last step, we will combine facial animations and interactions, creating instances that can show if they agree or disagree with us.

Practical sessions

Here are some additions you could make to the code:

- Extend the undo/redo functionality to the node trees.

- In addition to the existing undo/redo operations, add code to support reverting and re-reverting any operations in node trees. It would be helpful to be able to undo accidental changes, like deleting a connection or node.

- Create an **Apply changes** button for updating the instances.

  Implement a simpler way to update the copies of a changed node tree for all instances that are using this tree.

- Load node trees from a running instance into the editor.

  This is a good idea for debugging purposes, but probably also fun to watch what happens in real time in the node tree of an instance.

- Add a real-time debug visualization of the loaded node tree.

  Visual debugging could help a lot with understanding what happens in a node tree. You could start by highlighting the currently active node in the graph of the selected instance (see the previous task) and later also highlight the currently active output pin plus the outgoing connections to other nodes.

- React to the creation of new links in imnodes.

  Instead of having to create a new node and then place a link, add the context menu to create a node when a new link is created but not attached. Connect the dangling link directly to the input or output pin of the new node.

- Let the sequence node also wait for grandchildren.

  You could add a cascade of notifications about entire sub-sequences having finished execution, not just wait and RandomWait nodes – maybe with an extra checkbox to control which child node in the chain is the last one to wait for.

- Add condition and loop nodes.

  Enable more control. The condition node needs access to data it should react on, either from the instance, the world, or from other nodes. The loop node must also wait for the child nodes to finish.

- Allow renaming and copy/paste for entire node trees, or between editor windows.

  Extend the current implementation by adding the ability to rename existing node trees. Creating a copy of an entire node tree may become handy to duplicate and adjust existing behavior, and a copy/paste operation of nodes or entire selections between two editor sessions would be a blast.

- Show more than one tree node in the editor window.

  Either by using dockable ImGui windows or just opening more editor windows, let the user work on multiple node trees at the same time.

  Caveat: If more than one window is shown, the internal ImGui IDs must be unique among all UI elements in the windows.

- Enhanced difficulty: Integrate a full C++ behavior tree library.

  Instead of this small and hand-crafted node tree version, add a full-featured behavior tree from a third-party library and add imnodes support for the tree management.

Additional resources

- Introduction to behavior trees: `https://robohub.org/introduction-to-behavior-trees/`

- Behavior Trees: Breaking the Cycle of Misuse: `https://takinginitiative.net/wp-content/uploads/2020/01/behaviortrees_breaking-the-cycle-of-misuse.pdf`

- A simple C++ behavior tree example: `https://lisyarus.github.io/blog/posts/behavior-trees.html`

- Node Graph Editors with ImGui: `https://github.com/ocornut/imgui/issues/306`

- imnodes extension for ImGui: `https://github.com/Nelarius/imnodes`

10

Advanced Animation Blending

Welcome to *Chapter 10*! In the previous chapter, we added a bit more *real-life behavior* to the instances. After a brief overview of behavior trees, we added a visual node editor to visually draw the behavior of the instances by using a simple finite state machine. At the end of the chapter, we extended the code and implemented interaction as an additional form of behavior.

In this chapter, the instances will come even more to life. We start with a short exploration of the world of face animations made by morph target animations. Then we will add extra functionality to load morph meshes into the application and enable control over the face animations of the instances. Next, we add a graph node to be able to use face animations in the node trees as well. At the end of the chapter, additive blending will be implemented, allowing us to move the head of the instances independently of the skeletal and face animations.

In this chapter, we will cover the following topics:

- How to animate facial expressions
- Adding face animations to code and GPU shaders
- Using face animations in node trees
- Implementing additive blending

Technical requirements

The example code is in the chapter10 folder, in the 01_opengl_morphanim subfolder for OpenGL and 02_vulkan_morphanim subfolder for Vulkan.

How to animate facial expressions

After implementing behavior in *Chapter 9*, life in our virtual world has become a lot more vivid. The instances can walk or run around by themselves, do simple tasks at random times, react to a collision with another instance, and won't leave the virtual world beyond the invisible borders.

But the instances still appear a bit sterile and lifeless. They roam around like robots, always looking forward, keeping a straight face. No emotions are visible, and there are no reactions to interactions other than playing a waving animation.

So, let's give the instances the ability to show emotions by adding facial expressions. The most common way to add face animations to any kind of *living* virtual object is **morph target animations**.

To get the idea of morph target animations, here's a simple example. In *Figure 10.1*, three different weights of a morph target animation are shown:

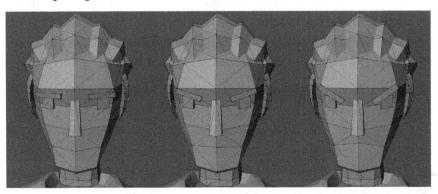

Figure 10.1: Three different weights during an angry morph target animation

The left face has an *angry* morph target animation applied to 0%, showing only the original face. The middle face has the morph target applied to 50%, blending halfway between the original face and the full morph, and for the right face, the full morph target animation has been applied.

As you can see, the eyebrows have been rotated, the mouth vertex has been moved a bit upward in the final state, and the vertex positions are only interpolated between the original and the final mesh. But these small vertex position changes create an entirely different facial expression for the model.

Morph target animations may have a different name in your tool, such as **per-vertex animation**, **shape interpolation**, **shape keys**, or **blend shapes**. All these names describe the same technique: multiple deformed versions of a mesh are stored in keyframes, and the animation of the mesh is done by interpolating the vertex positions between the positions in the keyframes.

There's an important difference between skeletal animals and morph target animations when it comes to cost: a skeletal animation only affects the properties of the model's nodes, while morph animations replace an entire mesh of the model's virtual skin, and the mesh needs to be duplicated for every morph animation the model should play, raising the overall size of the model as a file on disk and in memory.

Models have quite a small number of bones but many vertices for the skin, so recalculating the positions for a large number of vertices in every frame adds extra computation costs to morph animations. Luckily, the morph animations happen entirely in the vertex shader and are only linear interpolations between two positions saved as vectors. Thus, the additional computational burden of a morph animation remains negligible in our example code.

In Blender, morph target animations can be controlled by the **Shape Keys** options on the **Data** tab. *Figure 10.2* shows the setting used for the right face of *Figure 10.1*, with the **Value** set to 1.000 to apply 100% of the **Angry** morph:

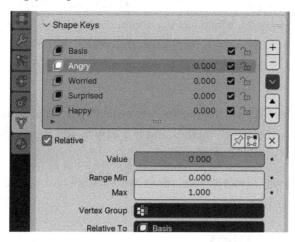

Figure 10.2: Shape keys in Blender controlling morph target animations

Creating and modifying shape key-based morph target animations in Blender is beyond the scope of this book. Blender has some basic documentation about shape keys, a link is included in the *Additional resources* section, and there are plenty of videos around showing how to work with shape keys in Blender.

If you have a model file containing morph target animations available, like the two models in the assets folder of *Chapter 10*, or if you have created your own set of morph animations in any other existing model, you are ready to go for the next step: using the Open Asset Importer Library to import these extra animations.

Let's now learn how to add morph target animations to our application.

Adding face animations to code and GPU shaders

Morph target animation data is stored in two places in an Assimp model file.

The first part of the morph animation data, the meshes, reside in the mAnimMeshes array of an aiMesh node, and the number of meshes is stored in the mNumAnimMeshes variable of the aiMesh. Every element of the mAnimMeshes array contains the exact same number of vertices as the original mesh, allowing us to interpolate the vertex positions between different versions of the mesh.

This interpolation is not limited to blending between the original mesh and one of the morph target meshes. Also, blending between two morph target meshes is possible, or mixing positions of more than two meshes. Be aware that the outcome of mixing meshes may not always be as expected as the effect of the morph target animations heavily depends on the intention of the animator.

The second part of the morph animation data, the keyframe data, is in the mMorphMeshChannels array of an aiAnimation node, which has the number of keyframes stored in a variable called mNumMorphMeshChannels. The keys in every keyframe contain the points in time for the specific key, plus the numbers of the morph mesh to use and the weight of the morph mesh in a linear interpolation.

We will only use the mesh data to interpolate between different facial expressions, so we ignore the animation data for the morph meshes. But it is easy to add support for the morph target animations on top of the code of this chapter.

As the first step on the way to morph animations, we will learn how to load the additional mesh data and extract the vertices.

Loading morph meshes

Since every vertex in a morph mesh replaces the position and the normal of the same vertex in the original mesh, only a subset of vertex data is needed for the replacement vertices. We will create a *lightweight* version of a vertex named OGLMorphVertex in the OGLRenderData.h file in the opengl folder, containing only the position and normal:

```
struct OGLMorphVertex {
  glm::vec4 position = glm::vec4(0.0f);
  glm::vec4 normal = glm::vec4(0.0f);
};
```

To collect the replacement morph vertices into a mesh, we also create a new `struct` called `OGLMorphMesh` that contains all the vertices in a `std::vector`:

```
struct OGLMorphMesh {
  std::vector<OGLMorphVertex> morphVertices{};
};
```

As all the morph meshes depend on the original meshes, we add a `OGLMorphMesh` vector to the default mesh, `struct OGLMesh`:

```
struct OGLMesh {
  ...
  std::vector<OGLMorphMesh> morphMeshes{};
};
```

For Vulkan, the two new structs are named `VkMorphVertex` and `VkMorphMesh`, residing in the `VkRenderData.h` file in the `vulkan` folder. The `VkMorphMesh` vector is added to the `VkMesh` struct.

Right before the end of the `processMesh()` method in the `AssimpMesh` class, we add a new code block to extract the morph mesh data from the model file. First, we check if we have any morph meshes attached to the current mesh:

```
int animMeshCount = mesh->mNumAnimMeshes;
if (animMeshCount > 0) {
```

If we find morph meshes, we iterate over all morph meshes, extracting the mesh data and the number of vertices:

```
for (unsigned int i = 0; i < animMeshCount; ++i) {
  aiAnimMesh* animMesh = mesh->mAnimMeshes[i];
  unsigned int mAninVertexCount =
    animMesh->mNumVertices;
```

Per definition, the number of vertices in the morph mesh must match the number of vertices in the original mesh. It does not hurt to do an addition check here, skipping the entire morph mesh and printing an error when a vertex count mismatch is detected:

```
if (animVertexCount != mVertexCount) {
  Logger::log(1, "%s error: morph mesh %i vertex
    count does not match (orig mesh has %i vertices,
    morph mesh %i)\n",
```

```
    __  FUNCTION__, i, mVertexCount, animVertexCount);
    continue;
}
```

Next, we check whether the morph mesh contains position data and create a temporary `OGLMorphMesh` if the check succeeds:

```
if (animMesh->HasPositions()) {
    OGLMorphMesh newMorphMesh{};
```

It may sound silly to check whether the morph mesh has vertex positions, but morph meshes can also override other data, such as normals, colors, or texture positions. It is possible to encounter a morph mesh without position data.

Then, we loop over all vertices and extract the vertex positions:

```
for (unsigned int i = 0; i < animVertexCount; ++i) {
    OGLMorphVertex vertex;
    vertex.position.x = animMesh->mVertices[i].x;
    vertex.position.y = animMesh->mVertices[i].y;
    vertex.position.z = animMesh->mVertices[i].z;
```

If normal data is stored in the morph mesh too, we extract the normals. Without normal data, we set the vertex normal to zero:

```
if (animMesh->HasNormals()) {
    vertex.normal.x = animMesh->mNormals[i].x;
    vertex.normal.y = animMesh->mNormals[i].y;
    vertex.normal.z = animMesh->mNormals[i].z;
} else {
    vertex.normal = glm::vec4(0.0f);
}
```

Finally, we place the vertex into the temporary `OGLMorphMesh`, and after all the vertices are processed, the `OGLMorphMesh` is added to the `morphMeshes` vector of the `OGLMesh` for this `AssimpMesh` object:

```
    newMorphMesh.morphVertices.emplace_back(vertex);
    }
    mMesh.morphMeshes.emplace_back(newMorphMesh);
    }
  }
}
```

Accessing any alternative morph meshes is now as simple as checking the morphMeshes vector for a size greater than zero, and if we have any morph meshes, extracting the vertex data and interpolating between the positions and normals of the original vertices and the vertices of the selected morph mesh.

At this point, all valid morph meshes found in the model file are available as part of the AssimpMesh mesh data. To use these morph meshes for face animations, we must add some code and logic to the application.

Storing all morph meshes in a single buffer

To use the vertices of the morph meshes in a shader, we store the vertex data of all morph meshes into a single SSBO. Using a single SSBO is needed due to the instanced rendering of the model instances on the screen – we need the vertex data of all meshes available at all times during the rendering since we cannot tell when a specific model instance will be drawn to the screen. Splitting the rendering depending on the selected morph mesh would also be possible, but that would be quite a costly alternative as we must filter the instances on every draw call.

The morph mesh SSBO plus some related variables are added to the AssimpModel class. First, three new private variables are added to the AssimpModel.h header file: mNumAnimatedMeshes, mAnimatedMeshVertexSize, and mAnimMeshVerticesBuffer:

```
unsigned int mNumAnimatedMeshes = 0;
unsigned int mAnimatedMeshVertexSize = 0;
ShaderStorageBuffer mAnimMeshVerticesBuffer{};
```

In mNumAnimatedMeshes, we store the number of morph meshes for this model. Right now, the code supports only a single mesh containing morph meshes, so the number in mNumAnimatedMeshes is equal to the number of morph meshes in this specific mesh.

But since we are doing only face animations, the limit of a single mesh with morph meshes is no problem. Also, a task in the *Practical sessions* section is available to extend the code accordingly and add support for multiple meshes containing morph meshes.

The value in mAnimatedMeshVertexSize is used to find the start of vertex data for the selected morph clip in the SSBO. By multiplying the mesh vertex size and the index of the morph clip, we can jump directly to the first vertex of the morph clip.

Finally, all vertex data is stored in the mAnimMeshVerticesBuffer SSBO.

We also add two public methods called hasAnimMeshes() and getAnimMeshVertexSize() to the AssimpModel.cpp class implementation file. Thanks to the *descriptive* method names, no further explanation should be required.

Filling the SSBO is done in the loadModel() method of the AssimpModel class. When all meshes are collected into the mModelMeshes vector, we can iterate over all meshes to add the vertex data to the new buffer:

```
for (const auto& mesh : mModelMeshes) {
  if (mesh.morphMeshes.size() == 0) {
    continue;
  }
```

As the first step of collecting the vertices in the mAnimMeshVerticesBuffer SSBO, we check if we have any morph meshes in this mesh. If we have a mesh without additional morph meshes, we simply continue with the next mesh.

Then, we create a temporary OGLMorphMesh called animMesh to collect all vertices and resize the morphVertices vector in the animMesh:

```
OGLMorphMesh animMesh;
animMesh.morphVertices.resize(
  mesh.vertices.size() * mNumAnimatedMeshes);
```

Now we can copy all vertices of the morph mesh into animMesh, using the number of vertices to calculate the correct position:

```
for (unsigned int i = 0; i < mNumAnimatedMeshes; ++i) {
  unsigned int vertexOffset = mesh.vertices.size() * i;
  std::copy(mesh.morphMeshes[i].morphVertices.begin(),
    mesh.morphMeshes[i].morphVertices.end(),
    animMesh.morphVertices.begin() + vertexOffset);
  mAnimatedMeshVertexSize = mesh.vertices.size();
}
```

Finally, we upload the collected vertices to the SSBO:

```
mAnimMeshVerticesBuffer.uploadSsboData(
  animMesh.morphVertices);
}
```

Whenever we need the morph animations of this model now, we can bind the buffer to a specified shader binding point. This binding can be achieved by using the new public method, bindMorphAnimBuffer():

```
void AssimpModel::bindMorphAnimBuffer(int bindingPoint) {
  mAnimMeshVerticesBuffer.bind(bindingPoint);
}
```

To use face animations on a per-instance basis, we must add a couple of variables and methods and extend some data structures.

Adding face morph settings to the code

The most important change to enable face animations is a new enum class called faceAnimation, which resides in the Enums.h file:

```
enum class faceAnimation : uint8_t {
  none = 0,
  angry,
  worried,
  surprised,
  happy
};
```

All supported morph animations are stored in the faceAnimation enum the same way as actions or node types. Instead of using the morph animation from the model files, we will use only a fixed set of face animations in the code.

Similar to other data types, we add a mapping from the enum values to strings. It is a lot easier to use the enum value in code and show the user-friendly string in the UI. The new map named micFaceAnimationNameMap will be added to the ModelInstanceCamData struct in the ModelInstanceCamData.h file:

```
    std::unordered_map<faceAnimation, std::string>
      micFaceAnimationNameMap{};
```

Filling the map with strings happens in the init() method of the renderer class files, OGLRenderer.cpp or VkRenderer.cpp, the best place is next to the existing mapping code.

Fixed morph mapping vs. dynamic loading from the model

The reason to hard code all morph target animation clips in the `faceAnimation` enum and `micFaceAnimationNameMap` is to keep the code simple.

While populating the list of morph target clips from the model file is easy, maintaining a dynamic list in the UI becomes quite complex. For instance, adding code to choose a morph clip in a node tree would create a hard dependency between the tree and a single model – using the same tree for other models will become impossible.

To avoid a model-tree dependency, only a predefined set of morph animations will be used. Any model can support all morph animations, none of them, or a partial number of clips with matching indices, filling any gaps with empty morph animations.

For the instance part, two new variables named `isFaceAnimType` and `isFaceAnimWeight` are added to the `InstanceSettings` struct:

```
faceAnimation isFaceAnimType = faceAnimation::none;
float isFaceAnimWeight = 0.0f;
```

In `isFaceAnimType`, we store the current face animation clip. Due to the extra none value in the `faceAnimation` enum, we do not need another Boolean to switch the face animations on or off. The interpolation weight between the default face mesh and the face animation can be controlled by `isFaceAnimWeight`, with `0.0f` showing only the default mesh and `1.0f` the morph mesh.

is stands for "InstanceSettings", not for "it is"

To bring up the sidenote again, and to avoid confusion: The `is` in the `InstanceSettings` variable names is just the abbreviation of the `struct` name, not something to define a state. So, `isFaceAnimType` stands for "Instance Settings Face Animation Type", not a Boolean controlling whether the face animation is enabled.

We also need to give the renderer the information about the face animations for every instance. Let's extend the renderer as the next step.

Filling the per-instance buffer data in the renderer

As for all other shader-related data, we need an SSBO to hand the data over to the GPU. To fill the SSBO, a `std::vector` of some data type is needed. So, the renderer class header file `OGLRenderer.h` will get two new private variables called `mFaceAnimPerInstanceData` and `mFaceAnimPerInstanceDataBuffer`:

```
std::vector<glm::vec4> mFaceAnimPerInstanceData{};
ShaderStorageBuffer mFaceAnimPerInstanceDataBuffer{};
```

For the Vulkan renderer, the data type of the buffer differs. We need to add the following lines to the `VkRenderer.h` file:

```
std::vector<glm::vec4> mFaceAnimPerInstanceData{};
VkShaderStorageBufferData mFaceAnimPerInstanceDataBuffer{};
```

Even though we need only three values, we will use a `glm::vec4` here to tackle possible data-alignment problems. You should try to avoid the three-element vector (`glm::vec3`) to transport data via an SSBO to the GPU since you may get a mismatch between the vector or struct on the CPU side and the buffer on the GPU side.

The per-instance face animation SSBO will be added to the `draw()` call of the renderer class file, `OGLRenderer.cpp` or `VkRenderer.cpp`, more specifically in the loop over the instances of the model:

```
for (const auto& model : mModelInstCamData.micModelList) {
  ...
  mFaceAnimPerInstanceData.resize(numberOfInstances);
  ...
    for (size_t i = 0; i < numberOfInstances; ++i) {
```

We also add the resizing of the vector containing the morphing data before the loop; see the highlighted part in the previous code snippet.

And since we have already extracted the `InstanceSettings` struct of the current instance in the loop, adding the face animation is done in just a couple of lines.

First, we add an empty `glm::vec4` named `morphData`, plus we check whether the instance has a face animation set:

```
glm::vec4 morphData = glm::vec4(0.0f);
if (instSettings.isFaceAnimType !=
  faceAnimation::none) {
```

If we should animate the face of the instance, we fill three elements of `morphData`:

```
morphData.x = instSettings.isFaceAnimWeight;
morphData.y =
    static_cast<int>(instSettings.isFaceAnimType) - 1;
morphData.z = model->getAnimMeshVertexSize();
```

Now we set the weight of the face animation, the clip number decreased by one to honor the none element of the `faceAnimation` enum, and the number of vertices to skip between two morph meshes.

The current shader code uses the number of vertices and the clip number to calculate the first vertex of the desired morph animation, but it is possible to an absolute value here. An absolute value could become handy if we plan to extend the code to support multiple meshes with morph target animations (see the *Practical sessions* section).

Finally, we store the `morphData` in the vector used to fill the SSBO:

```
    }
    mFaceAnimPerInstanceData.at(i) = morphData;
```

As a last step for the face animations, the vertex shaders must be made aware of the new buffers.

Extending the shader to draw face animations

As morph target animations only change vertex data, we need to add the new SSBOs and a bit of logic to the vertex shader. There is no need to touch a compute or fragment shader, a fact that simplifies the face animation implementation a lot.

To prevent distortions for models without face animations, we will use a separate set of shaders to draw the meshes containing morph animations. First, we add two new `private` shader variables to the renderer header file `OGLRenderer.h`:

```
Shader mAssimpSkinningMorphShader{};
Shader mAssimpSkinningMorphSelectionShader{};
```

For the Vulkan renderer, more work is needed here since the shaders are part of the pipelines. We need to add two `VkPipelineLayout` handles, two `VkPipeline` handles, two `VkDescriptorSetLayout` handles, and two `VkDescriptorSet` handles in the `VkRenderData.h` file:

```
VkPipelineLayout rdAssimpSkinningMorphPipelineLayout;
VkPipelineLayout
  rdAssimpSkinningMorphSelectionPipelineLayout;
```

```
VkPipeline rdAssimpSkinningMorphPipeline;
VkPipeline rdAssimpSkinningMorphSelectionPipeline;
VkDescriptorSetLayout
  rdAssimpSkinningMorphSelectionDescriptorLayout;
VkDescriptorSetLayout
  rdAssimpSkinningMorphPerModelDescriptorLayout;
VkDescriptorSet rdAssimpSkinningMorphDescriptorSet;
VkDescriptorSet
  rdAssimpSkinningMorphSelectionDescriptorSet;
```

With these handles, two new Vulkan pipelines are created to draw the models with and without the special selection handling. For further Vulkan implementation details, check out the VkRenderer.cpp file.

We need to adjust the selection vertex shader to draw the morphed face meshes in the selection buffer. Without the selection shader, the head of the instances would no longer be selectable by clicking the mouse button.

For the shader code itself, we can reuse and extend the existing files. Copy the following four files to the new file names:

- assimp_skinning.vert to assimp_skinning_morph.vert
- assimp_skinning.frag to assimp_skinning_morph.frag
- assimp_skinning_selection.vert to assimp_skinning_morph_selection.vert
- assimp_skinning_selection.frag to assimp_skinning_morph_selection.frag

The fragment shaders with the .frag extension will not be changed, but for further changes or debugging it is always better to use separate files for the new shaders.

In both vertex shader files ending with .vert, add the following lines to define the new MorphVertex struct, matching the OGLMorphVertex struct defined in the OGLRenderData.h file in the opengl folder:

```
struct MorphVertex {
  vec4 position;
  vec4 normal;
};
```

For Vulkan, the name of the original struct is VkMorphVertex, defined in VkRenderData.h in the vulkan folder.

Then, add two new SSBOs named `AnimMorphBuffer` and `AnimMorphData` on binding points four and five:

```
layout (std430, binding = 4) readonly restrict
    buffer AnimMorphBuffer {
  MorphVertex morphVertices[];
};
layout (std430, binding = 5) readonly restrict
    buffer AnimMorphData {
  vec4 vertsPerMorphAnim[];
};
```

The first buffer, `AnimMorphBuffer`, contains the vertices of all morph available animations. In the second buffer, `AnimMorphData`, all instance settings are handed over from the CPU to the GPU.

Inside the `main()` method of the vertex shader, we calculate the offset to the vertices for the desired face animation by multiplying the vertex count and the index of the face animation clip for every instance:

```
int morphAnimIndex =
  int(vertsPerMorphAnim[gl_InstanceID].y *
      vertsPerMorphAnim[gl_InstanceID].z);
```

It is no problem to cast the `float` values to `int` here to avoid another struct with separate integer and floating-point values and to use `glm::vec4` as a "transportation object." The first inaccurate integer represented by a float would be $2^{24}+1$, and that value is large enough even for bigger meshes with many face animations ($2^{24}+1$ would be ~16 MiB of vertex data).

Then we extract the vertices from the morph mesh by using the `gl_VertexID` internal shader variable (`gl_VertexIndex` for Vulkan):

```
vec4 origVertex = vec4(aPos.x, aPos.y, aPos.z, 1.0);
vec4 morphVertex = vec4(morphVertices[gl_VertexID +
  morphAnimOffset].position.xyz, 1.0)
```

Now we can mix the positions of the original vertex and the replacement vertex from the morph mesh according to the weight factor:

```
gl_Position = projection * view * worldPosSkinMat *
  mix(origVertex, morphVertex,
  vertsPerMorphAnim[gl_InstanceID].x);
```

We do the same extraction and calculation work for the vertex normals since a position change of a vertex may also affect the normal of the triangle the vertex is part of:

```
vec4 origNormal =
    vec4(aNormal.x, aNormal.y, aNormal.z, 1.0);
vec4 morphNormal =
    vec4(morphVertices[gl_VertexID +
    morphAnimOffset].normal.xyz, 1.0);
normal = transpose(inverse(worldPosSkinMat)) *
    mix(origNormal, morphNormal,
    vertsPerMorphAnim[gl_InstanceID].x);
```

For a better selection of meshes with and without morph animations, we also need some small changes in the AssimpModel class and the renderer.

Finalizing the face animation code

In the AssimpModel class, two new drawing methods are added:

```
    void drawInstancedNoMorphAnims(int instanceCount);
    void drawInstancedMorphAnims(int instanceCount);
```

The names say what the methods are doing: drawInstancedNoMorphAnims() draws all meshes without morph animations, and drawInstancedMorphAnims() draws only the meshes with morph animations.

To filter the meshes in both methods, a quite simple check is used – we loop over all the meshes and look at the size of the morphMeshes vector inside the mesh. For the drawInstancedNoMorphAnims() method that draws only non-morph meshes, we simply skip the meshes without extra morph meshes:

```
for (unsigned int i = 0; i < mModelMeshes.size(); ++i) {
  if (mModelMeshes.at(i).morphMeshes.size() > 0) {
    continue;
  }
  OGLMesh& mesh = mModelMeshes.at(i);
  drawInstanced(mesh, i, instanceCount);
}
```

And for the morph-mesh-only version, we reverse the check:

```
    ...
    if (mModelMeshes.at(i).morphMeshes.size() == 0) {
      continue;
    ...
    }
```

The reason for using two separate methods lies in the draw() method of the renderer class files, OGLRenderer.cpp or VkRenderer.cpp. There, we replace the normal instanced draw call for the animated models with the no-morph version:

```
model->drawInstancedNoMorphAnims(numberOfInstances);
```

Drawing the meshes with morph animations is done after checking whether the model contains any morph meshes, as shown in the following code of the OpenGL renderer:

```
        if (model->hasAnimMeshes()) {
          mAssimpSkinningMorphShader.use();
          ...
          model->bindMorphAnimBuffer(4);
          mFaceAnimPerInstanceDataBuffer.uploadSsboData(
            mFaceAnimPerInstanceData, 5);
          model->drawInstancedMorphAnims(numberOfInstances);
        }
```

In this case, we use the new morphing shader, bind the two SSBOs containing the vertex data and the per-instance settings, and use the draw call that only draws meshes with morph animations.

For a simple test, you can set the morphData values in the renderer to some fixed values and check whether the instances run around angry or smiling. But to have full control of the new settings, we will also add a combo box and a slider to the UI.

Adding UI elements to control face animations

For the UI, the amount of code is small. We just need a combo box, mapping the isFaceAnimType value of InstanceSettings to the string from micFaceAnimationNameMap, and a float slider linked to isFaceAnimWeight. With a model without a face animation, we simply disable the combo box and the slider.

Figure 10.3 shows the expanded combo box with the four face animations plus the None setting to disable face animations:

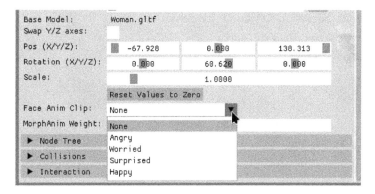

Figure 10.3: UI settings to control the face animations of an instance

We can choose the face animation clip now, and by using the weight slider, we can control how much of the face animation morph will be used.

As the last step for the face animations implementation, we will cover how to add the new settings to the YAML configuration file.

Saving and loading the new instance settings

Luckily, the current state of the YAML parser and emitter code allows us to add face animations with truly little effort. Since the face animation settings are set per instance, we need to extend the YAML emitter output operator for `InstanceSettings` in the `YamlParser.cpp` file in the `tools` folder.

Right after the output of the optional node tree setting, we check whether a face animation is configured and output the instance settings if a clip was set:

```
if (settings.isFaceAnimType != faceAnimation::none) {
  out << YAML::Key << "face-anim-index";
  out << YAML::Value << settings.isFaceAnimType;
  out << YAML::Key << "face-anim-weight";
  out << YAML::Value << settings.isFaceAnimWeight;
}
```

To output the faceAnimation enum, we also need a definition of the output operator for the new data type:

```
YAML::Emitter& operator<<(YAML::Emitter& out,
    const faceAnimation& faceAnim) {
  out << YAML::Flow;
  out << static_cast<int>(faceAnim);
  return out;
}
```

In the YamlParserTypes.h file, we also need a simple decode() method for the new faceAnimation data type:

```
template<>
struct convert<faceAnimation> {
  static bool decode(const Node& node, faceAnimation& rhs) {
      rhs = static_cast<faceAnimation>(node.as<int>());
      return true;
    }
};
```

The encode() method is not shown here, it essentially does the same as all other enum encode() methods do: it casts the node data to an int.

Finally, we just must extend the decode() method for the ExtendedInstanceSettings, adding the two new values:

```
        if (node["face-anim"]) {
          rhs.isFaceAnimType =
            node["face-anim"].as<faceAnimation>();
          rhs.isFaceAnimWeight =
            node["face-anim-weight"].as<float>();
        }
```

The encode() method extension is also super simple:

```
        if (rhs.isFaceAnimType != faceAnimation::none) {
          node["face-anim"] = rhs.isFaceAnimType;
          node["face-anim-weight"] = rhs.isFaceAnimWeight;
        }
```

Make sure to bump the version of the configuration file since we added new data to it. In this case, changing the file version is less crucial since parser versions from previous chapters simply do not know the new settings.

And that's it! When you select an instance now, you can change the type and strength of the facial expression, as shown in *Figure 10.4*:

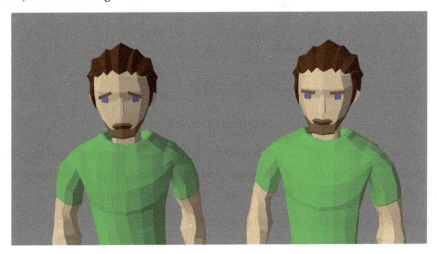

Figure 10.4: A "worried" instance next to the default face mesh

The face animations can be controlled for every instance, and changes to one instance do not affect other instances. It is up to you if you want the instances to be angry, worried, happy, or even surprised, and how much of that expression will be shown.

Adding more morph clips to the application is also easy. The most complex thing for new clips will be most probably the vertex animation in a tool such as Blender. In the code, it is just adding a new value to the `faceAnimation` enum `class` and a new string to the name mapping in the `micFaceAnimationNameMap` variable of the `ModelInstanceCamData` struct.

To be able to use the new face animations in a node tree too, we need to create a new node type, allowing us to control both the animation clip and the weight of the desired morph target animation. So, let's add the all-new **FaceAnim** node.

Using face animations in node trees

Creating a new node type is easy. First, we add a new class, FaceAnimNode, consisting of the `FaceAnimNode.h` header and the implementation file, `FaceAnimNode.cpp`, both placed in the graphnodes folder. We can borrow most of the implementation from the WaitNode, adding ImGui elements and a bit of logic to control the face animation during the execution time. *Figure 10.5* shows the final layout of the FaceAnim node:

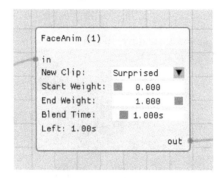

Figure 10.5: The new FaceAnim node

The node allows us to choose one of the face animation clips, including the None setting to disable face animations on an instance, starting and ending weights for the animation in both play directions, and a timer to control how long the animation replay will take.

Before we can add the new FaceAnim node, we must extend the enum containing the node types and the graph node factory class.

Adjusting the code for the new FaceAnim node

Similar to WaitNode, the FaceAnim node delays the control flow until the timer reaches zero and informs the parent node about it once the animation replay has ended.

Next to adding the two new files, creating the new node type needs two extra steps.

First, we must extend the graphNodeType enum in the Enums.h file:

```
enum class graphNodeType : int8_t {
  ...
  faceAnim,
  NUM
};
```

Next, the constructor and the makeNode() method of the GraphNodeFactory class must be made aware of the new node. In the constructor, we add the node title string to mGraphNodeTypeMap:

```
  mGraphNodeTypeMap[graphNodeType::faceAnim] = "FaceAnim";
```

In makeNode(), we add a case block for the new node type:

```
case graphNodeType::faceAnim:
  newNode = std::make_shared<FaceAnimNode>(nodeId);
  break;
```

Now we can adjust the implementation of the new FaceAnimNode class.

Adding the FaceAnim node

As we will blend manually between the two weight values, we will map the blend time to a range between zero and one in the update() method once the node is active:

```
float morphTimeDiff = 1.0f;
if (mFaceAnimBlendTime != 0.0f) {
  morphTimeDiff = std::clamp(mCurrentTime /
    mFaceAnimBlendTime, 0.0f, 1.0f);
}
```

By doing a simple division, surrounded by a check to avoid a division by zero, the time difference in morphTimeDiff will go from one to zero.

Then we interpolate the final weight by using the product of the time difference and weight difference:

```
float morphWeightDiff =
  mFaceAnimEndWeight - mFaceAnimStartWeight;
float currentWeight =
  mFaceAnimEndWeight - morphWeightDiff * morphTimeDiff;
```

On every run of the update() method, we continuously sent the new weight via the fireNodeOutputCallback to the renderer:

```
instanceUpdateType updateType =
  instanceUpdateType::faceAnimWeight;
nodeCallbackVariant result;
bool extra = false;
result = currentWeight;
fireNodeActionCallback(getNodeType(), updateType,
  result, extra);
```

Before doing the weight update, we send the desired animation clip index in the activate()
method:

```
instanceUpdateType updateType =
  instanceUpdateType::faceAnimIndex;
nodeCallbackVariant result;
bool extra = false;
result = mFaceAnim;
fireNodeActionCallback(getNodeType(), updateType,
  result, extra);
```

To signal the face animation values to the renderer, the instanceUpdateType enum needs to be
extended by two new values, faceAnimIndex and faceAnimWeight:

```
enum class instanceUpdateType : uint8_t {
  ...
  faceAnimIndex,
  faceAnimWeight
};
```

We also need the faceAnimation type in the nodeCallbackVariant variant to use the new data
type in the callbacks between the classes:

```
using nodeCallbackVariant = std::variant<float, moveState, moveDirection,
faceAnimation>;
```

Since we use the fireNodeOutputCallback in the node, both the GraphEditor and the
SingleInstanceBehavior classes need to be extended.

In the GraphEditor.cpp file in the graphnodes folder, the faceAnim node type must be added to
the createNodeEditorWindow() method to bind the node action callback to the newly created
faceAnim nodes:

```
        if (nodeType == graphNodeType::instance ||
            nodeType == graphNodeType::action ||
            nodeType == graphNodeType::faceAnim {
          newNode->setNodeActionCallback(
            behavior->bdNodeActionCallbackFunction);
        }
```

A similar check exists in the `SingleInstanceBehavior` copy constructor; we also have to add the `faceAnim` node type here to bind the node action callback:

```
if (node->getNodeType() == graphNodeType::instance ||
    node->getNodeType() == graphNodeType::action ||
    node->getNodeType() == graphNodeType::faceAnim {
  newNode->setNodeActionCallback(
    mBehaviorData->bdNodeActionCallbackFunction);
}
```

In addition to a manipulation of the `InstanceSettings` variables when changing the face animation settings, we add two new setters to the `AssimpInstance` class for simplified access to the new `InstanceSettings` variables.

Enabling instance and renderer to react to face animation changes

Updating the `InstanceSettings` by reading all data first plus writing all data back at the end is good if we need to adjust more than multiple values. For a single change, separate setters are easier to use. We add the two new `public` methods `setFaceAnim()` and `setFaceAnimWeight()` to the `AssimpInstance` class:

```
void setFaceAnim(faceAnimation faceAnim);
void setFaceAnimWeight(float weight);
```

Both methods update the two values in the `InstanceSettings` data of the instance, plus a bit of extra logic to handle the none value of the `faceAnimation` enum.

As the last step for the new node, the `updateInstanceSettings()` method of the renderer class, `OGLRenderer.cpp` or `VkRenderer.cpp`, needs to know what to do when an instance wants to change the face animation settings.

To do that, in the `switch` block for the node type, a new `case` block for the new `faceAnim` node type must be added:

```
switch (nodeType) {
  ...
  case graphNodeType::faceAnim:
```

Then, we check for the type of face animation update we have received. Since we need to react to a change to the face animation clip index and the clip weight, a new `switch`/`case` statement with the two update types is added:

```
switch (updateType) {
  case instanceUpdateType::faceAnimIndex:
    instance->setFaceAnim(
      std::get<faceAnimation>(data));
    break;
  case instanceUpdateType::faceAnimWeight:
    instance->setFaceAnimWeight(
      std::get<float>(data));
    break;
  default:
    break;
```

We also need to close the case block for the `faceAnim` node type:

```
  }
  break;
```

For the two new update types, `faceAnimIndex` and `faceAnimWeight`, the newly added methods in the `AssimpInstance` class will be called, using the data from the `nodeCallbackVariant` variant as parameters.

This last step completes the chain from the new node to the renderer, allowing us to use the face animations in the node editor. The FaceAnim node to the node tree of the man's model can be used to change the wave animations of all instances to let the instance wave with a smiling face, as shown in *Figure 10.6*:

Figure 10.6: Combined "Wave" action and "Happy" face animation in a node tree

More additions to the node tree are possible. You can make the models angry before punching or kicking, or surprised before playing the picking animation to simulate that the instance has seen something on the ground. And with more skeletal and face animation clips, even more funny and crazy combinations can be created.

Being able to see someone's mood in their face helps us as humans to evaluate possible next steps, and bringing facial expressions into the application enables a much broader way to interact with the instances. By using morph target animations, even our basic low-poly models take on much more personality.

But morph target animations have three severe limitations, which we'll discuss next.

Limitations of morph target animations

When using morph target animations, we must take care of these three limits:

- The number of vertices in the mesh must be identical in all animations and frames. It is not possible to add or remove vertices within a frame or during an animation, or to change the vertex assignment to triangles. You can only move the vertices around.

- The entire mesh of the morphing part of the model must be replicated for every morph key in an animation. For smaller parts of the model's body, this may be okay, but having a high-detail part of the body several times in memory may create a noticeable overhead.

- Only vertex position changes are supported, the morphing is usually done by a simple linear interpolation. Small rotations can be simulated by position changes but moving vertices by a large rotation or scaling, like for turning the head or moving the hands around, will result in visual distortions during the interpolation.

You can test the third limit by yourself in Blender. To do that, add a morph target-based rotation of the head, and you will see the rotation also affects the volume of the head. The larger the rotation angle gets, the bigger the distortion during the animation becomes.

Figure 10.7 shows the result of around 50% of a head rotation by 180 degrees:

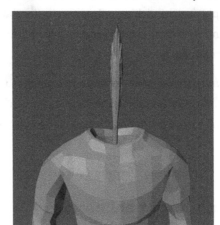

Figure 10.7: Distorted volume while rotating the head with a morph target animation

Morph target animations must be created and tested carefully while animating a model. They are a valuable addition to animations, but they still have some drawbacks.

How do we create advanced animations that may need rotations without using morph target animations, such as a fancy head movement animation to let the model look around in the virtual world?

That's what we'll learn next as we dive into additive blending.

Implementing additive blending

Additive blending is an alternative method of animation blending. While *normal* animation blending is used to interpolate between two skeletal animation clips and morph target animations are changing vertex positions of a mesh, additive blending *stacks* two different skeletal animations on top of each other.

The technical part of additive blending is astonishingly simple, but the effect achieved by the combination of two different skeletal animations leads to a much more natural appearance of a 3D model.

Let's explore the similarities and differences between additive blending and the animation blending methods we already know.

How additive blending works

The basic idea of additive blending comes from the desire to split up model animations into multiple and especially independent parts.

A skeletal animation usually delivers an animation for the entire model, allowing the model to either run, walk, punch, or jump. Blending between skeletal animations will smooth the transition between these two clips but won't add new movements. So, there are two different approaches: splitting the skeleton or stacking animations.

Splitting the skeleton into two or even more animation domains and playing a different clip for each part of the skeleton is called **layered blending**. Layered blending is a simple and cost-effective way to mix animations since every node of the skeleton is affected only by the transforms of a single animation clip, just the animation clips are different for the nodes.

But splitting the model skeleton into multiple parts with each part playing a different skeletal animation may lead to extra effort to synchronize clips across the body. Failures in a synchronous replay on a split-skeleton animation may lead to visual artifacts, just think of different replay speeds for the clips.

We don't handle layered blending in the book, but a task in the *Practical sessions* section is available to implement layered animation blending for the models. In contrast, additive blending allows *adding up* skeletal animations on top of other skeletal animations. While the basic movement created by the basic skeletal animation is applied normally, property changes of one or even more other skeletal animations are added to the nodes of the model, creating a concatenated motion with what's provided by the basic animation. Additive blending is more expensive to calculate than layered blending because we need to calculate multiple animations, and we also have to mix all the animations together. As an example, this simple addition of property changes allows us to add a head movement to the normal skeletal animations. The model will be able to run, walk, punch, or jump from a skeletal animation *and* move the head around at the same time. As a bonus, facial animations are not affected by additive blending, so a model can walk, look to the right, and smile, and all three animations are running in parallel.

For the technical implementation part, an additive animation is done by adding the differences in the node transformations between the current pose and a reference pose to another skeletal animation.

Let's use another example to explain the technical side. *Figure 10.8* shows the first and the last keyframe for an animation that only rotates the head node of the model to the right (from the model's perspective), while all other nodes remain in the T-pose:

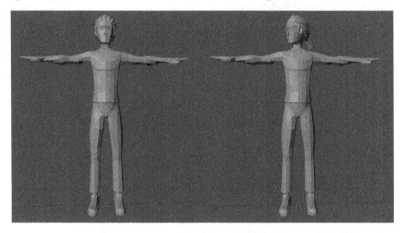

Figure 10.8: Start and end pose for the additive animation "head look right"

As the reference pose, we use the first keyframe, with the entire model in the T-pose. To calculate the values for an additive animation, we take the desired keyframe and simply subtract the translation, rotation, and scale values of the reference pose from the destination pose.

If the model remains in the T-pose, all values for the additive animation will be zero. And nothing is added to the running skeletal animation, for instance, the walking cycle.

When we advance further in the animation clip in *Figure 10.8*, the rotation of the head will lead to a bigger difference in the rotation value of the head node between the current pose and the reference pose. But we will get only a difference for the head node, all other node transformations are still identical to the reference pose.

Adding the difference of the head node rotation to the currently running skeletal animation clip is easy. Since we collect the transformation properties for all nodes, a combination of two skeletal animations is just a simple per-node addition of the values for translation and scale, and a quaternion multiplication for the rotation value.

This addition only changes the values for nodes that have changed in the animation clip of the additive animation clip compared to the reference pose. All nodes without changes in the additive animation will remain unaltered in the skeletal animation.

How to create suitable animations

Creating animations to use in additive blending is out of the scope of this book, similar to creating face animations. You can use a tool like Blender, or use the man's model from *Chapter 10*, which already contains four extra animations altering only the head.

If you create extra animations by yourself, make sure to prefix the clip names with something common, like an underscore, or the letters ZZZ_ to keep them grouped together. At least Blender tends to sort the clips by name during the export and since we store several clip mappings based on the index number of the clip in the YAML configuration file, adding the new clips at the start or somewhere in-between the existing clips would lead to broken config files.

Implementing additive animations in our application is also surprisingly simple.

Extending the code to support additive animations

To bring the additional data to the GPU, we add four new variables to the struct PerInstanceAnimData in the OGLRenderData.h file in the opengl folder:

```
struct PerInstanceAnimData {
    ...
    unsigned int headLeftRightAnimClipNum;
    unsigned int headUpDownAnimClipNum;
    ...
    float headLeftRightReplayTimestamp;
    float headUpDownReplayTimestamp;
};
```

As always for Vulkan, the file is called VkRenderData.h and resides in the vulkan folder.

We split the head animation into two parts and use separate variables to control both the left/right animation and the up/down animation of the head. It's impossible to move the head to the left and right at the same time, so we can combine those two directions into a single control variable. The same holds true for moving the head up and down.

Then, we create a new private compute shader called mAssimpTransformHeadMoveComputeSha der in the renderer class file, OGLRanderer.cpp:

```
Shader mAssimpTransformHeadMoveComputeShader{};
```

For Vulkan, we add a new VkPipeline handle named rdAssimpComputeHeadMoveTransformPip eline to the VkRenderData.h file:

```
VkPipeline rdAssimpComputeHeadMoveTransformPipeline;
```

Since not all models may have additive head animations, we could skip the extra calculations if no head animations were set. We also add the new variables in the PerInstanceAnimData struct to the compute shader file, assimp_instance_transform.comp. The new head animation variables will be ignored, but we need to expand the struct to the same size in both shaders.

Next, we copy the assimp_instance_transform.comp file to assimp_instance_headmove_ transform.comp and load the new file into the new mAssimpTransformHeadMoveComputeShader compute shader during the init() method of the OGLRenderer.cpp. For Vulkan, we create the new rendering pipeline loading the head transform compute shader in the createPipelines() method of VkRenderer.cpp.

In the new shader file, most of the additions are just copy and paste work. We must do the following steps in the extended compute shader, using the code for the rotational part of the left/ right head movement as examples:

1. Extract the animation clip numbers for both head animations:

    ```
    uint headLeftRightClip =
        instAnimData[instance].headLeftRightAnimClipNum;
    ```

2. Extract the inverse scale factors for both head animations:

    ```
    float headLeftRightRotInvScaleFactor =
        lookupData[headLeftRightClip * clipOffset +
            node * boneOffset + lookupWidth].x;
    ```

3. Calculate the index values for accessing the lookup data of the head animations:

    ```
    int headLeftRightRotLookupIndex =
        clamp(int(instAnimData[instance]
            .headLeftRightReplayTimestamp *
            headLeftRightRotInvScaleFactor) + 1, 0,
            lookupWidth - 1);
    ```

4. Get translation, rotation, and scale values for both the reference pose at the first lookup positions and the desired head animation clip timestamps:

```
vec4 headLeftRightBaseRotation =
    lookupData[headLeftRightClip * clipOffset + node *
    boneOffset + lookupWidth + 1];
...
vec4 headLeftRightRotation =
    lookupData[headLeftRightClip * clipOffset + node *
    boneOffset + lookupWidth +
    HeadLeftRightRotLookupIndex];
```

5. Calculate the difference between the transform values of the current pose and the references pose, using a quaternion multiplication for the rotation:

```
vec4 headLeftRightRotationDiff =
    qMult(qInverse(headLeftRightBaseRotation),
        headLeftRightRotation);
```

6. Add up the differences for translation, rotation, and scale for both head animations to a single value for each transform:

```
vec4 headRotationDiff =
    qMult(headUpDownRotationDiff,
        headLeftRightRotationDiff);
```

7. Add the summed-up differences to the first and second clip transforms, again using a quaternion multiplication for the rotation:

```
vec4 finalRotation =
    slerp(qMult(headRotationDiff, firstRotation),
        qMult(headRotationDiff, secondRotation), blendFactor);
```

The instances also need to carry information about the head movements, so we add the two new variables, isHeadLeftRightMove and isHeadUpDownMove, to the InstanceSettings struct in the InstanceSettings.h file:

```
float isHeadLeftRightMove = 0.0f;
float isHeadUpDownMove = 0.0f;
```

We map the positive ranges between 0.0f and 1.0f to a head movement to the left and upwards, and the negative range from 0.0f to -1.0f to move the head to the right or down. A movement value of zero will use the values of the reference pose for both animations, resulting in no head movement at all.

Filling the new data in the PerInstanceAnimData struct is done in the draw() call of the OGLRenderer or VKRenderer class, in the same part of the code as the facial animations. Following the mapping explained before, selecting the clip number is done as shown here:

```
if (instSettings.isHeadLeftRightMove > 0.0f) {
  animData.headLeftRightAnimClipNum =
    modSettings.msHeadMoveClipMappings[
    headMoveDirection::left];
} else {
  animData.headLeftRightAnimClipNum =
    modSettings.msHeadMoveClipMappings[
    headMoveDirection::right];
}
```

For head movement, we use the absolute value of the timestamp:

```
animData.headLeftRightReplayTimestamp =
  std::fabs(instSettings.isHeadLeftRightMove) *
    model->getMaxClipDuration();
```

Hard coding the clip numbers in the code is a bad idea, different models have these new animations on other clip indices, or not at all. Let's add another mapping, this time between the additive blending clip numbers and the four possible directions of the head movement.

Creating mappings for the new head animations

For a mapping between clips and head animations, a new enum class called headMoveDirection is created in the Enums.h file:

```
enum class headMoveDirection : uint8_t {
  left = 0,
  right,
  up,
  down,
  NUM
};
```

The corresponding string map micHeadMoveAnimationNameMap to show the names in the UI is added to the ModelInstanceCamData struct:

```
std::unordered_map<headMoveDirection, std::string>
  micHeadMoveAnimationNameMap{};
```

And since the mapping is model-related, the new msHeadMoveClipMappings mapping is added to the ModelSettings struct in the ModelSettings.h file:

```
std::map<headMoveDirection, int> msHeadMoveClipMappings{};
```

The AssimpModel class also gets a new public method to check whether all the mappings in msHeadMoveClipMappings are active:

```
bool hasHeadMovementAnimationsMapped();
```

Failing to find at least one of the head animations leads to a disabled additive head animation.

In the draw() call of the OGLRenderer.cpp files, we switch the compute shader based on the availability of all head animation mappings:

```
if (model->hasHeadMovementAnimationsMapped()) {
  mAssimpTransformHeadMoveComputeShader.use();
} else {
  mAssimpTransformComputeShader.use();
}
```

For Vulkan, we use the availability of head move animations to choose the pipeline to bind for the compute shader in the runComputeShaders() method of the VkRenderer.cpp file:

```
if (model->hasHeadMovementAnimationsMapped()) {
  vkCmdBindPipeline(mRenderData.rdComputeCommandBuffer,
    VK_PIPELINE_BIND_POINT_COMPUTE,
    mRenderData.rdAssimpComputeHeadMoveTransformPipeline);
} else {
  vkCmdBindPipeline(mRenderData.rdComputeCommandBuffer,
    VK_PIPELINE_BIND_POINT_COMPUTE,
    mRenderData.rdAssimpComputeTransformPipeline);
}
```

The UI part for the head animations can be copied mostly from other parts of the code in the UserInterface class. A combo box to select the clip, a loop over all four values in the headMoveDirection enum, two buttons, and two sliders to test the animations are all we need to create a new UI section, as shown in *Figure 10.9*:

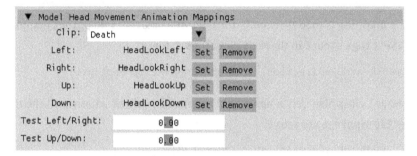

Figure 10.9: UI control for the head movement/animation clip mapping

Clip mapping and clips are taken from the model of the currently selected instance, making it easy to configure the additive head animations for all models.

To use the head animation in node trees, another new node type is needed.

Adding a head animation node

Thanks to the previous FaceAnimNode node, adding a new HeadAnimNode is done in minutes. You can follow the steps in the *Using face animations in node trees* section to create the new node as you have to do the same actions as with the FaceAnimNode. Only a couple of minor changes are needed, like the names of the enum class entries.

For the UI part of the new node, you can reuse the FaceAnimNode class code for the controls and copy the code to switch the two sections on or off from the InstanceNode class code.

The final **HeadAnim** node to be used in a node tree looks like in *Figure 10.10*:

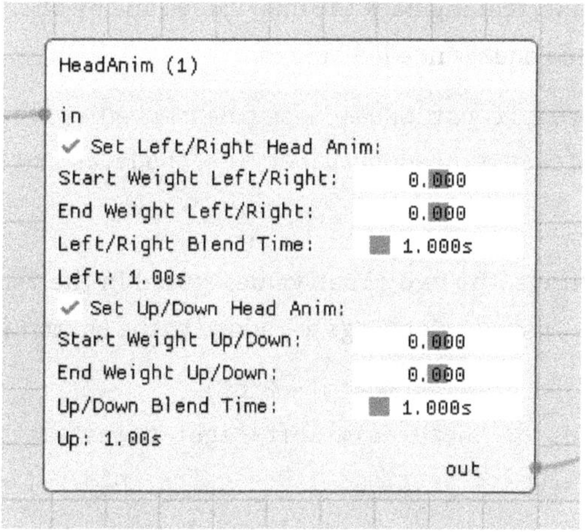

Figure 10.10: The HeadAnim node

Like the Instance node, we can control which head animation values we want to change, and for each animation, we can adjust the starting and ending weight plus the time it takes to blend between the two weight values. And like the FaceAnim node, the HeadAnim node delays the control flow until both timers are expired and signals the end of the execution to the parent node.

We close the chapter with the changes needed to save and load the settings for the additive head animations.

Saving and loading the head animation settings

Similar to the new tree node, implementing the YAML configuration file changes to save and load head animation settings is a matter of minutes.

For the `ModelSettings` YAML emitter output in the `YamlParser.cpp` file, we add the clip mappings directly from the map if all four clips are configured. We also need a new emitter output for the `headMoveDirection` enum, casting the value to an int:

```
YAML::Emitter& operator<<(YAML::Emitter& out,
    const headMoveDirection& moveDir) {
  out << YAML::Flow;
  out << static_cast<int>(moveDir);
  return out;
}
```

To load the mapping back, we add a section to the decode() method for the ModelSettings in the YamlParserTypes.h file, reading back the map values one by one. A new decode() method for the headMoveDirection enum is needed here too:

```
static bool decode(const Node& node, headMoveDirection& rhs) {
    rhs = static_cast<headMoveDirection>(node.as<int>());
}
```

And for the instance settings, the two float values stored in the isHeadLeftRightMove and isHeadUpDownMove of the InstanceSettings are added to the emitter in YamlParser.cpp:

```
if (settings.isHeadLeftRightMove != 0.0f) {
  out << YAML::Key << "head-anim-left-right-timestamp";
  out << YAML::Value << settings.isHeadLeftRightMove;
}
if (settings.isHeadUpDownMove != 0.0f) {
  out << YAML::Key << "head-anim-up-down-timestamp";
  out << YAML::Value << settings.isHeadUpDownMove;
}
```

And the two values are also to the decode() method for the ExtendedInstanceSettings data type in YamlParserTypes.h:

```
if (node["head-anim-left-right-timestamp"]) {
  rhs.isHeadLeftRightMove =
    node["head-anim-left-right-timestamp"].as<float>();
}
if (node["head-anim-up-down-timestamp"]) {
  rhs.isHeadUpDownMove =
    node["head-anim-up-down-timestamp"].as<float>();
}
```

After all these additions, you can add some HeadAnim nodes to the node tree of the man's model, creating animations like the one shown in *Figure 10.11*:

Figure 10.11: The instance looks up while waving and smiling

The instance can now turn the head at any time in a natural manner, we just need to add the new HeadAnim node to the control flow. If you go back to *Figure 10.6*, you will see that a small addition like the head movement makes an enormous difference in the appearance of the instance.

You can let your imagination flow about other possibilities for the new head movement. Do you want the head to follow the camera or any other nearby instance? Do you want to nod the head to signal *yes* and shake the head slightly if the answer to a question is *no*? Do you want to make the player look up or down to move the player's point of interest toward the sky or the floor? Some ideas are listed in the *Practical sessions* section if you want to extend the code.

Summary

In this chapter, we added both facial expressions and separate head animations to the instances. We started with a brief exploration of face animations. Then we implemented face animations in the form of morph target animations to code and shaders, enabling the instances to smile or be angry. Next, we added a tree node for the face animations, enabling us to use the new facial expressions in the node trees. Finally, we looked at additive animation blending and added head movement by using additive blending, including a new tree node and UI controls.

In the next chapter, we will leave the animation controls for a while and give the instances literally a room to live in by adding level data to the virtual world, like a game level. We start by checking the formats supported by the Open Assimp Importer Library and search for available level files. Then, we explore reasons why we should separate level data from models and instances. Finally, we load the level data from a file and add the level-related data to the application and renderer.

Practical sessions

Here are some additions you could make to the code:

- Add support for multiple meshes containing morph target animations.

- Currently, only one mesh of a model can have morph target animations. For a simple head animation, this limit is fine. But if you want to control more than one part of the face, using multiple morph targets may be helpful.

- Add blending between two morph targets. For even better and more natural facial expressions, a direct blending between two morph targets would be nice. A detour via the neutral position is no longer needed, then, but a direct path between anger and worry is available.

- Add more morph targets.

- You may try to let the models *speak*. You could add expressions for different vowels and consonants, including the direct blending from the previous task. With such animations, you could mimic instances speaking to you during interactions.

- Add layered/masked animations.
  In contrast to additive animation blending, layered blending uses different skeletal animation clips for distinct parts of the model's virtual body. For instance, all but the right arm uses the running animation and only the right arm plays the waving animation. As noted in the *How additive blending works* section, layered animations may need additional effort to synchronize the two animation clips. You need to add some logic to mask out parts of the model's skeleton.

- Let the instance turn their head toward you on interaction. This is a feature of many games: if you start interacting with an instance, they turn their head around to look directly toward you.

- Let nearby instances *judge* you. This is like the previous task: you could also add the additive head-turning animation to instances walking near you. Add a random facial expression too, enabling the instances to show some sort of emotion when they pass near you.

- Let the instances smile and wave at the nearest instance passing by.

  This is a combination and extension of the two previous tasks: use the interaction logic to find the nearest instance for every instance in the virtual world, then move the head towards that instance. Play the smiling morph animation and a new additive animation with only the right arm waving. You might want to use a layered animation for the arm here.

- Add more additive blending animations.

  Turning the head around is a good start, but what about doing an entire animation of someone looking around? Try to add more layers of additive blending animations to make instances make gestures in interaction.

- Optimize C++ and shader code for better performance.

  The current C++ and GLSL shader code and the data structures on the CPU and GPU were created to explain and explore the features we added here, like morph target animations and facial expressions. There is a lot of room left for optimization, both on the CPU and the GPU. You could try to squeeze more frames per second out of the application, for instance, by optimizing the data types sent to the GPU, by moving more work to compute shaders, or by removing the busy-waits for the shader results on Vulkan. You could also check if data compression has a positive or negative outcome on the frame times. For an easy comparison, add a checkbox to the UI to switch between the default code and the optimized version.

Additional resources

- Layered animations in Unreal Engine: `https://dev.epicgames.com/documentation/en-us/unreal-engine/using-layered-animations-in-unreal-engine`
- Additive animations in Unreal Engine: `https://dev.epicgames.com/documentation/en-us/unreal-engine/additive-vs.-full-body?application_version=4.27`
- Unity Animation Layers: `https://docs.unity3d.com/Manual/AnimationLayers.html`
- Godot Animation Trees: `https://docs.godotengine.org/en/latest/tutorials/animation/animation_tree.html`
- Blender: `https://www.blender.org`
- Blender Shape Keys: `https://docs.blender.org/manual/en/latest/animation/shape_keys/introduction.html`

Join our community on Discord

Join our community's Discord space for discussions with the author and other readers:

`https://packt.link/cppgameanimation`

Part 4

Enhancing Your Virtual World

In the last part of the book, you will give the inhabitants of your virtual worlds a place to live. You will explore the differences between instance and level data, and you will implement a loader for level data, either found on the internet or created by yourself. You will also learn how collision detection between instances and level geometry is handled, allowing the instances not only to avoid walls but also to walk on the floor of the loaded level. Then, you will be introduced to pathfinding and navigation within the level, enabling the instances to roam around between waypoints in the game map. Finally, you will be presented with a collection of ideas and resources to upgrade the animation editor to a small game engine.

This part has the following chapters:

- *Chapter 11, Loading a Game Map*
- *Chapter 12, Advanced Collision Detection*
- *Chapter 13, Adding Simple Navigation*
- *Chapter 14, Creating Immersive Interactive Worlds*

11

Loading a Game Map

Welcome to *Chapter 11*! In the previous chapter, we added facial expressions to the instances. After a brief introduction of morph target animations, we extended the application to load morph meshes and added UI elements to control the face animations of an instance. Also, a new graph node type was added to allow using face animations in node trees. Finally, we implemented additive blending to move the heads of the instances independently of any skeletal and face animations.

In this chapter, we will take a short break from character control and add a game level and level assets to the virtual world. We will start by exploring reasons why level data should be handled differently than models and instances; plus, we will look at suitable file formats to import level data with the Open Asset Importer Library and where to find game levels. Then, we will load level data and assets from files into the application and update the quadtree to become an octree. As the last step, we will add the level-related data to the renderer to draw the game map to the screen, giving us an idea of what the home for the inhabitants of our virtual world will look like. In this chapter, we will cover the following topics:

- Differences between map and model data
- Choosing a file format for a map
- Importing a game map
- Sending the map data to the GPU

Technical requirements

The example code for this chapter is available in the chapter11 folder, in the 01_opengl_level subfolder for OpenGL and the 02_vulkan_level subfolder for Vulkan.

Differences between map and model data

There are some interesting differences between handling models and level data, allowing us to apply optimizations in data handling. In the code for this book, we will do these optimizations after loading the level data. For larger levels, doing a precalculation during level creation is the better approach.

Let's take a closer look at some of the differences.

Level data does not move around

The most significant difference between models and levels is simple: while the properties of a model instance can change, such as position, rotation, and speed, and they play animations, react to events, and so on, a level's architecture typically remains unchanged.

Non-movable and non-animated polygons of a level have a big advantage: some data can be precalculated, either at creation time or at loading time for collision detection or lighting, for example. At runtime, only a lookup into the precalculated data is needed. Plus, we do not have to upload the data in every frame to the GPU again. All triangles can be processed at loading time and then uploaded once into GPU memory, residing there until the level data may be removed from the application by the user.

What about doors, buttons, elevators, or anything that does move in a level?

Movable parts of a level, such as sliding or revolving doors, elevators, buttons and switches, locker doors, mechanical platforms... in short, anything that can move inside a level, are usually modeled and used like an animated model instead of static level data.

Just think of a revolving door as a 3D model of a door, having a single node placed on the hinges. And on interaction, the model rotates around the hinge. Or, for a sliding door, the door model is translated a specific amount to one side, opening the passage to another room. In contrast to those doors, a static wall or a static floor in a level will never move or rotate.

Doing split collision detection for static data also helps us to improve performance.

Using a separate collision detection for level data

For collision detection, we can add a quadtree or octree containing only the level data. This tree must be recreated when the level is loaded and can be kept read-only during runtime, skipping costly operations of adding and removing instances. We then use the AABBs of the instances to check the level-data tree if an instance is colliding with level geometry. Using different tree structures for instance and level data also allows us to configure the trees according to the specific needs. A level octree may need entirely different values for maximum depth and number of triangles per node due to many triangles in the map, while there are only a few instances running around in the virtual world. In addition to the improvements for static data, a game level may contain other data that is not needed for models.

Level data may contain additional data

Both CPU and GPU time are scarce resources at runtime, and any data that can be made available in lookup tables or calculated in a shader can save precious milliseconds when creating the next frame. We saw the effect in *Chapter 2* while moving parts of the animation calculation to a compute shader, and again in *Chapter 7* after adding animation lookup tables to GPU memory. In both chapters, a significant frame time boost was achieved for the same number of instances on the screen.

For level data, similar accelerations can be done. Four examples of such additional data are spatial division, lightmaps, navigation meshes, and hierarchical level of detail. Let's take a brief look at these extra data types. Links to more detailed explanations can be found in the *Additional resources* section at the end of the chapter.

Spatial division

We talked about the spatial division of a level when diving into collision detection in *Chapter 8*. Saving spatial division data to the level file is needed to avoid doing the same calculations at loading time, or even at runtime of the game.

Creating **Binary Space Partition (BSP)** trees or dividing the virtual world into an octree may take a long time, depending on the number of triangles in a level and the overall level complexity. This kind of computation can be moved to level creation time, adding only an optimized lookup version to the final level file.

Lightmaps

Even though the principle of lightmaps was introduced in **id Software**'s **Quake** nearly thirty years ago, this technique is still in use today. During level creation, the light effects of static lights are "baked" into a texture, with bright pixels depicting the parts of the level geometry where the light of a static light source shines onto a surface, and dark pixels where shadows are on the level surface.

The lightmap texture is then added as a secondary texture, darkening the areas where the light from a light source does not reach the level geometry and simulating a shadow. Using a lightmap can drastically speed up light calculations by keeping a reasonable visual effect, since less expensive per-pixel calculations are needed.

Navigation mesh

A **navmesh**, or **navigation mesh**, is an addition for enemies, NPCs, or any other computer-controlled objects. The level geometry will be overlayed with an extra mesh made of triangles or other polygons, but only in those places where computer-controlled objects should be able to move around. A navmesh accelerates pathfinding for the objects and can help to prevent collision checks when placed correctly.

We will come back to navigation meshes in *Chapter 13*, when we add simple navigation to the instances.

Hierarchical level-of-detail

Model files can include so-called level-of-detail meshes. When drawing models that are far away from the camera, the mesh complexity can be lowered without affecting the visual quality as the model will cover only a few pixels of the screen. By using different mesh resolutions, the overall number of triangles to draw the models can be reduced.

Level data can leverage level-of-detail meshes even more, replacing groups of objects with a simpler representation. For example, instead of drawing a large number of visually indistinguishable rocks at a great distance, the **Hierarchical Level-of-Detail** (**HLOD**) version of the same area could be merged to a single mesh with adjusted textures, delivering a similar visual quality with a fraction of the polygons and textures.

Level data may be partial or incomplete

Your fancy animated 3D model should be fully available all the time, not only half of the model, or even less. But for level data, the sheer size of a level could be too much for a PC or console to handle at once, especially when taking the additional level data into account, like for lighting, navigation, or collision detection. But also texture size and quality, or the number and distribution of computer-controlled characters can raise the memory requirements by and large. Plus, the currently loaded level part could have much more detail, using the available resources to draw the visible area instead of keeping invisible and unused data in memory.

Keeping the immersion for the player alive is part of the level design. The level may be hidden behind a winding passage, where none of the two-level parts is visible, allowing the game engine to discard the area where the player is coming from and loading the part they are heading to. Another widely used example for level switches is to use elevators and load new level data as the next floor of a building, spaceship, or similar.

By using precomputed data wisely, the time to render a single frame could be reduced to deliver a greater experience to the player. Or the visual details could be adjusted with the now unused CPU power, allowing to show more objects on the screen, or more detailed objects, while still maintaining the same frame time.

After the differences between maps and instances are clear, let's see which file formats are mostly used for level data, and how to get game maps.

Choosing a file format for a map

The Open Asset Importer Library knows several old and new formats for 3D character models, but – sadly – support for level data is pretty limited.

We will explore file formats of level files mostly found on the internet first, and then look at alternatives if the available formats do not fit our needs.

Using levels in file formats supported by Assimp

A couple of file formats are used to create game level data, either by creating data from scratch or by using buildings and landscapes from other games as templates.

If you want to get some game maps to import, you should check out these websites:

- **Sketchfab**: https://sketchfab.com/
- **Free3D**: https://free3d.com

On both sites, an enormous number of free and paid animated and non-animated models, levels, and assets can be searched and downloaded. Several models come with a Creative Commons license, allowing you to use models in free and even commercial projects.

Usually, you will find levels in the following formats:

- Khronos Group glTF (`.gltf`/`.glb`): The open source glTF format can not only be used for models like the animated Woman and Man models we are using in the chapters, but also entire levels can be exported as glTF files.

- Collada (`.dae`): Collada is an old but fully open XML-based file format. Collada is also managed by the Khronos Group, and even an ISO standard for the file format has been created.

- Wavefront (`.obj` + `.mtl`): Many levels can be found in the Wavefront file format. Files in Wavefront format are pure text (no binary components) and the format is well documented and widely supported.

- Universal Scene Description (`.usd`/`.usdz`): The **Universal Scene Description** (**USD**) format is quite new compared to the other file formats. USD is also open source and well documented, but the support in Assimp is still experimental due to the complexity of the file format.

- Autodesk FBX (`.fbx`): The "Filmbox" format is proprietary and mostly undocumented, but tools such as Blender and Assimp can read and write this file format. Using FBX is more or less at your own risk as it is possible that only specific versions are working as expected.

If none of these models fits your needs, you may have to extend a file format, or even build a custom file format.

Extending existing formats or creating a custom format

Creating new game levels from scratch or modifying existing game levels may require additional information that is not available in the original file format, such as baked-in light maps, tree data, navigation meshes, or level-of-detail data. See the *Level data may contain additional data* section for more information.

File formats such as glTF have the built-in ability to create extensions, while other file formats may be hard or impossible to extend without breaking existing importers. In such a case, you could invent your own file format from scratch or use a combination of one of the standard file formats for level data and add a custom format to store additional data.

A custom file format was created earlier in this book in the *Adding a YAML parser* section of *Chapter 5*: the YAML configuration file to store all settings of the models, instances, cameras, collision detection, and node trees. Although we are relying on a standard textual format to store the data on disk, the contents of the file are tailored to fit the needs of our example application.

Storing the same data in a binary format would also be possible, for instance, when decoding the text information will take too long.

But creating an entirely new file format should the last resort since you will have to write all the code to read and write the data, keep track of different versions of the file format during read and write operations, and maybe even support different operating systems and hardware architectures. Maintaining such an organically grown file format can become a nightmare.

A better way is to use standard formats and bundle all files into an archive, for instance, into a ZIP file. You don't have to care about missing files when the level is distributed to players or other developers, but at the same time, you do not need to reinvent the wheel by creating a new, all-encompassing file format.

Such archives are more common than you might think. Formats such as WAD from the original DOOM and PAK/PK2/PK3 for the Quake series were created to collect all game data in a single file, and these file types even support patching as files in new archives replace files of the same name in old archives.

 Building your own levels

What if you can't find a suitable game level map on the internet? You still have the option to create a small map by yourself, for instance, with Blender. Creating a map is out of the scope of this book, but you will find suitable tutorials and videos on the internet. You can find links to two example videos in the *Additional resources* section.

After we explored the reasons why separating model and level data in the application, we will now implement new code for loading and processing level data.

Importing a game map

As the first step to load a level, we will add a new C++ class named `AssimpLevel`. You can think of the `AssimpLevel` class as a mix of the two classes, `AssimpModel` and `AssimpInstance`, containing the static vertex data of the model class and dynamic properties such as the position, rotation, or scale of the instance class.

The `AssimpLevel` class consists of two new files, `AssimpLevel.h` and `AssimpLevel.cpp`. Both files are in the model folder, but we will borrow most of the methods and members from the two classes, `AssimpModel` and `AssimpInstance`.

Let's do a brief walkthrough of the `AssimpLevel` class.

Adding a C++ class to hold the level data

Since the level and model/instance data are so similar, we can reuse parts of the functionality we already have in the `AssimpModel` and `AssimpInstance` classes, such as loading the model file or doing matrix operations.

For the static data, we can copy the following methods and members from the `AssimpModel` class, exchanging the `model` part in the name with `level` to be consistent with the class name:

- The `loadModel()` method, but without bones, animations, and lookup table creation
- The `processNode()` method, again without the bone-specific part
- The entire `draw()` method
- The `getTriangleCount()`, `getModelFileName()`, and `getModelFileNamePath()` methods
- The `setModelSettings()` and `getModelSettings()` methods
- The `mTriangleCount` and `mVertexCount` member variables
- The `mRootNode`, `mNodeList`, `mRootTransformMatrix`, `mModelMeshes`, `mVertexBuffers`, and `mModelSettings` member variables to store the viable level data
- The `mTextures` and `mPlaceholderTexture` member variables for the textures

For the dynamic data, the following methods and members can be copied from the `AssimpInstance` class, again replacing the word `model` with `level` in the names:

- The `updateModelRootMatrix()` and `getWorldTransformMatrix()` methods
- The `mLocalTranslationMatrix`, `mLocalRotationMatrix`, `mLocalScaleMatrix`, `mLocalSwapAxisMatrix`, `mLocalTransformMatrix`, and `mModelRootMatrix` member variables

To have all the variable level data in one location, we create the `LevelSettings.h` file in the model folder, containing the `LevelSettings` struct:

```
struct LevelSettings {
  std::string lsLevelFilenamePath;
  std::string lsLevelFilename;
  glm::vec3 lsWorldPosition = glm::vec3(0.0f);
  glm::vec3 lsWorldRotation = glm::vec3(0.0f);
  float lsScale = 1.0f;
  bool lsSwapYZAxis = false;
};
```

As you can see, these level settings are also a mix of data taken partially from model settings (filenames) and instance settings (position, rotation, scale, axis swap). The LevelSettings data type will be used to simplify the level settings in the user interface and to save and load level-related data.

We also make the loaded level data available to other parts of the application by adding a vector of AssimpLevel shared pointers called micLevels and the micSelectedlevel int that holds the currently selected level from the vector:

```
std::vector<std::shared_ptr<AssimpLevel>> micLevels{};
int micSelectedLevel = 0;
```

The main work to manage the AssimpLevel objects in the micLevels vector will be handled by the renderer class, so we add methods and callbacks as the second step.

Adding callbacks and renderer code

Similarities between the new level functionality and existing model functions also continue in the callbacks. Three new callback definitions named levelCheckCallback, levelAddCallback, and levelDeleteCallback must be added to the Callbacks.h file:

```
using levelCheckCallback = std::function<bool(std::string)>;
using levelAddCallback = std::function<bool(std::string)>;
using levelDeleteCallback =
  std::function<void(std::string)>;
```

For the models, we have the same set of callbacks. The first callback, levelCheckCallback, is used to check if a level file with the same name is already loaded, and the other two callbacks, levelAddCallback and levelDeleteCallback, are used to load a new level from a file and to delete an existing level object.

Like for most of the callbacks, we will also make the functions available in the ModelInstanceCamData struct in ModelInstanceCamData.h:

```
levelCheckCallback micLevelCheckCallbackFunction;
levelAddCallback micLevelAddCallbackFunction;
levelDeleteCallback micLevelDeleteCallbackFunction;
```

In the renderer class, four new methods are added to handle the level management. And again, the new methods, hasLevel(), getLevel(), addLevel(), and deleteLevel(), are mostly copies from the equivalent model methods:

```
bool hasLevel(std::string levelFileName);
std::shared_ptr<AssimpLevel> getLevel(std::string
  levelFileName);
bool addLevel(std::string levelFileName);
void deleteLevel(std::string levelFileName);
```

While hasLevel() is examining the micLevels vector to see if a level with the same file name is already loaded, getLevel() returns a shared pointer to the existing AssimpLevel object, or a nullptr if no level with the requested file name exists.

As the names suggest, addLevel() will try to load a level data file from local storage and add the new AssimpLevel object to micLevels, and deleteLevel() will delete the requested level from micLevels if it exists.

We also add a null level to stop micLevels being empty:

```
void OGLRenderer::addNullLevel() {
  std::shared_ptr<AssimpLevel> nullLevel =
    std::make_shared<AssimpLevel>();
  mModelInstCamData.micLevels.emplace_back(nullLevel);
}
```

The connection between the three new callbacks and the hasLevel(), addLevel(), and deleteLevel() methods is created in the init() method of the renderer, allowing us to use the level calls in the UserInterface class.

So, let's go for the third step on the path to level data management and add new elements to the user interface.

Extending the UI with level property controls

Just like for the AssimpLevel class, we can simply copy and adjust existing control elements from other parts of the createSettingsWindow() method in the UserInterface class to create the new CollapsingHeader named **Levels**.

In *Figure 11.1*, the resulting user interface part for the level data is shown:

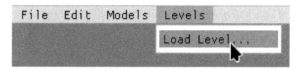

Figure 11.1: User interface controls for the level data

The **Levels** combo box is filled from the file names of the levels within the miclevels vector in the ModelInstanceCamData struct. The **Delete Level** button for the level data has the same function as the **Delete Model** button from the **Models** section of the UI, removing the currently selected level, and the controls for axis swap, position, rotation, and scaling are taken from the **Instances** UI section, along with the **Reset Values to Zero** button to set all controls to default values.

In addition to the new control elements, a new main menu entry named **Levels** is created. *Figure 11.2* shows all the elements of the main menu at this point:

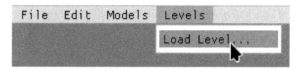

Figure 11.2: The new Levels main menu entry

Clicking on **Load Level...** opens the well-known ImGui-based file dialog, configured with a list of supported file formats for level data. See *Choosing a file format for a map* section about the extensions in the filter.

The **Delete Model** and **Load Level...** UI elements utilize the callbacks to add and delete an AssimpLevel object from the application, creating a seamless workflow for the user when adding level data to the virtual world.

The significant difference between level data and model instances in terms of user experience is the missing visual selection and modification functionality for the level data. Since you will adjust the level data a few times until you are happy with position, rotation, and scale, the extra code to continuously move the level data around like instances will be used only once or twice. It is even more probable that a visual selection harms the workflow if the level data is selected when the desired instance is missed by some pixels.

As the last step of level data management, we will add the names of the loaded level files and the per-level settings to the YAML config file.

Saving and loading the level configuration

Storing the loaded levels and the level settings in the YAM configuration file is quick and straightforward.

After adding an Emitter output operator overload for the LevelSettings data type, we can copy and adjust the emitting code block for models or cameras in the createConfigFile() method of the YamlParser class in the tools folder to save the level data. In addition, we must also emit the selected level number in the settings map of our configuration file.

Also, two new methods named getLevelConfigs() and getSelectedLevelNum() are added to the YamlParser class:

```
std::vector<LevelSettings> getLevelConfigs();
int getSelectedLevelNum();
```

Both methods follow the same process as the model and camera counterparts. The first method, getLevelConfigs(), tries to load the level data from the YAML file, and getSelectedLevelNum() returns the index of the selected level at the time the configuration was saved.

In the YamlParserTypes.h file, a simple pair of encode() and decode() methods for the LevelSettings data type must be added to read back the data from the YAML file. We should also increase the mYamlConfigFileVersion value as the configuration structure has changed.

Now we can add level data from a file, place the level in the virtual world, and store and reload the configuration. Adding the level data to the undo/redo stack is left as an exercise for you, but the basic principle level data undo/redo is identical to the undo/redo functionality for models.

Since the level data may contain overlapping elements, such as bridges, tunnels, or multiple floors of a building, instances could be on the same location in two dimensions. The existing collision detection would be triggered even if the instances are walking at different heights in the level, causing false reactions to non-existing collisions.

We have to extend the quadtree to become an octree to support collision detection in all three dimensions. Let's check out how to upgrade the quadtree.

Converting the quadtree to an octree

Updating the quadtree to an octree is astonishingly simple, and most of the work can be triggered by using the Rename function of the Refactoring functionality of the IDE. For brevity, we will just do a brief walkthrough of the required changes here. Please check the example code in the subfolders within the chapter11 folder for the full octree code.

First, we change the name of the quadtree folder to octree. In the CMakeLists.txt file, the two occurrences of quadtree must be also renamed octree to match the folder name. And we rename the QuadTree class Octree and change BoundingBox2D to BoundingBox3D.

Next, we extend the Octree class by using eight instead of four children. *Figure 11.3* shows the quadrant IDs of the octree:

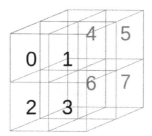

Figure 11.3: Quadrant IDs in the octree

The four existing child quadrant IDs, 0 to 3, will be used for the four front-facing octants, and the four back-facing octants will receive the new IDs 4 to 7. Moving the four new octants to the back of the octree cuboid allows us to retain most of the logic from the quadtree. Adding the new logic to find the correct octant becomes merely an act of copying and pasting the code, taking front- and back-facing octants into account.

Then, we update all QuadTree-related include statements, classes, and method calls in the code to Octree, and all BoundingBox2D occurrences to BoundingBox3D. The bounding box upgrade includes the change of all glm::vec2 types of the old BoundingBox2D parameters to use glm::vec3 instead. We also change the name of getTopLeft() to getFrontTopLeft() and add the getBack() method to reflect the availability of the third dimension.

Finally, all callback function types in the code will be renamed from quadTree to octree to reflect the functionality change in all other places in the code too.

Now we can use the octree to detect collisions in three dimensions. Sadly, the **Instance Positions** window still shows a top-down view of the instances, and we are unable to see if any instances are placed at different heights. We must adjust the rendering of the mini window containing the instances so that we can see any instances placed at different heights.

Creating an interactive octree view

The new octree view is created in three steps:

1. For a better overview of the octree and the instances, the new view can be scaled, rotated, and translated by using the mouse. It may still take some extra rotations to align the octree with the camera view, but that is hard to do due to the orthogonal display and the symmetry of the octree. Fading out far away parts of the octree or highlighting the octant containing the camera may help to focus on the current area of interest. On the other hand, using a perspective projected octree may make it easier to find the right alignment, but the perspective will distort the distances between the instances, and we just create a copy of the main level rendering.

2. The lines of the octree quadrants and the instances are collected into a temporary data structure. We will use an OGLLineMesh here as this data type contains just the bare minimum; we need to draw ImGui lines.

3. To achieve the desired view, all points of the octree quadrants and the instance bounding boxes must be transformed by the scaling, rotation, and translation from the first step. This transformation is done in the same way as we did for the cameras and instances: by creating a matrix and a matrix-vector multiplication for each point. There should be no surprises in the matrix operations; only the translation may need an explanation.

Let's step through the interactive part first.

Adding interactivity

To be able to change the octree view with the mouse button and mouse movements, we need three new private variables named mOctreeZoomFactor, mOctreeRotation, and mOctreeTranslation in the UserInterface class:

```
float mOctreeZoomFactor = 1.0f;
glm::vec3 mOctreeRotation = glm::vec3(0.0f);
glm::vec3 mOctreeTranslation = glm::vec3(0.0f);
```

The names of the variables are self-explanatory, so we do not need to dive into the details here.

Right after creating the **Instance Positions** window in the createPositionsWindow() method of the UserInterface class, we add a check to see if the current window has been hovered over:

```
if (ImGui::IsWindowHovered(
    ImGuiHoveredFlags_RootAndChildWindows)) {
```

Without the check, the mouse buttons and motions would trigger the octree view changes in all windows, leading to unwanted results.

Then, we get a reference to the internal io structure of ImGui:

```
ImGuiIO& io = ImGui::GetIO();
mOctreeZoomFactor += 0.025f * io.MouseWheel;
mOctreeZoomFactor = std::clamp(mOctreeZoomFactor,
  0.1f, 5.0f);
```

In ImGui's io structure, many internal states are available, like changes made to the mouse wheel or the mouse position.

We use the mouse wheel here to adjust the zoom factor of the octree view. Setting upper and lower bounds for the zoom factor helps to avoid losing the overview.

Next, we check if the right mouse button has been pressed and rotate the view according to the mouse movement while the right mouse button is still pressed:

```
if (ImGui::IsMouseDown(ImGuiMouseButton_Right)) {
  mOctreeRotation.y += io.MouseDelta.x;
  mOctreeRotation.x += io.MouseDelta.y;
}
```

Using the right mouse button to change the rotation is also used for the camera, so this kind of view change should be known from working with the application.

Finally, we check for the middle mouse button, moving the octree around with the mouse motion:

```
if (ImGui::IsMouseDown(ImGuiMouseButton_Middle)) {
  mOctreeTranslation.x += io.MouseDelta.x;
  mOctreeTranslation.y += io.MouseDelta.y;
}
}
```

If you wonder why we don't use the left mouse button here: Pressing the left mouse button above an ImGui window activates the internal window movement. We have only the right and middle mouse buttons left to achieve two different view changes.

Once we have the transformation we want to see, we can get the lines from the octree and the instances.

Collecting the lines

To store the lines before drawing, we add a `private` variable named `mOctreeLines` to the `UserInterface` class:

```
OGLLineMesh mOctreeLines{};
```

After clearing the vertices vector inside `mOctreeLines`, we get the octree lines:

```
mOctreeLines.vertices.clear();
const auto treeBoxes =
    modInstCamData.micOctreeGetBoxesCallback();
```

For every octree quadrant, we get a `BoundingBox3D` object, containing the minimum and maximum point positions. A conversion to an `AABB` is simple:

```
AABB boxAABB{};
boxAABB.create(box.getFrontTopLeft());
boxAABB.addPoint(box.getFrontTopLeft() +
    box.getSize());
```

Then, we use the `getAABBLines()` method to create all lines for the AABB as an `OGLLineMesh` and add the lines to the `mOctreeLines` mesh:

```
std::shared_ptr<OGLLineMesh> instanceLines =
    boxAABB.getAABBLines(white);
mOctreeLines.vertices.insert(
    mOctreeLines.vertices.end(),
    instanceLines->vertices.begin(),
    instanceLines->vertices.end());
```

Next, we get AABB lines for every instance, coloring colliding instances red and all other instances yellow. The currently selected instance also gets an additional green border to be able to stop the instance easily.

At the end of the loops over both the octants and the instances, `mOctreeLines` contains vertices of all lines that should be drawn to the ImGui window. We now need to transform the vertices to match the selected scaling, rotation, and translation.

Calculating the view and drawing the lines

Since storing intermediate results is faster than allocating and calculating a new transformation matrix for the octree lines in every frame, we add three more `private` member variables named `mScaleMat`, `mRotationMat`, and `mOctreeViewMat`:

```
glm::mat3 mOctreeViewMat = glm::mat3(1.0f);
glm::mat4 mRotationMat = glm::mat4(1.0f);
glm::mat4 mScaleMat = glm::mat4(1.0f);
```

Then, scaling and the two rotations are applied to create the final view matrix:

```
mScaleMat = glm::scale(glm::mat4(1.0f),
  glm::vec3(mOctreeZoomFactor));
mRotationMat = glm::rotate(mScaleMat,
  glm::radians(mOctreeRotation.x),
  glm::vec3(1.0f, 0.0f, 0.0f));
mOctreeViewMat = glm::rotate(mRotationMat,
  glm::radians(mOctreeRotation.y),
  glm::vec3(0.0f, 1.0f, 0.0f));
```

Now we loop over the vertices in `mOctreeLines` in groups of two since we need a starting point and ending point for each line:

```
for (int i = 0; i < mOctreeLines.vertices.size(); i += 2) {
```

Inside the loop, we extract the vertex pair for each line and transform the vertex positions by multiplication with the `mOctreeViewMat`:

```
OGLLineVertex startVert = mOctreeLines.vertices.at(i);
OGLLineVertex endVert = mOctreeLines.vertices.at(i+1);
glm::vec3 startPos = mOctreeViewMat *
  startVert.position;
glm::vec3 endPos = mOctreeViewMat * endVert.position;
```

Next, we add the point coordinates to the center of the drawing and add the translational part:

```
ImVec2 pointStart =
  ImVec2(drawAreaCenter.x + startPos.x +
    mOctreeTranslation.x,
    drawAreaCenter.y + startPos.z +
    mOctreeTranslation.y);
ImVec2 pointEnd =
```

```
ImVec2(drawAreaCenter.x + endPos.x +
  mOctreeTranslation.x,
  drawAreaCenter.y + endPos.z +
  mOctreeTranslation.y)
```

We don't need a separate translation matrix here because the movement of the octree lines is only related to the ImGui window, not the position of the vertices in 3D.

At the end of the loop, we draw an ImGui line from the start point to the end point using the colors of the line and a fixed alpha value:

```
drawList->AddLine(pointStart, pointEnd,
ImColor(startVert.color.r, startVert.color.g,
  startVert.color.b, 0.6f));
```

If we start the application after these changes, the octree view can be rotated by pressing the right mouse button, moved around by pressing the middle mouse button, and zoomed in and out by using the mouse wheel.

Figure 11.4 shows a view of the octree in the **Instance Positions** window:

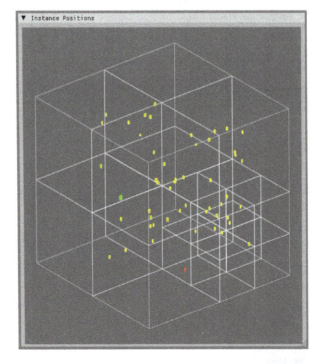

Figure 11.4: A rotated octree with instances and two subdivision levels

You can see the bounding boxes for all instances in three dimensions. Colliding instances are drawn in red, all other instances are yellow (the same colors as for the AABB debug lines), and the currently selected instance has an extra outline in green.

Another important fact to see is the subdivision level of the octree. At the root level of the octree, one subdivision is divided into eight octants – this has happened because of the number of instances. In the far lower right octant, another subdivision was needed to limit the instance count per octant.

When the application is running, the movement of the instances and changes in the octree subdivision can be seen in real time. And the view can be changed to focus on any interesting area of the octree.

One drawback of the default octree implementation is the growing overhead. A subdivision may produce a lot of empty nodes, especially if the threshold per node is small and the tree depth is high. For our implementation, each subdivision into eight octants adds a memory overhead of roughly one kilobyte in memory usage, even if we need to store only one or two instance AABBs in one of the child octants.

Also, each subdivision adds another step to the traversal costs. Even though the traversal complexity grows only on a logarithmic basis, the overhead in memory and traversal time may become significant in larger levels. In this case, a data structure such as a sparse voxel octree could be used instead. A link to a paper describing the principles of sparse voxel octrees is available in the *Additional resources* section.

A shortcoming of the current level loading is a missing "feeling" about the dimensions of the loaded level data. If the level is not flat but contains areas with different heights, it is hard to imagine the edges of the level data.

To get a better orientation, we will also add an AABB for the level data.

Building an AABB for the level data

Axis-aligned bounding boxes are a great tool to avoid estimating or guessing the dimensions of an object. We are using model instance AABBs as a solution to detect collisions by allowing the application to compare the maximum extents of two instances.

While unused areas between the vertices of the instances and the bounding box are a trade-off between speed and complexity for collision detection, the situation is different for level data. The AABB lines will help us to see the maximum extent of the level in all three dimensions, especially when the level data has large unused areas.

Creating the AABB is done quick and simple. First, we add a new private member variable called mLevelAABB in the AssimpLevel.h file to store the AABB:

```
AABB mLevelAABB{};
```

To generate and retrieve the bounding box data, we add two new public methods, generateAABB() and getAABB():

```
void generateAABB();
AABB getAABB();
```

Splitting the generation of the AABB data from the retrieval is a clever idea as the levels may contain a lot of meshes and vertices. A recalculation is only needed if we adjust the level properties such as the scaling or position since the level data does not move or change other properties by itself.

We already have the transformation matrix for the level data, so calculating the bounding box for the level in generateAABB() is only a loop over all vertices of all meshes:

```
updateLevelRootMatrix();
mLevelAABB.clear();
for (const auto& mesh : mLevelMeshes) {
  for (const auto& vertex : mesh.vertices) {
    mLevelAABB.addPoint(mLevelRootMatrix *
      glm::vec4(glm::vec3(vertex.position), 1.0f));
  }
}
```

A crucial step here is changing the w element of the vertex position. We are using the last element of the position to transport one texture coordinate to the shader. For a correct matrix multiplication, we must set the last element of position to 1.0f.

To trigger an automatic update of the level AABB during property changes of the level, we add a simple callback to Callbacks.h:

```
using levelGenerateAABBCallback = std::function<void(void)>;
```

In the ModelInstanceCamData struct, another callback function is added:

```
levelGenerateAABBCallback
  micLevelGenerateAABBCallbackFunction;
```

We bind the micLevelGenerateAABBCallbackFunction callback to the generateLevelAABB() method in the init() method of the renderer, along with the other level data callbacks.

To get a nice interactive display in the user interface, we add a Boolean named settingChangedForAABB to the **Levels** section. On every slider or checkbox change, or when pressing the **Reset Values to Zero** button, we trigger a recalculation of the level's AABB.

And what about other static level elements? These objects are called **assets** and can be added to a level. Assets also need collision checks to prevent the instances from running right through each other, but assets are mostly not animated; they remain in the place intended by the level designers.

We will use a shortcut here and utilize the non-animated models to mimic static level assets. For dynamic assets, such as buttons or doors, animated models can be used; see the *Level data does not move around* section for a brief explanation. In the *Practical sessions* section, a task to add dynamic assets to the virtual world is available.

So, let's see what changes are needed for the non-animated models.

Using non-animated models as assets

To avoid adding a new AssimpAsset class with mostly the same functionality as the non-animated models, we will extend the current AssimpModel class and the renderer a bit.

For the model class, we change the getAABB() method to return either a dynamic AABB for models with animations or a static AABB for models without animations:

```
AABB AssimpModel::getAABB(InstanceSettings instSettings) {
  if (mNumAnimatedMeshes > 0) {
    return getAnimatedAABB(instSettings);
  } else {
    return getNonAnimatedAABB(instSettings);
  }
}
```

The new method, getAnimatedAABB(), is just a new name for the old getAABB() method, and it calculates the AABB from the lookup data as before. The other new method, getNonAnimatedAABB(), is mostly the updateModelRootMatrix() method from the AssimpInstance class.

First, we calculate a separate matrix for scaling, rotation, axis swap, and translation:

```
    glm::mat4 localScaleMatrix = glm::scale(glm::mat4(1.0f),
      glm::vec3(instSettings.isScale));
    glm::mat4 localSwapAxisMatrix;
    if (instSettings.isSwapYZAxis) {
```

```
    glm::mat4 flipMatrix = glm::rotate(glm::mat4(1.0f),
      glm::radians(-90.0f), glm::vec3(0.0f, 0.0f, 1.0f));
    localSwapAxisMatrix = glm::rotate(flipMatrix,
      glm::radians(-90.0f), glm::vec3(0.0f, 1.0f, 0.0f));
  } else {
    localSwapAxisMatrix = glm::mat4(1.0f);
  }
  glm::mat4 localRotationMatrix = glm::mat4_cast(
    glm::quat(glm::radians(instSettings.isWorldRotation)));
  glm::mat4 localTranslationMatrix =
    glm::translate(glm::mat4(1.0f),
    instSettings.isWorldPosition);
```

Then, the transformation matrices and the root transformation matrix from the model file are combined into a single transform matrix:

```
  glm::mat4 localTransformMatrix =
    localTranslationMatrix * localRotationMatrix *
    localSwapAxisMatrix * localScaleMatrix *
    mRootTransformMatrix;
```

To create the bounding box data, all vertices of the model mesh are transformed to the new positions and the positions are added to a local variable named modelAABB:

```
  AABB modelAABB{};
  for (const auto& mesh : mModelMeshes) {
    for (const auto& vertex : mesh.vertices) {
      modelAABB.addPoint(localTransformMatrix *
        glm::vec4(glm::vec3(vertex.position), 1.0f));
    }
  }
```

For the w element of the vertex position, the same adjustment as for the level data AABB is needed. By setting the last value to 1.0f, we guarantee a correct matrix multiplication when computing the final position.

With the resulting AABB, the extents of the non-animated instance vertices are able to detect AABB collisions with animated models and to draw the debug lines.

Performance considerations for asset AABBs

Currently, the AABB for non-animated instances is calculated for every instance in every frame, like the AABB for the animated instances. If the calculation becomes a bottleneck, for example, if a lot of static assets are placed in the virtual world, changing the AABB computation only on property changes in the UI can be done easily.

Once the level data has been loaded and processed and the AABBs are calculated, we are ready to draw the level triangles to the screen.

Let's extend the renderer to add the level data to the rendering process.

Sending the level data to the GPU

With every addition of new features, it becomes simpler to reuse code in the application. In the case of level data, mesh data is encapsulated in the `AssimpLevel` class, and drawing the level's triangles can be done in a small loop over all loaded levels.

As the first step, we create a new shader to draw the level data.

Creating a new shader

Since we need to draw the level triangles only once, using a separate shader for the level data is a clever idea. Add the `private` shader named `mAssimpLevelShader` to the header file of the renderer class:

```
Shader mAssimpLevelShader{};
```

The shader will use the two new files, `assimp_level.vert` for the vertex shader and `assimp_level.frag` for the fragment shader. We load the files along with the other shaders in the `init()` method of the renderer:

```
if (!mAssimpLevelShader.loadShaders(
    "shader/assimp_level.vert",
    "shader/assimp_level.frag")) {
  return false;
}
```

The fragment shader file, assimp_level.frag, is just a copy of the assimp.frag file without any changes. For the vertex shader file, assimp_level.vert, we can copy the assimp.vert file and keep the in and out layout portion and the Matrices uniform buffer.

We don't need the selection buffer since no visual selection has been implemented for the level data, and we can change the buffer at binding point 1 to contain only a single 4x4 matrix:

```
layout (std430, binding = 1) readonly restrict
    buffer WorldTransformMatrix {
  mat4 worldTransformMat;
};
```

Uploading only small data elements like a single matrix to a uniform buffer on the GPU is not the best idea as every upload may add a small delay to the frame. For a real game, or a game engine, the world transform matrix would be part of a bigger buffer, but for the sake of simplicity we just do the single upload here.

In the main() method of the vertex shader, we use the worldTransformMat to transform the position and normal vertices to the final position given by the matrix created from the level properties:

```
void main() {
  gl_Position = projection * view * worldTransformMat *
    vec4(aPos.x, aPos.y, aPos.z, 1.0);
  color = aColor;
  normal = transpose(inverse(worldTransformMat)) *
    vec4(aNormal.x, aNormal.y, aNormal.z, 1.0);
  texCoord = vec2(aPos.w, aNormal.w);
}
```

Then, in the draw() method of the renderer, we loop over all levels and skip the null level by checking for the existence of any triangles:

```
for (const auto& level : mModelInstCamData.micLevels) {
  if (level->getTriangleCount() == 0) {
    continue;
  }
```

As the last step of the level display process, the vertex drawing is triggered:

```
    mAssimpLevelShader.use();
    mShaderModelRootMatrixBuffer.uploadSsboData(
      level->getWorldTransformMatrix(), 1);
    level->draw();
  }
```

We use the new `mAssimpLevelShader`, upload the transformation matrix of the level to the shader, and call the `draw()` method of the `AssimpLevel` object.

Drawing the level AABB on the screen requires a few more methods and member variables in the renderer.

Drawing the level AABB

The level AABB vertices are stored in a new `private` member variable named `mAllLevelAABB` in the renderer class:

```
    AABB mAllLevelAABB{};
```

Also, two new private methods named `generateLevelAABB()` and `drawLevelAABB()` are added to the renderer class:

```
    void generateLevelAABB();
    void drawLevelAABB(glm::vec4 aabbColor);
```

We also split generating and drawing the AABB lines here to avoid costly calculations in every frame we draw.

Generating the level AABB in `generateLevelAABB()` is done in a simple loop. After clearing the level AABB data, we loop over all loaded levels:

```
  mAllLevelAABB.clear();
  for (const auto& level : mModelInstCamData.micLevels) {
    if (level->getTriangleCount() == 0) {
      continue;
    }
```

The check for a level without triangles skips the null level since there is nothing to draw to the screen. Then, we generate the AABB of each level and add the minimum and maximum extents of each level to mAllLevelAABB:

```
level->generateAABB();
mAllLevelAABB.addPoint(level->getAABB().getMinPos());
mAllLevelAABB.addPoint(level->getAABB().getMaxPos());
}
```

The resulting AABB contains all the level data of all the loaded levels. If you want to have separate AABBs for each level, you could use a vector of AABBs instead the single AABB.

Drawing the level AABB in the drawLevelAABB() method needs little explanation:

```
mAABBMesh = mAllLevelAABB.getAABBLines(aabbColor);
mLineVertexBuffer.uploadData(*mAABBMesh);
mLineShader.use();
mLineVertexBuffer.bindAndDraw(GL_LINES, 0,
  mAABBMesh->vertices.size());
```

We use the getAABBLines() method of the AABB to create the line data, upload the lines to the mLineVertexBuffer, call use() on LineShader, and then call bindAndDraw() on the mLineVertexBuffer object to draw the axis-aligned bounding box of the level data.

Then, in the draw() method of the renderer, we call drawLevelAABB() when rdDrawLevelAABB is set to true:

```
if (mRenderData.rdDrawLevelAABB) {
  glm::vec4 levelAABBColor =
    glm::vec4(0.0f, 1.0f, 0.5, 0.5f);
  drawLevelAABB(levelAABBColor);
}
```

The color has been chosen randomly, you may change the color value or even add a 3-element float slider to the UI to control the color value.

Showing the level AABB lines on screen is done by a new Boolean variable called rdDrawLevelAABB in the OGLRenderData struct in the OGLRenderData.h file:

```
bool rdDrawLevelAABB = false;
```

For the Vulkan version of the code, the variable will be created in the VKRenderData struct in the VkRenderData.h file.

In the UserInterface class, we add a checkbox for rdDrawLevelAABB in the **Levels** section of the createSettingsWindow() method, allowing us to toggle the level's AABB lines.

That's all! In *Figure 11.5*, an example map from Sketchfab has been loaded next to the woman model, and the level's AABB was activated:

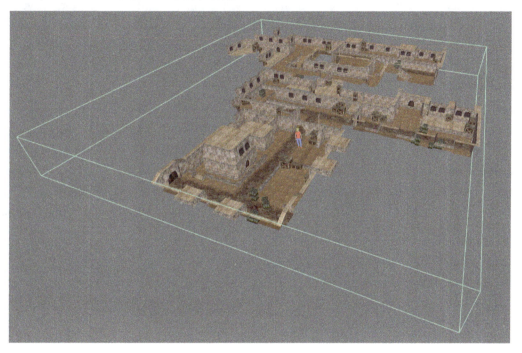

Figure 11.5: Example map (unscaled) and an instance of the woman model (source: Counter Strike 1.6 map "de_dust" by Zarudko at https://skfb.ly/6QYJw)

As a gamer, you may know this map: It's "de_dust" from Counter Strike 1.6. The map is available at Sketchfab in several versions and formats, along with other popular game maps.

The bounding box around the level data helps us to see the dimensions of the level. Especially for unused areas like in the front right of *Figure 11.5*, finding the boundaries of the level data would be hard without the AABB lines.

You will also notice the unusual size ratio between the level map and the model instance. The map and model have been loaded with their default scaling values, and the size values have been chosen arbitrarily by the author of the files. Resizing one or both objects is easy thanks to the scaling slider for model and level data, but getting a reasonable ratio between levels, models, and other objects from various sources and artists can become challenging.

To create a plausible virtual world, the sizes of the game character models must match the sizes of furniture, buildings, environmental objects, and so on. Even a small mismatch in the proportions of different objects will be visible when comparing game characters and objects with the real world. A good way to adjust the different elements is to use one fixed-size object with a known size, such as a block from Minecraft, which has a (virtual) edge length of one meter, or even a simple line of a defined length in the virtual world. By resizing all objects to their real-world sizes compared to the known object, models from different sources can be made to match visually.

Summary

In this chapter, we added static level data to the virtual world. After exploring the differences between level maps and models, we looked at suitable file formats for level data and how to find cool game maps. Then, we added support for level data to the application and replaced the quadtree with an octree to support collision detection in three dimensions. Finally, we added the new level data and a level AABB to the renderer. We will extend the level data in the next two chapters to create a virtual world where the instances can roam around freely and by themselves.

In the next chapter, we will continue the collision detection from *Chapter 8*. First, we will extend the existing code to support collisions between instances and the level geometry. To ensure the instances are always on the ground, we will introduce gravity in the virtual world. As the last step, we add inverse kinematics to the legs of the instances, allowing the model to climb stairs or slopes with natural motion.

Practical sessions

Here are some additions you could make to the code:

- Add a door or a button to the level.

  Since the animated level data is more like an animated character model placed at a fixed position in the level than static level data, you could try to add doors, switches, or buttons to the level, and instead of waving back on interaction, the button could play a "pressed" animation, and a door could revolve around the hinge or slide to one side.

- Add dynamic level loading.

  You could use the information about the current position of the playable character to decide when to load or unload parts of the level. Maybe add a new mapping of coordinates where a specified level data file is loaded, and another coordinate where the level data is removed from the application. If you have added animated level objects from the first task to the dynamic level part, make sure to save the status of these objects on unloading and restore the state when reloading the level data. The player could open a door or activate a switch, and upon returning to the level part, the player could see the object in the exact same state as they left it. To prevent crashes or data corruption caused by assets that are not fully loaded or destroyed, use atomic operations or locking mechanisms such as mutexes. Also, loading and level data and assets may need synchronization to restore the correct state of all elements.

- Expert difficulty: Load dynamic level parts asynchronously.

  Loading a level file, processing the data, and adding the vertex data takes some time, resulting in a visible hitch in the application. Use `std::async` or a full worker thread to trigger the loading when a condition to load is met, for instance, when the player is at a specific world position. Be aware that adding any asynchronous code requires extra measures against data races.

Additional resources

- Efficient sparse voxel octrees: `https://www.nvidia.com/docs/IO/88972/nvr-2010-001.pdf`
- Blender map creation 1: `https://www.youtube.com/watch?v=IKkOLeAuEHI`
- Blender map creation 2: `https://www.youtube.com/watch?v=hdyBgQ77Sdg`
- What is a lightmap?: `http://wiki.polycount.com/wiki/Light_map`
- Navigation mesh explanation: `https://medium.com/@mscansian/a-with-navigation-meshes-246fd9e72424`
- HLOD: `https://gamma.cs.unc.edu/HLOD/`
- How to write glTF custom extensions: `https://gltf-transform.dev/extensions`
- itch.io Assets: `https://itch.io/game-assets`
- Sketchfab for models, maps, and assets: `https://sketchfab.com`
- Free3D: `https://free3d.com`
- Counter Strike 1.6 map "de_dust" by Zarudko: `https://skfb.ly/6QYJw`

12

Advanced Collision Detection

Welcome to *Chapter 12*! In the previous chapter, we added the ability to load static level data to the virtual world. Now the instances no longer have to run in thin air; they can get a virtual home. First, we explored the differences between model and level data, which file formats are mostly used for level data, and where to find game maps on the internet. Then, we added code to load level data and replaced the two-dimensional quadtree with a three-dimensional octree. Finally, we implemented the level data rendering, including debug data for wireframe, octree, and level AABB lines.

In this chapter, we will extend the level data from the previous chapter. First, we will add a specialized octree for the level data and update the code to also support collision detection between instances and level geometry. Then, we will add a simplified form of gravity to the virtual world to keep the instances at ground level instead of having them floating around. As the last step, we will introduce inverse kinematics for the instance legs to allow the instances to climb slopes and stairs with more natural leg motions and to prevent the feet from clipping into the ground or floating in the air.

In this chapter, we will cover the following topics:

- Enhancing collision detection for level data
- Using gravity to keep the instances at floor level
- Adding inverse kinematics

Technical requirements

The example code for this chapter is available in the chapter12 folder, in the 01_opengl_adv_ collision subfolder for OpenGL, and the 02_vulkan_adv_collision subfolder for Vulkan.

Enhancing collision detection for level data

To speed up collision detection between instances and level geometry, we will create spatial partitioning for the level data, like the octree. But instead of adding the level triangles to the instance octree, we build a specialized octree for the triangle data alone.

Adding a new octree type

Using a separate data structure for level data makes more sense than trying to mix both data types in the existing octree for several reasons:

- The level data is static while the instance positions change frequently. We need to do costly updates to a quite heavily utilized octree on every instance position change, possibly resulting in a lot of additional split and merge operations when removing and re-adding the instances.

- The number of subdivisions for level data and instances may be completely different, depending on the level's complexity and the number of instances. Having only a small number of instances roaming around a detailed level may lead to a huge overhead when searching for nearby triangles or instances.

- We are using an octree for the level data for simplicity, but other data structures, like BSP trees or **boundary volume hierarchies (BVHs)**, are more common. Since BSP trees and BVHs cannot be dynamically updated as quickly as our octree, a split between level data and instances would still be necessary.

With two different octrees, we can overcome these mentioned problems. The level data octree is kept unchanged after adding all the level triangles, both octrees have their own subdivisions, depending on the amount of data per octant, but we can still combine the information by using the instance bounding boxes in the level octree.

As the first step for the level octree, we add a new struct named MeshTriangle to the OGLRenderData.h file in the opengl folder:

```
struct MeshTriangle {
  int index;
  std::array<glm::vec3, 3> points;
```

```
    BoundingBox3D boundingBox;
};
```

For Vulkan, the triangle `struct` will be added to the `VkRenderData.h` file in the `vulkan` folder.

The `index` member is mostly for debugging purposes and will be added to a log output line in case some triangles cannot be added to the octree. In the `points` array, we save the world positions of each of the three points of a triangle. The world position is needed to create the proper bounding box for the triangle, we will use the world position also later for collision detection. And the `boundingBox` member contains the AABB for every triangle of the level data mesh.

Using bounding boxes instead of the real triangle data in the octree simplifies the query operations a lot since we do not have to check the exact outline of every triangle when searching for collision. We may end up with more triangles to check by using the AABB, but the AABB checks are cheap since we only need a maximum of six simple `float` comparisons. As most parts of a level geometry are either wall or ground, the additional size of the AABB does not matter.

Next, we add the new octree class named `TriangleOctree`. The new triangle octree will be implemented in the two new files, `TriangleOctree.h` and `TriangleOctree.cpp`, in the `octree` folder.

The `TriangleOctree` class is a copy of the normal `Octree` class, with a few exceptions:

- We store the triangle data in the tree instead of the instance index.
- Since the level data octree will be kept read-only, we don't need the methods to update or remove objects or merge octants.
- We handle only static data in the triangle octree, a search for intersections between triangles of the level does not return any useful information for us. So, the `findAllIntersections()` and `findIntersectionsInDescendants()` methods can be skipped too.

In addition to the reasons to use a separate octree for the level data mentioned in the *Adding a new octree type* section, we also use a different approach for objects not fitting in a single octant.

In the instance octree, a bounding box of an instance will be only in rare cases larger than a single octant, for instance when an instance is scaled by a large factor. But within the level octree, the bounding box of many triangles may not fit into a single subdivided octant. The creator of a level will try to minimize the number of triangles in a level for good rendering performance, resulting in areas of the level made of only a few large triangles.

We could overcome the size problem with one of the following three methods:

1. Keep a large triangle in the octant big enough to contain the entire triangle. This solution would store additional objects in a parent node, not only in a leaf.

2. Add the triangle to all affected subdivided octants. We would only have data in the leaves but would duplicate the triangle data in the worst case 8 times.

3. Split the triangle on the octant boundaries and add only the sub-triangles to each octant. Again, we would have an additional triangle per affected octant, plus possible problems with rounding errors in the split lines.

To keep the code simple, we will use the first method and add any triangle exceeding the dimensions of a subdivided octant only in the parent octant.

We can achieve the storage process for oversized triangles with a two-step check in the add() and split() methods. First, we iterate over all child octants to find possible intersections of the triangle with the boundaries of the child octant:

```
int intersectingChildren = 0;
for (int i = 0; i < node->childs.size(); ++i) {
  BoundingBox3D childBox = getChildOctant(box, i);
  if (childBox.intersects(triangle.boundingBox)) {
    intersectingChildren++;
  }
}
```

If we find an intersection with a child octant, we increment the intersectingChildren variable. Then, for the add() method, we check how many child octants the triangle would intersect. In case of more than one octant, the triangle is kept in the current octant:

```
if (intersectingChildren > 1) {
  node->triangles.emplace_back(triangle);
} else {
  int i = getOctantId(box, triangle.boundingBox);
  if (i != -1) {
    add(node->childs.at(i), depth + 1,
      getChildOctant(box, i), triangle);
  }
}
```

And if we found only an intersection with a single child octant, we hand over the triangle recursively to the child octant.

For the split() method, we do the same, and keep the triangle in the current octant if we find more than one intersection with the future child octants:

```
if (intersectingChildren > 1) {
  newTriangles.emplace_back(triangle);
} else {
  int i = getOctantId(box, triangle.boundingBox);
  if (i != -1) {
    node->childs.at(i)
      ->triangles.emplace_back(triangle);
  }
}
```

The query() methods to query the triangle octree for collisions with a bounding box and getTreeBoxes() boxes to show octree debug lines remain the same as in the original octree, only the data type for the private query() method needs to be adjusted.

After the TriangleOctree is ready, we can add the level data to the new octree and query for the tree for collisions.

Filling the level data octree

Like the instance octree, we need to add the TriangleOctree.h header to the renderer header, and then add a new private member named mTriangleOctree and the two private methods initTriangleOctree() and generateLevelOctree():

```
std::shared_ptr<TriangleOctree> mTriangleOctree = nullptr;
void initTriangleOctree(int thresholdPerBox, int maxDepth);
void generateLevelOctree();
```

To have default values for threshold and depth and to be able to control the settings via UI later, two new variables named rdLevelOctreeThreshold and rdLevelOctreeMaxDepth are stored in the OGLRenderData struct in the OGLRenderData.h file in the opengl folder:

```
int rdLevelOctreeThreshold = 10;
int rdLevelOctreeMaxDepth = 5;
```

Again, for Vulkan, the two variables are added to the VkRenderData struct in the VkRenderData.h file in the vulkan folder.

During the init() method of the renderer, initTriangleOctree() is called to create an octree with the given threshold and maximum depth:

```
void OGLRenderer::initTriangleOctree(int thresholdPerBox,
  int maxDepth) {
  mTriangleOctree = std::make_shared<TriangleOctree>(
    mWorldBoundaries, thresholdPerBox, maxDepth);
}
```

The world boundaries are updated during level AABB generation, so our triangle octree is exactly the same size as the level data after the level was loaded.

Filling the level data octree is done in the generateLevelOctree() method. We just walk through the important parts here since the outer code is only a loop over all levels in the micLevels vector of the ModelInstanceCamData struct.

For every level in micLevels, we get the level meshes in the form of optimized meshes for drawing the level. Then, we iterate over all the indices of the level mesh:

```
std::vector<OGLMesh> levelMeshes =
  level->getLevelMeshes();
glm::mat4 transformMat =
  level->getWorldTransformMatrix();
glm::mat3 normalMat =
  level->getNormalTransformMatrix();
for (const auto& mesh : levelMeshes) {
  int index = 0;
  for (int i = 0; i < mesh.indices.size(); i += 3) {
```

For Vulkan, the levelMeshes vector will contain the VkMesh data type.

We must use the indices to draw the triangles since the triangle data is stored based on indices; using the vertices directly would not give us the correct information to deduce the triangles' vertices. We also retrieve the world and normal transformation matrices from the level. The normal transformation matrix is just the transpose of the inverse world transform matrix, the getNormalTransformMatrix() method has been added to keep the additional transformations in the AssimpLevel class.

Next, we create an empty `MeshTriangle` and use the transformation matrix of the level to transform the level vertices to the world position:

```
MeshTriangle tri{};
tri.points.at(0) = transformMat *
  glm::vec4(glm::vec3(mesh.vertices.at(
  mesh.indices.at(i)).position), 1.0f);
tri.points.at(1) = transformMat *
  glm::vec4(glm::vec3(mesh.vertices.at(
  mesh.indices.at(i + 1)).position), 1.0f);
tri.points.at(2) = transformMat *
  glm::vec4(glm::vec3(mesh.vertices.at(
  mesh.indices.at(i + 2)).position), 1.0f);
```

Now it is time to create the boundaries for each triangle:

```
AABB triangleAABB;
triangleAABB.clear();
triangleAABB.addPoint(tri.points.at(0));
triangleAABB.addPoint(tri.points.at(1));
triangleAABB.addPoint(tri.points.at(2));
```

Using an AABB makes it easy to calculate the bounding box coordinates. From this AABB, we create a `BoundingBox3D` and store the result in the `boundingBox` member of the `MeshTriangle` struct:

```
tri.boundingBox = BoundingBox3D(
  triangleAABB.getMinPos() -
  glm::vec3(0.0001f),
  triangleAABB.getMaxPos() -
  triangleAABB.getMinPos() + glm::vec3(0.0002f));
```

Adding a small offset is needed to keep triangles that are coplanar to one of the X, Y, or Z planes in the level. Without the offset, the dimension for the bounding box of a triangle could become zero in one or more dimensions, making it impossible for us to detect collisions with that triangle.

Finally, we store and increment the debug index number and add the triangle to the level data octree:

```
tri.index = index++;
mTriangleOctree->add(tri);
}
```

By calling generateLevelOctree whenever level data has been added or removed, we assure that our octree has the correct world positions for all triangles. The best way to achieve the update on level changes is to tie the octree update to the already implemented AABB update for level data.

To achieve this coupling, we add a new private method named generateLevelVertexData() and call AABB and octree generation there:

```
void OGLRenderer::generateLevelVertexData() {
  generateLevelAABB();
  generateLevelOctree();
}
```

Then, all occurrences of generateLevelAABB() are replaced by the new generateLevelVertexData() method, and whenever the level data or other properties, such as rotation or scaling, are changed, the level octree is also updated.

With an up-to-date level octree, we can finally check if the instances collide with level geometry.

Detecting instance/level collisions

By using the same strategy as we used in the *Adding a quadtree to store nearby model instances* section in *Chapter 8*, for instance/instance collisions, finding collisions between instances and level triangles is easy. All we must do is loop over all instances, get the bounding box of the instance, and query the triangle octree for collisions with that bounding box. The octree delivers us all the triangles where the bounding box of the triangle collides with the bounding box of the instance, even if the instance is not stored inside the triangle octree.

To implement collision detection between instances and level data, follow these steps:

1. First, we add a new member named isCollidingTriangles to the InstanceSettings struct in the InstanceSettings.h file to store the colliding triangles:

    ```
    std::vector<MeshTriangle> isCollidingTriangles{};
    ```

2. Then, a new public method called setCollidingTriangles() of the AssimpInstance class is created, storing the incoming triangle data in the instance settings:

    ```
    void AssimpInstance::setCollidingTriangles(
        std::vector<MeshTriangle>& collidingTriangles) {
      mInstanceSettings.isCollidingTriangles =
        collidingTriangles;
    }
    ```

3. Next, we create a new private method called checkForLevelCollisions() in the renderer. We start by getting the instance settings and skipping the null instance:

```
void OGLRenderer::checkForLevelCollisions() {
  for (const auto& instance :
      mModelInstCamData.micAssimpInstances) {
    InstanceSettings instSettings =
      instance->getInstanceSettings();
    if (instSettings.isInstanceIndexPosition == 0)
      continue;
  }
```

4. Then, we simply query the triangle octree with the bounding box of the instances:

```
std::vector<MeshTriangle> collidingTriangles =
  mTriangleOctree→query(instance->getBoundingBox());
```

5. Just knowing that we have collisions is nice, but we want to store the collision data for further actions, such as reacting to collisions or drawing debug lines. So, we store the vector of MeshTriangles in the instance settings:

```
instances.at(i)->setCollidingTriangles(
  collidingTriangles);
    }
  }
```

The method checkForLevelCollisions() is called to the draw() method of the renderer, after the instances have been rendered and before the UI is drawn. Now all instances are checked in every frame for collisions with the level geometry, and if colliding triangles were found, we store them in the InstanceSettings of the instance.

Although you could have trust in the general functionality of collision detection to work, seeing is believing. We add extra debug lines for the various level data now, allowing us to draw viable information as overlaying lines on the screen.

Drawing debug lines

If we would like to see the collisions in real time on the screen, we can highlight the affected triangles in the level geometry. To achieve this highlighting, we will follow these steps:

1. We add a new `private` member, `mLevelCollidingTriangleMesh`, to store the colliding triangle meshes to the renderer:

    ```
    std::shared_ptr<OGLLineMesh>
      mLevelCollidingTriangleMesh = nullptr;
    ```

2. Then, in `checkForLevelCollisions()`, we clear the mesh:

    ```
    mLevelCollidingTriangleMesh->vertices.clear();
    ```

3. Next, we iterate over all colliding triangles, adding the vertices pairwise to the mesh storage to create a line for every side of the triangle:

    ```
    for (const auto& tri : collidingTriangles) {
      OGLLineVertex vert;
      vert.color = glm::vec3(1.0f, 0.0f, 0.0f);
      vert.position = glm::vec4(tri.points.at(0), 1.0f);
      mLevelCollidingTriangleMesh->vertices.push_back(vert);
      vert.position = glm::vec4(tri.points.at(1), 1.0f);
      mLevelCollidingTriangleMesh->vertices.push_back(vert);
      vert.position = glm::vec4(tri.points.at(1), 1.0f);
      mLevelCollidingTriangleMesh->vertices.push_back(vert);
      vert.position = glm::vec4(tri.points.at(2), 1.0f);
      mLevelCollidingTriangleMesh->vertices.push_back(vert);
      vert.position = glm::vec4(tri.points.at(2), 1.0f);
      mLevelCollidingTriangleMesh->vertices.push_back(vert);
      vert.position = glm::vec4(tri.points.at(0), 1.0f);
      mLevelCollidingTriangleMesh->vertices.push_back(vert);
    }
    ```

4. Now we have saved the outlines of the detected triangles for all instances. Rendering the triangles to the screen can be done with a simple line draw call:

    ```
    mLineVertexBuffer.uploadData(*mLevelCollidingTriangleMesh);
      if (mLevelCollidingTriangleMesh->vertices.size() > 0) {
    ```

```
        mLineShader.use();
        mLineVertexBuffer.bindAndDraw(GL_LINES, 0,
          mLevelCollidingTriangleMesh->vertices.size());
    }
```

Running the application with instance/level collision and debug drawing results in a picture similar to *Figure 12.1*:

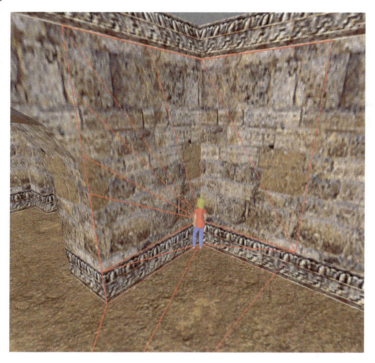

Figure 12.1: Collision between an instance and the level geometry

In *Figure 12.1*, the instance collides with the ground and several walls. All the triangles were detected by using their bounding boxes, so don't be alarmed if a triangle is highlighted while the instance is still a bit away from the triangle itself. In this case, the bounding box of the triangle was hit, spanning a larger area than the triangle itself. But the number of false positives among the detected collisions is low and may only affect the performance of the collision detection by a small amount.

To add a proper reaction of the instance to a collision with the level geometry, we will enhance the node tree next.

Extending the node tree to support level geometry collisions

Thanks to the good foundation built in the last chapters, adding a new collision type takes a matter of minutes by following these steps:

1. First, we add the new event type to the `nodeEvent` enum in the `Enums.h` file:

```
enum class nodeEvent : uint8_t {
    ...
    instanceToLevelCollision,
    NUM
};
```

2. We also add some text to the `micNodeUpdateMap` during the `init()` method of the renderer to add a name in the node tree:

```
mModelInstCamData.micNodeUpdateMap[
    nodeEvent::instanceToLevelCollision] =
    "Inst to Level collision";
```

3. Then, in `checkForLevelCollisions()`, trigger the new event if we have at least one colliding triangle:

```
if (collidingTriangles.size() > 0) {
    mModelInstCamData.micNodeEventCallbackFunction(
        instSettings.isInstanceIndexPosition,
        nodeEvent::instanceToLevelCollision);
}
```

4. The event informs the node tree of the instance that a collision with level geometry occurred. As an example, we could just let the instance turn around by 180 degrees, as shown in *Figure 12.2*:

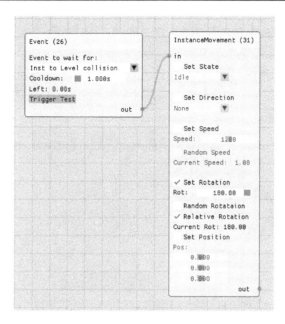

Figure 12.2: An Event node reacting to instance/level collisions

In the Event node in *Figure 12.2*, the instance would instantly turn around when running into a collision with the level. Also, a cooldown of 250 milliseconds has been added. Using a cooldown should give the instance a bit of time to walk far enough away from the affected level geometry to avoid immediately re-triggering a level collision.

But right now, collision detection has a huge drawback: the instances keep walking at the same height level, thus running through hills or walking in the air when the elevation changes.

To keep the instances on the ground, let's add a simple form of gravity to the application.

Using gravity to keep the instances on the floor

Gravity is literally always around us, accelerating objects downwards until they hit some other, immovable object, such as the ground. We mostly don't realize the effects of gravity while walking around or standing still; we only realize its power when something falls down and most probably breaks when it hits the ground.

Before we can add gravity, we need to find a way to detect if a triangle in the level geometry belongs to the ground or not.

Finding ground triangles in level data

For real-world levels, extra attributes could be used to mark areas of a level as walkable or not. Since we want to keep the ground-level technique as generic as possible, we will use a different approach and use the triangle normal to check if the area around us belongs to the floor or a wall, and up to which angle a sloped area can be walked on.

We store the normal of each triangle as 3-element vector inside the MeshTriangle struct, along with the other triangle data:

```
struct MeshTriangle {
  ...
  glm::vec3 normal;
  BoundingBox3D boundingBox;
};
```

When generating the triangle octree in generateLevelOctree(), the normal from the first vertex of the triangle is taken:

```
        tri.normal = glm::normalize(normalMat *
          glm::vec3(mesh.vertices.at(
          mesh.indices.at(i)).normal));
```

Due to the indexed structure of the level data, using one of the normals of the vertices could lead to artifacts caused by reusing the same vertex for different triangles. In this case, we could alter the calculation of the normal to be the cross product of two edges of every triangle:

```
        glm::vec3 edge1 = glm::vec3(mesh.vertices.at(
          mesh.indices.at(i + 1)).position -
          mesh.vertices.at(mesh.indices.at(i)).position);
        glm::vec3 edge2 = glm::vec3(mesh.vertices.at(
          mesh.indices.at(i + 2)).position -
          mesh.vertices.at(mesh.indices.at(i)).position);
        tri.normal = glm::normalize(normalMat *
          glm::cross(edge1, edge2));
```

To be able to control the ground slope in the user interface, we add a new variable called rdMaxLevelGroundSlopeAngle to the OGLRenderData struct:

```
    float rdMaxLevelGroundSlopeAngle = 0.0f;
```

For Vulkan, as always, the variable will be added to the VkRenderData struct.

Then, in checkForLevelCollisions(), we add a new check to find out if the angle between an upward-pointing vector and the normal of the triangle is larger than the maximum configurable ground slope:

```
if (glm::dot(tri.normal, glm::vec3(0.0f, 1.0f, 0.0f))
    >= glm::cos(glm::radians(
    mRenderData.rdMaxLevelGroundSlopeAngle))) {
```

Inside the if block, we can now limit the event sending code to be triggered only for walls, no longer for ground triangles. We also change the color of the debug lines for triangles detected as ground triangles to blue while wall triangles remain red:

```
    vertexColor = glm::vec3(0.0f, 0.0f, 1.0f);
} else {
    vertexColor = glm::vec3(1.0f, 0.0f, 0.0f);
    mModelInstCamData.micNodeEventCallbackFunction(
        instSettings.isInstanceIndexPosition,
        nodeEvent::instanceToLevelCollision);
    }
```

In the **Levels...** section of the UserInterface class, we add a float slider to enable controlling the maximum ground slope interactively:

```
ImGui::Text("Max Ground Slope:");
ImGui::SameLine();
ImGui::SliderFloat("##MaxSlope",
    &renderData.rdMaxLevelGroundSlopeAngle,
    0.0f, 45.0f, "%.2f", flags);
```

Now the application draws collisions with walls and ground in different colors, as shown in
Figure 12.3:

Figure 12.3: Separate collisions for ground and walls

As you can see in *Figure 12.3*, wall collisions are now marked by red triangle edges, while ground
collisions are highlighted by blue triangle edges. The slope angle can be configured by a slider,
allowing finetuning of which slope of a hill or edge will be still seen as the ground.

In addition to the distinct colors for collisions between instances and walls or the ground, the
event reporting also differs. For a ground collision, no instance/level geometry collision event
will be generated, allowing the instances to run around in the level and only collide with walls.

After we can check if an instance collides with a ground polygon, it's time to add the gravity to
the code.

Adding basic gravity

For our application, we are using only simple gravity. We just move the instance down by some
amount every frame, without thinking about more complex patterns, such as acceleration over
time. If you want to implement more details, the *Addition resources* section contains the ISBNs of
books that dive into advanced physics and collision detection topics. Also, a task in the *Practical
sessions* section implements enhanced gravity.

To be able to add a gravity effect to an instance, we create a new public method named applyGravity() to the AssimpInstance class:

```
void AssimpInstance::applyGravity(float deltaTime) {
  glm::vec3 gravity =
    glm::vec3(0.0f, GRAVITY_CONSTANT * deltaTime, 0.0f);
  mInstanceSettings.isWorldPosition -= gravity;
}
```

The private variable GRAVITY_CONSTANT is defined in the AssimpInstance.h header and set to 9.81, similar to the real gravity on earth. The gravity is then applied in the instances loop in the draw() method of the renderer:

```
        if (mRenderData.rdEnableSimpleGravity) {
          instances.at(i)->applyGravity(deltaTime);
        }
```

The rdEnableSimpleGravity variable has been added to the OGLRenderData struct in the OGLRenderData.h file for OpenGL, and to the VkRenderData struct in the VkRenderData.h header for Vulkan.

In the **Levels...** collapsing header of the createFrame() method in the UserInterface class, a checkbox is used to control the gravity:

```
    ImGui::Text("Simple Gravity:  ");
    ImGui::SameLine();
    ImGui::Checkbox("##EnableGravity",
      &renderData.rdEnableSimpleGravity);
```

We will use this checkbox to prevent all instances from falling when no level geometry is loaded.

One last step is needed to enable instances to roam around on the floor of the levels. Let's create the final parts of the code the finish the ground handling for the instances.

Keeping the instances on the ground triangles

With the code from the previous sections of this chapter, we can detect collisions between instances and level walls and floors and the handle wall collision. For ground collisions, we need special handling since the instance will, most of the time, stay on the floor of the level.

A naive idea for ground collision would be to move the instance upward a bit after gravity is applied. Sadly, applying gravity and moving the instance back leads to oscillations if the amounts of vertical movement are not identical. But instead of moving the instance up, we can avoid applying gravity in the first place, leaving the instance on the ground triangle once the collision is detected.

The functionality to keep instances on the ground triangles of the level will be implemented by the following steps:

1. For every instance, we store the "on ground" state by using a new Boolean variable named isInstanceOnGround in the InstanceSettings struct in the InstanceSettings.h file:

```
bool isInstanceOnGround = false;
```

2. In the AssimpInstance class, a public setter for the state will be added too:

```
void AssimpInstance::setInstanceOnGround(bool value) {
  mInstanceSettings.isInstanceOnGround = value;
}
```

3. Then we update the applyGravity() method to disable adding the gravity to the vertical position if the instance is found to reside on the ground:

```
if (!mInstanceSettings.isInstanceOnGround) {
  mInstanceSettings.isWorldPosition -= gravity;
}
```

To set the isInstanceOnGround instance variable in the renderer, a new checking code will be added to the draw() method of the renderer, right below the query() call to the triangle octree. This way, we make sure we are using the most recent triangle colliding data.

4. First, we set the local instanceOnGround Boolean to true, which prevents instances from falling if the gravity is disabled. Next, we calculate the gravity with the same formula as the instance, and we initialize the current footPoint of the instance with the world position:

```
bool instanceOnGround = true;
if (mRenderData.rdEnableSimpleGravity) {
  glm::vec3 gravity =
    glm::vec3(0.0f, 9.81 * deltaTime, 0.0f);
  glm::vec3 footPoint =
    instSettings.isWorldPosition;
```

We need the foot point in the next step to have a valid position for the instance in case the ground detection fails.

5. Now, we set `instanceOnGround` to false as the default setting for ground-level detection, and we iterate over all colliding triangles:

```
instanceOnGround = false;
for (const auto& tri : collidingTriangles) {
```

6. Then, the same angle check between the normal vector of the triangle and an upwards pointing vector as in `checkForLevelCollisions()` is used to find out if the triangle is a ground triangle and thus considered walkable:

```
if (glm::dot(tri.normal, glm::vec3(0.0f, 1.0f,
    0.0f)) >= glm::cos(glm::radians(
    mRenderData.rdMaxLevelGroundSlopeAngle))) {
```

7. If the triangle is walkable ground, we try to get the intersection between a virtual ray pointing upwards, originating from the instance after it has already been sunk slightly into the ground:

```
std::optional<glm::vec3> result =
    Tools::rayTriangleIntersection(
    instSettings.isWorldPosition - gravity,
    glm::vec3(0.0f, 1.0f, 0.0f), tri);
    if (result.has_value()) {
        footPoint = result.value();
        instances.at(i)->setWorldPosition(
            footPoint);
        instanceOnGround = true;
    }
}
```

Checking the instance after applying the gravity value is required because no collision will be reported if the instance is exactly at the same level as the ground triangle.

The helper function `rayTriangleIntersection()` in the `Tools` class implements the Möller-Trumbore algorithm to find an intersection between a ray and a triangle. This algorithm detects if a ray intersects the triangle and returns the exact point of the intersection.

A visualization of the algorithm is shown in *Figure 12.4*:

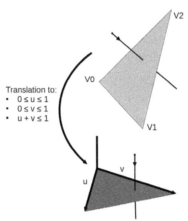

Figure 12.4: Visualization of the Möller-Trumbore algorithm

The Möller-Trumbore algorithm uses the barycentric coordinates of the triangle created by the three vertices V0, V1, and V2 to check if the ray is inside or outside of the triangle. To simplify the detection process, the algorithm transforms both the triangle vertices and the ray so that two of the triangle sides are mapped to the X and Y axes of the Cartesian coordinate system, defining a unit triangle. The barycentric coordinates of the intersection point stay intact during these transformations. The final test for intersection just needs to check if the x and y coordinates of the intersection point are inside the triangle by testing for valid barycentric coordinates. A link to the mathematical backgrounds of the algorithm is available in the *Additional resources* section.

8. As the last step in the draw() call part of the new renderer code, we set the ground flag to the instance and apply the gravity:

    ```
    instances.at(i)-setInstanceOnGround(instanceOnGround);
    instances.at(i)->applyGravity(deltaTime);
    ```

    The extra check for rdEnableSimpleGravity around applyGravity() that was added in the *Adding basic gravity* section can be removed. We already ensure that no gravity will be added if rdEnableSimpleGravity is false by setting the default value of instanceOnGround to true.

Running the application with collision triangle debug draw enabled and the ground slope adjusted will result in an image similar to *Figure 12.5*:

Figure 12.5: Instances walking at different heights of the level

In *Figure 12.5*, we can see that the instances are walking on their own level, with the left instance climbing up a small slope. In the running application, you will see that climbing down a hill is also working as expected.

After level gravity is enabled, the instances are running on the level floor. But on an uneven floor, one either intersects with the floor when going up a hill, or one of the feet is still in the air when going down a slope. You can see this effect on the right foot of the left instance: the entire foot is clipping into the ground triangle.

Let's fix the instance feet by adding inverse kinematics.

Adding inverse kinematics

The word "kinematics" is defined as the mechanics behind the motion of an object, but without referencing the forces that cause this motion. So, every part of our daily motion can be described in terms of kinematics as the movement of our bones.

The two types of kinematics

The type of animation of our characters in the previous chapters is called **forward kinematics**. An example of forward kinematics is shown in *Figure 12.6*:

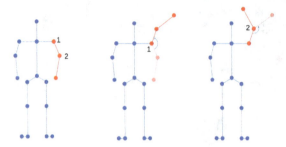

Figure 12.6: Raising the hand of the simple skeleton by using Forward Kinematics

The skeleton in *Figure 12.6* raises its simplified hand by rotating at bone number one, the shoulder, and number two, the elbow.

During the movement or rotation of the skeletal bone, all the other nodes attached to it are also affected. Rotating the arm around the shoulder does not change the elbow or the forearm, as we only change one bone at a time. Next, the forearm is rotated around the elbow, bringing the hand to the final position. This final position of the hand is defined by the concatenation of the changes of all the bones before the hand.

But... what happens if we only know the desired final position of the hand?

If we want to move the hand of the skeleton in *Figure 12.7* to the green target point, or we want to put the foot onto the green target block, our only option with forward kinematics would be trial and error.

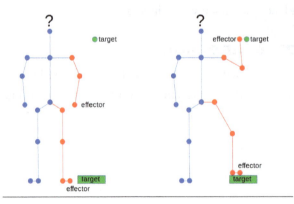

Figure 12.7: How to move the hand to the target, or put the foot on the box?

We would have to adjust all the nodes on the arm or the leg over and over again until we reach a matching position. This is where **inverse kinematics** comes into play. Instead of rotating the nodes directly, we calculate bone positions matching the final movement and read the node rotations from the final bone positions,

In inverse kinematics, the name **effector** is used to describe the part of the skeleton that should reach the **target**. If the target is too far away to be reached by the effector node, we should at least try to find a position as close as possible to the target. In addition to effector and target, a **root node** must be chosen. The root node is the first unchanged node of the skeleton.

Although many inverse kinematics solver algorithms have been created, we will use one of the basic algorithms: FABRIK, the **Forward And Backward Reaching Inverse Kinematics** solver. FABRIK is easy to understand and implement and finds good solutions for the nodes. So, let's dive into inverse kinematics with FABRIK.

Understanding the FABRIK basics

FABRIK was introduced in 2011 by Dr. Andreas Aristidou. The FABRIK algorithm solves the inverse kinematics problem by moving the nodes of a bone chain one by one closer to the target and then rescaling the bones back to the original length. Also, FABRIK moves along the chain of bones in both directions, forward and backward, hence its name.

We will use a simple robotics arm to describe the steps to solve an inverse kinematics problem with FABRIK. Four nodes of the arm define three bones, and the target and the effector were drawn in every step, with the blue node attached to the ground as the root node and the outer red node used as the effector. All the steps are shown in *Figure 12.8* to *Figure 12.11*.

Let's step through a single iteration of the algorithm. First, we will examine the *forward* solving part of FABRIK.

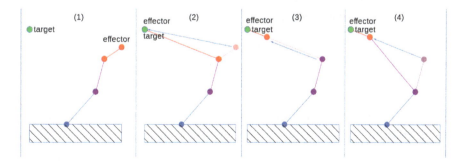

Figure 12.8: Doing inverse kinematics using FABRIK forward iteration – part 1

The start situation is shown in *Figure 12.8* (**1**):

1.   As shown in *Figure 12.8* (**2**), we will *move* the effector to the position of the target as the first step. You can see that moving the node stretches the red bone far beyond its original length.

2.   We must correct the length of the red bone, so we need to save the length of our bone before moving the effector. By using the saved length, we scale the red bone back to its original length, right after the effector has been moved, as shown in *Figure 12.8* (**3**). Scaling back the red bone to the previous length rips apart our robotics arm, as seen in *Figure 12.8* (**3**), but this is an intended behavior during a FABRIK iteration.

3.   Then, we will move the outer node of the purple bone back to the end of the red bone, scaling it again to an arbitrary length. *Figure 12.8* (**4**) shows the result after the robotics arm has been reconnected.

4.   The purple bone is scaled back to its previous length, as shown in *Figure 12.9* (**5**), moving the end node away from the blue bone.

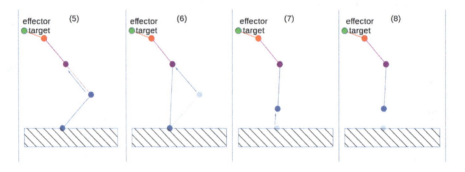

Figure 12.9: Inverse kinematics using FABRIK forward iteration – part 2

5.   Finally, we will repeat *steps 4* and *5* of the purple bone movement with the blue bone. We will reconnect the arm every time and scale the bone back to its original length, as shown in *Figure 12.9* (**6**) and *Figure 12.9* (**7**).

     Figure 12.9 (**8**) shows the result after the *forward* steps of the FABRIK algorithm are finished. But having the robotic arm disconnected from the ground is not the result we want. To fix the arm, we will repeat the same steps, but this time *backward* on the same chain of bones.

     In the *backward* part of FABRIK, we will swap the target, effector node, and root node. We use the original connection point of the arm as the target, the end of the blue bone becomes the effector, and the original effector node is the new root node.

6. As the first step in the backward operation, we will reconnect the arm to the ground, as shown in *Figure 12.10* (**9**).

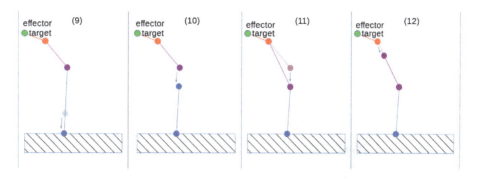

Figure 12.10: Inverse kinematics using FABRIK backward iteration – part 1

7. Then, we scale the blue bone back to its previous size and move the purple bone in the same way as we did initially in *steps 2* and *3*. In *Figure 12.10* (**10**), *Figure 12.10* (**11**), and *Figure 12.10* (**12**), the results of adjusting the blue and purple bones are shown.

8. Now, the lower node of the red bone will move, and the red bone is scaled back to its previous size, as shown in *Figure 12.11* (**13**) and *Figure 12.11* (**14**).

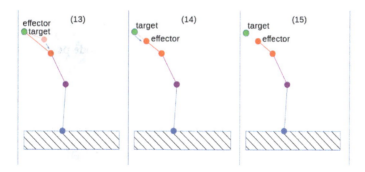

Figure 12.11: Inverse kinematics using FABRIK backward iteration - part 2

Figure 12.11 (**14**) moves the effector away from the position of the target, but again, this is the intended behavior in FABRIK if the target cannot be reached. In *Figure 12.11* (**15**), a single FABRIK iteration has ended.

For the next iterations of FABRIK, *steps 2* to *9* are repeated until the effector node reaches the target position, or until we hit the maximum number of iterations.

By using simple pseudo-code, FABRIK can be melted down to this procedure:

```
NodePositions := OrigNodePositions
StoreOriginalBoneLengths
RootNodePos := NodePositions[LastPosition];
For NumIterations; Do
    EffectorPos := NodePositions[0]
    If TargetIsCloseToEffector
        Return
    SolveForward(TargetNodePos)
    SolveBackwards(RootNodePos)
EndFor
```

The `SolveForward` and `SolveBackwards` methods are similar, so we can look only at pseudo-code for the forward-solving part of FABRIK:

```
NodePositions[0] = TargetNodePos
For i = 1; i < NodePositions.Size; i += 1
    BoneDirection = NodePositions[i] - NodePositions[i-1]
    NewOffset = BoneDirection * BoneLengths[i - 1]
    NodePositions[i] = NodePositions[i-1] + NewOffset
EndFor
```

The backward-solving part just starts with the saved root node position and iterates over the bones in the opposite direction.

As you can see, the number of steps is small and the actions in these steps are simple. Armed with the new knowledge, let's add a FABRIK solver.

Implementing the FABRIK inverse kinematics algorithm

The inverse kinematics solver using the FABRIK algorithm is implemented by the following steps:

1. For the FABRIK inverse kinematics solver, we create a new class, `IKSolver`, by adding the `IKSolver.h` and `IKSolver.cpp` files to the `tools` folder.

2. Next to the constructor and a setter for the number of iterations, a `public` method named `solveFABRIK()` is added:

    ```
    std::vector<glm::vec3> solveFARBIK(
      std::vector<glm::mat4>& nodeMatrices,
    glm::vec3 targetPos);
    ```

3. We also add the two private members, mNodePositions and mBoneLengths, and three private methods, solveFABRIKForward(), solveFABRIKBackwards(), and calculateOrigBoneLengths():

```
std::vector<glm::vec3> mNodePositions{};
std::vector<float> mBoneLengths{};
void solveFABRIKForward(glm::vec3 targetPos);
void solveFABRIKBackwards(glm::vec3 rootPos);
void calculateOrigBoneLengths();
```

4. In mNodePositions, we store the world positions of the nodes during calculation, and in mBoneLengths, the required original bone lengths are saved. The name of the calculateOrigBoneLengths() method speaks for itself; we don't need to dive into details there. But let's do a quick walkthrough of the three remaining methods.

5. The forward part of FABRIK is handled in solveFABRIKForward(). First, we set the first element of mNodePositions to the target position:

```
void IKSolver::solveFABRIKForward(glm::vec3 targetPos) {
  mNodePositions.at(0) = targetPos;
  for (size_t i = 1; i < mNodePositions.size(); ++i) {
    glm::vec3 boneDirection =
      glm::normalize(mNodePositions.at(i) -
      mNodePositions.at(i - 1));
    glm::vec3 offset = boneDirection *
      mBoneLengths.at(i - 1);
    mNodePositions.at(i) =
      mNodePositions.at(i - 1) + offset;
  }
}
```

6. Then we loop over the remaining nodes, calculate the new direction of the bone after moving the previous node, and calculate the new position of the node by using the original length. Finally, we move the node to the new position, retaining the length.

7. In solveFABRIKBackwards(), we do the same operations as in *steps 5 and 6* but in the opposite direction along the node chain. We start with the root node position as the target and adjust the node positions one by one:

```
void IKSolver::solveFABRIKBackwards(glm::vec3 rootPos) {
  mNodePositions.at(mNodePositions.size() - 1) = rootPos;
```

```
    for (int i = mNodePositions.size() - 2; i >= 0; --i) {
      glm::vec3 boneDirection =
        glm::normalize(mNodePositions.at(i) -
        mNodePositions.at(i + 1));
      glm::vec3 offset = boneDirection * mBoneLengths.at(i);
      mNodePositions.at(i) =
        mNodePositions.at(i + 1) + offset;
    }
  }
```

8. The last method, solveFARBIK(), is used to control the iterations of FABRIK plus the comparison of the effector and target positions. We start with a simple check for an empty node matrix vector. In this case, we return an empty vector:

```
std::vector<glm::vec3> IKSolver::solveFARBIK(
    std::vector<glm::mat4>& nodeMatrices,
    glm::vec3 targetPos) {
  if (nodeMatrices.size() == 0) {
    return std::vector<glm::vec3>{};
  }
```

9. Then, we resize and fill the mNodePositions vector:

```
    mNodePositions.resize(nodeMatrices.size());
    for (int i = 0; i < nodeMatrices.size(); ++i) {
      mNodePositions.at(i) =
        Tools::extractGlobalPosition(
        nodeMatrices.at(i));
    }
```

10. In the helper method extractGlobalPosition(), the translational part of the node matrix is extracted and returned. Now we can calculate the bone lengths, and we store the position of the root node for the backward part of FABRIK:

```
    calculateOrigBoneLengths();
    glm::vec3 rootPos =
      mNodePositions.at(mNodePositions.size() - 1);
```

11. We need to store the root node position because we alter the mNodePositions vector during the forward calculations. Without saving the original root node, the backward part would be impossible to solve.

12. Then, we start a loop with the maximum number of iterations:

```
for (unsigned int i = 0; i < mIterations; ++i) {
  glm::vec3 effector = mNodePositions.at(0);
  if(glm::length(targetPos - effector) <
      mCloseThreshold) {
    return mNodePositions;
  }
```

At the start of the loop, we compare the positions of the effector node and the desired target. If the positions are close together, we return the current node positions as solutions.

13. Now comes the FABRIK solving part. We call the forward solver method with the target position and then the backward solver method with the saved root node position:

```
  solveFABRIKForward(targetPos);
  solveFABRIKBackwards(rootPos);
}
```

14. After both solving parts are finished, we continue with the next iteration. Finally, we return the positions FABRIK found for the nodes:

```
  return mNodePositions;
}
```

It's possible that the effector node is unable to reach the target position, i.e., because the node chain is too short. In this case, the best position FABRIK could find will be returned.

Before we can continue with the last part of the FABRIK, we need to make sure to configure the root and effector nodes of the model. Here, we will use only the feet to create a natural appearance while walking up or down a hill.

Defining the node chain for the instance's feet

To be able to configure the nodes for the feet, two new members of the ModelSettings struct in the ModelSettings.h file are added:

```
std::array<std::pair<int, int>, 2> msFootIKChainPair{};
std::array<std::vector<int>, 2> msFootIKChainNodes{};
```

In the msFootIKChainPair array, we store the node IDs of the effector and the root node for the left foot and right foot. We only need this pair for the user interface since the contents of the msFootIKChainNodes array will be calculated from the effector and root node IDs.

For the user interface, we use the names from the bone name list of the instance's model. Since we have a 1:1 relationship between the bone IDs and the names, iterating over the list to create a combo box is easy.

Together with a Boolean variable to enable or disable inverse kinematics and an iteration slider, the user interface for the section about inverse kinematics for the model's feet looks like *Figure 12.12*:

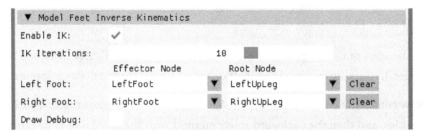

Figure 12.12: Configured inverse kinematics for the Women model

For *Figure 12.12*, the Women model was used as an example. For other models, the node names may be different.

Inverse kinematics depends on the model

The ability to configure inverse kinematics for the feet of a model depends heavily on the model's skeleton. It's likely that some models you find on the internet may miss some parent-child relationships between nodes of the skeleton, for instance between leg and feet nodes, leading to non-working inverse kinematics.

The FABRIK algorithm has another part that adjusts the world positions of the original nodes by using the calculated positions. We skipped the code for the final part in the *Implementing the FABRIK inverse kinematics algorithm* section since we have to split the FABRIK algorithm for technical reasons – the node data used by the FABRIK algorithm resides on the GPU, but some of the calculations are easier to handle on the CPU.

Let's combine the node positions now.

Adjusting the node positions

Due to the usage of compute shaders, the matrices containing the rotation, translation, and scale plus the data for the world positions of the nodes only reside in GPU memory. Plus, the node positions are calculated for performance reasons in a compute shader. We need to copy the data back and forth between the CPU and the GPU to adjust the node rotations to the results delivered by the FABRIK solver. After calculating the final node positions for all instances with FABRIK, the rotation data for every node from target to effector is updated. The resulting transform matrices are uploaded to the GPU, and a compute shader is used to calculate the new transform matrices. Since all child nodes of a node are affected by the transform matrix, we have to perform these steps for each node individually.

Keeping the node transformations separate

To simplify using the data calculated in the compute shaders, we will not combine the rotation, translation, and scale data for the TRS matrix into a single matrix. Instead, we store the values in a new struct.

In the three shaders files, `assimp_instance_matrix_mult.comp`, `assimp_instance_transform.comp`, and `assimp_instance_headmove_transform.comp`, we add the following TRSMat struct at the top:

```
struct TRSMat {
  vec4 translation;
  vec4 rotation;
  vec4 scale;
};
```

Be aware that the rotation element is a quaternion; we just use a vec4 for the transport to the shader since GLSL does not support quaternions directly.

To avoid adding translation, rotation, and scale to a matrix in one shader and extracting the values again in another shader, we will keep the decomposed transformation data as separate values in the SSBO:

```
uint index = node + numberOfBones * instance;
trsMat[index].translation = finalTranslation;
trsMat[index].rotation = finalRotation;
trsMat[index].scale = finalScale;
```

Creating the final TRS matrix is moved into the matrix multiplication shader, along with the createTRSMatrix(), createTranslationMatrix(), createScaleMatrix(), and createRotationMatrix() helper methods. The TRS matrices will be created on the fly instead of doing a lookup in the main() method of the assimp_instance_matrix_mult.comp shader:

```
mat4 nodeMatrix = createTRSMatrix(index);
```

```
    ...
    nodeMatrix = createTRSMatrix(parent) * nodeMatrix;
```

Since the calculation was done entirely on the GPU, the only change in the renderer code to reflect the TRS data split is the size calculation for the `mShaderTRSMatrixBuffer` SSBO:

```
    size_t trsMatrixSize = numberOfBones *
        numberOfInstances * 3 * sizeof(glm::vec4);
```

Instead of a `glm::mat4` for the full TRS matrix, we use three `glm::vec4` instances here, keeping the node transform split into translation, rotation, and scale like in the compute shader.

In the `OGLRenderData.h` file, a matching `TRSMatrixData` struct is added:

```
  struct TRSMatrixData{
    glm::vec4 translation;
    glm::quat rotation;
    glm::vec4 scale;
  };
```

For Vulkan, the addition of `TRSMatrixData` happens in the `VkRenderData.h` file.

Right after the final node positions were calculated by the compute shaders, but before the instances are rendered, new code will be added for the animated instances.

Adding the code for the animated instances

We start by retrieving the current contents of the TRS buffer:

```
        mTRSData =
            mShaderTRSMatrixBuffer.getSsboDataTRSMatrixData();
```

Then we iterate over the two feet and calculate the size of the node chain for each foot:

```
        for (int foot = 0; foot <
            modSettings.msFootIKChainPair.size(); ++foot) {
            int nodeChainSize =
                modSettings.msFootIKChainNodes[foot].size();
            if (nodeChainSize == 0) {
                continue;
            }
```

If the foot node chain is empty, we continue immediately since we don't have anything to calculate here. But if we have a valid foot node chain, we iterate backward over the node chain, and in each node chain, we iterate forward over all instances:

```
for (int index = nodeChainSize - 1; index > 0;
    --index) {
  for (size_t i = 0; i < numberOfInstances; ++i) {
```

The order of the loops – foot first, then the node chain, and instance last – has a good reason: it is much easier to handle cases where one of the foot node chains is empty or the foot node chains have different sizes, as we can skip an entire loop or use a different number of iterations. Iterating the node chain backward is necessary because the foot chain vector contains the nodes in order from the effector to the root node, but the world position update starts with the root node as the first node.

In the inner loop, we extract the node IDs of the current node and the previous node from the foot node chains:

```
int nodeId =
  modSettings.msFootIKChainNodes[foot].at(index);
int nextNodeId =
  modSettings.msFootIKChainNodes[foot]
  .at(index - 1);
```

By using the two node IDs, we extract the world position of the nodes:

```
glm::vec3 position = Tools::extractGlobalPosition(
  mWorldPosMatrices.at(i) *
  mShaderBoneMatrices.at(i * numberOfBones +
  nodeId) *
  model->getInverseBoneOffsetMatrix(nodeId));
glm::vec3 nextPosition =
  Tools::extractGlobalPosition(
  mWorldPosMatrices.at(i) *
  mShaderBoneMatrices.at(i * numberOfBones +
  nextNodeId) *
  model->getInverseBoneOffsetMatrix(nextNodeId));
```

After multiplying the inverse of the bone offset node, the current node position, and the instance world position, we get the world position of the two adjacent nodes of the foot node chain.

With the two positions, we calculate the normalized toNext vector:

```
glm::vec3 toNext = glm::normalize(nextPosition -
    position);
```

To calculate the desired rotation for the node, we need to find a quaternion that rotates the bone from the current world rotation to the rotation computed by the FABRIK algorithm.

Creating the new world positions

We extract the new world positions of the same nodes calculated by FABRIK, calculate the normalized toDesired vector between the new world positions, and compute the rotation angle between the toNext and toDesired vectors as a quaternion, nodeRotation:

```
int newNodePosOffset = i * nodeChainSize + index;
glm::vec3 toDesired = glm::normalize(
    mNewNodePositions.at(foot)
    .at(newNodePosOffset - 1) -
    mNewNodePositions.at(foot)
    .at(newNodePosOffset));
glm::quat nodeRotation = glm::rotation(toNext,
    toDesired);
```

At this point, we have the world-level rotation between the current position of the bone and the new position of the same bone of the model's skeleton.

Now we extract the world-level rotation of the current node and calculate the local rotation that would be needed to match the world-level rotation of the node:

```
glm::quat rotation = Tools::extractGlobalRotation(
    mWorldPosMatrices.at(i) *
    mShaderBoneMatrices.at(i * numberOfBones +
    nodeId) *
    model->getInverseBoneOffsetMatrix(nodeId));
glm::quat localRotation = rotation *
    nodeRotation * glm::conjugate(rotation);
```

Finally, we read the current local rotation of the node, concatenate the new rotation, and store the rotation back to the TRS data:

```
        glm::quat currentRotation = mTRSData.at(i *
          numberOfBones + nodeId).rotation;
        glm::quat newRotation = currentRotation *
          localRotation;
        mTRSData.at(i*numberOfBones + nodeId).rotation =
          newRotation;
    }
```

By running the `mAssimpMatrixComputeShader` and uploading the updated TRS data, the new node matrices for all the nodes in the foot node chain are recalculated. As the last step, we read back the contents of the `mShaderBoneMatrixBuffer` to have the new node matrices available for the next node in the foot node chain.

We are just one step away from a working inverse kinematics implementation. What's left now is detecting the collisions between the foot position and the ground triangle. Let's tackle the last section of this chapter.

Detecting feet-to-ground collisions

The general idea behind detecting collisions between instance feet and the ground is the same as for the instances. We use the ray-to-triangle check to find the intersection of a ray with the triangle below or above the defined foot node. This intersection point is then used as the target position for the FABRIK solver.

For both feet of every instance, we use the same method to extract the world position as in the last step of the FABRIK solver code:

```
        int footNodeId =
          modSettings.msFootIKChainPair.at(foot).first;
        glm::vec3 footWorldPos =
          Tools::extractGlobalPosition(
          mWorldPosMatrices.at(i) *
          mShaderBoneMatrices.at(i * numberOfBones +
          footNodeId) *
          model->getInverseBoneOffsetMatrix(footNodeId));
```

We also calculate the offset of the foot node from the ground:

```
float footDistAboveGround = std::fabs(
    instSettings.isWorldPosition.y - footWorldPos.y);
```

This footDistAboveGround offset is needed to let the foot hover above the sloped ground triangle at the same distance as the foot would be on a plain ground triangle. Then, we use the AABB of the instance to calculate the full and half height of the bounding box:

```
AABB instanceAABB = model->getAABB(instSettings);
float instanceHeight = instanceAABB.getMaxPos().y -
    instanceAABB.getMinPos().y;
float instanceHalfHeight = instanceHeight / 2.0f
```

With the two height values, we create a ray to detect the intersection with the ground triangle. Next, we set a default value for the final hitPoint of the intersection and iterate over the colliding triangles:

```
glm::vec3 hitPoint = footWorldPos;
for (const auto& tri :
    instSettings.isCollidingTriangles) {
      std::optional<glm::vec3> result{};
```

Then we check every colliding triangle for an intersection with a ray starting at the half height of the instance, pointing at most the entire instance height down:

```
result = Tools::rayTriangleIntersection(
    footWorldPos +
    glm::vec3(0.0f, instanceHalfHeight, 0.0f),
    glm::vec3(0.0f, -instanceHeight, 0.0f), tri);
```

Using an upper and lower limit for the ray helps prevent the misdetection of any nearby triangles. Next, we check if we have found an intersection:

```
if (result.has_value()) {
    hitPoint = result.value() +
       glm::vec3(0.0f, footDistAboveGround, 0.0f);
}
```

Here, we add the footDistAboveGround to the resulting value to keep the original distance from the animation to the ground. *Figure 12.13* shows a simplified example of how keeping the foot-to-ground distance affects the instance:

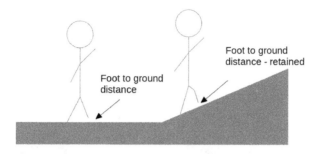

Figure 12.13: Retaining the distance of the foot above the ground

Now we can run the inverse kinematics solver to calculate the adjusted node positions.

Running the FABRIK solver

First, we clear the vector containing positions to solve. Then, we place the matrices of the nodes in the current foot node chain in mIKWorldPositionsToSolve:

```
mIKWorldPositionsToSolve.clear();
for (int nodeId :
    modSettings.msFootIKChainNodes[foot]) {
  mIKWorldPositionsToSolve.emplace_back(
    mWorldPosMatrices.at(i) *
    mShaderBoneMatrices.at(i * numberOfBones +
    nodeId) *
    model->getInverseBoneOffsetMatrix(nodeId));
}
```

As the final step of the inverse kinematics, we let FABRIK solve the node positions for the intersection point we have found, and insert the results into the mNewNodePositions vector for the foot we are working on:

```
mIKSolvedPositions = mIKSolver.solveFARBIK(
    mIKWorldPositionsToSolve, hitPoint);
mNewNodePositions.at(foot).insert(
    mNewNodePositions.at(foot).end(),
```

```
mIKSolvedPositions.begin(),
mIKSolvedPositions.end());
```

At this point, the foot positions are ready for the node matrix and TRS updates from the *Detecting foot to ground collisions* section.

Enabling and configuring inverse kinematics after loading a level will render an image similar to *Figure 12.14* to the screen:

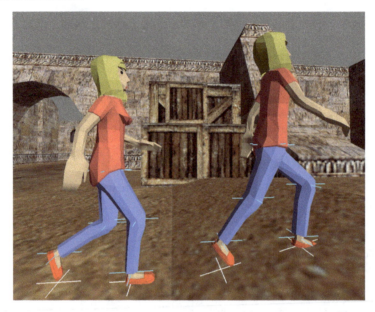

Figure 12.14: The right foot of the right instance has less intersection on sloped ground

As you can see in the right instance in *Figure 12.14*, the right foot no longer fully intersects the ground triangle. Also, the angle of the right knee has been adjusted to allow the foot to be placed on the higher part of the ground triangle.

There is still some intersection with the toes on the left. Fixing the remaining intersection by aligning the toes to the ground slope is a task in the *Practical sessions* section. But even with this minimal intersection, it's a lot of fun to watch the instances going up and down on hills much more like a real human.

Limitations of FABRIK

Animations created by using a FABRIK solver for inverse kinematics usually look good, but the algorithm has some limitations that should be addressed.

The biggest problem arises when note rotations create unnatural bone positions. For example, a human cannot bend their knees forward, but our instances on the screen can do so. Without checking and restricting the rotations of the nodes, the bones of the instances can end up in virtually any position. A task in the *Practical sessions* section handles this issue by limiting node rotations.

Another problem emerges if the target is too far away from the effector, thus becoming unreachable. FABRIK solves unreachable targets by stretching the entire bone chain from the root node to the effector node in a straight line, causing the instance to walk around with stiff legs like a robot. Since we can detect if the target cannot be reached by the effector, handling these situations is easier than unlimited node rotations. There is a task in the *Practical sessions* section to solve problems with unreachable targets.

Summary

In this chapter, we enhanced the collision detection in our level. First, we added a separate and specialized octree for the level data, allowing us to do a quick check for collisions between instances and level geometry. Then, we added simple gravity to the virtual world and adjusted the collision detection to allow instances to walk on the level floor. Finally, we added inverse kinematics for the feet of the instances, bringing a more natural foot and leg movement on sloped grounds by avoiding the feet floating above the ground or clipping into ground triangles of the level.

In the next chapter, we will add a final extension to the level data and add simple navigation. We will start with a brief roundup of several ways to implement navigation in games. Next, we will explore the A* pathfinding algorithm and implement it in the application. Then, we will add waypoints to the map, serving as targets for A* calculations. Finally, we will implement waypoint navigation to the instances, enabling the instances to move to random waypoints or to patrol between a set of defined waypoints.

Practical sessions

Here are some additions you could make to the code:

- Add a more complete gravity.

  Instead of just manipulating the vertical position of the instances, use a more complex way to apply gravity by using vertical acceleration. Since gravity is used in two places, in the instance for the speed and in the renderer for the collision detection, synchronization between both code parts is needed.

- Add collision detection for the third-person camera.

  In real games, the camera is also a normal object in the virtual world. And instead of clipping through the level data, the camera always stays inside the same boundaries as the character it follows, connected by a spring arm structure to allow adjustments if the camera is unable to keep the exact position behind the character. You can try to add a bounding box for the third-person camera and check the boundaries against the level octree too. Remember to also check and change the distance and height of the camera if a collision occurs.

- Enhance stair and cliff detection.

  To enable the instances climbing stairs, basic logic has been added to the code that compares the step height of stairs with the instance position. This idea may not work for different kinds of game maps, plus the instance may fall off a cliff when the stair detection returns the wrong result. Enhance the logic to have better stair detection and also prevent the instance from falling down when it "thinks" it is standing in front of a step when it is actually on the edge of an abyss.

- Align the instance's feet to follow the slope and normal if the floor.

  Right now, the feet of the instances may still intersect the ground, depending on the slope of the ground and the instance position. Add some code, and maybe even more nodes to the model(s), to align the feet of the instance to the ground triangle. This adjustment should work for forward/backward inclination and for a sideway rotation of the feet to match the ground.

- Handle unreachable targets.

  Implement logic to detect if the effector cannot reach the target and add some kind of default rotations for the nodes, for instance, taken from the current frame of the animation clip.

- Move the node update part of FABRIK to a compute shader.

  To keep the FABRIK code for updating the final node rotations simple and easy to follow, a CPU/GPU combination was used. The downside of the current code is the need to copy both TRS matrix data and final node positions from GPU memory at the start of every update of the node chain. By creating a compute shader for the node rotation updates, you can keep the entire node update process on the GPU.

- Extended difficulty: Write a compute shader for inverse kinematics.

  The FABRIK inverse kinematics algorithm is simple and straightforward. Implementing the same algorithm in a compute shader should not be too hard. You can use the matrix multiplication compute shader as an example of how to do loops in GLSL code without hard coding the loop variable.

- Extended difficulty: Add node limits to the inverse kinematics algorithm.

  In the default version, inverse kinematics does not worry about unnatural bone rotations when solving for the position. For a game character, it looks strange if a knee or an elbow is bent in the wrong direction. By adding per-node limits for all three rotation axes, the target may not be reachable, but the character still looks like a human. But be warned: adding node limits may influence the stability of the inverse kinematics algorithm.

- Extended difficulty: Use a **bounding volume hierarchy** (**BVH**) for collision detection.

  The idea of a bounding volume hierarchy was mentioned in the *Using spatial partitioning to reduce complexity* section of *Chapter 8*, and the book *Real-Time Collision Detection* by Christer Ericson has an entire chapter about BHVs. Replacing the octree with a BHV to detect collisions may be a long task since the creation of the hierarchy already adds a significant amount of complexity to collision detection.

Additional resources

- Introduction to the Jacobian Matrix: https://medium.com/unity3danimation/overview-of-jacobian-ik-a33939639ab2

- *Collision Detection in Interactive 3D Environments* by *Gino van den Bergen*, published by *CRC Press*: ISBN 978-1558608016

- *Game Physics Engine Development* by *Ian Millington*, published by *CRC Press*: ISBN 978-0123819765

- *Game Physics* by *David H. Eberly*, published by *Morgan Kaufmann*: ISBN 978-0123749031

- *Real-Time Collision Detection* by *Christer Ericson*, published by *CRC Press*: ISBN 9781000750553

- FABRIK publications: http://www.andreasaristidou.com/FABRIK.html

- Inverse kinematics in Unreal Engine: https://dev.epicgames.com/documentation/en-us/unreal-engine/ik-setups?application_version=4.27

- Full body inverse kinematic: https://dev.epicgames.com/documentation/en-us/unreal-engine/control-rig-full-body-ik-in-unreal-engine

- Möller-Trumbore algorithm for ray-triangle intersection checks: http://www.lighthouse3d.com/tutorials/maths/ray-triangle-intersection/

Join our community on Discord

Join our community's Discord space for discussions with the author and other readers: https://packt.link/cppgameanimation

13

Adding Simple Navigation

Welcome to *Chapter 13*! In the previous chapter, we created a separate octree to enhance collision detection, allowing us to detect collisions between instances and level geometry in a quick and computationally cheap way. Then we added simple gravity to the application to keep the instances on the ground of the map, eventually resulting in the instances walking on the level floor and small hills. Finally, we used inverse kinematics on the feet of the instances to keep both feet on the ground when climbing hills or sloped areas of a map.

In this chapter, we will add pathfinding and navigation. We start with a brief overview of methods used for navigation in computer games, followed by an exploration and the implementation of the A* path-finding algorithm. Next, we will add navigation targets to the application, enabling a simple way to place path destinations in the virtual world. At the end of the chapter, we will implement the navigation toward the waypoints, allowing the instances to walk or run toward a defined target.

In this chapter, we will cover the following topics:

- An overview of different ways to navigate
- The A* path-finding algorithm
- Adding navigation targets to the map
- Navigating instances to a target

Technical requirements

The example code for this chapter is available in the `chapter13` folder, in the `01_opengl_navigation` subfolder for OpenGL and the `02_vulkan_navigation` subfolder for Vulkan.

An overview of different ways to navigate

Pathfinding and navigation have been used in video games for much longer than one might think. Let's explore a couple of navigation methods.

Distance-based navigation

One of the oldest games using a simple algorithm to mimic intelligent behavior for enemies is **Pac-Man** by **Namco**. Each of the four ghosts (Blinky, Pinky, Inky, and Clyde) has a slightly different kind of "character," created only by the target point of the ghost's movement.

While the red ghost (Blinky) is chasing Pac-Man directly, the pink ghost (Pinky) and the blue ghost (Inky) will try to get in front of Pac-Man, effectively trying to surround the player. The fourth ghost (the orange Clyde) has "a mind of its own" and switches between chasing the player and running away.

The decision about the new path to choose is made only at the intersections in the game's maze and is based entirely on the distance to the target tile for all possible ways at the intersection. The game does not use more advanced look-ahead path planning, sometimes leading to a bad decision. *Figure 13.1* shows such a decision situation at an intersection:

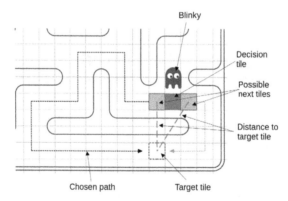

Figure 13.1: Navigation decision of the red ghost in Pac-Man

In *Figure 13.1*, the green box is the field triggering a decision to go left or right and the two dashed green lines are the direct distances to the red-outlined target tile. Even though the right path is shorter, the left path will be chosen due to the shorter decision distance on the left, creating erratic behavior of the ghost. A link is available in the *Additional resources* section with in-depth information about the internals of ghost navigation.

Simple distance-based navigation is still used in games today, for instance, to find the spot where an enemy could intercept the player, based on the speed and direction of both entities. Planning the path to the player is then done with a graph-based navigation algorithm.

Graph-based navigation

In a graph, search algorithms use the nodes of a graph to describe locations on a game map and the edges to describe the connections between the nodes. By building a graph of the map, the shortest path between two locations can be found in an organized manner.

Several graph algorithms are used in navigation. The most common ones are:

- **Depth-First Search (DFS)**
- **Breadth-First Search (BFS)**
- Dijkstra's algorithm
- A* (pronounced "A star")

DFS and BFS algorithms

Both of these are simple algorithms. While DFS traverses the graph "depth-first," from the start node to the most distant node, BFS visits the nearest nodes first, advancing in "rings" to the next nodes. *Figure 13.2* shows an example graph made of six nodes named A to F:

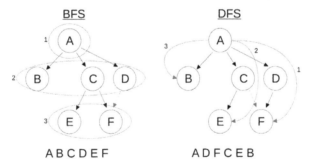

Figure 13.2: BFS and DFS

The BFS algorithm on the left side of *Figure 13.2* starts with the closest nodes (B, C, and D) after the root node (A) and then traverses to nodes E and F. The DFS algorithm on the right side of *Figure 13.2* traverses child node D and D's child node (F) first, advancing to nodes C and E, and, finally, to node B.

Dijkstra's algorithm

Dijkstra's algorithm adds weights to the edges of a graph. The weights can be seen as costs or distances to travel from one node to another, depending on the problem to solve. Dijkstra's algorithm traverses the entire graph, building a table containing the shortest paths from a start node to all other nodes of the graph.

Figure 13.3 shows the starting graph and the result after all steps of the algorithm:

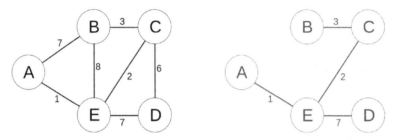

Figure 13.3: A graph and the shortest distances from A to all other nodes

By using Dijkstra's algorithm, any weighted graph can be traversed to find the paths with the lowest costs (or distances) from one node to all other nodes, but the algorithm must be rerun for every start node. For a full description of the algorithm, a link in the *Additional resources* section is provided showing the steps of finding the shortest distances for the graph in *Figure 13.3*.

A* algorithm

A* uses Dijkstra's algorithm as a basis, but two additions are made:

- A so-called **heuristic** is added to each node, stating the estimated distance from each node to the target node.

- The algorithm searches from a start node to a specified target node and usually terminates when the target node has been reached.

By combining the distance from the start node to a node and the estimated distance from the same node to the target node and using the shortest sum while traversing to the next node, A* does a directed search toward the target node. So, instead of doing an undirected search like BFS or DFS, A* always heads in the direction of the target node. We will discuss A* in depth in the *The A* path-finding algorithm* section.

One drawback of the algorithms in this section is that they have to recreate the entire path if the target is not static. For dynamic targets, algorithms like LPA*, D*, or D*-Lite could deliver better results. Also, several other path-finding algorithms have been created since the introduction of A*, aiming for special environments like in robotics, or to further optimize the outcome path-finding process, like in Theta*.

Before exploring A*, let's look at another popular navigation type in video games, using triangles or other polygons to describe the walkable area for bots and NPCs, and also take a short look at machine learning as an alternative version to create navigation data.

Mesh-based navigation

Simple games like Pac-Man and many strategy games use distance-based navigation by dividing the world into a grid, usually built from rectangular or hexagonal structures. But the needs of three-dimensional games (like an open world) or first- and third-person exploration and fighting games are different. Due to overlapping parts of the virtual world, a three-dimensional structure is needed to be able to guide computer-controlled characters through the map.

Most games with three-dimensional maps use either navigation meshes, area awareness, or a combination of both.

Navigation meshes

Navigation meshes (also called **NavMeshes**) were introduced in games around the year 2000. A navigation mesh is an additional data structure made of polygons (triangles in most implementations), overlaying the level geometry. The polygons in a navigation mesh mark the walkable area of a level, omitting any objects and structures a computer-controlled character could collide with.

By using a navigation mesh, a bot or NPC can walk around in the virtual world while avoiding costly collision checks with static level geometry if the character stays on the navigation mesh. Only if the character can leave the navigation mesh are collision checks required. In combination with a graph-based algorithm like A*, fine-grained control of the behavior of computer-controlled characters is possible. A link to a comprehensive introduction to pathfinding with navigation meshes is available in the *Additional resources* section. *Figure 13.4* shows a simple example:

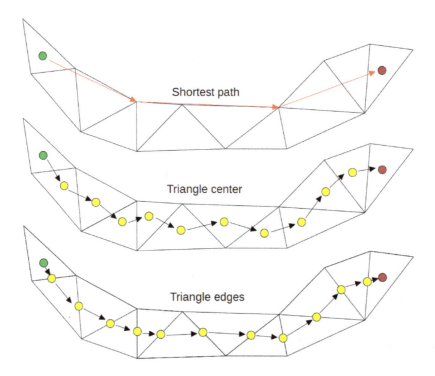

Figure 13.4: Navigation mesh with start (green), target (red), and path from start to target

In *Figure 13.4*, the top picture shows the shortest possible path from the starting triangle (green) to the target triangle (red) by using the next vertex in a line of sight to the next sharp corner of the mesh.

In comparison, the path in the middle picture uses the triangle centers as graph nodes for the path-finding algorithm, and the bottom picture uses the inner triangle edges as graph nodes.

The path's quality depends on the mesh and which part or parts of a triangle will be used for the graph node. Combinations of the methods in *Figure 13.4* are possible, so both the center and the middle of triangle edges could be used as graph nodes. The resulting path can also be smoothed by skipping to the next directly visible node and by using splines for the curves.

Be aware that if the edge navigation mesh is too close to walls or borders in a narrow passage, an instance may collide with the walls, generating additional movement corrections or leading to an impassable part of the mesh. Static obstacles in a level should also be bypassed at a safe distance.

As a rule of thumb, use the distance between the edges and the center of the axis-aligned bounding box of an instance as the minimum distance between the edges of the navigation mesh and the adjacent level geometry. By keeping the instance away from walls at any time, no collision can occur during normal navigation.

Generating a navigation mesh from level data

Usually, a navigation mesh will be created by hand and added to the level data. But we need a solution for levels found on the internet, so we will do a shortcut in the code and use the same upward-facing triangles as "possibly walkable ground" that are used for the detection if the instance collides with the level ground.

In combination with adjacency relations between all ground triangles, an estimation of the walkable area in the level can be achieved. A couple of enhancements to the ground area creation code are available as tasks in the *Practical sessions* section.

By using navigation meshes, two kinds of navigation are possible: free roaming through the virtual world and patrolling between waypoints.

Free navigation

With free navigation, any point on a map can be a target point for the start and destination. Moving from one part of the level to another may be costly to calculate; in the worst case, the entire mesh must be checked during pathfinding. Also, the path of the character may be entirely different between two path plannings, depending on the exact position of the start and target.

Waypoint navigation

A better approach for mesh-based navigation is to define waypoints on the navigation mesh that are visible to each other. For instance, every door in a group of rooms will be a waypoint or every fork in the road. When a bot moves through the virtual world, a waypoint is set as the next target after reaching the desired waypoint. If the player is spotted and then lost, the bot can return to the nearest waypoint. By making sure that the computer-controlled character can always "see" at least one waypoint, path planning to that next waypoint becomes cheap and easy to calculate.

Area awareness system

In 1999, **id Software** used a system called **area awareness** in **Quake III Arena**. Instead of two-dimensional graphs, a simplified three-dimensional representation of the levels was created, containing all information about the level structure, other bots, and the player.

The bots can traverse the awareness areas not only by walking, jumping, or swimming but also by using a teleporter, a jump pad, or even by doing a rocket jump. With such a large repertoire of actions, a bot can easily follow the player around in the level or try to cut off the player's path.

A full description of the area awareness system is available in a link to a PDF document in the *Additional resources* section.

Using machine learning to generate navigation data

A more recent way to create navigation data for computer-controlled characters is machine learning, mostly in the form of so-called **reinforced learning**. During reinforced learning, an agent representing the character explores the virtual world on its own in a large amount of "trial-and-error" style rounds, but with added rewards for achieving a defined task or a punishment for failing to complete the task.

Such a task could be something like "Reach a defined target point with maximum health," "Don't fall off the level," or "Complete the level in minimum time." By taking the rewards and punishments of previous explorations into account, the agent optimizes its behavior to maximize rewards and minimize punishments. When the data generated by these agents is used in games, the enemies can utilize the strategies from machine learning to appear even more natural when moving around in the virtual world.

Two challenges of machine learning are making the usage time- and cost-expensive:

- Goals, rewards, and punishments must be clearly defined and adjusted during the calculations. Even if we humans think that the goals and rewards are well-defined, the machine learning algorithm could find unexpected ways to maximize rewards. A failure in the setup may result in discarding the data and doing a complete restart of the entire machine learning cycle.

- Since machine learning is exploring the virtual world by trial and error, progress is non-deterministic and may happen only in insignificant amounts. Even for simple tasks, thousands of game rounds must be played to achieve the desired results while the game is running. Creating a complex AI that explores big levels of the game may need a significant amount of computational resources, leading to excessive development costs.

Even though machine learning may produce better results than algorithm-based navigation, it is recommended to check the trade-offs between possible improvements and additional costs. A link to a video showing the progress of letting a machine learn how to drive a car is available in the *Additional resources* section.

After the short round-up of navigation methods, let's dive into the A* algorithm next.

The A* path-finding algorithm

The A* algorithm was published in 1968 in the earlier days of computing. A* is the result of the path planning for an AI-controlled mobile robot called **Shakey**. The robot was developed at the Stanford Research Institute. Its software included computer vision and natural language processing, and it was able to do simple tasks like driving to a place in the lab on its own, without describing every single action in advance. A link is available in the *Additional resources* section with more details about the project and the robot.

But what makes A* different from Dijkstra's algorithm?

Estimating the distance to the target

While Dijkstra's algorithm only uses the weights between nodes, A* adds a heuristic value to every node. The heuristic function calculates an estimated cost of the cheapest path from every node to the selected target. In many cases, such as for large worlds and many nodes, calculating the minimal costs between every pair of nodes is computationally expensive, so an "educated guess" for the costs is cheaper to calculate and also good enough.

For the heuristics function, any distance calculation function can be used. In most cases, either the so-called **L1 norm** will be used, known as the **Manhattan distance**, or the **L2 norm**, known as the **Euclidean distance**. *Figure 13.5* shows the idea behind both distance calculations:

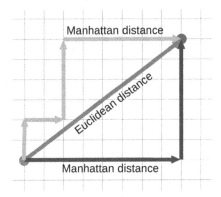

Figure 13.5: Manhattan and Euclidean distances from start to target

The Manhattan distance is modeled after the path of a taxicab in Manhattan. The streets are organized in parallel lines, crossing at an angle of 90 degrees. Like a cab in Manhattan, the blue paths in *Figure 13.5* can only use the grid lines between the start and the target. It also does not matter whether we use straight, direct lines, as in the dark blue path, or a staircase version, like the light blue path; the distance for both paths is identical.

In contrast, the Euclidean distance for the green path in *Figure 13.5* is calculated by using the Pythagorean theorem. This means squaring the lengths of the distances in both directions, summing up the squares, and calculating the square root of the sum.

Whether Manhattan distance, Euclidean distance, or any other distance calculation will be used for the heuristics function of A* heavily depends on the needs of the application. For instance, obstacles, hills, or enemies in a game map may need to be considered when estimating the distances. An intuitive way to find the best function is by drawing the paths for every heuristic function and a set of combinations for the start and target node and comparing the results.

By using the heuristic value to the target node, A* tries to minimize the costs of the path to the target for every iteration.

Minimizing path costs

In every iteration, A* uses the sum of the known costs of the path *from the start* node and the estimated costs *to the target* node for every neighbor of the current node to calculate the minimal costs to reach the target node. Then, the algorithm chooses the neighboring node with the minimum costs, makes that neighboring node the current node, and starts the next iteration.

In addition, A* saves a reference to the current node in each visited neighboring node if the overall cost from the start to the target over this neighbor is minimal among all neighboring nodes. Storing the parent node in a node allows backtracking to the best path from target to source after the target node has been reached.

To visualize the algorithm, let's step through a small example.

Exploring the A*algorithm

Figure 13.6 shows a graph with nodes A, B, C, and D, plus the heuristics table from every node to the desired target node, D. The start node, in this case, is node A.

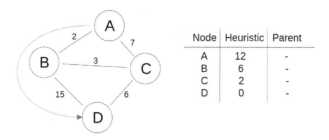

Figure 13.6: A graph to traverse plus estimated distances to the target node, D

We can immediately see the shortest path from node A to node D: ABCD. But for the computer, the A* algorithm must walk through the nodes to find this path.

For the first iteration, we visit the neighbors of node A, as shown in *Figure 13.7*:

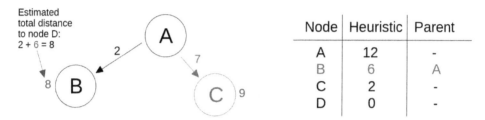

Figure 13.7: Visiting nodes B and C

Here, we calculate the estimated distance as the sum of the known distance from A and the heuristic value of each node. The sum for node B is lower, so we proceed to node B. We also remember the parent node for B since A is the direct predecessor of B.

Then, we look at all neighbors of node B, as shown in *Figure 13.8*:

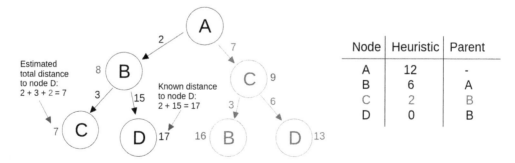

Figure 13.8: Visiting nodes C and D

We do the same calculations for node C and sum up the costs from A to B, B to C, and the heuristic from C to D. In an optimized version of A*, our search could be already over since we reached the target node, D.

But we continue here by checking the remaining neighbors of node D in case there is an even shorter path available. So, we update the parent node of nodes C and D, and visit node C as the last yet unvisited neighbor of node D, as shown in *Figure 13.9*:

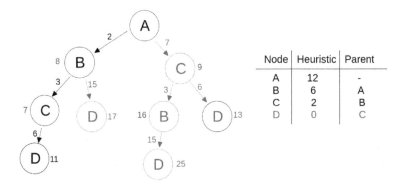

Figure 13.9: The shortest path from A to D is ABCD

Indeed, the path to node D via nodes B and C is much shorter than the path via B. So, we set node C as the new parent node for node D. After all the neighboring nodes of the target node D have been visited, A* has fulfilled its job to find a path from node A to node D.

By backtracking the parent nodes, we get the path from the target to the start. By reversing the node order, we now have the shortest path from the start to the target: ABCD.

As you can see, even in this very simple example, A* cares about the total estimated costs to the target when choosing the node to proceed with. If the algorithm learns about a shorter distance while working on a node, the parent node used to backtrack the best path is also updated. In the *Additional resources* section, a link to a website with a deep dive into A* is available.

After an overview of the algorithm, let's add the path-finding code.

Implementing A*-based navigation

Since we will not have a simple two-dimensional terrain in most maps, a two-dimensional grid for navigation cannot be used. Instead, we will use a navigation mesh to find a path from a source object to a target object in the virtual world.

As already stated in the *Navigation meshes* section, creating the meshes is at least a partially manual job, depending on the editor used to create the game map. Some editors can create a navigation mesh based on the map's elements, but in most cases, the generated mesh must be corrected manually. The navigation mesh must be stored on the same map as the rest of the level data or in a separate data file.

To support both in-map and separate navigation mesh, the path-finding class is kept modular when it comes to the walkable ground meshes. For instance, if your navigation mesh is saved with a special name in the map file, you could import the navigation polygons and their adjacency properties into the path-finding class. You also have to import the navigation triangles into a separate triangle octree and do an additional ray-to-triangle intersection to find both the ground-level triangle and the navigation mesh triangle. The A* path-finding algorithm has also been implemented as a separate method, allowing you to easily add other algorithms or a different heuristics function.

In the example code in this chapter, we will use the same idea as for the ground-level detection and use the normal of each mesh triangle to decide whether it is walkable or not. This method will result in having all upward-facing triangles in the navigation mesh, even if the triangles may be unreachable by any instance. But to demonstrate the general idea of pathfinding and navigation in a game map, creating a navigation mesh from the ground triangles of the map is sufficient and delivers reasonable results.

We will use the Euclidean distance to calculate the distance between nodes and for the heuristic function, as the triangles in the map are most probably not arranged in a rectangular grid. To speed up the distance calculations, we will extend the mesh triangle data structure.

Preparing the mesh triangles

The MeshTriangle struct is defined in the OGLRenderData.h file for OpenGL and in the VkRenderData.h file for Vulkan. At the end of the MeshTriangle struct, we add the two new arrays, edges and edgeLengths:

```
struct MeshTriangle {
  std::array<glm::vec3, 3> edges{};
  std::array<float, 3> edgeLengths{};
};
```

In the edges array, we store the three edges of each triangle. We order the edges by using the same winding as the original triangles. As we will need the lengths of the edges during the calculation of any adjacent triangles, we store the length of each edge in the corresponding edgeLengths element.

Now we can jump directly into the implementation of the path-finding class.

Adding the path-finding class

The path-finding class (named PathFinder) will reside in the tools folder where all other helper classes created in the previous chapters are stored, like AABB or IKSolver. To keep the naming consistent, the header file is named PathFinder.h and the implementation will go into the PathFinder.cpp file.

On top of the PathFinder.h header, right after all the #include directives, we add two struct entries. The first new struct is named NavTriangle:

```
struct NavTriangle {
  int index;
  std::array<glm::vec3, 3> points{};
  glm::vec3 center{};
  glm::vec3 normal{};
  std::unordered_set<int> neighborTris{};
};
```

We don't reuse MeshTriangle here as we need a couple of different variables. While index, the points array, and the normal vector are the same, we also need to store the world position of the center of each triangle in the center variable and the surrounding triangles in neighborTris. The instance will navigate from one triangle center to the next, and the triangles stored in neighborTris are used to find the triangle with the shortest distance to the target.

For the neighbor triangles, std::unordered_set has been chosen over a plain std::vector to have an automatic removal for duplicate entries.

The second struct is called NavData and contains the data for the A* algorithm:

```
struct NavData {
  int triIndex;
  int prevTriIndex;
  float distanceFromSource;
```

```
    float heuristicToDest;
    float distanceToDest;
};
```

In the triIndex variable, we store the triangle index of the corresponding NavTriangle. By using the index, we can do a simple lookup to find triangle data like position or neighbor triangles. As soon as we visit a neighboring node of a triangle, we add the index of the triangle with the shortest path so far to prevTriIndex, allowing us to backtrack the shortest path at the end of the pathfinding run.

The remaining three variables (distanceFromSource, heuristicToDest, and distanceToDest) are the workhorses of the A* algorithm. Here we store the aggregated distance from the source to the current node, the result of the heuristic function for the distance between the current node and the target, and the sum of both distances. By comparing the values of distanceToDest for all neighboring nodes, A* chooses the next node toward the target node.

After the two new structs, the PathFinder class is declared, starting with the two public methods, generateGroundTriangles() and findPath():

```
    void generateGroundTriangles(OGLRenderData& renderData,
        std::shared_ptr<TriangleOctree> octree,
        BoundingBox3D worldbox);
    std::vector<int> findPath(int startTriIndex,
        int targetTriIndex);
```

By calling generateGroundTriangles(), all upward-facing triangles in the triangle octree are located and the neighbor information for each "walkable" triangle is created. Once the ground data is ready, findPath() can be used to find a path from the start triangle to the target triangle. The result of findPath() is the path found by A* as a vector of triangle indices to step on, ordered from the start triangle to the target triangle, or an empty vector if no valid path exists.

Also in the PathFinder class is the private member called mNavTriangles:

```
    std::unordered_map<int, NavTriangle> mNavTriangles{};
```

We store the calculated ground triangles in the mNavTriangles map. A mapping between the index and the triangle data is used for fast access by using the triangle index, also stored as part of a NavData element.

Let's step through the ground triangle generation code next.

Generating ground triangles

The ground triangles are generated by utilizing the triangle octree generated by the renderer. Since we will make a lot of requests to the triangle octree, it will be given as the second parameter in the generateGroundTriangles() method.

After clearing any previously generated navigation triangles, we get all triangles from the octree by a query with the world boundaries given as the third parameter:

```
mNavTriangles.clear();
std::vector<MeshTriangle> levelTris =
  octree->query(worldbox);
```

Then we loop over all level triangles to find the subset of upward-facing triangles:

```
std::vector<MeshTriangle> groundTris{};
NavTriangle navTri;
for (const auto& tri: levelTris) {
  if (glm::dot(tri.normal,
    glm::vec3(0.0f, 1.0f, 0.0f)) >=
      std::cos(glm::radians(
      renderData.rdMaxLevelGroundSlopeAngle))) {
        groundTris.emplace_back(tri);
```

Comparing the dot product of a triangle's normal and an upward-facing vector with the cosine of the rdMaxLevelGroundSlopeAngle value is known from the collision detection in *Chapter 12*. If the current triangle fulfills the check, we add it to the groundTris vector.

Next to the ground triangles in groundTris, we fill the NavTriangle named navTri with minimal data and add navTri to the mNavTriangles map:

```
    navTri.points = tri.points;
    navTri.normal = tri.normal;
    navTri.index = tri.index;
    navTri.center = (tri.points.at(0) +
      tri.points.at(1) + tri.points.at(2)) / 3.0f;
    mNavTriangles.insert(std::make_pair(tri.index,
      navTri))
  }
}
```

We use different sets of data in the groundTris vector and the mNavTriangles map here since a query to the triangle octree returns a vector of MeshTriangles but we maintain a better fitting map of NavTriangles for the ground triangles.

Now we can iterate over all ground triangles and query the triangle octree for all colliding triangles in the level:

```
for (const auto& tri : groundTris) {
    std::vector<MeshTriangle> nearbyTris =
      octree->query(tri.boundingBox);
```

This query works well as, in *Chapter 12*, we had to make the bounding box of every triangle in the generateLevelOctree() method of the renderer classes OGLRenderer or VkRenderer a bit bigger to avoid a size of zero in any of the three dimensions. With this minimal size change, the bounding boxes of adjacent triangles in the level data are colliding now, and the triangle octree returns all neighbor triangles.

Then we get a reference to the same ground triangle in the mNavTriangles map and iterate over all triangles reported by the octree query:

```
NavTriangle& navTri = mNavTriangles.at(tri.index);
for (const auto& peer : nearbyTris) {
```

Using a reference for the ground triangle is important because we will update the neighbor triangles directly on the NavTriangle object in the map.

And even though these two nested loops look awful, the overall computation time is still small because the octree query reports only a small number of neighbor triangles. We can even sort out more triangles by simple checks:

```
if (tri.index == peer.index) {
    continue;
}
if (glm::dot(peer.normal,
  glm::vec3(0.0f, 1.0f, 0.0f)) <
    std::cos(glm::radians(
    renderData.rdMaxLevelGroundSlopeAngle))) {
    continue;
}
```

The query for colliding triangles may also report the ground triangle we are currently inspecting, so we return immediately if we find it in the results. We also remove all triangles not facing upward from the list of possible neighbors as we are only interested in adjacent ground triangles.

In case of triangulation errors made by Assimp, we also need to check if the peer triangle is in mNavTriangles:

```
if (mNavTriangles.count(peer.index) == 0) {
  continue;
}
```

If we find a valid neighbor triangle, we get the neighbor triangle from the mNavTriangles map:

```
NavTriangle peerNavTri =
  mNavTriangles.at(peer.index);
```

Finally, we can do a loop over all three vertices of both triangles to check for adjacency:

```
for (int i = 0; i < 3; ++i) {
  for (int j = 0; j < 3; ++j) {
```

Inside the loop, we calculate the distance of every vertex from the edges of the other triangle:

```
glm::vec3 pointToPeerLine =
  glm::cross(tri.points.at(j) -
  peer. points.at(i), tri.points.at(j) -
  peer.points.at((i + 1) % 3));
float pointDistance =
  glm::length(pointToPeerLine) /
  peer.edgeLengths.at(i);
glm::vec3 peerPointToTriLine =
  glm::cross(peer.points.at(j) -
  tri. points.at(i), peer.points.at(j) -
  tri.points.at((i + 1) % 3));
float peerPointDistance =
  glm::length(peerPointToTriLine) /
  tri.edgeLengths.at(i);
```

By calculating the distance from all vertices to every edge of the other triangle, we can detect if the triangles share a vertex or a side, or if a vertex of one triangle is on the edge of the other triangle.

If the distance is small enough, we add the index of the current peer triangle to the set of neighbor triangles of the currently inspected ground triangle:

```
if ((pointDistance < 0.01f ||
    peerPointDistance < 0.01f)) {
  navTri.neighborTris.insert(peerNavTri.index);
}
```

After the generateGroundTriangles() method has finished the calculations, the mNavTriangles map contains all possibly "walkable" ground triangles, and for every triangle, a list of triangles sharing at least a side or a vertex.

A note on the navigation mesh quality

The quality of the generated ground triangle mesh heavily depends on the map: Since the upward-facing triangles in the map may not form a perfect triangle mesh that shares vertices between triangles, the generated ground triangles in the mNavTriangles map may contain more neighbors than a separate navigation mesh would have. More triangles in a level usually also bring better quality here.

With a navigation mesh of ground triangles at hand, we can go for the A* algorithm.

Finding a path between two ground triangles

The implementation of the findPath() method follows the A* algorithm and should be easy to understand.

Preparing the data

We start by extracting the center points of the target and start triangles:

```
NavTriangle targetTri = mNavTriangles.at(targetTriIndex);
glm::vec3 targetPoint = targetTri.center;
NavTriangle startTri = mNavTriangles.at(startTriIndex);
glm::vec3 startPoint = startTri.center;
```

We will need the center point to calculate the distances between the nodes.

Next, we create two sets called navOpenList and navClosedList and a map named navPoints:

```
std::unordered_set<int> navOpenList{};
std::unordered_set<int> navClosedList{};
std::unordered_map<int, NavData> navPoints{};
```

In the navOpenList variable, we store all neighbors of nodes that are candidates for the next iteration, and in navClosedList, we save all nodes that were already fully explored. The navPoints map contains data about all known nodes, like the distances and the parent node.

Prior to the first iteration of the A* algorithm, we set the currentIndex variable to the start triangle and create the navigation data for the start triangle:

```
int currentIndex = startTriIndex;
NavData navStartPoint{};
navStartPoint.triIndex = startTriIndex;
navStartPoint.prevTriIndex = -1;
navStartPoint.distanceFromSource = 0;
navStartPoint.heuristicToDest =
   glm::distance(startPoint, targetPoint);
navStartPoint.distanceToDest =
   navStartPoint.distanceFromSource +
   navStartPoint.heuristicToDest;
navPoints.emplace(std::make_pair(startTriIndex,
   navStartPoint));
navOpenList.insert(startTriIndex);
```

The distance to the target point is calculated as Euclidean distance by using a call to glm::distance and the distance to the start point is set to zero as we are still at the start point. We also add the start node to both the list of open nodes and the map containing the navigation data.

Running the main loop

For the main loop of the A* algorithm, we start a while loop that ends if we hit the target triangle. The loop is *not* guaranteed to end at some point in time (for instance, if the target triangle is outside of the reachable mesh), so we will need to add an exit condition at the end of the loop:

```
while (currentIndex != targetTriIndex) {
  NavTriangle currentTri = mNavTriangles.at(currentIndex);
  glm::vec3 currentTriPoint = currentTri.center;
```

```
    std::unordered_set<int> neighborTris =
      currentTri.neighborTris;
```

For every loop iteration, we extract the current triangle from the mNavTriangles map and get the center point in world coordinates and the neighbor triangles.

Next, we loop over all neighbor triangles and extract the center point of the triangle:

```
    for (const auto& navTriIndex : neighborTris) {
      NavTriangle navTri = mNavTriangles.at(navTriIndex);
      glm::vec3 navTriPoint = navTri.center;
```

If the neighboring node is not fully explored and not even visited yet, we continue inside the two if conditions and add the node to the open list:

```
      if (navClosedList.count(navTriIndex) == 0) {
        if (navOpenList.count(navTriIndex) == 0) {
          navOpenList.insert(navTriIndex);
```

As a reminder, the closed list contains all fully explored nodes, and the open list contains all known neighbors but not yet fully explored nodes of any of the nodes (even already closed nodes). At this point, we know that this is a new node to visit, so we create new navigation data:

```
          NavData navPoint{};
          navPoint.triIndex = navTriIndex;
          navPoint.prevTriIndex = currentIndex;
```

For the distance calculation, we get the distance from the current index (our parent node) and add the distance between the two nodes to the distance from the source:

```
          NavData prevNavPoint =
            navPoints.at(navPoint.prevTriIndex);
          navPoint.distanceFromSource =
            prevNavPoint.distanceFromSource +
            glm::distance(currentTriPoint, navTriPoint);
          navPoint.heuristicToDest =
            glm::distance(navTriPoint, targetPoint);
          navPoint.distanceToDest =
            navPoint.distanceFromSource +
            navPoint.heuristicToDest;
          navPoints.emplace(
```

```
                    std::make_pair(navTriIndex, navPoint));
        }
```

As the last step of the code block, we add the new navigation data to the navPoints map that contains data about all currently known nodes.

If the neighboring node is already in the list of open nodes, we check if we need to update the existing navigation data:

```
    } else {
      NavData& navPoint = navPoints.at(navTriIndex);
```

Here, we get a reference to the navigation data to be able to update the information in place. For the existing navigation point, we calculate the new estimated distance from the known distance to the source and the heuristic value to the target:

```
      NavData possibleNewPrevNavPoint =
        navPoints.at(currentIndex);
      float newDistanceFromSource =
        possibleNewPrevNavPoint.distanceFromSource +
        glm::distance(currentTriPoint, navTriPoint);
      float newDistanceToDest = newDistanceFromSource +
        navPoint.heuristicToDest;
```

If the new path through this node is shorter than the previously known path, we update the navigation data to reflect the new, shorter path:

```
      if (newDistanceToDest < navPoint.distanceToDest) {
        navPoint.prevTriIndex = currentIndex;
        navPoint.distanceFromSource =
          newDistanceFromSource;
        navPoint.distanceToDest = newDistanceToDest;
      }
```

After all neighboring nodes have been checked, we add the current node to the closed list, marking it as fully explored:

```
    navClosedList.insert(currentIndex);
```

If our open list becomes empty, we return an empty vector:

```
if (navOpenList.empty()) {
  return std::vector<int>{};
}
```

We check for an empty open list before going on since the next step involves a loop over all elements of the open list.

Extracting the best node

Once we have collected all the new nodes and updated the distances of all existing nodes, we need to find the node with the shortest combined distance from start to target. We will use a priority queue here to minimize the costs to access the node having the smallest distance. The priority queue will sort all nodes according to a comparison function into a tree structure and allow accessing the largest or smallest node as the topmost element.

First, we create the comparison function for the priority queue:

```
auto cmp = [](NavData left, NavData right) {
  return left.distanceToDest > right.distanceToDest;
};
```

By default, a priority uses `std::less` as a comparison function, resulting in a queue with the maximum value as the top element. But by using the `cmp` function, we will have the minimum distance to the destination as the top element.

Now we can fill the queue by pushing all triangles in the open list:

```
std::priority_queue<NavData, std::vector<NavData>,
  decltype(cmp)> naviDataQueue(cmp);
for (const auto& navTriIndex : navOpenList) {
  NavData navPoint = navPoints.at(navTriIndex);
  naviDataQueue.push(navPoint);
}
```

Next, we declare an empty navigation data variable and extract the index with the minimum distance from the queue by a call to `top()`:

```
NavData nextPointToDest{};
nextPointToDest = naviDataQueue.top();
currentIndex = nextPointToDest.triIndex;
```

The new triangle index will be used for the next loop of `while`, looping until the target triangle has been found as the triangle with the minimal distance.

As a final step for the A* algorithm, we erase the node from the open list:

```
navOpenList.erase(currentIndex);
}
```

Once we have found the target triangle, the outer `while` loop ends, and we can collect and return the shortest path

Backtracking the shortest path

Since we have saved the parent node with the shortest distance so far in the navigation data for every triangle, we just need to follow the chain along the parent nodes, starting from the target node until we hit the start node. The start node is marked by a parent node of `-1`, so we know when to stop.

First, we create a new vector named `foundPath` and store `currentIndex` in it:

```
std::vector<int> foundPath{};
foundPath.emplace_back(currentIndex);
```

The main `while` loop ends when `currentIndex` is identical to the requested `targetIndex`, so we could use any of the two variables here.

Then, we get the navigation data of the current triangle and loop over all parents until we hit the start triangle:

```
NavData navPoint = navPoints.at(currentIndex);
while (navPoint.prevTriIndex != -1) {
  foundPath.emplace_back(navPoint.prevTriIndex);
  navPoint = navPoints.at(navPoint.prevTriIndex);
}
```

As we started the backtracking at the target triangle and ended on the start triangle, the order of the triangles in `foundPath` is also from target to start. To fix the order, we reverse the vector:

```
std::reverse(foundPath.begin(), foundPath.end());
```

Finally, we return the reversed path:

```
return foundPath;
```

We can call findPath() now with any combination of start and target triangles and get a path back if such a path exists. If no path from start to target exists, findPath() returns an empty vector by the check for the empty open list.

The starting point of the pathfinding is known; it's the instance. But what about the target? Let's add some configurable navigation targets to the virtual world.

Adding navigation targets to the map

Before we start, let us imagine which properties a possible navigation target must have:

- It should come in any shape and number.
- It should be easy to select and move around.
- It can be placed anywhere on the ground.
- Ideally, it should be able to move by itself.

So, our ideal target is a model instance! And since we already have all the ingredients for this list, implementing navigation targets becomes easy.

Adjusting model and instance

First, we add a new Boolean variable named msUseAsNavigationTarget to the ModelSettings struct:

```
bool msUseAsNavigationTarget = false;
```

The AssimpModel class also needs two simple public methods named setAsNavigationTarget() and isNavigationTarget() to set and query the new variable:

```
void setAsNavigationTarget(bool value);
bool isNavigationTarget();
```

In the UserInterface class, a checkbox will be added to set the state of a model with a simple mouse click. *Figure 13.10* shows the **Models** layout with the new checkbox:

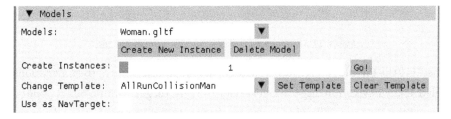

Figure 13.10: The Models part of the UI with the new navigation target checkbox

By setting the **Use as NavTarget** checkbox in *Figure 13.10*, we can control whether or not a model should be used as a navigation target.

For the instances, we add the five variables to the `InstanceSettings` struct:

```
bool isNavigationEnabled = false;
int isPathTargetInstance = -1;
int isPathStartTriangleIndex = -1;
int isPathTargetTriangleIndex = -1;
std::vector<int> isPathToTarget{};
```

To control the navigation on a per-instance basis, `isNavigationEnabled` is used. The two variables `isPathTargetInstance` and `isPathToTarget` should not need an explanation; their names state what they are for. In `isPathStartTriangleIndex`, the index of the triangle is saved where the instance currently resides, and `isPathTargetTriangleIndex` is filled with the triangle index of the target instance.

In the `AssimpInstance` class, simple `public` setter and getter methods for the new variables are added:

```
void setPathStartTriIndex(int index);
void setPathTargetTriIndex(int index);
int getPathTargetTriIndex();
void setPathTargetInstanceId(int instanceId);
void setPathToTarget(std::vector<int> indices);
std::vector<int> getPathToTarget();
```

In the **Instances** collapsing header of the `UserInterface` class, a couple of new controls are added too:

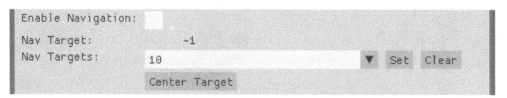

Figure 13.11: New navigation controls for the instances

When checking the **Enable Navigation** checkbox, the remaining parts of the navigation controls are enabled. If any navigation target model exists, the **Nav Targets** combo box is populated with the indices of the instances, allowing us the set the instance number to use as the target. In the case that a target was set, **Nav Target** shows the index of the current target, or -1 if no target was selected. To find the target without switching instances, Center Target can be pressed, centering the target in the middle of the screen.

For the combo box with the navigation targets, a callback named getNavTargetsCallback will be added to the Callbacks.h file:

```
using getNavTargetsCallback = std::function<std::vector<int>(void)>;
```

The corresponding method in the renderer class files OGLRenderer.cpp and VkRenderer.cpp is called getNavTargets() and collects the indices of all instances from models enabled as navigation targets:

```
std::vector<int> targets;
for (const auto& model : mModelInstCamData.micModelList) {
  if (!model->isNavigationTarget()) {
    continue;
  }
```

We loop over all models, and if the model is not a navigation target, we continue with the next model. If the model is marked as a navigation target, we store all indices in a vector named targets and return the vector:

```
    std::string modelName = model->getModelFileName();
    for (auto& instance : mModelInstCamData.
        micAssimpInstancesPerModel[modelName]) {
      InstanceSettings settings =
        instance->getInstanceSettings();
      targets.emplace_back(
        settings.isInstanceIndexPosition);
  }
}
return targets;
```

To place the targets on the ground, we also need gravity to apply.

Adding gravity for non-animated instances

Gravity is currently only affecting any animated instances since we needed them to stay on the ground for collision detection and inverse kinematics in *Chapter 12*. Thanks to keeping the code for animated and non-animated models mostly similar, adding gravity for non-animated instances is done with only a couple of small changes.

First, copy the entire code block with the `mLevelCollisionTimer.start()` and `mLevelCollisionTimer()` calls below the call that adds the current instance to the instance octree, as shown in the following code block:

```
mOctree->add(
    instSettings.isInstanceIndexPosition);
mLevelCollisionTimer.start();
...
mRenderData.rdLevelCollisionTime +=
    mLevelCollisionTimer.stop();
```

Then, add a call to `updateInstancePosition()` below the new code:

```
instances.at(i)->updateInstancePosition(
    deltaTime);
```

Finally, move the retrieval of the matrix containing the world transforms from the start of the block after the instance position update:

```
mWorldPosMatrices.at(i) =
    instances.at(i)->getWorldTransformMatrix();
```

That's all!

Now the gravity and ground collisions are also calculated for non-animated instances, the instance position is updated, and the most recent world transforms are collected and added to the `mWorldPosMatrices` array, which is then uploaded to a Shader Storage Buffer Object.

Saving and loading the new model and instance data

Storing the new values in the YAML configuration file and restoring the settings should need no further explanation. The Boolean to use a model as a navigation target is stored in the `ModelSettings` struct and all new path-finding and navigation variables for the instance are stored in the `InstanceSettings` struct. Adding the new values to the YAML emitter and parser is only a matter of copying and pasting. The YAML configuration version should be updated, too, to reflect the new values.

We have ground triangles, a path-finding algorithm, and the start and target points of a path. What's left is the logic to make an instance follow the path. So, let's add the last part now.

Navigating instances to a target

To calculate or update the path to the target instance, we need to add more code to the renderer. We start by adding the code to compute the actual path from an instance to the target position.

Calculating the path to the target

The best place for the path update code is in the loop over all animated instances in the `draw()` call of the renderer class `OGLRenderer.cpp` or `VKRenderer.cpp`, right after the ground and collision detection code that was just copied for the non-animated instances. We have the final world position of the instance available, including any gravity updates, and can use this position as the starting point of the path-finding algorithm.

First, we check if navigation is enabled for the instance and get the instance index of the target:

```
if (instSettings.isNavigationEnabled) {
  int pathTargetInstance =
    instSettings.isPathTargetInstance;
```

Then, we do a sanity check of the target instance to avoid a crash when accessing the `micAssimpInstances` vector:

```
if (pathTargetInstance >=
    mModelInstCamData.micAssimpInstances.size()) {
  pathTargetInstance = -1;
  instances.at(i)->setPathTargetInstanceId(
    pathTargetInstance);
}
```

Next, extract the index of the triangle the target is currently on plus the world position of the target:

```
int pathTargetInstanceTriIndex = -1;
glm::vec3 pathTargetWorldPos = glm::vec3(0.0f);
if (pathTargetInstance != -1) {
  std::shared_ptr<AssimpInstance>
    targetInstance =
    mModelInstCamData.micAssimpInstances.at(
    pathTargetInstance);
  pathTargetInstanceTriIndex =
    targetInstance->
      getCurrentGroundTriangleIndex();
```

```
        pathTargetWorldPos =
          targetInstance->getWorldPosition();
    }
```

As the target instance may move by itself or may be moved by the user, the target triangle index must be retrieved before every path update. This triangle index update ensures that the instance is following the target, regardless of the target being a static waypoint or another instance that roams around in the level.

Now we check if both the current instance and the target instance have a valid ground triangle and if we or the target moved away from the saved triangle. Only if all conditions are met do we recalculate the path at all, avoiding costly computations when no changes to the source or target occurred:

```
    if ((instSettings.isCurrentGroundTriangleIndex > -1 &&
        pathTargetInstanceTriIndex > -1) &&
        (instSettings.isCurrentGroundTriangleIndex !=
        instSettings.isPathStartTriangleIndex ||
        pathTargetInstanceTriIndex !=
        instSettings.isPathTargetTriangleIndex)) {
        instances.at(i)->setPathStartTriIndex(
      instSettings.isCurrentGroundTriangleIndex);
      instances.at(i)->setPathTargetTriIndex(
        pathTargetInstanceTriIndex);
```

In the case of any changes, we adjust the start and the target triangle of the current instance. With the most recent data for the triangles, we can call findPath():

```
    std::vector<int> pathToTarget =
        mPathFinder.findPath(
        instSettings.isCurrentGroundTriangleIndex,
        pathTargetInstanceTriIndex);
```

The result may be empty if no valid path has been found. In that case, we disable the navigation of the instance and invalidate the target instance by setting it to -1:

```
    if (pathToTarget.size() == 0) {
      instances.at(i)->setNavigationEnabled(false);
      instances.at(i)->setPathTargetInstanceId(-1);
    } else {
```

```
            instances.at(i)->setPathToTarget(pathToTarget);
        }
```

If the path was valid, we set the path indices in the instance.

Since the path will only update on changes, we get the saved or just updated path of the instance now:

```
        std::vector<int> pathToTarget =
            instances.at(i)->getPathToTarget();
```

To avoid awkward movement when starting or ending the path to a target, we remove the start and target triangles from the instance path:

```
        if (pathToTarget.size() > 1) {
          pathToTarget.pop_back();
        }
        if (pathToTarget.size() > 0) {
          pathToTarget.erase(pathToTarget.begin());
        }
```

The path is created between the center of the ground triangle the instance is currently standing on to the ground triangle the target resides. If the instance is already closer than the triangle center, the path would point backward, and the instance may never leave the current ground triangle. We could also remove the elements in the PathFinder class, but if we want to use the data generated in findPath() anywhere else, the triangles may be needed. So, we cut off the triangle indices here.

As the last step for pathfinding, we rotate the instance toward the next path point or the target, depending on whether we have a path left in pathToTarget or not:

```
        if (pathToTarget.size() > 0) {
          int nextTarget = pathToTarget.at(0);
          glm::vec3 destPos =
            mPathFinder.getTriangleCenter(nextTarget);
          instances.at(i)->rotateTo(destPos, deltaTime);
        } else {
          instances.at(i)->rotateTo(pathTargetWorldPos,
            deltaTime);
        }
```

The call to `getTriangleCenter()` of the `PathFinder` class returns the center of the requested triangle in world coordinates. This center point is then fed into the `rotateTo()` method of the instance, so let's look at the implementation of the rotation method next.

Rotating the instance to reach the target

The new `public` method called `rotateTo()` must be added to the `AssimpInstance` class.

First, we check if the instance walks or runs right now. Rotating the instance while standing idle on the ground may look strange:

```
if (mInstanceSettings.isMoveState != moveState::walk &&
    mInstanceSettings.isMoveState != moveState::run) {
  return;
}
```

Then, we get the rotation vector of the current instance and the vector from our position toward the target position:

```
glm::vec3 myRotation = get2DRotationVector();
glm::vec3 twoDimWorldPos =
  glm::vec3(mInstanceSettings.isWorldPosition.x,
    0.0f, mInstanceSettings.isWorldPosition.z);
glm::vec3 toTarget = glm::normalize(glm::vec3(
  targetPos.x, 0.0f, targetPos.z) - twoDimWorldPos);
```

We are only interested in a rotation around the Y axis, so we use the two-dimensional rotation vector of the instance and reduce the vector to the target and also to the values of the X and Z dimensions.

By using the two vectors `myRotation` and `toTarget`, we can calculate the angle between the two vectors via the dot product:

```
float angleDiff = glm::degrees(std::acos(
  glm::dot(myRotation, toTarget)));
```

Finally, we calculate a quaternion containing the rotation between the two vectors, extract the Euler angles, and use the y element of the angle to rotate the instance:

```
if (angleDiff > 6.0f) {
  glm::quat destRoation =
    glm::rotation(toTarget, myRotation);
```

```
        glm::vec3 angles = glm::eulerAngles(destRoation);
        rotateInstance(glm::degrees(angles.y) *
          deltaTime * 2.0f);
    }
```

The multiplication with `deltaTime` makes the instance rotation smooth since the angle in every frame is small. The initial comparison of the `angleDiff` value makes sure we have a small "dead zone" left, leading to fewer rotations if the path is nearly straight and avoiding oscillations in case the rotation oversteers a bit.

If the target is moving around in the level, the dead zone also reduces the number of corrections when the path of the instance is recreated. By carefully tuning the amount of oversteering and the dead zone angle, a chasing instance will behave more naturally since both parameters could reduce the number of directional changes while following the target.

To make the calculated path visible, we should also add a visual output for the renderer.

Adding debug lines for the path

Drawing the path to the screen is astonishingly easy. Next to adding a control Boolean named `rdDrawInstancePaths` to the `OGLRenderData` struct for OpenGL, respective to the `VkRenderData` struct for Vulkan, a new line mesh in the renderer and a checkbox in the `UserInterface` class, creating the lines between all path points is easy. The best place for the new code is after the code added in the *Calculating the path to the target* section.

First, we check if we should create the lines at all and if we have a valid target:

```
      if (mRenderData.rdDrawInstancePaths &&
        pathTargetInstance > -1) {
```

Then, we set the desired color and a height offset for the path and create a vertex to draw the line:

```
        glm::vec3 pathColor = glm::vec3(0.4f, 1.0f, 0.4f);
        glm::vec3 pathYOffset = glm::vec3(0.0f, 1.0f, 0.0f);
        OGLLineVertex vert;
        vert.color = pathColor;
```

Next, we add the world position of the current instance as the starting point for the lines:

```
        vert.position = instSettings.isWorldPosition +
          pathYOffset;
        mInstancePathMesh->vertices.emplace_back(vert);
```

If we have a valid path, we extract the world position of the first triangle center of the path as the second point for the first line. Since we already removed the starting triangle, the line will be drawn to the next triangle in the path:

```
if (pathToTarget.size() > 0) {
  vert.position = mPathFinder.getTriangleCenter(
    pathToTarget.at(0)) + pathYOffset;
  mInstancePathMesh->vertices.emplace_back(vert);
```

Then, we create a new temporary line mesh and retrieve the vertices of the path segments by calling getAsLineMesh() of the PathFinder class:

```
std::shared_ptr<OGLLineMesh> pathMesh =
  mPathFinder.getAsLineMesh(pathToTarget,
  pathColor, pathYOffset);
mInstancePathMesh->vertices.insert(
mInstancePathMesh->vertices.end(),
  pathMesh->vertices.begin(),
  pathMesh->vertices.end());
```

The helper method getAsLineMesh() just extracts the center points of the ground triangles on the path, adds the desired offset to the world position of the vertices, and creates lines from the vertices.

Now, we add the last position as a possible starting point for the last line:

```
vert.position = mPathFinder.getTriangleCenter(
  pathToTarget.at(pathToTarget.size() - 1)) +
  pathYOffset;
mInstancePathMesh->vertices.emplace_back(vert);
}
```

As a final step for the line creation, we add the world position of the target:

```
vert.position = pathTargetWorldPos + pathYOffset;
mInstancePathMesh->vertices.emplace_back(vert);
```

If the path is empty after removing the first and/or last element, we skip the code inside the if condition and draw only a line from our own position to the target. This happens only if we have a valid target, and the start and target triangles are directly next to each other. If an error occurs during pathfinding and the path is empty, we reset the target instance, and the line is no longer drawn.

To draw the created lines, a new `private` method called `drawInstancePaths()` is created in the renderer class `OGLRendere.cpp` or `VkRender.cpp` that just sends the lines to the shader. After enabling the navigation debug draw by enabling the **Enable Navigation** checkbox under the **Navigation** header and the **Draw Instance Path** checkbox under the **Levels** header, navigation paths for the instances will be drawn as green lines, similar to *Figure 13.12*:

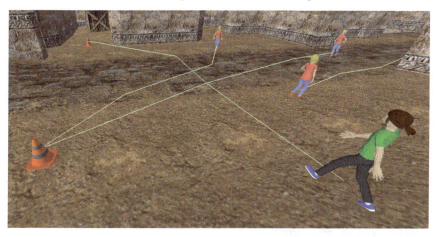

Figure 13.12: Debug lines showing the path of the instances

In *Figure 13.12*, the model of a traffic cone was added and marked as a navigation target. Then, the instances were instructed to walk to their desired targets.

The jagged paths between the instances and the targets are a result of large ground triangles in the selected level map. Since the instances are moving from triangle center to triangle center, the paths have larger angles as the distances between the center points are quite large. A level with smaller ground triangles will have much smoother paths for the instances.

Summary

In this chapter, we implemented a simple path-finding navigation. After an overview of methods to allow computer-controlled instances to navigate in a game map, we explored and implemented the A* path-finding algorithm, supported by a custom navigation mesh creation. Then, we modified models to use them as navigation targets in the virtual world and enabled instances to use instances of the special models as path targets. As the last step, we added navigation to the instances, allowing them to walk or run toward a random target.

In the next and last chapter of the book, we will take a step back from the implementation side and take a look at different ways to enhance immersion and visual quality. We will start with the audible side and discuss methods and tools to add sound effects and music to the application. Then, we will check out ideas to fill the world with more life, followed by a discussion about ideas to enhance the visuals in the virtual world. We will look at quests and interactions between instances and, finally, explore the impact of daytime and weather changes.

Practical sessions

Here are some additions you could make to the code:

- Smooth the path even with large ground triangles.

  By looking up the next couple of path segments, it may be possible to create an average of the segments. For sharper turns, the transitions between the triangles could be smoothed by using splines.

- Clean up the generated triangle neighbor list.

  Right now, the list of adjacent triangles is quite large. This fact can be seen when the neighbor mesh debug drawing for a level is activated. Try to find a solution to include only triangles sharing parts of an edge.

- Add a minimum distance between walls and path lines.

  For the generated ground triangles, some of the center positions may be so close to a wall that the instance will collide when following the path. In some cases, the paths even go through edges of level geometry when the triangles are seen as adjacent. When creating the ground triangles, try to find the outlines of the mesh and reduce the size by a configurable amount.

- Use the instance AABB to detect narrow passages.

  Some maps may have passages where the navigation needs to be exact. In the absence of a real navigation mesh, you could try to use the bounding box of the instance along the path to find possible collisions and adjust the path to avoid a collision with the level structures.

- Advanced difficulty: Create a navigation mesh in an editor and load that mesh.

  If you are confident working with a tool like Blender, you could try to create a navigation mesh as a separate mesh of a level, or even as a separate file, saved next to the level file. Then, load the navigation mesh into the `PathFinder` class to have a collision-free ground for the instances.

Additional resources

- Ghost navigation in Pac-Man: `https://gameinternals.com/understanding-pac-man-ghost-behavior`
- Dijkstra's algorithm: `https://graphicmaths.com/computer-science/graph-theory/dijkstras-algorithm/`
- Quake III Arena's area awareness system: `http://www.kbs.twi.tudelft.nl/docs/MSc/2001/Waveren_Jean-Paul_van/thesis.pdf`
- Navigation meshes: `https://www.gamedev.net/tutorials/programming/artificial-intelligence/navigation-meshes-and-pathfinding-r4880/`
- Shakey the Robot: `https://www.sri.com/hoi/shakey-the-robot/`
- Introduction to A*: `https://www.redblobgames.com/pathfinding/a-star/introduction.html`
- Using A* with navigation meshes: `https://medium.com/@mscansian/a-with-navigation-meshes-246fd9e72424`
- Navigation meshes in Unreal Engine: `https://dev.epicgames.com/documentation/en-us/unreal-engine/basic-navigation-in-unreal-engine`
- Implementing A* in an Unreal Engine project: `https://www.youtube.com/watch?v=xakl29fupCA`
- Training an unbeatable AI in Trackmania: `https://www.youtube.com/watch?v=Dw3BZ6O_8LY`
- Recast Navigation: `https://github.com/recastnavigation/recastnavigation`
- Optimization for Smooth Paths: `https://www.gameaipro.com/GameAIPro3/GameAIPro3_Chapter20_Optimization_for_Smooth_Paths.pdf`
- Toward More Realistic Pathfinding: `https://www.gamedeveloper.com/programming/toward-more-realistic-pathfinding`

14

Creating Immersive Interactive Worlds

Welcome to *Chapter 14*! In the previous chapter, we added pathfinding and navigation to the instances. We started with a brief overview of navigation methods in computer games. Then we explored and implemented the A* algorithm to find a path between the instance position and a point in the virtual world. Next, we enhanced the models to serve as navigation targets and extended the instances to find a path to one of the targets. At the end of the chapter, we added the ability for an instance to follow the path and reach the desired target.

In this chapter, we will explore different ideas to enhance the example code for more immersion and visual quality. We will look at the audible side for tools and methods to add sound effects and music to the application. Also, we will implement a simple audio manager class to play sounds and background music. To please not just the ears but also the eyes, we will collect some ideas about how to enhance the visual appearance next and implement two of the graphical enhancements to the application. We will end the book with this chapter by looking at the effects of daytime and weather changes on the virtual world and add a basic day/night cycle to the application.

In this chapter, we will cover the following topics:

- Adding sound effects and background music
- Enhancing visuals
- Extending immersion with daytime and weather

Technical requirements

The example code for this chapter is available in the `chapter14` folder: the `01_opengl_ideas` subfolder for OpenGL and the `02_vulkan_ideas` subfolder for Vulkan.

Adding sound effects and background music

Running the example code from *Chapter 13* provides a lot of features, such as face animations, level loading, collision detection, and pathfinding and navigation. But sadly, all the animations on the screen are running in dead silence. No bleeping or beeping, no sound, and no music. Just silence.

But sound and music are an important part of games for very good reasons. Whether you are enjoying the calm meadows or deep caves of Minecraft, grooving to the happy music of one of the Super Mario titles and hearing the sound effects as acoustic feedback of our actions, prefer roaming through the haunting worlds of the Dead Space or Silent Hill series while listening carefully to the environment sounds to be aware of your surroundings, or driving cars to the pumping music and fat sounds of racing games such as the Need for Speed series – without music and sound, games wouldn't deliver the same experience for the player.

To add sound output, we can include a freely available sound library, allowing us to easily play sound effects or music. Let's look at some of the libraries first.

Using an audio library

Most audio libraries are written in C, but bindings for C++ can be found, encapsulating the operating-system-specific low-level function calls in an object-oriented manner. Just using the C functions and building a custom abstraction is also possible, similar to GLFW, OpenGL, and Vulkan.

Simple DirectMedia Layer

Simple DirectMedia Layer (**SDL**) is a cross-platform library for multimedia hardware components of a computer. SDL manages audio and can serve as a framework for window functions, graphics context, and input handling, like GLFW. In addition, there are several official libraries that provide support for importing and exporting images, custom networking, and font rendering to display text on the screen.

OpenAL

OpenAL is a cross-platform library that focuses on multi-channel, three-dimensional audio. By using 3D audio, the sound can be modeled to be in front of or behind the player, not just to the left or right, deepening the immersion.

PortAudio

PortAudio is another cross-platform audio library. It targets real-time audio playback and recording. PortAudio can be used if the scope of SDL and OpenAL is too large for the project, and the goal is to just have some audio playing.

FMOD

Although **FMOD** is a proprietary sound engine, it can be included in the list of freely available libraries as a non-commercial license exists, allowing us to use FMOD for free. A paid FMOD license is only needed if the final application or game will be distributed commercially. FMOD supports 3D engines such as Unreal and Unity, so you might even get in touch with FMOD if you are working on a game at some point in time.

After exploring *which software* for sound and music replay could be included, let's check out *what* could and should be played.

Playing sound effects

Since sound plays a key role in our lives, we will have some expectations of what we should hear in a game or a simulation. Failing to meet these expectations may harm immersion.

The game character's footsteps

Probably the most important sound effects a player wants to hear are the footsteps of the character on the ground. By adjusting the sound in relation to the ground material and the speed of the character, instant feedback about the environment is delivered to the player. There is a significant difference between silently sneaking through grass or running on metal ground, and the player should be made aware of the "loudness" of the character's actions, and by using collision detection and ground triangle discovery, as described in the *Finding ground triangles in level data* section of *Chapter 12,* the material type of the ground triangle can be found easily.

Other character sounds

The character makes a lot more sounds, not just footsteps. Jumping and landing, climbing a ladder, swimming, or being hurt by an enemy character should also give audible feedback to the player for additional information about what happens with the character in the virtual world.

Local sound sources

Not only does the player-controlled character need sound effects, but also for the computer-controlled characters and inanimate objects in the virtual worlds audio effects should be played. Hearing doors opening and closing, the hammering of a blacksmith, or the call of a bird, and listening to the crackles of fireplaces, the sound of a waterfall, or wind in a high place in the world will intensify immersion greatly.

Ambient sounds

Ambient sounds are a mix of different sounds and frequencies coming from locations far away, losing some of their information on the way to the listener. A large group of people, the wind in a forest, or a street some meters away all produce well-known sounds for us that should be added to corresponding places of the virtual world.

Weather effects

If the world includes some kind of weather system, the sounds and effects should be added too. A distant thunderstorm or the silence of the ground after a snowfall can change the perception of the virtual world by the player.

But not only can sound effects be useful for immersion; playing music can also help to keep a player's attention.

Playing music

Since the early days of computer games, music has been added to games to keep players interested. As a result, we may still remember the music of a game when we see the title but not details of the gameplay or the game's characters.

Menu music

The first screen a player will see when starting the application is most probably some kind of main menu. Throwing a player directly into the action, without being able to configure the controls for the virtual character, the visual quality, or the sound volume first, may not be the best idea. While the player explores the options in the menu, music can help to prevent the player from getting lost or bored straight away.

Ambient music

Similar to ambient sounds, ambient music helps to prevent dead silence in a game. Playing no sounds at all may be intended to build up tension, but running for hours and hours in silence through a game can become boring. Adding a music track with a style and tempo that fits the gameplay helps the player to enjoy even slow passages of the game.

Adaptive music play

When the player moves into a different area in an open world or enters an environment with a different style, or another room, changing the music to match the new place is a good idea. The famous "hearing boss music" moment when entering a room, combined with the sound of doors locking, will create unforgettable moments for a player.

Allowing custom music

An interesting option for music selection is to let the player add local music to the list of tracks played in the game or even replace the music entirely. Seeing the game's character exploring a virtual world while listening to some favorite music tracks may be a plus for players.

To experience the difference audio replay can make, we will add a C++ class to manage sound effects and music replay.

Hands-on: Implementing an audio manager

The audio manager class consists of two distinct parts. On one hand, we need a high-level interface between the audio manager and the renderer and other classes. On the other hand, the encapsulated low-level interface linking the audio manager functionality to the audio library of the operating system would allow us to replace the audio library with another variant.

We will start with a brief overview of the high-level interface and dive into the low-level implementation afterward.

Defining the high-level interface

The new AudioManager class, consisting of the AudioManager.h header file and the AudioManager. cpp implementation file will be added to the tools folder. We will add the basic functions a usual music/sound player should have:

- Initializing and cleaning up the audio library
- Loading music tracks from files on the file system
- Loading sound effects from files on the file system

- Playing and stopping music and sound effects
- Pausing, resuming, and skipping the music tracks to the next and previous
- Retrieving, shuffling, and clearing the current playlist
- Changing the volume of music and sound effects

For instance, the public setMusicVolume() and getMusicVolume() methods are added to the AudioManager class to control the music volume:

```
void setMusicVolume(int volume);
int getMusicVolume();
```

In addition, the private member variable named mMusicVolume is used to store the current volume of the music:

```
int mMusicVolume = 64;
```

For the remaining functionalities in the list of functions, public methods and private member variables are created. Check the AudioManager.h file to see the full number of methods and member variables that are available in the AudioManager class.

Now we must add a member variable for an object of the AudioManager class along with the initialization and cleanup calls of the audio functionality to the application code. To keep the renderer for the video part only, the AudioManager member variable and methods will be added to the Window class.

Adding the AudioManager class to the Window class

The two primary steps to add the audio functions to the Window class are the same as for all other classes: including the AudioManager.h header file at the top of the Window.h header file and declaring the private member variable named mAudioManager:

```
#include "AudioManager.h"

...

    AudioManager mAudioManager{};
```

Then, in the init() method of the Window class in the Window.cpp file, we try to initialize the AudioManager object:

```
if (!mAudioManager.init()) {
  Logger::log(1, "%s error: unable to init audio,
    skipping\n", __FUNCTION__);
}
```

Note that we use the Logger class to print an error message, but we *do not* end the window initialization if the AudioManager initialization fails. Audio replay should be kept optional, and we continue without music and sound replay instead of failing the application startup process.

Loading the music tracks into the AudioManager can be done right after the initialization call:

```
if (mAudioManager.isInitialized()) {
    mAudioManager.loadMusicFromFolder("assets/music", "mp3"));
}
```

Here, we are trying to load all MP3 files in the assets/music folder into the AudioManager if the initialization is successful. Again, we don't fail if no music files are found in the asset folder.

Adding music tracks to the playlist

In the AudioManager class, support for loading MP3 and OGG files from the local folder assets/music into a playlist has been implemented. You can add your own music to the assets/music folder as the playlist will be populated when the application is started. In the *Practical sessions* section, a task is available to add a **Refresh** button to the UI, allowing you to add or remove music tracks at application runtime.

Finally, we need to clean up the AudioManager when shutting down the application. So, we add a call to the cleanup() method of AudioManager to the cleanup() method of the Window class:

```
void Window::cleanup() {
    mRenderer->cleanup();
    mAudioManager.cleanup();
    ...
}
```

Since we created the AudioManager in the Window class, we need to create callback functions to access the music and sound-effect functions from the renderer or the user interface.

Using callbacks to make the AudioManager class available everywhere

By using these callback functions, changing the music track or playing footstep sounds can be done from anywhere in the code. As an example, we will use the functionality to play a specific music track here, given the track name as a parameter.

First, we add the function signature for the callback named `playMusicTitleCallback` to the `Callbacks.h` file:

```
using playMusicTitleCallback =
  std::function<void(std::string)>;
```

Next, we create a variable named `micPlayMusicTitleCallbackFunction` to the `ModelInstanceCamData` struct in the `ModelInstanceCamData.h` file:

```
playMusicTitleCallback micPlayMusicTitleCallbackFunction;
```

We use the `ModelInstanceCamData` struct to avoid spreading the callback functions all over the code.

Then, the callback variable will be bound to the corresponding `AudioManager` function in the `init()` method of the `Window` class:

```
ModelInstanceCamData& rendererMICData =
  mRenderer->getModInstCamData();
RendererMICData.micPlayMusicTitleCallbackFunction =
  [this](std::string title) {
    mAudioManager.playTitle(title);
  };
```

Here, we get a reference to the variable containing the `ModelInstanceCamData` struct of the renderer class and assign the `playTitle()` method of the `AudioManager` class by using a lambda function.

The same three steps of creating the callback function signature, adding a variable to the `ModelInstanceCamData` struct, and binding the callback function to the method of the `AudioManger` class must be repeated for every audio method that should be available in the renderer.

Now, let's look at the implementation of the low-level part of the audio manager. We will use SDL as the audio functions are easy to use.

Using SDL for the low-level layer

Although SDL can handle more features than audio, it is possible to use only a subset of the functions provided by the SDL library. So, instead of using SDL for window and keyboard handling, which is done by GLFW in the application, we will only use the sound replay and mix functionality of SDL.

To use audio replay with SDL, we need the core SDL library plus the separate mixer library named SDL_mixer.

Installing SDL and SDL_mixer on Windows

For Windows, precompiled versions of SDL and SDL_mixer are available on GitHub. Go to the releases page at the following two URLs and download the latest stable development zip files for Visual Studio, containing both devel and VC in their names. As an example, the current development package of the main SDL library for Visual Studio is named SDL2-devel-2.30.9-VC.zip. Here are the URLs:

- SDL: https://github.com/libsdl-org/SDL/releases
- SDL_mixer: https://github.com/libsdl-org/SDL_mixer/releases

Now, unpack the two zip files to your computer, but take care to avoid spaces and special characters like German umlauts in the path names to avoid problems since even in 2024 many tools have still problems with special characters in the paths.

Next, add two **environment variables** to help the CMake search scripts find the headers and libraries:

- The first variable is named SDL2DIR and must point to the folder where the main SDL library was unpacked.
- The second variable is named SDL2MIXERDIR and must point to the folder of the SDL_mixer library.

Figure 14.1 shows an example of the environment variables:

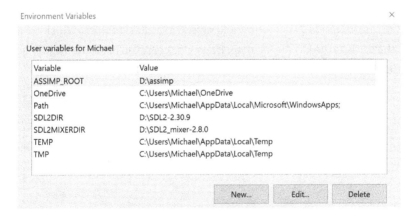

Figure 14.1: Example environment variables for SDL

After installing the two libraries and adding the environment variables, the code for this chapter can be compiled. The CMake build script takes care of placing the two DLL files next to the executable file.

Installing SDL and SDL_mixer on Linux

On Linux, the SDL libraries can be added by using the integrated package management. On Ubuntu or Debian, you can use the apt package manager to install the main SDL library, the SDL_mixer library, and all development headers and libraries by issuing the following command:

```
sudo apt install libsdl2-dev libsdl2-mixer-dev
```

For an Arch-based distribution, use the pacman package manager to add the two libraries to the system with the following command:

```
sudo pacman -S sdl2 sdl2_mixer
```

To add SDL and SDL_mixer to the AudioManager class in order to use the SDL functions, we must include the two SDL headers after the existing #include directives in the AudioManager.h header file:

```
#include <SDL.h>
#include <SDL_mixer.h>
```

Since SDL is a C library, all structures only use raw pointers. The audio manager is one of the places where you will find variables with raw pointers in the code:

```
std::unordered_map<std::string, Mix_Music*> mMusicTitles{};
Mix_Chunk* mWalkFootsteps;
```

The mMusicTitles variable is a map containing several SDL music objects, which are accessible by the name of the track as the key for the map. Every track is saved in a variable named Mix_Music, where the prefix Mix states that this is a variable used by the SDL_mixer library.

In the mWalkFootsteps variable, a so-called chunk of audio (using the terms of SDL) is stored. An SDL_mixer chunk can be played by calling the respective sound effect's replay function.

Before sound effects or music can be played, the audio part of SDL must be initialized properly, and at the end of the application, the audio functions must be ended too.

Initializing and shutting down SDL and the SDL_mixer

As the first step in the init() method of the AudioManager class, we try to initialize the audio part of SDL:

```
if (SDL_Init(SDL_INIT_AUDIO) < 0) {
  return false;
}
```

The SDL prefix of both SDL_Init() and the SDL_INIT_AUDIO flag denotes that we are using the core functionality of SDL. If we cannot initialize the audio part of SDL, we stop the initialization of the AudioManager right here. Beware that the initialization of the audio device can fail for various reasons, for instance, if the audio device is in use by another application that forbids sharing the device.

Next, we try to set the parameters for the audio device by calling Mix_OpenAudio():

```
if (Mix_OpenAudio(44100, MIX_DEFAULT_FORMAT, 2, 8192) < 0) {  return
false;
}
```

Now, we are in the realm of SDL_mixer, which is visible on the Mix prefix of Mix_OpenAudio. The first parameter of Mix_OpenAudio is the replay frequency in Hz. We are using the well-known value of 44.1 kHz, introduced by Sony's **compact disc** specifications. As the second parameter, the internal audio format is configured. MIX_DEFAULT_FORMAT stands for 16-bit signed integer values, which is also a common value in the audio world.

The third parameter is the number of output channels to use. One output channel uses mono replay, and the two channels from the initialization call are for stereo output. Depending on the audio hardware and driver support, up to eight output channels for a 7.1 system are possible.

With the fourth and last parameter, an internal audio buffer in the SDL_mixer library is configured. A small buffer value may cause audio dropouts if the CPU load gets too high while filling the buffer, and a large buffer leads to delays since the buffer needs to be filled before the samples can be played. The unit of the buffer parameter is "sample frames," so we configure SDL_mixer to reserve space for 2,048 frames, every frame contains two 16-bit signed integers, one for every output channel.

At the termination time of the application, the cleanup() method of the AudioManager is called by the cleanup() method of the Window class. Inside the cleanup() method of the AudioManager class, we close the audio device and signal both SDL_mixer and SDL to run their respective cleanup code:

```
Mix_CloseAudio();
Mix_Quit();
SDL_Quit();
```

Note that we did not call Mix_Init() in the init() method, but we have to call Mix_Quit() here. SDL manages the mixer initialization for us without an explicit call to Mix_Init().

Now we are ready to play music and sound effects. Let's start with a look at the music replay code.

Controlling music replay

Loading a music track is done by calling Mix_LoadMUS() with the C-style character array as a parameter:

```
Mix_Music* music = Mix_LoadMUS(fileName.c_str());
```

SDL_mixer supports several music formats, such as WAV, MP3, and OGG. The return value of Mix_LoadMUS() is a pointer to the Mix_Music struct.

To clean up a loaded music track, Mix_FreeMusic() must be called with the pointer to the above Mix_Music struct:

```
Mix_FreeMusic(music);
```

A music track can be played by calling Mix_PlayMusic() with two parameters:

```
Mix_PlayMusic(music, 0);
```

The first parameter is a pointer to a valid Mix_Music struct, while the second parameter tells SDL_mixer the number of loops to play. A loop value of 0 disables looping and a value of -1 will loop the music infinitely.

Stopping the music is done by calling Mix_HaltMusic():

```
Mix_HaltMusic();
```

Since there is only one music track playing at a time, no parameters are needed, and in case the current track should be paused or resumed, the two Mix_PauseMusic() and Mix_ResumeMusic() calls are available:

```
Mix_PauseMusic();
Mix_ResumeMusic();
```

Finally, the music volume is controlled by `Mix_VolumeMusic()`:

```
Mix_VolumeMusic(volume);
```

The parameter for `Mix_VolumeMusic()` is an int value between 0 and 128 to set the new volume, or a value of -1 to query the current volume of the music.

By using the default `SDL_mixer` calls, we can only play one music track once or with an infinite number of loops. If a dynamic music system is required, a manual implementation is needed, or even a different sound replay API should be considered. For the simple ability to advance to the next track in a playlist at the end of a track, we just need to implement a callback.

Adding a callback for continuous music playback

`SDL_mixer` supports a callback to inform the application that the current music track has finished the number of loops. In this callback, we can simply forward to the next track in the playlist.

Sadly, `SDL_mixer` is a C audio library, and the callback must fulfill the C-style calling convention. The C++ calling convention is not compatible with the C calling convention and allows only calling static member functions of the `AudioManager` class. We need to add a small hack to be able to call a non-static method of the `AudioManager` class that has access to the playlist and the current position in the playlist.

First, we declare a raw pointer named `mCurrentManager` as private member variable, plus the private static `staticMuscFinishedCallback()` member method for the C-style callback and a private non-static member `musicFinishedCallback()` for the translated callback:

```
static AudioManager* mCurrentManager;
static void staticMusicFinshedCallback();
void musicFinishedCallback();
```

In the `init()` method of the `AudioManager` class, we set the `mCurrentManager` pointer to the current instance and call the callback hook setup method `Mix_HookMusicFinished()` with the static callback method:

```
mCurrentManager = this;
Mix_HookMusicFinished(staticMusicFinshedCallback);
```

Whenever a music track ends now, `staticMusicFinishedCallback()` is called by `SDL_mixer`. To translate the callback to C++, we use the pointer to the current `AudioManager` instance stored in `mCurrentManager` to call the non-static callback `musicFinishedCallback()` method:

```
if (mCurrentManager)  {
```

```
        mCurrentManager->musicFinishedCallback();
    }
```

Inside `musicFinishedCallback()`, we can now add code to advance one track in the playlist, enabling a continuous replay of all tracks in the playlist:

```
    if (mMusicPlaying) {
        playNextTitle();
    }
```

After the music replay is implemented, let's go to the sound effect replay code.

Playing sound effects

Using `SDL_mixer` to play sound effects has some subtle differences compared to playing music. The main difference is that by default eight sound effects can be played at the same time since `SDL_mixer` allocates eight internal sound channels for the sound effect output.

Note that these internal sound channels are not the same as the two output sound channels configured when we initialized the audio device.

Allocating more or even less than these eight sound channels can be done by calling `Mix_AllocateChannels()` with the number of desired channels as a parameter:

```
    Mix_AllocateChannels(1);
```

We will use only one channel in the `AudioManager` for now to allow a simple implementation of the footstep sound replay.

As `SDL_mixer` has only one channel available now, a second sound effect cannot be played if another sound effect is still playing. So, by limiting the number of channels to only one, we can avoid creating a complex system to switch between walking and running footstep sounds for the example implementation.

Loading a sound file from the file system is similar to the music loading process. We call `Mix_LoadWav()` with the C-style character array of the file name and store the returned result in a `Mix_Chunk` struct:

```
    Mix_Chunk* mWalkFootsteps;
    mWalkFootsteps = Mix_LoadWAV(fileName.c_str());
```

Cleaning up the sound effect is done by calling Mix_FreeChunk():

```
Mix_FreeChunk(mWalkFootsteps);
```

Playing and stopping the replay of a sound effect is also like playing or stopping the music. A sound effect will be played by using Mix_PlayChannel():

```
mSoundChannel = Mix_PlayChannel(-1, mRunFootsteps, 0);
```

The first parameter of Mix_PlayChannel() is the sound channel to use. The special value of -1 just uses the next available sound channel for the sound effect replay. The second parameter is a pointer to the Mix_Chunk struct to play, and the third parameter is again the number of loops.

As the return parameter of Mix_PlayChannel(), we get the sound channel number, on which this sound effect is played. We save the channel number in the mSoundChannel member variable to be able to stop the replay with Mix_HaltChannel():

```
Mix_HaltChannel(mSoundChannel);
```

Like for the music, we can control the volume of the sound channel by calling Mix_Volume() with the channel number and desired volume as parameters:

```
Mix_Volume(mSoundChannel, volume);
```

After we know how to play sound effects, we need to add a bit of code to the renderer to play a footstep sound whenever our instance is walking or running.

Using the footstep sound effects in the renderer

The implementation of the footstep replay will be just the bare minimum to show how and where the callbacks for the sound effects could be added. A full-featured sound effects replay system requires much more work and is out of the scope of this book.

To add the footstep sounds, the following piece of code needs to be added to the handleMovementKeys() method of the renderer, right after we set the next state of the instance by calling setNextInstanceState(). At this point, we have all data about the current movement state of the instance.

First, we retrieve the current animation state of the current instance and check if the instance is in the idle/walk/run cycle:

```
if (currentInstance->getAnimState() ==
  animationState::playIdleWalkRun) {
```

We only want to add sound effects at the same time as the walking and running animations replay.

Then we check for the movement state of the instance and call the proper callback for the state:

```
switch (state) {
  case moveState::run:
    mModelInstCamData.
      micPlayRunFootstepCallbackFunction();
    break;
  case moveState::walk:
    mModelInstCamData.
      micPlayWalkFootstepCallbackFunction();
    break;
```

When the instance is in the running state, we play the sound effect for running footsteps. And if the instance is in the walking state, we play the walking footsteps.

If the instance is neither running nor walking, we stop the footstep sounds:

```
  default:
    mModelInstCamData.
      micStopFootstepCallbackFunction();
    break;
}
```

And if the instance is not in the idle/walk/run cycle, we also stop any sounds. This way, we catch all the actions like jumping or punching where no sound effect is available yet:

```
} else {
  mModelInstCamData.
    micStopFootstepCallbackFunction();
}
```

To hear the footsteps sounds, the following steps are required:

1. Start the application and load a configuration with animation mapping.
2. Select (or create) a first-person or third-person camera.
3. Select an instance and set the instance by clicking on **Use Selected Instance** in the **Camera** section of the **Control** window of the UI.
4. Press F10 to switch to view mode.

If you move around the controlled instance now by using the mouse and the *W/A/S/D* keys, you should hear two different footstep sounds, depending on the instance walking or running around in the virtual world.

Extending the audio manager class

To outline a possible expansion of the AudioManager class to support more channels to achieve a more game-like sound management, we would need to keep track of the channel playing the footstep sound returned by the Mix_PlayChannel() call. By reserving one channel exclusively for the local footstep sounds, we can achieve the same behavior, but we would be able to play more sound effects at the same time.

Handling multiple sound effects can be achieved by adding a creating a pool of sound channels and adding a callback to the Mix_ChannelFinished() SDL function, similar to Mix_HookMusicFinished(). SDL triggers the Mix_ChannelFinished() callback whenever a channel has finished the current sound clip, or when Mix_HaltChannel() is called and delivers the number of the finished sound channel in the callback.

The sound channel pool can be updated when a sound effect is played and when the effect replay has finished. By using the distance to the object creating the sound effect and scaling down the volume of the channel with Mix_Volume() or by using Mix_SetDistance(), the different distances of the source can be modeled. In addition, Mix_SetPanning() can be used to adjust the position of the sound source to the left and right.

Several tasks in the *Practical sessions* section are available to evolve the sound replay from the current state.

As an example of how to use the AudioManager callbacks from the UserInterface class, a simple music replay control has been added to the user interface. In the **Music & Sound** section of the **Control** window, you will find a combo box and some buttons to play the music from the playlist created from the assets/music folder.

Using the music player in the UI

Adding music replay functionality to the UserInterface class is a quick and simple task. By using the callbacks to the AudioManager class, a basic music player is implemented with only a few code blocks to the UI.

In *Figure 14.2*, the ImGui section with a basic music player using the AudioManager class is shown:

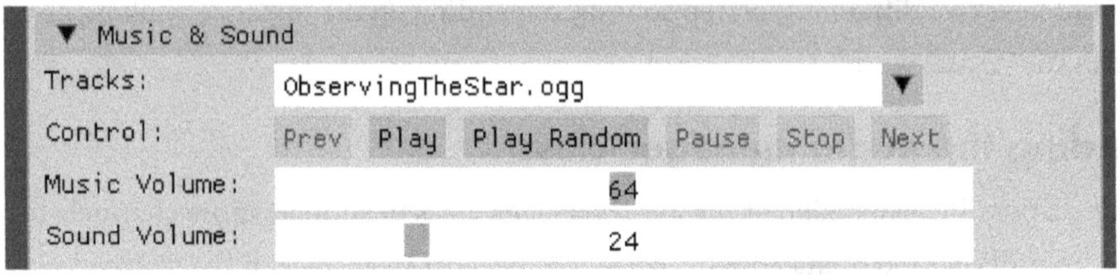

Figure 14.2: A music player based on the AudioManager added to the user interface

The desired music track to play can be chosen by using the **Tracks** combo box, the current track can be played by pressing the **Play** button, or a random track from the playlist will be chosen from the shuffled playlist by pressing **Play Random**. The other four buttons, **Prev, Pause, Stop**, and **Next**, do exactly what the label states, and by using the sliders, the volume of music and sound effects can be set to a value between 0 (for silence) and 128.

Alternative sound manager implementations

The AudioManager class used for the application uses a straightforward implementation with direct control through C++ callback functions. For an advanced sound system, an event- or message-based implementation could be used. Such an implementation can use event managing code already in the game, and events or messages also decouple the sound effects replay from the code that is requesting to replay a sound effect or a music change.

After having sound and music available in the virtual world, an update to the graphics of the application may appear also on the to-do list. Let's explore some visual enhancements now.

Enhancing visuals

The OpenGL and Vulkan renderers in the example code support only a minimal set of features to bring an image to the screen: Both renderers can only draw textures triangles and colored lines. Adding one or more of the following enhancements will be a fantastic extension to the quality of the images.

Bringing colors to the world by using physically based rendering

Right now, we are using only the textures of the Assimp objects to render the model instances and level geometry to the screen. By using **physically based rendering**, short **PBR**, we could also model surface properties in the form of materials. With such PBR materials, it is easy to create surfaces that have a shininess and reflectivity of metal or make surfaces like concrete or bricks look more natural.

Figure 14.3 shows spheres drawn by the Vulkan PBR example code from Sascha Willems (the code is available at `https://github.com/SaschaWillems/Vulkan/tree/master/examples/pbribl`):

Figure 14.3: Different PBR materials

On the left side of *Figure 14.3*, the reflectiveness of the environment is set to a high value, resulting in a golden sphere. Between the spheres, the reflection settings change gradually, and on the right side, no reflectiveness at all is set.

A link to the source code of the PBR rendering and other examples is available in the *Additional resources* section.

Adding transparency

A virtual world without windows and objects made of transparent materials may feel a bit strange since we are surrounded by transparent objects in the real world. However, rendering transparency is tricky due to the physics behind the color changes of the light on the path through more than one transparent object, requiring multiple transparent pixels on the same screen position to be drawn from back to front to calculate the correct final color for a pixel.

Two different approaches exist, called ordered and order-independent transparency. While ordered transparency requires all transparent objects to be sorted from back to front, order-independent transparency rearranges the pixels to be drawn by itself into the correct order. Both methods have advantages and disadvantages, so the best way to choose is to test both versions.

Figure 14.4 shows two transparency examples from LearnOpenGL (`https://learnopengl.com/`) by Joey de Vries (`https://x.com/JoeyDeVriez`):

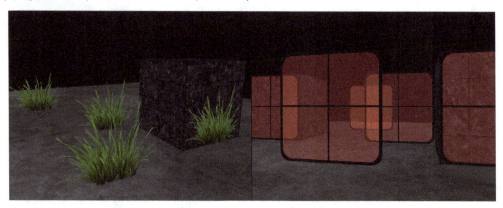

Figure 14.4: Transparent plants (left) and translucent red glass (right)

On the left side of *Figure 14.4*, partially transparent plants are rendered. By discarding pixels in the empty areas of the texture, a realistic effect of a plant can be achieved. On the right side of *Figure 14.4*, colored glass is rendered. Imitating glass for windows and other translucent objects by using transparent textures helps to create a better copy of the real world.

Looking up at a beautiful sky

If you start the virtual world created with the example code of the book and load a level that is partially made to be outside of a building, you will not see some sort of sky but just the default background color. Adding a beautiful sky to the scene requires not just a simple sky texture, but also a so-called cubemap and a distorted sky texture.

A cubemap is a special kind of rendering object that represents the six sides of a cube, and the sky texture is projected onto the cubemap. The resulting skybox will create a seamless background that follows the view of the virtual camera, placing the level geometry and the instances into a realistic environment.

Figure 14.5 shows a skybox as environment around a wooden box, created with code from LearnOpenGL (`https://learnopengl.com/`) by Joey de Vries (`https://x.com/JoeyDeVriez`):

Figure 14.5: A wooden box with a skybox as the background

The effect of using a skybox can be seen best when moving the view around. In a static picture like in *Figure 14.5*, the difference between the wooden box and the skybox can be seen.

We will implement a skybox to our virtual world at the end of this section.

Playing with light and shadows

The current vertex shaders are using a hard-coded light source as virtual sun, emitting white light from a fixed position into the world. This basic lighting helps to identify the dimensions of the level geometry and the instances, even by using only flat shading. By adding more lights to the virtual world, other light-emitting objects can be modeled in a more realistic way, such as lamps, lanterns, fire, or torches. The flickering light of a fire in a dark place can be used to create various kinds of tension since it could mean a safe place to stay the night or an enemy position.

The scene in *Figure 14.6* is illuminated by several thousand different colored light sources:

Figure 14.6: Multiple lights in a virtual world (image courtesy of Hannes Nevalainen)

The image in *Figure 14.6* is a tech demo for the jMonkeyEngine made by Hannes Nevalainen, and the effect of many individual lights can be seen. The full video is available in the *Additional resources* section.

When lights are added, shadows should be implemented too. For a simple start, the shadows of the objects cast by the virtual sun could be projected to the ground by using the so-called shadow mapping, creating the impression of lights and shadows taken from the real world. Shadows for the other lights can be added too, although the implementation is more complex. But the visual results will compensate for the effort as a lamp casting only the lit part of a window to the ground will bring a big smile to the programmer's face.

Figure 14.7 was created from the Vulkan example code made by Sascha Willens (the code is available at `https://github.com/SaschaWillems/Vulkan/tree/master/examples/pbribl`), showing the shadows of trees created by using cascaded shadow maps:

Figure 14.7: Cascaded shadow maps of trees

Similar to the skybox, the effect of using shadow maps can be seen much better when light, objects, and/or cameras are moving. Shadows like in *Figure 14.7* are a great addition to the virtual world.

Swimming in realistic water

If water was added as part of the extended level environment, the visual appearance should also be checked and enhanced. While using a simple, static transparent water texture may be fine for the first implementation, the urge to create better water may come up at some point.

By using a combination of reflection, refraction, and distortion of the light hitting the virtual water surface, realistic water can be created, and if the player should be able to dive into the water, a different kind of distortion could be utilized to create the illusion of being underwater.

Figure 14.8 shows a water simulation made in WebGL by Evan Wallace (the code is available at `https://github.com/evanw/webgl-water/blob/master/index.html`):

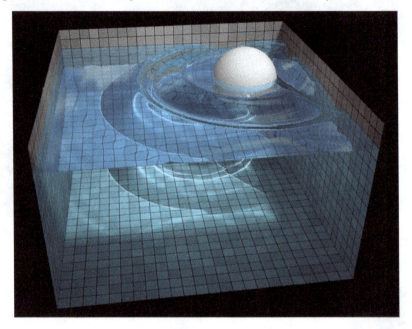

Figure 14.8: Realistic water with waves and underwater caustics (courtesy of Evan Wallace)

In *Figure 14.8*, the waves of the sphere falling into the water can be seen. Also, the refraction of the walls created by the water and the refraction of the light on the bottom of the pool are clearly visible.

Adding stunning post-processing effects

For even more realism in the virtual world, post-processing effects can be added to the renderers. The list of possible effects is long, so here is just a brief list of ideas that can be implemented quite quickly while creating great visuals:

- Lens flares for the illusion of looking through a camera
- God rays: visible rays in haze when the direct view into the sun is blocked
- Bloom effect simulating glowing objects
- Motion blur blurring the image when the view is moved
- Depth of field blurring the world around a sharp center
- Screen Space Ambient Occlusion darkening gaps and edges
- Screen Space Reflection, a cheap way to create reflective surfaces

All these effects are created by using shaders and have different performance impacts. Nevertheless, even a bunch of the effects listed here will give the visual appearance a huge boost.

Figure 14.9 shows two post-processing effects, Bloom and **Screen Space Ambient Occlusion** (**SSAO**). The Bloom effect was created with code from LearnOpenGL (`https://learnopengl.com/`) by Joey de Vries (`https://x.com/JoeyDeVriez`) and the SSAO picture is made with code from Sascha Willems' Vulkan examples (the code is available at `https://github.com/SaschaWillems/Vulkan/tree/master/examples/pbribl`):

Figure 14.9: Bloom (left) and SSAO (right)

On the left side of *Figure 14.9*, the Bloom effect is shown. The characteristic part of the Bloom effect is the halo effect around the light sources. For the green light source, the light even overlaps the top left edge of the wooden crate.

On the right side of *Figure 14.9*, SSAO is shown. The SSAO effect may be subtle, but it is visible: look at the floor below the curtains on the right side of the white line. The shadow creates the illusion of a darker room behind the curtains.

Upgrading to ray tracing

As the next step to realism, ray tracing can be added as an optional enhancement.

Ray tracing uses virtual light rays emitted from the camera to compute the resulting pixel color by following the ray through the collisions with objects in the virtual world. Instead of just using the object color, the virtual ray is reflected by the physical rules and followed until the amount of light added falls below a threshold.

With ray tracing, effects like a global illumination of the world, causing dark areas to be lit by light being reflected from the objects, or realistic reflections could be achieved. Imagine running through a room full of mirrors and seeing your character multiple times, drawn in a correct physical way.

Figure 14.10 shows a scene created by a ray tracing example from Sascha Willems Vulkan code (the code is available at `https://github.com/SaschaWillems/Vulkan/tree/master/examples/pbribl`):

Figure 14.10: Real-time ray tracing scene

The reflections on the floor, the spheres, and the teapot in *Figure 14.10* are calculated in real time by using ray tracing with the Vulkan API on an Nvidia RTX 4000 series GPU.

The FPS counter was included to show how fast the current GPU generation is able to create ray tracing images. Only a few decades ago, a single frame of the same picture required several days to render.

Ray tracing should be optional

Note that the calculations for ray tracing require lots of computing power and creating complex scenes in real time needs both a GPU and a graphics API that support ray tracing. Right now, only Vulkan and DirectX 12 are able to use the ray tracing capabilities of modern GPUs. You need to check the availability of hardware and software support before switching to a graphics pipeline with ray tracing enabled.

Diving into virtual reality

Even though virtual reality (VR) is still a small niche, implementing VR support can be a great step ahead for immersion. Being able not just to see the virtual world on a flat screen but to stand right in the middle of the world can become a memorable moment for a player. Using head tracking to move the virtual camera simultaneously to the head of the player and adding virtual hands for the VR controllers creates a lot of new opportunities for interaction.

Figure 14.11 shows a scene from the Godot XR Tool Demo (the code is available at `https://github.com/GodotVR/godot-xr-template`):

Figure 14.11: Godot XR Tools Demo

The most notable detail of *Figure 14.11* is the two virtual hands. By using the integrated sensors of the Valve Index® controllers, not only the position of the controllers can be deduced in all 6 degrees of freedom, but also the individual fingers can be tracked to allow gestures or actions depending on the position of a finger.

After the theoretical part of this section, we will now add a skybox to the application, acting as the global background.

Hands-on: Adding a skybox to the virtual world

A virtual sky is a great addition to a virtual world, especially above any open areas, as shown in *Figure 14.5*.

Exploring the technical details

From the technical side, a skybox is drawn from a texture applied on the inside of a unit cube. *Figure 14.12* shows the cube and the coordinates around the virtual camera placed in the center of the cube:

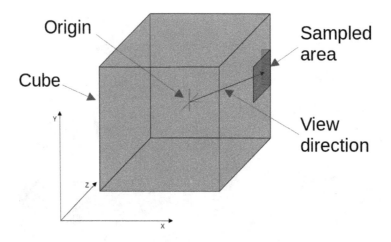

Figure 14.12: The sampled area from the inside of a cubemap

In *Figure 14.12*, the red area of the cube will be sampled to create the background of the current frame. Note that the area is wrapping around the corner of the cube, but that is nothing to worry about. Both graphics libraries take care of such edge cases (pun intended) and will sample the respective areas of the two affected cube sides.

The cubemap texture is usually stored as a set of six separate images or as a single image with the sides of the cube at specific locations in the image. *Figure 14.13* shows a skybox texture made by Jockum Skoglund (aka hipshot – https://opengameart.org/content/stormy-days-skybox) in a commonly used format plus the cube faces:

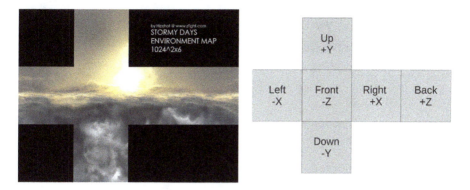

Figure 14.13: A cubemap texture and the cube face of each picture

On the left side of *Figure 14.13*, an example cubemap texture for a skymap is shown. You will find many cubemap textures as this kind of cross. On the right side of *Figure 14.13*, the cube faces for each of the smaller sub-images of the cubemap texture are listed. Remember that OpenGL and Vulkan with an inverted viewport have the negative Z-axis pointing into the virtual world, hence -Z for the front image.

Another noteworthy detail is the distortion of a cubemap image. Since the cubemap texture is applied to a cube but the virtual sky around us can be seen as a sphere, the pixels of a cubemap texture must be adjusted to appear as if the image was taken with a camera from inside a sphere. In *Figure 14.14*, the discrepancy between the projection inside a cube and inside a sphere is shown:

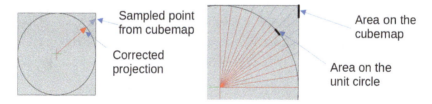

Figure 14.14: Sampled point of a cube vs. the corrected projection of a sphere

As you can see on the left side of *Figure 14.14*, the difference between a sample point taken from the cubemap and the position on the surface of the sphere gets larger the more we get near the edge of one side of the cubemap. On the right side of *Figure 14.14*, an area sampled from the cubemap and the required projection onto the surface of a sphere are highlighted as black bars. You can see that both the size and the angle of the areas differ. When building a cubemap texture for a skybox, a spherical distortion of the images for each of the cube faces must be applied to create a plausible sky.

Implementing the skybox

Adding the skybox to the code needs only a few components:

- New vertex and mesh types

- A new vertex buffer

- A unit cube model containing the coordinates of the faces.

- A new shader

- Loading a cubemap texture from a file

We start with creating a new vertex type called OGLSkyboxVertex and a new mesh type called OGLSkyboxMesh in the OGLRenderData.h file in the opengl folder:

```
struct OGLSkyboxVertex {
  glm::vec4 position = glm::vec4(0.0f);
};
 struct OGLSkyboxMesh {
   std::vector<OGLSkyboxVertex> vertices{};
};
```

As always, for Vulkan, the two new struct elements must be added to the VkRenderData.h file in the vulkan folder. For all the details of the Vulkan implementation, check the renderer class file, VkRenderer.cpp.

While we could reuse the vertex buffer of the models, doing so would waste a lot of resources since the cube only needs the position data for the vertices. The new vertex buffer class called SkyboxBuffer uses only the position element of the new vertex, struct OGLSkyboxVertex:

```
glVertexAttribPointer(0, 4, GL_FLOAT, GL_FALSE,
  sizeof(OGLSkyboxVertex),
  (void*) offsetof(OGLSkyboxVertex, position));
glEnableVertexAttribArray(0);
```

For the cube model, we create a class called SkyboxModel returning an OGLSkyboxMesh consisting of 36 vertices, using two triangles for each side. In all three axes, the model coordinates are either 1.0 or -1.0, defining a unit cube.

The new vertex shader named skybox.vert outputs a vec3 with 3-dimensional texture coordinates. We need 3-dimensional coordinates here since we are inside a cube:

```
layout (location = 0) out vec3 texCoord;
```

In the main() method of the vertex shader, we invert the projection matrix and transpose the view matrix first:

```
mat4 inverseProjection = inverse(projection);
mat3 inverseView = transpose(mat3(view));
```

For the view matrix, we can use a cheaper transpose operation instead of taking the inverse matrix since we need to get rid of the translational part to stop the cube moving around with the camera.

By multiplying the inverse matrices with the incoming point positions of the cube, we calculate the texture coordinates in world space:

```
texCoord = inverseView * (inverseProjection * aPos).xyz;
```

Now, the texture coordinates to sample are from the inside of the cube, as shown in Figure *14.12*.

As the last step for the vertex shader, we set the GLSL-internal variable gl_Position to the incoming vertex position:

```
gl_Position = aPos.xyww;
```

By setting the z component of gl_Position to the value of the w component, we make sure to draw the pixels of the cubemap on the far-Z plane, creating a background that will not be overwritten by other pixels.

The new fragment shader, skybox.frag, uses the incoming texture coordinates to look up the texture data in the cubemap:

```
layout (location = 0) in vec3 texCoord;
layout (location = 0) out vec4 FragColor;
uniform samplerCube tex;
void main() {
  FragColor = texture(tex, texCoord);
}
```

Please note that the type of the texture tex is a samplerCube and not a sampler2D like on the other fragment shaders.

Loading the cubemap texture is done in the Texture class. In the new loadCubemapTexture() method, we load an image shown in *Figure 14.13* and extract the six images. And since the values of the values of the texture map side definitions are in ascending order, we can just use the first side definition GL_TEXTURE_CUBE_MAP_POSITIVE_X and add an integer value for the remaining sides to upload:

```
glTexImage2D(GL_TEXTURE_CUBE_MAP_POSITIVE_X + face, 0, GL_SRGB8_
ALPHA8, cubeFaceWidth, cubeFaceHeight, 0, GL_RGBA, GL_UNSIGNED_BYTE,
subImage.data());
```

For the full implementation of the cubemap texture loading, please check the details in the Texture class.

Drawing the skybox

Bringing the skybox to the screen is now done in two steps. First, we upload the unit cube model data to the vertex buffer in the init() method of the OGLRenderer.cpp renderer class file:

```
mSkyboxModel.init();
OGLSkyboxMesh skyboxMesh = mSkyboxModel.getVertexData();
mSkyboxBuffer.uploadData(skyboxMesh.vertices);
```

Then, before drawing the level data, we draw the skybox by using the new shader, binding the texture and drawing the cube from the vertex buffer:

```
mSkyboxShader.use();
mSkyboxTexture.bindCubemap();
mSkyboxBuffer.bindAndDraw();
mSkyboxTexture.unbindCubemap();
```

For Vulkan, we also upload the skybox model and the texture in the init() method of the VkRenderData.cpp file, bind the skybox pipeline, and draw the skybox model before the level data in the draw() method.

For both OpenGL and Vulkan renderers, a simple change should be made when drawing the skybox as the first object: disabling the depth test function. Without the depth test, the skybox texture overwrites all values of the previous color buffer, acting as the global background for the remaining objects, such as level data and instances. And that's all.

If everything was added correctly, the new and glorious sky above the level can be seen in *Figure 14.15* (the image is made from glTF level created by Zarudko (`https://skfb.ly/6QYJw`) using a texture created by Jockum Skoglund (aka hipshot – `https://opengameart.org/content/stormy-days-skybox`) as the skybox):

Figure 14.15: Example level with an activated skybox

As you can see in *Figure 14.15*, the skybox brings a real-world feel to levels with open areas. And since the cube does not move when the view changes like the level data, the illusion of an infinitely distant sky is created.

But even with great graphics and cool sound effects and music, there's room for improvement. The environment of the virtual world is still somehow static, so let's add changes to the world itself.

Extending immersion with daytime and weather

Although they are natural phenomena in our lives, the cycle between day and night, weather effects, and different seasons are rarely used in computer games. But all these aspects can be a great boost for immersion in a game. Slight changes to the virtual world depending on an internal clock may help to create an environment that a player wants to stay in for a much longer time to experience the full cycle.

Adding a day/night cycle

A day/night cycle adds some sort of familiarity to a game. Seeing the sun rise or enjoying a colorful sunset, watching the changes when running through the world around noon or late at night... every aspect will remind the player of being in a more realistic world. And if not only the light changes, but also other characters and animals react to the time of day, the immersion will become better and better. For instance, it may be good to see some animals only at night, and kids only in the morning, characters appearing at work at some time and leaving for a pub in the afternoon.

The in-game time could be running much faster than real time, reducing an entire day to a couple of minutes. Such a speedup can help if events that are frequently needed only occur at a specific time of the day.

One of the most popular examples of the day/night cycle is Minecraft. A full day in Minecraft lasts 20 minutes by default, split into a 10-minute day and a 10-minute night. And since the light level changes, enemy spawning and food and tree growing behave completely differently in the day and the night.

Figure 14.16 shows the same spot in our application at noon and at night:

Figure 14.16: Day and night in the example code from **Chapter 14**

As you can see in *Figure 14.16*, even a simple change in the overall brightness of the virtual world could make an enormous difference. And changing more properties of the world depending on the time of day will bring more immersion for the player.

Allowing forward time travel

When working with time, one fact should not be underestimated: the time waiting for an event to happen can be boring and passes slowly. Instead of keeping the player waiting for the entire day or night to pass, special "time travel" events could be added, such as sleeping through the night, or waiting at a fireplace to let the time pass, having the game fast-forwarding the in-game time.

Playing in real time

Thinking about the time in a game, the idea of synchronizing the time in the virtual world to the time of the real world can be an interesting option. Only a few games utilize such a feature. Also, solving tasks or quests may be more complicated if they are bound to a special time of the day. But being "now" in a game may be fun.

Worshipping the weather god

Not only may the time of day change the world, but weather changes can also greatly influence characters, animals, and the environment. During a thunderstorm, the best advice is to stay inside, heavy rain may be so loud that other sounds never reach the player's ears, and fresh snow will also absorb noises. So, roaming around in various weather states can give entirely different impressions of the same world.

Environmental changes such as the addition of fog also change the perception of the virtual world.

Figure 14.17 shows different types of fog in our application:

Figure 14.17: The effect of fog in the example code from Chapter 14

On the left side of *Figure 14.17*, the virtual world is completely without fog, showing a clear day. In the middle of *Figure 14.17*, heavy fog was added, causing the world to fade out after a short distance. Fog was used in several old games to hide the appearance and disappearance of objects due to rendering limitations in early game engines. Finally, on the right side of *Figure 14.17*, the light color was adjusted to a green tone, creating the illusion of toxic fog in the streets of the map.

Listening to the oracle of seasons

The next evolutionary step after a day/night cycle and weather would be the implementation of the four seasons. The rotation between Spring, Summer, Fall, and Winter is a great opportunity to bring even more reality into the virtual world as the actions of characters or the appearance of animals will change throughout the year.

Like the length of the in-game day, a virtual year should be shortened to a reasonable amount of real time, or a forward time travel functionality should be allowed if all tasks in the current season have been finished. Letting the player wait for no reason will kill their enthusiasm.

A good example of the changing world properties depending on the season is "Legend of Zelda: Oracle of Seasons" by Nintendo for the GameBoy Color. Despite the age of the game, the changes of the seasons have been implemented with great detail, allowing the player to enter some areas of the world only in specific seasons. For instance, rivers are only frozen in Winter and snow fields elevate the parts of the landscape, while only in Summer, flower tendrils enable Link to climb up walls.

In "Stardew Valley" by Eric Barone, seasons are also a key element of the gameplay. Each of the four seasons influences different parts of the game, like crop growth. A season is 28 in-game days long, and by accelerating the time, an entire year in Stardew Valley elapses in 26 hours of in-game time.

For the application, we will create simple day/night light changes and fog as examples. Let's start with day and night.

Hands-on: Adding day and night

Changing the light source's color and position is easy. Most of the fragment shaders already contain a fixed light source definition to allow better visualizations of the instances and the level data.

Implementing light control

As the first step, we add two new variables called `lightPos` and `lightColor` to the `Matrices` uniform in all vertex and fragment shaders where `Matrices` exists:

```
layout (std140, binding = 0) uniform Matrices {
    ...
  vec4 lightPos;
  vec4 lightColor;
};
```

In `lightPos`, we will hand over the current position of the light source, allowing us to simulate the position of the Sun or Moon in the virtual world, and in `lightColor`, we transport the color of the light source to the GPU, enabling us to simulate sunrise, noon, sunset, and so on.

Since we defined the uniform buffer containing the view and projection matrix on the CPU to use `glm::mat4` as the data type, we must add the two `glm::vec4` vectors for the light position and color as the first two elements of a `glm::mat4` that will be uploaded to the GPU before drawing the frame:

```
glm::mat4 lightMatrix = glm::mat4(lightPos, lightColor,
    glm::vec4(), glm::vec4());
matrixData.emplace_back(lightMatrix);
```

Now all fragment shaders containing the light source definitions can be adjusted with a better light control for the surfaces.

We start the new shader code in the `main()` method by defining the ambient light level:

```
float ambientStrength = 0.1;
vec3 ambient = ambientStrength * max(vec3(lightColor),
    vec3(0.05, 0.05, 0.05));
```

The ambient light level is used to simulate the light scattering from other surfaces, enabling some sort of minimal lighting in the virtual world. By limiting the minimal ambient light, we also prevent the resulting picture from becoming pitch black.

Next, we calculate the diffuse part by using the angle between the triangle normal and the direction of the light source:

```
vec3 norm = normalize(vec3(normal));
vec3 lightDir = normalize(vec3(lightPos));
```

```
float diff = max(dot(norm, lightDir), 0.0);
vec3 diffuse = diff * vec3(lightColor);
```

The diffuse lighting of a surface changes with the angle between the surface and the light source. As the dot product of two normalized vectors equals the cosine of the angle between the two vectors, we can use the result of the dot() call directly as a multiplier of the light source color.

As the last step for the fragment shader code changes, we add up ambient and diffuse light and multiply the resulting light value by texture data and vertex color:

```
FragColor = vec4(min(ambient + diffuse, vec3(1.0)), 1.0)*
    texture(tex, texCoord) * color;
```

We can now control the position and color of the light source from the application, and by sending a spherical position and a color, various times of the day can be simulated.

Adding a UI control

To control the light values, a new UI section will be created, enabling fine-grained settings of all light-related values. *Figure 14.18* shows the new **Environment** section in the UserInterface class:

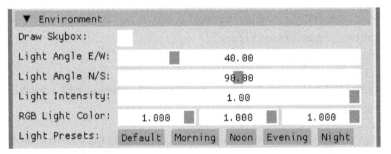

Figure 14.18: UI controls for light parameters and skybox

By splitting the light angle into east/west and north/south, we can move the light around to any position of the virtual sky. The light intensity can be used to lower the overall brightness of the light without manually touching the color values.

With the separate light color values, we can adjust the light to match the natural colors of the Sun or the Moon, at least within the limitations of the available color space, and by using a set of predefined color values, we can set the light color, intensity, and position immediately to a specific time of the day.

Figure 14.19 shows three different light settings for the virtual world (this image is created using the map by Zarudko (`https://skfb.ly/6QYJw`) and the skybox image is by Jockum Skoglund (aka hipshot – `https://opengameart.org/content/stormy-days-skybox`)):

Figure 14.19: The virtual world in the morning, at noon, and in the evening

You can see in *Figure 14.19* that just changing the color of the light source can create entirely different moods in the virtual world. Combined with the skybox from the *Enhancing visuals* section, you can already create truly immersive worlds.

Summary

In this chapter, we explored ideas and tools to show how to upgrade the current animation editor to a small game engine with a built-in editor.

First, we looked at a couple of audio libraries and when to play sound effects and music in a game. Sound effects and music are essential parts of the player's experience, creating a basic form of immersion as the experience of the real world will be transferred to the virtual world.

Then, we explored visual enhancements to the graphics of the application. Extending the basic renderer with transparency, a skybox, dynamic lights and shadows, realistic water, and post-processing effects such as God rays and motion blur will bring the visuals to the next level. Even though it's optional due to the limited target group, adding support for ray tracing and VR could become viable options as both features are a big step forward in terms of visual quality and immersion.

As the last step, we explored a day/night cycle, weather, and seasons as elements to change the environment of the virtual world. Already, a simple cycle of a day adds a lot of interesting opportunities to the virtual world, such as only meeting computer-controlled characters or animals at a certain time of the day or enemies that only appear at night. Weather effects and seasons also multiply the options to change behavior depending on the current environment.

So... what to do next? Well, that's completely up to you!

You could start by learning how to use **Blender** to create your own animated characters, animals, objects, and levels. The created assets don't have to be of the quality of recent games; even low-poly worlds are charming and have many fans. There are lots of books, tutorials, and videos available, handling many different art styles for virtual worlds.

What about adding more objects? Vehicles and animals would enrich the virtual world, and doors and buttons lead to a lot more ways to interact with the world. For better gravity, you might even add a physics engine to the application, enabling other cool features such as force distribution on collisions between objects.

You might also explore the world by using a camera with orthogonal projection. Watching the player, other characters, and the environment in an isometric projection or only from the side could open new ways of expressing a story. Since both the isometric projection and the side view are only different views of the three-dimensional world, all options mentioned in this chapter also apply when using the orthogonal projection.

Another idea could be the creation of a storyline and quests for the player to handle. Forcing the player to move between various locations and interact with different characters to unlock more quests, items, or doors, or just to receive the next piece of the mental puzzle about a quest could engage the player to stay longer in your game.

Or you could dive into the networking part of SDL and create a small network server, allowing you to explore the virtual worlds with your friends. Roaming around the levels and solving quests as a team is satisfying and brings new complexity to the quest system since you may or may not allow the players to use their shared knowledge of a quest over a long distance.

But this is the most important next step: stay curious and experiment with the code.

Practical sessions

Here are some additions you could make to the code:

- Add a button to reload the music tracks from the asset folder.

  A nice-to-have feature to dynamically add or remove tracks.

- Add more sound effects for the instances.

  You could map a sound clip to every action of the instances, creating more realistic effects when controlling the selected instance.

- Play the step sound depending on the floor material.

  Here, you need to load more than one pair of footstep sounds for walking and running. The appropriate sound effect could be chosen by using the mesh type of the ground triangle as the index into the footstep sounds.

- Add sounds for nearby instances.

  The SDL_mixer library allows us to set the volume and balance per channel. Using the distance and angle of the surrounding instances can be used to calculate the effective volume and direction of the sounds.

- Play ambient sound at special places on the map.

  Similar to the waypoint models, you could use small models as markers to play an ambient sound. And like the sounds for nearby instances, the volume and balance of the ambient sound can be adjusted to match the expectation.

- Add markers for music changes.

  This task is closely related to the ambient sound. You could use models and/or nodes to switch the music when your controlled instance enters a specific area of the map or interacts with other instances.

- Adjust level color and fog depending on the level location.

  Not only can the music be changed when roaming through the level; also, the light and fog settings can be adjusted. For instance, when entering a cave, the ambient light can be lowered and the fog density can be raised.

Additional resources

- SDL: `https://www.libsdl.org`
- OpenAL Soft: `https://github.com/kcat/openal-soft`
- PortAudio: `https://www.portaudio.com`
- FMOD: `https://www.fmod.com`
- *Game Physics Engine Development* by *Ian Millington*, published by *CRC Press*: ISBN 978-0123819765
- *Game Physics by David H. Eberly*, published by *Morgan Kaufmann*: ISBN 978-0123749031
- Open-source physics engine: `https://www.tapirgames.com/blog/open-source-physics-engines`
- Vulkan examples by Sascha Willems: `https://github.com/SaschaWillems/Vulkan`
- Ordered transparency: `https://learnopengl.com/Advanced-OpenGL/Blending`
- Order-independent transparency: `https://github.com/nvpro-samples/vk_order_independent_transparency`
- OpenGL skybox: `https://learnopengl.com/Advanced-OpenGL/Cubemaps`
- How to create cubemaps: `https://paulbourke.net/panorama/cubemaps/`
- OpenGL multiple lights: `https://learnopengl.com/Lighting/Multiple-lights`
- Multiple lights demo by Hannes Nevalainen: `https://www.youtube.com/watch?v=vooznqE-XMM`
- OpenGL shadow maps: `https://learnopengl.com/Guest-Articles/2021/CSM https://learnopengl.com/Guest-Articles/2021/CSM`
- WebGL water simulation: `https://madebyevan.com/webgl-water/`
- OpenGL realistic water: `https://medium.com/@vincehnguyen/simplest-way-to-render-pretty-water-in-opengl-7bce40cbefbe`
- OpenGL water caustics: `https://medium.com/@martinRenou/real-time-rendering-of-water-caustics-59cda1d74aa`
- OpenGL lens flares: `https://john-chapman.github.io/2017/11/05/pseudo-lens-flare.html`
- OpenGL God rays: `https://github.com/math-araujo/screen-space-godrays`
- OpenGL bloom effect: `https://learnopengl.com/Advanced-Lighting/Bloom`

- OpenGL motion blur: `https://www.nvidia.com/docs/io/8230/gdc2003_openglshadertricks.pdf`

- OpenGL depth of field: `https://lettier.github.io/3d-game-shaders-for-beginners/depth-of-field.html`

- OpenGL SSAO: `https://lettier.github.io/3d-game-shaders-for-beginners/ssao.html`

- OpenGL SSR: `https://lettier.github.io/3d-game-shaders-for-beginners/screen-space-reflection.html`

- Vulkan raytracing: `https://nvpro-samples.github.io/vk_raytracing_tutorial_KHR/`

- OpenXR: `https://www.khronos.org/openxr/`

- Godot XR Demo template: `https://github.com/GodotVR/godot-xr-template`

- Blender: `https://www.blender.org`

- Open Game Art for assets: `https://opengameart.org/`

Join our community on Discord

Join our community's Discord space for discussions with the author and other readers:
`https://packt.link/cppgameanimation`

www.packt.com

Subscribe to our online digital library for full access to over 7,000 books and videos, as well as industry leading tools to help you plan your personal development and advance your career. For more information, please visit our website.

Why subscribe?

- Spend less time learning and more time coding with practical eBooks and Videos from over 4,000 industry professionals
- Improve your learning with Skill Plans built especially for you
- Get a free eBook or video every month
- Fully searchable for easy access to vital information
- Copy and paste, print, and bookmark content

At www.packt.com, you can also read a collection of free technical articles, sign up for a range of free newsletters, and receive exclusive discounts and offers on Packt books and eBooks.

Other Books You May Enjoy

If you enjoyed this book, you may be interested in these other books by Packt:

Vulkan 3D Graphics Rendering Cookbook

Sergey Kosarevsky, Alexey Medvedev, Viktor Latypov

ISBN: 978-1-80324-811-0

- Master the core features of Vulkan 1.3, with a focus on bindless rendering
- Learn effective techniques for debugging and profiling Vulkan applications
- Build a glTF 2.0 physically based rendering pipeline from scratch
- Enhance visual quality with advanced glTF 2.0 PBR extensions
- Integrate multiple rendering techniques and optimizations into a single application
- Manage large-scale content efficiently in real-time 3D rendering engines
- Leverage Vulkan compute pipelines for advanced image and geometry processing

C++ Game Animation Programming

Michael Dunsky, Gabor Szauer

ISBN: 978-1-80324-652-9

- Create simple OpenGL and Vulkan applications and work with shaders
- Explore the glTF file format, including its design and data structures
- Design an animation system with poses, clips, and skinned meshes
- Find out how vectors, matrices, quaternions, and splines are used in game development
- Discover and implement ways to seamlessly blend character animations
- Implement inverse kinematics for your characters using CCD and FABRIK solvers
- Understand how to render large, animated crowds efficiently
- Identify and resolve performance issues

Packt is searching for authors like you

If you're interested in becoming an author for Packt, please visit authors.packtpub.com and apply today. We have worked with thousands of developers and tech professionals, just like you, to help them share their insight with the global tech community. You can make a general application, apply for a specific hot topic that we are recruiting an author for, or submit your own idea.

Share Your Thoughts

Now you've finished *Mastering C++ Game Animation Programming*, we'd love to hear your thoughts! Scan the QR code below to go straight to the Amazon review page for this book and share your feedback or leave a review on the site that you purchased it from.

https://packt.link/r/1835881939

Your review is important to us and the tech community and will help us make sure we're delivering excellent quality content.

Index

A

AABB lookup tables
creating 242

A* algorithm 416

acceleration
using 206- 208

action node 272

additive animation 19

additive blending
code, extending to support additive
animations 327-330
head animation node, adding 332, 333
head animation settings, saving 333-335
implementing 324
mappings, creating for head
animations 330-332
working 325-327

Advanced Vector Extensions (AVX) 234

animation clips
actions, mapping to 211-213

animation performance
data model, adjusting 56-58
data representation, analyzing 54-56
hotspots, locating in code 53
profiling 51-53

animations
blending between 190

A* path-finding algorithm 421
A*-based navigation, implementing 424
distance, estimating to target 421
exploring 422-424
ground triangles, generating 428-431
mesh triangles, preparing 425, 426
path, between two ground triangles 431
path costs, minimizing 422
path-finding class, adding 426, 427

A-pose 18

application handling
undo and redo functionality,
implementing 119

area awareness 419

artificial intelligence (AI) 260

asset AABBs
performance considerations 363

assets 361
non-animated models, using as 361-363

AssimpModel null object
creating 101

audio library
FMOD 453
OpenAL 453

PortAudio 453

Simple DirectMedia Layer (SDL), using 452

audio manager

  callback, adding for continuous music
      playback 463

  class, extending 467

  footstep sound effects, using
      in render 465-467

  high-level interface, defining 455

  implementing 455

  music player, using in UI 467, 468

  music replay, controlling 462

  SDL, using for low-level layer 458

  sound effects, playing 464

Autodesk FBX 346

axis-aligned bounding box (AABB) 232, 233

  building, for level data 359-361

B

background music

  adding 452

behavior tree 260

binary data

  pros and cons 128, 129

binary file formats

  pros and cons 128

Binary Space Partition (BSP) 229, 230, 343

bind pose 18

bit fields

  using 201, 202

blending 19

bones 18

bounding circle 234

bounding spheres

  data, creating 248-251

  drawing 251-253

  implementing 247

  using, for collision detection 253-255

bounding volume hierarchy 231, 232, 236

Breadth-First Search (BFS) 415

C

cameras

  adding 159-161

  and configuration, switching between 178

  configuration file version, bumping 164

  configuration load and save,
      adjusting 162-164

  current first-/third-person cameras,
      limits 175

  deleting 159-161

  keyboard shortcuts, configuring for
      selection 178

  manual movement, disabling 174, 175

  moving, in third-person view 172-174

  orthogonal projection, adding 179-181

  renderer, adjusting 156, 157

  types, creating 164-166

  user interface controls, for projection
      settings 181, 182

camera settings

  setting 155

capsules 234, 235

clips 19

CMake

  used, for integrating imnodes 262, 263

code, to support behavior changes

  current implementation,
      limitations 290, 291

  events, adding 286-290

node tree copy, creating for instance 285

SingleInstanceBehavior, connecting with renderer 285, 286

Collada 346

collision detection

debug lines, drawing 380, 381

enhancing, for level data 372

instance/level collisions, detecting 378, 379

level data octree, filling 375-378

limitations 226

node tree, extending to support level geometry collisions 382

octree type, adding 372-374

compute relocation

finalizing 72, 73

compute shader 50

adjusting 196-200

data, relocating to 61

debugging 75

implementation, testing by scaling up 73-75

last preparations 61, 62

missing data, adding 58-61

node transforms, calculating 63-68

configuration file

contents, storing 140

creating 142, 143

errors, leading to corrupted files 148, 149

file dialog, adding to user interface 144, 145

loading 139, 145, 146

nodes, parsing 145, 146

output operator of emitter, overloading 141

relaxed configuration file loading 148

saving 139

scene, recreating from saved values 147

writing 142, 143

convex hull 235, 236

convex volume 235

D

data tables

uploading, to GPU 194-196

DebugLog Node 271

deceleration

using 206-208

default configuration file

loading, at startup 149, 150

Depth-First Search (DFS) 415

Dijkstra's algorithm 416

distance-based navigation 414

E

edit modes

and view modes, switching between 110

effector 393

elevation angle 170

Euclidean distance (L2norm) 421

event node 272

F

FABRIK inverse kinematics algorithm

implementing 396-398

FABRIK solver

running 407, 408

face animations

adding, to code and GPU shaders 302

changes, rendering with instance and renderer installation 321-323

code, adjusting for FaceAnim node 318

code, finalizing 313, 314

controlling, with UI elements 314, 315

FaceAnim node, adding 319-321

face morph settings, adding
   to code 307, 308
instance settings, loading 317
instance settings, saving 315
morph meshes, loading 302-305
morph meshes, storing in single
   buffer 305-307
morph target animations,
   limitations 323, 324
per-instance buffer data, filling in
   renderer 309
shader, extending to draw 310-312
using, in node trees 317

FaceAnim node
adding 319-321
code, adjusting for 318

facial expressions
animating 300, 301

file formats
choosing, for map 345
custom format, creating 346, 347
existing formats, extending 346, 347

file formats, supported by Assimp
levels, using in 345, 346

finite state machine
using, to control animation flow 214-217

first- and third-person cameras
bone matrix, retrieving 167, 168
implementing 166, 167
parameters, computing 169-172

FMOD 453

**Forward And Backward Reaching Inverse
   Kinematics (FABRIK) 393**
basics 393-396
inverse kinematics algorithm,
   implementing 396-399

limitations 409
node chain, defining for instance's
   feet 399, 400

forward kinematics 392

framebuffer, adjusting 92-94
pixel, reading from texture 95, 96
selection shader, creating 94, 95

Free3D
reference link 345

free camera
defining, as default camera 158, 159

free navigation 419

G

game character
animating 18
bones 18
building blocks 19, 20
character data, updating 21, 22
data preparation 20
nodes 18

game map
AABB, building for level data 359, 361
C++ class, adding t hold level data 348
callbacks and renderer code,
   adding 349, 350
importing 347
interactive octree view, creating 354
level configuration, saving 352
non-animated models, using as
   assets 361-363
quadtree, converting to octree 353, 354
UI extension, with level property
   controls 350-352

geometry buffer (G-Buffer) 92

**Gilbert-Johnson-Keerthi (GJK) distance
   algorithm 236**

GPU

data tables, uploading 194-196

level data, sending to 363

graph-based navigation 415

A* algorithm 416

BFS 415

DFS 415

Dijkstra's algorithm 416

graphics cards 49

graph node classes

creating 271-273

graph nodes

base class 273-275

behavior struct, creating 278, 280

callbacks, using to propagate changes 278

storage class, creating for instances 278-280

gravity

basic gravity, adding 386, 387

ground triangles, finding in level data 384-386

instances, keeping on ground triangles 387-391

using, to instances on floor 383

grid 227

ground triangles

generating 428, 430

group of filters

adding 34

H

heuristic 416

Hierarchical Level-of-Detail (HLOD) 344

high-level interface

AudioManager class, adding to Window class 456, 457

callbacks, using 457

defining 455

highlight

adding, to selected instances 87

logic, adjusting to shaders and UI 89-91

renderer, preparing 87, 88

home computers 48

hotkeys

defining, for undo and redo functionality 122

I

idle/walk/run animations

mapping 209, 210

idle/walk/run logic

adding 204-206

id Software 419

ImGui elements

creating 267, 268

ImGui file dialog

using 32, 33

ImGui menu

adding, to allow direct access 122, 123

ImGui window

node editor, creating 264, 265

simple node, adding 266, 267

immersion

day/night cycle, adding 484

extending, with daytime and weather 483

forward time travel, adding 485

oracle of seasons 486

playing, in real time 485

weather god, worshipping 485

imnodes 261

default values, setting 264

integrating, CMake used 262, 263

links, maintaining between nodes 268-270

reference link 261

used, for creating UI elements 263

imnodes attributes

creating 267, 268

imnodes context

creating 264

INI format 131

instance behavior

structure, to control 260

instance bounding boxes, calculating 240

AABB debug lines, drawing 246, 247

AABB lookup tables, creating 242

AABB, using in model and renderer 243

colliding instances, retrieving 245

reacting, to collisions 245

three-dimensional bounding cube class, adding 240

window, creating to show quadtree plus contents 244

instance node 272

instances

debug lines, adding to path 445-447

navigating, to target 441

path, calculating to target 441-444

rotating, to reach target 444, 445

instances and models

settings structs, extending 202, 203

interaction

adding, between instances 291

debug information, drawing 294

handling code, extending 292-294

interaction control properties

creating 291, 292

interactive octree view

calculating 357, 359

creating 354

interactivity, adding 354, 355

lines, collecting 356

lines, drawing 357-359

inverse bind matrix 19

inverse kinematics 393

adding 391

FABRIK solver, running 407, 408

feet-to-ground collisions, detecting 405, 406

types 392, 393

J

JSON file format 131

K

k-d tree 230

key frames 19

Khronos Group glTF format 346

L

L1 norm 421

layered blending 325

level data, sending to GPU

level AABB, drawing 365-368

shader, creating 363, 364

light control

implementing 487

lightmaps 344

lookup tables

creating 191-194

importance 190

M

Manhattan distance (L1 norm) 421

map, versus model data 342
level data 342
level data, as partial or incomplete 345
level data, with additional data 343
separate collision detection, using for level data 343

mesh 19

mesh-based navigation 417
area awareness system 419
navigation meshes 417, 418

mesh triangles
preparing 425, 426

Minkowski difference
AABB debug lines, drawing 236

model abstractions 232

model file
animations, importing 30
code, checking 30
embedded textures, loading 26, 27
loading 25, 26
node hierarchy, parsing 27, 28
vertex buffers, adding for meshes 29

model instance
adding 36
bones, reusing 36, 38
drawing 42
dynamic model and management 39-42
framebuffer, adjusting 92-94
index, assigning to 97
instance-specific settings, storing 38, 39
mouse button, adding 96
pros and cons, of shooting virtual arrays 91
selecting, at mouse positions 98, 99
selecting, with point and click 91
texture, using 92

model viewer application
changes, reverting before application 116
code and User Interface elements, adding 116-118
current solution drawbacks 118
rollback method 116

morph animation 19

morph meshes
loading 302-305
storing, in single buffer 305-307

morph target animations 300
limitations 323, 324

move to instance function
button, creating 85, 86
coordinate arrows, adding 80-84
implementing 80

multi-core machines 49

multiple cameras
adding 154

music
adaptive music play 455
ambient music 455
custom music, allowing 455
Menu music 454

N

navigation mesh (navmesh) 344, 417-419
free navigation 419
generating, from level data 419
waypoint navigation 419

navigation targets
adding, to map 437
gravity, adding to non-animated instances 439

model and instance, adjusting 437-439

model and instance data, saving 440

navigation ways

distance-based navigation 414

graph-based navigation 415

machine learning, used to generate
navigation data 420

mesh-based navigation 417

overview 414

node computations

moving, to GPU 62

shader storage buffers, adding 63

node editor

extending 281, 282

node factory

adding 280

node matrices

creating 69-71

node positions

adjusting 400

code, adjusting for animated
instances 402-404

transformations, keeping separate 401, 402

world positions, creating 404, 405

nodes 18

node tree copy

creating, for instance 285

node trees

face animations, using in 317

loading 282-284

saving 282-284

non-player characters (NPCs) 260

null object 100

AssimpModel null object 101

implementing, to allow deselection 100

user interface, adjusting 102, 103

O

octree 228, 229

quadtree, converting to 353, 354

OpenAL 453

Open Asset Import Library (Assimp) 22-25

Open File dialog

used, for extending UI 31

OpenGL Shading Language (GLSL) 57

oriented bounding box (OBB) 233

P

parser class

adding 137

exceptions thrown by yaml-cpp,
handling 139

node type of yaml-cpp, using 137

sequences and maps, accessing 138

path, between two ground triangles

best node, extracting 435

data , preparing 431, 432

main loop, running 432-434

shortest path, backtracking 436

physically based rendering (PBR)

using 468, 469

Pierre Vigier

reference link 237

plain enums

using 201, 202

PortAudio 453

Q

quadtree 228

adding, to store nearby model instances 237

bounding box code, adjusting 237, 238

quadtree code
rewriting 238, 239
Quake III Arena 419

R

RandomWait Node 272
raster interrupt 48
ray tracing 475
redo functionality
creating 119
hotkeys, defining 122
implementing 119
limits and enhancements 123, 124
regular expression-style filter
adding 34
reinforced learning 420
RenderDoc 75
renderer code
adjusting 196-200
root node 18, 271, 393

S

Screen Space Ambient Occlusion (SSAO) 475
SDL_mixer
installing, on Linux 460
installing, on Windows 459
selector node 272
Separating Axis Theorem 233
sequence node 272
setting storage class
creating 120, 121
shader storage buffer objects (SSBOs) 50
Simple DirectMedia Layer (SDL) 452
and SDL_mixer, initialization 461
and SDL_mixer installation, on Linux 460
and SDL_mixer installation,
on Windows 459
and SDL_mixer, shutting down 461
using, for low-level layer 458
single camera
migrating, to array of cameras 154, 155
single filter
adding 34
SingleInstanceBehavior
connecting, with renderer 285, 286
Single Instruction, Multiple Data (SIMD) 234
skeletal animation 18
Sketchfab
reference link 345
skinning 19
sound effects
adding 452
ambient sounds 454
audio library, using 452
audio manager, implementing 455
character sounds 454
game character's footsteps 453
local sound sources 454
music, playing 454
playing 453
sound manager implementations,
alternatives 468
weather effects 454
spatial partitioning
binary space partitioning 229, 230
bounding volume hierarchy 231, 232
grid 227
k-d tree 230
octree 228, 229

quadtree 228

using, to reduce complexity 227

spherical linear interpolation (SLERP) 52

Standard Portable Intermediate
Representation (SPIR-V) 62

states

adding, to code 200

allowed changes, defining 213, 214

and animations, linking 209

loading 217

model settings, reading in renderer 220

new data types, storing 218, 219

saving 217

stationary cameras

adding 176

stationary follow camera

creating 176, 178

storage class

hooking up, to render 121

Streaming SIMD Extensions (SSE) 234

T

target 393

test node 271

text format

INI file format 131

JSON file format 131

selecting, for saving data 130

YAML file format 132, 133

textual data

loading 130

saving 129, 130

textual file formats

pros and cons 128

texture data type (float) 93

T-pose 18

translation, rotation, and scale (TRS) 52

U

UI control

adding 488

UI elements

creating, with imnodes 263

UI, extending with Open File dialog 31

filter, adding to display supported
file types 34

ImGui file dialog, using 32, 33

integrating, into CMakeLists.txt 31, 32

model, drawing to screen 36

model file, loading 35

undo functionality

creating 119

hotkeys, defining 122

implementing 119

limits and enhancements 123, 124

Universal Scene Description (USD) 346

V

view modes

and edit modes, switching between 110

and edit modes, toggling between 113, 114

and edit mode, toggling between 113-115

feature, switching in 111

outlook for future changes 115

state variable plus code, adding 111, 112

virtual skybox

drawing 482, 483

implementing 480-482

technical details, exploring 478, 479

visual enhancement
  beautiful sky, adding 470
  colors, bringing with PBR 469
  light and shadows 471-473
  post-processing effects, adding 474, 475
  ray tracing, upgrading to 475, 476
  realistic water 473, 474
  transparency, adding 469
  virtual reality 477
  virtual sky 478
visual node editor
  adding 261

W

wait node 272
  creating 275-278
Wavefront 346
waypoint navigation 419
weights 19

Y

yaml-cpp
  integrating, into CMake build 136
  obtaining 135, 136
YAML file
  format 132
  map 133
  maps and sequences combinations 134
  node 133
  sequence 134
  structure 133
YAML map 133
YAML node 133
YAML parser
  adding 135
  parser class, adding 137
  yaml-cpp, obtaining 135, 136

www.ingramcontent.com/pod-product-compliance
Lightning Source LLC
Chambersburg PA
CBHW060638060326
40690CB00020B/4440